IET COMPUTING SERIES 44

Streaming Analytics

Other volumes in this series:

Streaming Analytics

Concepts, architectures, platforms, use cases and applications

Edited by
Pethuru Raj, Chellammal Surianarayanan,
Koteeswaran Seerangan and George Ghinea

The Institution of Engineering and Technology

Published by The Institution of Engineering and Technology, London, United Kingdom

The Institution of Engineering and Technology is registered as a Charity in England & Wales (no. 211014) and Scotland (no. SC038698).

The Institution of Engineering and Technology
Futures Place
Kings Way, Stevenage
Hertfordshire, SG1 2UA, United Kingdom

www.theiet.org

British Library Cataloguing in Publication Data
A catalogue record for this product is available from the British Library

ISBN 978-1-83953-416-4 (hardback)
ISBN 978-1-83953-417-1 (PDF)

Typeset in India by MPS Limited
Printed in the UK by CPI Group (UK) Ltd, Croydon

Cover Image: Weiquan Lin via Getty Images

Contents

About the Editors

Pethuru Raj is the Chief Architect and Vice President in the Site Reliability Engineering (SRE) division of Reliance Jio Platforms Ltd., Bangalore, India. He focuses on emerging technologies such as the Internet of Things (IoT), Artificial Intelligence (AI), big and fast data analytics, blockchain, digital twins, cloud-native computing, edge & fog clouds, reliability engineering, microservices architecture (MSA), and event-driven architecture (EDA). He has authored and edited 20 technology books. He holds a CSIR-sponsored PhD from Anna University, India.

Chellammal Surianarayanan is an assistant professor of computer science at Government Arts and Science College, Tiruchirapalli, India. Her contributions include the development of an embedded system for lead shield integrity assessment system, portable automatic air sampling equipment, an embedded system of detection of lymphatic filariasis in its early stage, and the development of data logging software applications for atmospheric dispersion studies. She is a life member of the Computer Society of India and IAENG. She earned a Doctorate in Computer Science by developing computational optimization models for the discovery and selection of semantic services.

Koteeswaran Seerangan is an associate professor in the Department of Computer Science and Engineering, School of Computing, and Dean of Research Studies at Vel Tech Rangarajan Dr Sagunthala R&D Institute of Science and Technology, India. His research interests include big data and analytics, Internet of Things, and machine learning. He is a member of ACM and the IET, and a senior member of IEEE and life member of ISTE. He holds a PhD in computer science and engineering from Vel Tech Rangarajan Dr Sagunthala R&D Institute of Science and Technology, India.

George Ghinea is a professor in multimedia computing in the Department of Computer Science at Brunel University, London, UK. His research activities lie at the confluence of computer science, media and psychology. His work focuses on the area of perceptual multimedia quality and how one builds end-to-end communication systems incorporating user perceptual requirements. He has applied his expertise in areas such as eye-tracking, telemedicine, multi-modal interaction, and ubiquitous and mobile computing. He consults regularly for both public and private institutions. He is a member of the IEEE. He holds a PhD in computer science from the University of Reading, UK.

Preface

With the wider acceptance and leverage of path-breaking digitization and edge technologies (disappearing sensors, multifaceted actuators, disposable stickers, barcodes, and RFID tags, miniaturized microcontrollers, specialised chips, infinitesimal beacons and LED lights, etc.), all kinds of physical, mechanical, and electrical systems in our everyday environments are being turned into and tuned to be digitized entities. By attaching communication modules, these digitized elements get the connectivity feature. Through the communication-enablement, digitized entities in our personal, professional, and social places can find, bind, and interact with other digitized elements in the vicinity and also with remotely held systems (cloud-hosted applications, services, and databases) over the Internet, which is being touted as the largest, open, public, and affordable communication infrastructure. The connectivity may be direct or indirect (through a middleware solution). Thus, every commonly found and cheap thing in our midst becomes connected artifacts, which intrinsically have gained the much-needed wherewithal to join in the mainstream computing. These empowered entities are typically resource constrained. Formally these digitized and connected entities are termed as the Internet of Things (IoT).

On the other hand, electronics devices are increasingly instrumented to be powerful in their assignments with more compute, storage and networking resources. They natively come out with the connectivity feature and hence interactions with digitized entities and other electronics devices get innately enabled. Electronics devices are increasingly hooked into the Internet. For example, smartphones, CCTV cameras in important junctions, robots in manufacturing floors, drones in the open sky, kitchen utilities such as refrigerator, consumer electronics like TV in our lively and lovely home environments, etc. are being linked with the web to exhibit adaptive and adroit behavior. Thus, the nomenclature of the Internet of devices (IoD) became popular. Now, in order to hide the complexity of digital elements and electronics, the flourishing microservices concept got introduced in the device world. That is, every device is expressed and exposed as a service to the outside world. By introducing one or more service interfaces, the respective service implementation is separated out. Such a simplification comes handy in eliminating the dependency problem. Thus everything is being seen as a service and hence the term "the Internet of services (IoS)" started to get a lot of attention in the technology world. Precisely speaking, digital entities and devices are being presented as configurable, customizable, and composable services. In nutshell, the operational technologies (OT) are being merged with the information technologies (IT).

In other words, there is a technology-induced affinity between the physical and the digital/cyber/virtual worlds. Such a cool and strategically sound convergence has laid down a stimulating foundation for the ensuing digital era. Context-aware applications are easily envisaged and realized through the synchronization of the digital and physical worlds.

Now when the digitally empowered things and devices interact with one another purposefully, there will be a massive amount of multi-structured data getting generated in varying velocities, varieties, and volumes. That is, we have big, real-time and streaming data in plenty. Data is a strategic asset for any enterprising business. Experts point out that data is emerging as a fuel for the future of the human society. It is a universal truth that data can be transitioned into information and into knowledge. The process of converting data into knowledge is being technologically optimized and speeded up. Every bit of data has to be meticulously collected, cleansed, and crunched in order to extract actionable insights. The fast-evolving digitization and digitalization technologies and tools contribute immensely in the long-standing goal of data-driven insights and insights-driven decisions.

The leading market analysts and watchers have forecast that there will be trillions of digitized elements and billions of connected devices. With the surge in the adoption and adaption of microservices architecture (MSA) and event-driven architecture (EDA), it is estimated that there will be millions of microservices. When all these digitized entities, connected devices and microservices interact decisively, we will be bombarded with a tremendous amount of poly-structured data. Therefore, we increasingly come across big, fast, and streaming data. There are batch and real-time processing methods for making sense and money out of exponentially growing data heaps. With the faster maturity and stability of competent mechanisms and cloud infrastructures (highly organized and optimized IT infrastructure modules), big data analytics (BDA), and real-time analytics requirements and processes are being simplified and speeded up. That is, the transition of data into information and into knowledge is being accelerated and augmented through a host of powerful and pioneering technologies and tools. The knowledge thus discovered gets disseminated to business workloads and IT services to act upon the actionable insights with all the clarity and confidence Precisely speaking, the real digital transformation is being achieved across industry verticals through meticulous data gathering, preparation, storage, and analytics in time. In this book, we are to dig deep and deal with streaming data. IoT sensors and devices normally generate streams of data. Thus, garnering and processing data streams acquire special significance for a variety of industry verticals. Further on, it has to be real-time analysis of streaming data in order to produce trustworthy intelligence, which can be acted upon with all the sagacity and alacrity.

In a day, there can be zillions of personal, social, and business events, which ought to be minutely monitored and extracted as a series of events data and messages. Capturing and subjecting those value-adding events, which are generally arriving in a pre-defined sequence, are termed as the prime task for squeezing out viable and venerable insights. Thus, the aspect of event capture is becoming an important activity. Thus, sense and respond (S & R) applications can be designed, developed, and deployed through the blending of MSA and EDA styles. The futuristic applications, therefore, will be cloud-hosted, service-oriented, event-driven, process-aware, business-critical, people-centric, knowledge-filled. We can journey toward intelligent and real-time enterprises with all the required maturity and stability of digital technologies. The mix of microservices and event-driven architectures is all set to dismantle the currently running reactive systems. And hence governments, organizations, establishments, institutions, and corporates are to succulently and sufficiently be empowered to be proactive and pre-emptive in their operations, outputs and offerings.

With the steady of arrival of streaming analytics platforms, databases, specialized engines and processors, and a dazzling array of tools, streaming applications and cloud infrastructures, the activity of making sense out of streaming data gets accelerated, augmented, and automated. This book is exclusively prepared for conveying all about the fast-growing domain of streaming analytics. The recent spurt in the usage of Artificial Intelligence (AI) algorithms (machine and deep learning) has automated and advanced the analytics aspect significantly. By fluently leveraging AI algorithms in streaming analytics, the world of streaming analytics is bound to be prominent, prudent, and paramount.

Streaming data is a kind of continuous flow of data generated by various sources such as networked embedded systems, the IoT sensors and devices, cyber physical systems (CPS), server logs, business workloads, financial transactions, purchases through B2C e-commerce applications, geographical location data, smartphones, and industrial machineries. The requirement here to make sense out of the data getting streamed is to capture and process data on the fly. The classical analytical systems store and process but streaming analytics platforms do differently to emit out real-time insights. The data getting generated and transmitted is structured, semi-structured, and non-structured. The streaming analytics platforms have to have all the capabilities to transition input data into useful and usable data. For example, the data may be audio, video, text, binary, JSON, etc. Another important aspect is that, the data is being generated in huge volume. Thus, there is a need to set up and sustain a new set of data storage and processing systems that can elegantly handle streaming data.

There is also a need to develop and deploy streaming applications to process and extract insights from streaming data. The nature of application may differ extensively. Take a video conferencing or processing/analytics application. The resource requirements change hugely.

In this book, we would like to focus on the aspect of streaming data and its real-time analytics. The fundamental and foundational concepts around streaming data get explained in the first part of the book. The challenges widely associated with streaming data and analytics will be articulated and accentuated. Also, the fast proliferation of myriads data sources gets its own share of description in this book.

The second part of the book will primarily focus on the various tools for data virtualization and ingestion, integrated streaming analytics platforms, hot and warm databases, and 360-degree dashboards for knowledge visualization. The right and relevant data analytics algorithms and approaches will be described in order to adequately enlighten our esteemed readers.

Some chapters detail how machine and deep learning (ML/DL) algorithms handle streaming data in order to perform real-time analytics to bring forth personalized, predictive, and prescriptive insights.

The third and final portion of the book will delineate about the various industry use cases of streaming analytics. Streaming analytics use cases across cloud system operations, retail, self-driving vehicles, manufacturing, supply chain, healthcare, cyber security, and other prominent business domains will be discussed in the book to insist the strategic significance of automated streaming analytics. Finally, we will explain edge/fog computing and how streaming analytics can be accomplished in edge device clouds.

Pethuru Raj PhD
Vice President
Reliance Jio Platforms Ltd.
Bangalore, India
Technology Books: https://peterindia.net/MyBooks.html

Chapter 1

Streaming data processing – an introduction

Chellammal Surianarayanan[1]

Abstract

This chapter presents an overview about the basics of streaming data, core components of streaming data processing architecture, challenges associated with stream processing and recent tools for stream processing.

1.1 Introduction

Streaming data is a kind of continuous flow of data generated by various sources such as networking devices, the Internet of Things (IoT) sensors, server logs, applications in different domains, transactions in financial domains, geographical location data, mobile devices, and machine sensors. The word "streaming" describes that the data is continuously flowing with no beginning or end. In traditional systems, the number of sources that generated data was limited. In addition, the nature of data also remained structured. That time data processing systems were designed to accommodate only those structured data. But in streaming data, the nature or format of data is unstructured. The sources of streaming data themselves are many in number right from sensors, to server logs to different applications, the nature of the data also varies. Not only that the data generated by various sources are likely to contain structured, semi-structured, and unstructured data. For example, the data may be audio or video or text or standard excel data or machine-generated numbers, etc. Another important aspect is that the data is being generated in huge volume. Obviously, it is not possible to put any constraint on the sources of data generation; rather there is a need to establish a new set of data storage and processing systems that can handle streaming data.

1.2 Dependence of streaming data processing on the purpose of applications

Having understood that the streaming data is inherently associated with velocity, variety, and volume, the need for its time of processing is decided by the nature of

[1]Department of Computer Science, Government Arts and Science College, Srirangam, Affiliated to Bharathidasan University, India

the application and the purpose for which the application has been built. Since it is the application that decides how the data needs to be processed, utmost care must be given to analyze the needs of the applications. After analyzing the application needs, it will be sorted to set up appropriate storage and processing infrastructure for the streaming data.

To illustrate, the nature of applications is highly variant from one another, a few examples are discussed below. The nature of application may be a simple online video conferencing application, where streaming data is being transferred from source to target locations over network having sufficient bandwidth. In addition, on the destination site, advanced graphical display units and applications would be used to playing video.

In contrast to the above situation, consider another application of online analytical transaction processing (OLAP). An OLAP application basically analyzes a huge amount of data by employing various data mining algorithms in order to find interesting or hidden patterns or knowledge. Here, the task of analyzing data and taking higher level business decision can be well done with a batch processing approach.

In contrast to the above one, consider an earthquake monitoring application. Also, consider that the vibrations of earth surfaces are being acquired by seismic sensor once in a second. When the vibrations are found to be normal, there will be no need for processing the data. But when the vibrations cross a particular threshold, which is a predefined value set by domain experts, it becomes very crucial to take immediate action for giving alerts to the concerned departments and necessary actions will be taken according to the measured value. Here, one can understand that the data being acquired needs to be processed in real time to take the necessary decisions and actions.

Consider another example of autonomous car. Here also continuous detection of the presence of obstacles around the car for about a particular predefined distance that is being sensed. Whenever there is no obstacle found, smooth driving of the car continues. But when an obstacle is found, say for example, a small dog in front of the car, break has to be applied immediately in order to save the life of the dog. Here also, the need of taking actions immediately as soon as something is sensed which is understood.

Consider another example of healthcare monitoring application which monitors the crucial parameters like heart rate, respiratory rate, temperature, and blood pressure. When any of these vital parameters deviates from the predefined normal values, obviously, appropriate medical treatment and care should be given to the concerned person.

The above application scenarios clearly exhibit the need for handling the incoming streaming data in real time.

To provide more insight, consider a cyclone alert application where a number of sensors like thermometer, wind speed anemometer, wind direction sensing wind vanes, rainfall and precipitation sensors which are mounted at various heights of meteorological tower/mast continuously monitor various parameters in a normal data acquisition rate say for example once in a minute. Now consider that suddenly the wind starts blowing with a higher speed and it is more than the predefined threshold. Also, consider that this is due to a depression in the nearby sea. Hereafter, the data acquisition itself will be fast, say for example, once in 10 sec. When the values are normal within the specified data range, batch processing of data will be performed toward the usual atmospheric studies like dispersion studies or any other modeling whereas when the monitored parameters deviate from the predefined threshold, in this case, the data compulsorily needs to be analyzed in real time to study the movement of depression and to draw actionable insights.

Consider another scenario of an enterprise sharing its data and assets to other organizations for collaboration. Here, as long as the data is kept within an organization, the server logs may well be periodically scanned for any abnormal event log. But when the organization is in collaboration with other organizations, obviously mandatory need arises to monitor the incoming and outgoing network traffic in real time to prevent unwanted data loss or leakage as well as intruder.

Similarly, in the case of financial organizations, applications which sanction the loans need to follow up the transactions of the customers very carefully in real time as the event happens to detect fraudulent transactions and take proper counter actions. In addition, nowadays, in ATMs and through fraudulent messages, posters, and chat messages, many cyber-attacks occur very frequently. So, there is a need to filter out them in the respective domains.

In nutshell, the purpose of the application determines when the data needs to be processed. A few applications like legacy applications which had been built to manage an organization level business processing, applications which are built for OLAP, and normal server logs and OLTP within an organization can go casually with batch processing. In most of the modern use cases like fraud detection, cyber security, sensor data, online advertising, healthcare applications, etc., there is a need to process the streaming data in real time.

1.3 Key features of streaming data

Time sensitive—Each element in a data stream carries a time stamp. The data streams are time sensitive and lose significance after a certain time. For example, the data of the location from a user who is in mobility loses its meaning if that user moves away from the concerned location.

Continuous—Data streams are continuous in nature. A data stream consists of a series of data elements ordered in time. The data represents an "event" or a change in state that can happen in a system. According to the application in hand, the streams are processed.

Heterogeneous—Typically, in a streaming data application, data is likely to arrive from multiple sources. For example, in healthcare domain, stream data may arrive from different medical instruments such as electro cardio gram (ECG), magnetic resonance imaging (MRI) scan, and electronic health record (HER). Here, EHR will be a structured data whereas ECG and MRI data are images. So, streaming data might be a mix of different formats.

Imperfect—Due to the variety of their sources and different data transmission mechanisms, a data stream may have missed or damaged data elements. Also, the data elements in a stream might arrive out of order.

Volatile and unrepeatable—The data streams are highly volatile. Data streams are likely to be associated with drift. That is the incoming data may not have the same pattern.

1.4   Components of stream processing architecture

As mentioned earlier, the conventional data processing systems are limited in its infrastructure and they are more apt for handling batch processing where the arrived data are made into batches and processing of batches will be performed in regular intervals of time. These conventional infrastructures are insufficient to handle the streaming data generated from various resources.

A stream processing architecture must include software components to ingest and process large volumes of streaming data from multiple sources. A streaming data processing architecture consumes data as it comes, persists the incoming data (if needed), and includes various components for real-time analysis, visualization, actions, alerts, etc. Typical stream processing architecture is shown in Figure 1.1. The core components include the following:

- Stream processor/message broker
- ETL platform
- Data analytic engine
- Streaming data storage

Stream processor is fundamentally a message broker which receives data from different data sources. The message broker converts the received data into standard message streams on an ongoing basis. Other components can consume the messages from the broker. Conventionally message brokers such as Apache RabbitMQ, Microsoft Message Queue, and IBM MQ were used for exchanging messages across various components.

Though these brokers are based on message-oriented middleware and they are good at implementing the publisher/subscriber pattern, they are not designed specifically for dealing with large streams of data originating from multiple sources. Whereas recent stream processors such as Apache Kafka have been specifically designed to handle streams and it has a high throughput of 2 million writes/sec. Kafka not only supports the message distribution in publisher–subscriber pattern but also provides data retention by continuously logging the data in a persistent storage which then can be used later for any kind of offline processing. Along with asynchronous message communication to consumers and data retention, Kafka stores the data with redundancy which ensures high availability also.

Once the messages are received in Kafka, according to requirements of application, various tasks can be performed. As mentioned in the previous section, each and every application has its own purpose. According to the application requirements, other components would be designed. For example, there may

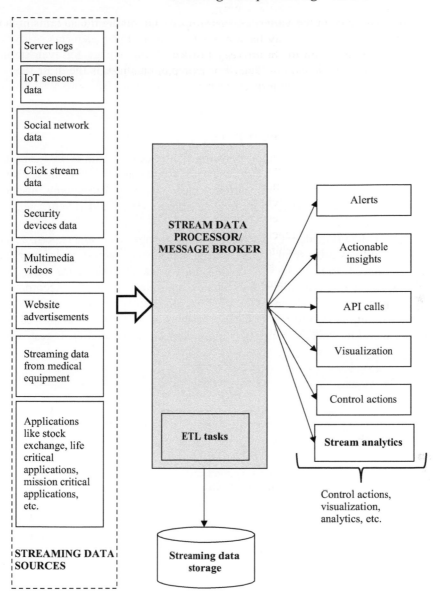

Figure 1.1   Typical streaming data processing architecture

be a requirement like, the data from different sources is required to be aggregated, transformed into suitable format, and then the data can be queried using different SQL tools. For example, ETL tools such as Apache Storm and Spark Streaming would extract the data from message queues and perform transformation for the user queries and provide user information to the users. The ETL tools are capable of processing message streams and storing the streams in persistent storage also.

The advent of hardware technology provides cheap storage for even storing huge volume of even streaming data. For example, data lake is the most flexible and inexpensive option for storing event data.

1.5   Stream analytics

One of the core tasks that is being performed on streaming data is analyzing the streaming data in real time. Like any other data, stream data is also being analyzed using a wide spectrum of disciplines that include statistics, data mining, machine learning, deep learning, visualization technologies, vision and robotics, etc. as shown in Figure 1.2.

Once the data is made into discretized streams, knowledge, and expertise from various disciplines are useful to extract the hidden and interesting information. Here, machine learning plays a crucial role. Data analysis starts after preprocessing it for missing values, consistency, and integrity checks. According to the application needs, clustering, classification, association rule mining algorithms, pattern recognition algorithms, and deep learning algorithms are employed. For example, there are specific clustering algorithms such as Isolation Forest which

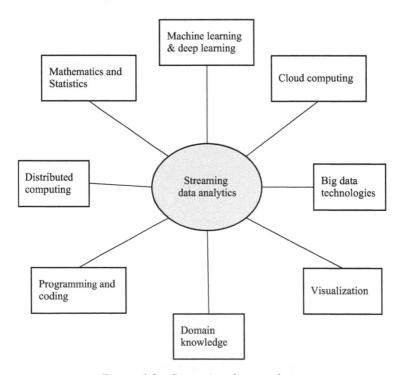

Figure 1.2   Streaming data analytics

isolates the outliers from the data. Similarly, Random Forest classifies the streaming data of even large volume into predefined labels. Naïve Bayes algorithm provides multiclass handling feature. Support vector machine transforms the incoming data into a higher dimensional space in order to convert the non-linearity associated in the incoming data by using kernel functions such as polynomial and sigmoid. Also, in financial and network domains also, machine learning algorithms are used to find fraudulent events in the incoming data. Recently, the advancement in hardware technology makes deep learning feasible through large neural network. Deep learning helps to classify images. For example, in health care domain, deep learning learns from a huge set of images and afterwards it recognizes the images that got affected with diseases. Also, in the object recognition as well as robotics, along with visualization technologies and deep learning makes many real-time applications automatic. Analysis cannot be done only with machine or deep learning. The analysis requires knowledge from various domains such as Big Data, distributed computing, statistics, mathematics, Internet technologies, programming and coding skills, visualization techniques, etc. More importantly, when the large sized streams are required to be stored and analyzed, cloud platforms turned out as the appropriate options. For example, streaming data can be stored into Amazon Redshift which is also integrated with real-time dashboard facility to keep the analyzed results updated to the users. Similarly, huge unstructured text streams can be analyzed using Elasticsearch. In addition, the data from Kafka can be stored in Cassandra.

1.6   Core attributes of stream processor

Low latency—Streaming data platforms are required to match the speed of the data acquisition from data sources with the requirements of the near real-time analytics.

Scalable—Streaming data processing architectures should be scalable to receive and ingest data from a large number of sources both internally and externally.

Diverse—Streaming data processing architecture should be capable of handling diverse data sources including both legacy RDBMS, CRM, ERP platforms to modern data sources like mobile devices, cloud sources, or the IoT.

Centralized—Another desirable feature of any stream processing architecture is that the capability to provide a centralized repository of technical and business metadata to enable common data formats and transformations among various applications.

Durable—The ability to land data in a data warehouse or Hadoop-based data lake environment is a key component to a streaming data processing architecture.

1.7   Benefits of stream processing

Accelerated data delivery—The primary benefit of data streaming is real-time insight. Organization can take advantage of fresh data. Thus, real-time streaming processing helps to accelerate data delivery.

Increased customer satisfaction and retention—The ability to quickly collect, analyze, and act on fresh data will provide a competitive edge in their market-place. The organization become more responsive to market trends, customer needs, and business opportunities. Real-time streaming processing supports customer retention.

Improved returns—The improved response times to different situations help businesses generate high returns compared to the businesses having no data streaming or processing systems.

Prevention of losses—Data streaming prevents other losses such as system outages, financial downturns, and data breaches.

Reduced infrastructure costs—In most of the application domains, there is no need to store all the data in warehouses. Only processed knowledge and insights are becoming more meaningful. This reduced the infrastructure cost involved.

Anomaly detection—The ability of stream processors to integrate and analyze, data in real-time, at huge volume opens up new applications in various domains. A few applications include location data, fraud detection, real-time stock trades, log monitoring, security systems, marketing, sales, predictive analytics, etc. Along with these applications, detection of anomaly in various domains in real time leads to the successful implementation of many life critical, safety critical, and mission critical applications.

1.8   Challenges with streaming data

Ordering of data—In streaming data, the data may arise from different sources. Since the data is moving through distributed system, maintaining the ordering of message from multiple sources is tedious. The continuous data streams may contain imperfection, missing data elements or damaged data elements.

Data consistency and data availability—Streaming data is directly influenced by CAP theorem while designing a solution. The domain expert and database architect have to appropriately make trade-off among, consistency, availability and partition according to the application needs.

Scalability and performance—Real-time streaming processors should process the incoming data within predefined time periods. As and when the data arrives, both the storage and processing layers should scale according to the size of the incoming data. For example, in a situation any fault, this size of data accumulated will still be larger. So, the stream processor should scale according dynamic demands, which is really a challenge to implement.

Lengthy transformation processes—In a stream processing architecture, the incoming data is stored in its raw form in object storages like JSON files rather than tables. Typically, organizations are using relational databases. So, storing unstructured data requires lengthy cleansing and transformation processes, creating engineering bottlenecks.

Fault tolerance—The data streaming should be fault tolerant. The chances of downtime affect the accuracy of the data streaming.

Unreliable network connectivity—In applications where edge devices are being used, processing of device data is challenging as the connectivity is unreliable due to limited bandwidth. In addition, such applications very often employ signal processing for time and frequency analysis. So, data loss, or missing packets due to poor connectivity or missing the ordering of data may lead to inaccurate analysis.

Choosing data formats, schemas, and frameworks—In general, there would be data coming in from different sources. So, the formats and the velocity with which they are coming will be different. Though streaming data processing can be employed on either on-premise or cloud-based large-scale data repository, choosing data formats, schemas and development frameworks will be really a challenging task as data is used by different varieties of people right from analysts to domain experts to top-level managers to operators. The structure of the data and the tools that analysts, data scientists, and domain experts have at their disposal will greatly impact the adoption and application of the entire platform. In addition, data schema and structure often change, which can potentially break data pipeline itself.

1.9   Recent data streaming tools

Google Cloud DataFlow—Dataflow is a fully managed streaming analytics service that minimizes latency, processing time, and cost through autoscaling and batch processing.

1.9.1   Amazon Kinesis

Amazon Kinesis is also streaming tools which allows streaming Big Data with Amazon Web Services (AWS). Enterprises can develop streaming applications by leveraging open-source Java libraries and SQL editor with Amazon Kinesis. The best thing about Kinesis is that it takes care of the major responsibilities of running applications and scaling them according to requirements. As a result, enterprises can easily reduce the need for managing servers and other complexities related to the development, integration, and management of applications for real-time analytics. One of the most crucial traits of Amazon Kinesis that makes it one of the top opensource data streaming tools is flexibility.

1.9.2   Apache Kafka

Apache Kafka is especially designed for distributed messaging system for gaining high throughput. When compared with other messaging systems, Kafka offers built in partitioning, replication and fault tolerance features. It is originally based on publish–subscribe model. Since it is distributed in nature, it can be scaled out easily. Kafka is very fast as it performs two million writes/sec. Kafka has the following core components

Kafka producer—Producer will produce or publish the messages on one or more topics. Every time, a producer first sends messages to Kafka broker which is then transferred into the topic.

Kafka broker—Kafka cluster consists of one or more servers called Kafka broker which has the great responsibility for maintaining the published data. Kafka maintains data retention also, where the broker keeps the messages for certain amount of time.

Kafka topic—Kafka topic is located within the Kafka broker. Topic is the area where the messages are stored and published. For each topic, Kafka maintains a minimum of one partition. Topics may have many partitions also. Each partitioned message has a unique sequence id termed as offset.

Kafka Zookeeper—Zookeeper serves as the coordination interface between the Kafka brokers and Kafka consumers. Kafka allows zookeeper to store information about topics, brokers, consumers, and so on.

Kafka consumer—Consumer consumes messages from brokers. Consumer subscribes to one or more topics and consumes published messages by pulling data from the brokers. Kafka can support a large number of consumers and retain a large amount of data.

In addition, Kafka provides various application programming interfaces (APIs), namely, *Producer API, Consumer API, Streaming API, and Connector API* which enable the communications between various components.

1.9.3 Apache storm

Apache storm is a distributed real-time computational system for processing data stream. It is extremely fast as it processes a one million tuples per second per node. Storm can be easily integrated with any programming language. Storm architecture is mainly designed for micro batch processing. Apache storm specifically aims at the transformation of data streams. There is a considerable difference from Hadoop, which relies on batch processing. Apache storm can be integrated with Hadoop to improve its capability for larger throughputs.

1.9.4 Azure stream analytics

The design of Azure stream analytics focuses on the delivery of mission-critical end-to-end analytics services. The in-built machine learning capabilities of Azure stream analytics also provide adequate support for intuitive data processing. The machine learning capabilities also help in easier identification of spikes and dips, slow positive and negative trends, and outliers pertaining to streamed data.

1.9.5 StreamSQL

StreamSQL is the exceptional transformation of SQL for providing a real-time data streaming tool. StreamSQL is so simple which makes it suitable even for non-developers. StreamSQL makes it easier for the development of applications to ensure the manipulation of data streams, real-time compliance, surveillance, and monitoring networks.

1.9.6 Spark streaming

Apache spark is a distributed platform used to process Big Data with a unique capability that it can keep huge data in memory. Hence, it gives higher performance than Hadoop. Spark platform consists of various components such as spark core, Spark SQL, MLLib, streaming data API, and graph API.

Apache Spark Core—Spark Core is the general execution engine for parallel and distributed processing. It performs various functions namely in-memory computing, scheduling, distribution, and monitoring of jobs and interactions with external storage systems.

Spark SQL—Spark SQL like functions help to query large sized structured data which is distributed in nature.

MLLib—The Machine learning library includes various algorithms such as Naïve Bayes, *support vector machine, Random Forest, linear regression*, and *K-means clustering*. These algorithms are useful in carrying out various mining functions.

Streaming Data API—Spark streaming API provides techniques to handle streaming data.

GraphX—GraphX library provides methods to handle graph data structure.

1.9.7   Apache Flink

Apache Flink is a framework for processing streaming data in real time. It provides an open source stream processing engine for high-performance, scalable, and accurate real-time applications. Flink is designed to run in all common cluster environments, performs computations at in-memory speed and at any scale. Flink is effective both as a batch and real-time processing framework but it considers streaming first. Apache Flink architecture is designed around *Kappa architecture*. The main idea behind kappa architecture is to handle both batch and real-time data through a single-stream processing engine Kappa that provides flexibility to developers to develop applications without thinking about the internals of the processing framework.

1.10   Conclusion

In stream processing, data is consumed as it is generated, computation is performed quickly and results are immediately produced in real time. The rise of stream analytics is the result of modern analytic-centric applications which span multiple domains, including manufacturing, finance, healthcare, telecommunications, cyber security, etc. In addition, stream processing has emerged from the confluence of various disciplines mathematics, statistics, parallel and distributed computing, signal processing, machine and deep learning, data mining, cloud computing, Big Data, etc. In addition, in modern data processing platforms, the complexity of traditional architecture is abstracted into single self-service platform that turns event streams into analytics ready data. These modern systems are built around business centric value. More important aspect is that these modern processing architectures are based on cloud-based platforms and these are deployed very quickly with no capital cost.

References

[1] O. Sowmaya, T. M. Amine, A. Soufiane, D. Abderrahmane, and A. Mohamed, A new architecture for real time data stream processing, *International Journal of Advanced Computer Science and Applications*, vol. 8, no. 11, pp. 44–51, 2017.

[2] A. Jain and P. Venkatramana Bhat, Analysis of bill of material data using Kafka and spark, *International Journal of Scientific and Research Publications*, vol. 6, no. 8, pp. 44–48, 2016.

[3] J. Quddus, Real time data pipeline with Apache Kafka and Spark, 07 June 2017. Available at: https://knowledgebase.hyperlearning.ai/en/articles/real-time-data-pipeline-with-apache-kafka-and-spark.

[4] J. Kreps, N. Narkhede, and J. Rao, Kafka: A Distributed Messaging System for Log Processing, 12 June 2011. Available at: https://cs.uwaterloo.ca/~ssalihog/courses/papers/netdb11-final12.pdf.

[5] F. Gurcan and M. Berigel, Real-time processing of big data streams: life-cycle, tools, tasks and challenges, in 2018 2nd International Symposium on Multidisciplinary Studies and Innovative Technologies (ISMSIT), October 2018, pp. 1–6, doi: 10.1109/ISMSIT.2018.8567061.

[6] C. N. Gireesh Babu, P. Anu, V. Ashwini, and M. Thungamani, Real time big data analysis using apache flink, *International Journal of Scientific Engineering and Applied Science (IJSEAS)*, vol. 3, no. 6, pp. 78–83, 2017.

Chapter 2

Event processing platforms and streaming databases for event-driven enterprises

Pethuru Raj[1], S. Usha[2] and N. Susila[3]

Abstract

The Internet of things (IoT) devices and sensors are found everywhere generating tons of multi-structured data every second. These tiny, trendy, networked and embedded computers communicate and correspond to produce a mammoth amount of poly-structured data. The real beauty is here. When the generated data gets collected, cleansed, and subjected to a variety of deeper and decisive investigations, it is possible to extract and emit out actionable insights out of voluminous IoT data. The discovered knowledge comes handy for product, solution and service that are provided to visualize and realize a plethora of next-generation, multifaceted, state-of-the-art, and intelligent devices, systems, and networks. These smart entities and elements are deployed in critical junctions and environments ranging from industrial plants, manufacturing floors, retail stores, airports to people residences to derive people-centric, event-driven, service-oriented, knowledge-filled, process-optimized, mission-critical, situation-aware, time-sensitive and composite services, and applications.

Thus, the world is tending to be deeply and decisively connected and cognitive. Such an extreme integration results in streams of event data and messages. To bring forth premium use cases, businesses have to be event streaming, storage, and processing systems in place to readily make sense out of the event data. The event-driven architecture (EDA) style toward event-driven applications is maturing and stabilizing. This chapter is dedicated to convey how streaming databases combine well with other EDA components to build and run futuristic streaming applications and services.

[1]Edge AI Division, Reliance Jio Platforms, Bangalore, India
[2]Department of CSE, RRCE, India
[3]Department of Information Technology, Sri Krishna College of Engineering and Technology Kuniamuthur, India

2.1   Introduction

Pioneering and ground-breaking products, equipment, appliances, wares, utilities, machineries, and instruments are being manufactured in large quantities and deployed across all kinds of important locations to intrinsically empower deeper automations. Now, these instrumented, interconnected, and intelligent devices interact with one another in the vicinity and also with far away software applications, services, and databases (cloud-hosted) in order to get adequately empowered to contribute building context-aware and cognitive use cases for industries as well as people at large. Precisely speaking, the increasingly digital era leads to the realization of billions of connected devices and trillions of digital entities. On purpose-interactions, these digital devices and sensors produce a tremendous amount of multi-structured data (interaction, collaboration, log, operational, performance/throughput, scalability, security, health, etc.). In other words, these are all categorized as event(ful) data, which continuously and consistently originates from business, social and personal applications, services and devices. For timely extraction of actionable insights, hidden patterns, useful trends and transitions, fresh possibilities and opportunities out of exponentially growing data volumes, appropriate digital infrastructure modules have to be in place. We will talk about a few incredible and indispensable systems that have laid down a stimulating and scintillating foundation for setting up and sustaining event-driven enterprises.

Consider an earthquake monitoring application. The vibrations of earth surfaces are being meticulously acquired by seismic sensors once in a second. When the vibrations are found to be normal, there is no need to process data. However, when the vibrations cross a pre-defined threshold value, then it is critical to process and emit out insights, which can be used by multiple systems to send alerts and to ponder about the next course of actions with all the confidence. Here both streaming and processing happen in real time. That is, real-time analytics of streaming data is being insisted to derive timely insights to act upon.

Thus, real-time processing of data streams is mandatory. Most of the personal and professional use cases depend upon real-time data analytics in order to be right and relevant to respective stakeholders.

2.2   The emergence of streaming data

Streaming data is a continuously flowing data. Data originating from many sources get captured and streamed to be processed. The streaming data getting processed and analyzed is capable of producing easily and elegantly usable details. Many industrial sectors have realized that capturing and processing such data is going to be a huge beneficial for them to proceed with visualizing a plethora of premium services and delivering them with all the astuteness.

As indicated elsewhere, immediate processing of streaming data provides a variety of advantages for business establishments. With the explosion of IoT devices and sensors, connected applications, centralized, consolidated, shared and automated IT infrastructure modules, data getting collected and streamed is growing rapidly. Here is a list of popular streaming data sources, channels, and advantages.

- Sensors attached (internally as well as externally) in transportation vehicles, machineries in manufacturing floors, medical instruments, defense equipment, home appliances, consumer electronics, etc. send data continuously to stream-handling and processing applications. The application then understands the performance and health condition of the systems and predicts when they need some rest and repair.
- Stock brokers, investment managers, and financial services providers continuously track changes in the stock market and do the necessary computation quickly and indulge in remedial actions to rearrange portfolios in order to get benefits out of stock price movements.
- Patient health is being minutely monitored, measured, and managed through streaming analytics, which is being even deployed in IoT edge devices to ensure low-latency communication, patient data privacy, bandwidth conservation, etc.
- Weather and structure monitoring is being accomplished through the analyses of continuously flowing data from weather sensors and satellites.
- House property recommendation is being fine-tuned through streaming analytics of house value, location, and other relevant data.
- Microgrid data is being subjected to a variety of investigations to ascertain the electricity utilization, need, and preservation in real time.

Benefits of streaming data—Streaming data brings in several new benefits and instigates fresh use cases. By performing simple and advanced analytics on streaming data on the fly, industries can benefit in many ways. Streaming data is dynamic. Also, real-time analytics is being demanded on flowing data in order to get all the timely benefits. Luckily there are state-of-the-art platforms for processing data streams. Log data analytics is one of the foremost applications for employing streaming analytics. The applications that need streaming analytics capability are becoming more in number as well as in complexity. Initially simple reports and actions were produced through streaming analytics. If there is a deviation or threshold break-in in key performance indicators (KPIs), the system immediately produces alarms. Operational metrics are being extensively used to produce something useful out of real-time streaming analytics.

The journey is on. Today, complex applications embed streaming analytics in order to be intrinsically intelligent in their operations, offerings, and outputs. Further on, in the beginning, simple queries were used for incoming data to emit out something useful and usable. Now with the faster maturity and stability of machine and deep learning (ML/DL) algorithms, streaming analytics is astutely emboldened with ML and DL models in order to do deeper and decisive analytics on all kinds of flowing data with all the alacrity.

Real-time insights are important for many industries to be right and relevant to their esteemed consumers. Batch processing is time-consuming and also works as per schedules. But use cases such as fraud detection, e-commerce, and e-business applications bat for real-time data processing. With streaming data, modern applications have to capture, filter, process, and react to that data in real-time. This opens up a new plethora of fresh use cases. In short, any industry can easily and elegantly benefit from continuous data through real-time processing. The typical use cases through streaming data include the following:

- Building location-based and context-aware applications
- Facilitating fraud detection and real-time stock trades
- Enabling marketing, sales, and business analytics
- Monitoring customer/user activity
- Monitoring and managing critical and capital assets including IT infrastructures
- Log, operational, transactional, security, and performance data analytics
- Inventory and replenishment management operations for retail stores and warehouses
- Intelligent supply chain systems
- Healthcare and structural monitoring
- By applying ML and DL algorithms, predictive and prescriptive analytics capabilities can be incorporated into mission-critical systems and applications.

There are a plenty of integrated platforms for simple and complex event processing platforms. Thus, complex business events are also captured and integrated with other decision-enabling and contextual information in order to emit out actionable insights in time. One significant impact of streaming data and its analytics is empowering the setup and sustenance of event-driven enterprises, which are slated to be open, dynamic, people-centric, extensible, adaptive, and business-aware.

2.3   Streaming data analytics

Streaming data is becoming popular and had laid down a stimulating platform for visualizing newer use cases for businesses in conjunction with streaming analytics tools. In the subsequent sections, we will be deliberating on a few streaming data analytics platforms and infrastructures. Also, some of the industrial use cases. Especially, the arrival of simple and complex event processing platforms has done a great job in receiving and processing event data/messages in real time to bring out actionable insights in the form of useful patterns, brewing trends and transitions, beneficial associations, etc. Also, event processing has enabled envisaging newer possibilities and opportunities. Especially, enterprises are bound to be event-driven. The event-centric business automation prospects brightened. The event-driven architecture (EDA) pattern has become popular and pioneer in realizing event-driven applications, which are decoupled, extensible, modern, dynamic, and supple. You can read more on this below. Another noteworthy facet is the emergence of streaming databases. We have talked about them in the latter part of this chapter.

2.4   The journey toward event-driven enterprises

Events turn out to be the key driver of modern enterprises. Visiting a web site, a credit card swipe, the turn of a gear, etc. are all noteworthy events, which are getting digitized to create fresh business value. Enterprises are putting required IT infrastructure, event processing platforms, databases, message queues and brokers, visualization tools, and business workloads in order to succulently capture and make sense out of discrete as well as complex events flowing from many sources. The business and technical implications of collecting and crunching business, people and social events are becoming enormous and strategically sound for organizations across the world. Event data/messages are streamed and hence the aspect of event stream processing is gaining dominance these days. Here are a few renowned use cases of event stream processing.

- *Contextualization*—It is vital to gain decision-enabling and value-adding context details for bringing forth correct and comprehensive answer for any complex problem. For example, a meteorologist gathers and interprets various event information getting streamed by satellites. Generally, there are event streams for temperature, humidity, pressure, wind speed, and precipitation. These event streams primarily add context and support information. In order to do accurate weather prediction, each event stream has to be captured, combined with other event streams, and crunched together.
- *Data analytics*—There are IoT devices and sensors producing event data continuously on various aspects. The data produced has to be gleaned and processed immediately in order to identify any threatening issue and to issue appropriate alerts and notifications in time. For example, a gas pipeline management software monitors and correlates signals coming from pressure and rate-monitoring sensors attached with gas pipelines. Thereby, any threshold break-in can be messaged to the concerned to keep things running without any hitch or hurdle.
- *Automated action*—There are breakthrough digital technologies and tools emerging to accomplish a variety of tasks without any interpretation and intervention of human beings. For such a situation, software systems and embedded devices are being empowered through artificial intelligence (AI) algorithms, models, and libraries. For an example, an AI-enabled credit card transaction processing software automatically identifies an unusual transaction, compares it to historical behavior, and alerts the card owner of if there is a sniff of a potential fraud.

- *On-device intelligence*—IoT edge devices are joining in the mainstream computing. Edge devices are also connected and integrated with remotely held software applications and databases. Purpose-specific and agnostic sensors are being attached on edge devices to empower devices to gain vision and perception capabilities. Streaming analytics platforms and AI frameworks are increasingly embedded in edge devices to enable them to decide and act independently and collaboratively with other devices in the vicinity. Thus, edge devices are not only computational and communicative but also sensitive, perceptive, and responsive. Thus, devices are being made intelligent by capturing and crunching event streams.

Events from a growing pool of data sources ranging from cloud infrastructure modules, business workloads, IT services, to portables, handhelds, implantable, and wearables can be gleaned and harnessed to support a number of fresh industrial use cases.

2.5   Briefing on EDA

Enterprises heavily depend on a myriad of digital technologies and tools to build and run highly scalable, available, and reliable applications. As elucidated elsewhere, microservices architecture (MSA) is one popular architectural pattern to construct production-grade, service-oriented, and enterprise-scale applications. Another interesting architectural pattern is EDA. EDA applications are made up of decoupled and distributed services, which are connected through asynchronous events. Such a loosely or lightly coupled nature simplifies adding newer services and databases without disrupting the functioning of currently running software systems. Another important consideration is enterprise integration. Increasingly enterprise business applications such as enterprise resource planning (ERP) and supply chain management (SCM) applications are being modernized and migrated to cloud environments. For eliminating security concerns, still some databases with customer, confidential, and corporate details are being kept in private cloud environments. Then there are some applications being rendered as a service by SaaS providers. Thus, linking up these different and distributed software applications, platforms, middleware solutions, and databases, enterprise integration mechanisms are being solicited. Event-driven integration is gaining dominance and prominence with the unprecedented adoption and adaption of the event driven architecture (EDA) pattern. Another popular use case for the surging popularity of EDA is event streaming and processing.

EDA has the wherewithal to plan and produce pioneering applications that are event-driven and adaptive to changes. EDA is being pitched and positioned as a keystone toward building enabling modern enterprises. Event-driven applications are inherently capable of responding quickly to all kinds of real-time events. Such a technologically inspired power empowers businesses to take intelligent decisions in an automated manner. Events have become a source of strength for building next-generation applications. Events contribute as a glue among decoupled applications, services, and databases in order to develop integrated systems.

The motivations for EDA adoption—Having understood the strategic significance of events, software developers and enterprise IT divisions are keenly planning and producing software solutions that natively leverage events to be distinct in their operations, outputs, and offerings. Enterprising businesses across the globe, therefore, embrace and capitalize the proven EDA pattern to come out with highly scalable and sustainable applications. Especially with the exponential growth of event-generating entities such as IoT devices and sensors, cyber physical systems (CPS), ambient intelligence (AmI), smart objects and sentient materials, the number of events is bound to go up significantly. The challenge is to capture each and every event with all the care and confidence and analyze event streams to uncover hidden patterns. The patterns unearthed empower every stakeholder in building modern applications that fully comply with the EDA style.

The surge in using event-driven applications gets emboldened with the ready availability of highly reliable and robust communication. Such a setup has laid down a beneficial foundation to initiate premium solutions and services across a variety of industry verticals. With edge computing flourishing ceaselessly, scores of sophisticated real-time and event-driven services and applications are to see a grandiose reality. Such applications are decisively impacting and improving the scalability, reliability, and responsiveness of applications. The diagram below clearly shows the participants of an EDA application.

2.6   Delineating event-driven reference architecture

There is no doubt on the efficacy of EDA in having modern applications across business domains. Wipro and Red Hat have cooperated together to come out with a reference architecture. On the one side, there are IoT devices emitting out a lot of event data and messages. The other major categories of event producers include business workloads and IT services. There are enterprise IT environments (traditional and private clouds) and public cloud environments hosting most of the production-grade business applications. The second key component of the EDA reference architecture is event brokers. There are message queues and brokers leveraging the proven publish–subscribe paradigm. In the recent past, Kafka acquires special significance for the event world for receiving and persisting event messages. Apache Kafka (https://kafka.apache.org/) is a distributed event streaming platform used extensively for accomplishing high-performance data pipelines, streaming analytics, data integration, and mission-critical applications.

This fully complies with the pub/sub messaging pattern. There are event-producing services, which publish (write) events to Kafka topics. On the other side, there are event-consuming services consuming (reading) events from Kafka topics. All these happen in real time. This is called event streaming. Further on, Kafka provides stream processing capabilities through Kafka Streams, which is a client library that facilitates writing Java and Scala applications that can consume event streams from Kafka, analyze, aggregate, enrich, and publish the output back into Kafka. Organizations increase process event streams to extract insights out of events and to make sound, sagacious, and speedy decisions.

Kafka is an excellent message-oriented middleware utilizing messages for linking up different and distributed applications. This can handle millions of event messages per minute. This acts as an extempore intermediary or as a cushion among data stores and high-throughput applications. When millions of event messages flow across, the message delivery should not be missed or messed up. Apache Kafka remains the default choice for all streaming use cases. This is fitted with a rock-solid and super-fast event-streaming backbone. Kafka enables several unique use cases such as activity tracking, log aggregation, change data capture (CDC), and processing IoT telemetry data streams. With Kafka streams, event streaming and processing capabilities are aggregated into a single product. In short, Kafka plays a very vital role in the event-filled world in not only capturing events but also making sense out of those captured events. In-memory data grids are also highly recommended as an event broker. Event processing systems are classified into two: simple and complex event processing solutions.

Stream processing is the real-time processing of data "in motion." Unlike batch processing, where data is collected over time and then analyzed, stream processing enables you to query and analyze continuous data streams and react to critical events immediately. Any standardized event processing platform (reliably store streams of events and process them) has to be empowered with many programming abstractions including SQL to query the fast-moving data. Increasingly ML libraries are also being attached to accomplish automated classification, clustering, and prediction tasks.

Streaming databases are being pitched as an excellent software solution for event capture, store, and processing. Event stores are now important ingredients. EventStoreDB (https://www.eventstore.com/) is a database technology that stores critical data in streams of immutable events. It was built and sustained for event sourcing. This event store solution facilitates building and using event-centric systems. Generally, event sourcing offers some great benefits over state-oriented systems.

Event sourcing is to persist data in which all changes in a system are stored as an immutable series of events in the order that they occurred. The current state is derived from that event log. This contrasts with state-oriented persistence that only keeps the latest version of the entity state. If there is a change occurring in traditional database systems, the state gets updated and hence the history along with the reason for the change is lost. More information can be found at this page [1].

Traditional SQL databases are also empowered with additional competencies to natively handle events. For enabling purpose-specific processing, rule engines are also being attached. The figure below vividly illustrates how event processing happens.

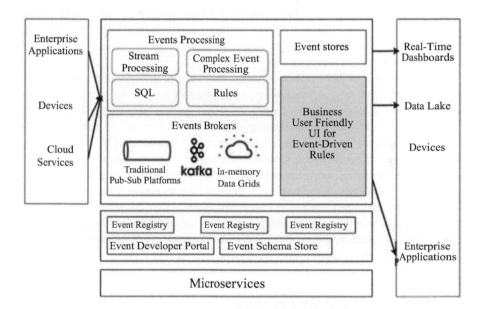

If handled by business users, most events can easily be mapped to business concepts. An intuitive and informative user interface allows users to define event processing rules based on the occurrence and recurrence of an event or a combination of events within a time-window.

2.6.1   Event-driven serverless architecture

Serverless computing refers to the growing concept of building and running software applications that do not require server management. For the serverless era to shine, functions are being touted as the highly optimized development and deployment unit. Server-side applications get disintegrated into a collection of functions in order to be micro-managed. Functions can respond to user requests individually and collectively. The advantage with serverless applications is that they get executed, scaled, and billed in response to the exact demand from users. With the widespread adoption of cutting-edge technologies such as MSA, containerization and container orchestration platforms, the aspects of subdividing complex applications into a dynamic pool of functions and executing functions on requests have laid down a breakthrough foundation for serverless applications to gain the momentum. The automation of server management operations gets speeded up and simplified through functions. Functions and their composites (applications) are fully managed through containerization technologies and tools and are provided as services.

Functions are being combined through workflow composers. The much-touted NoOps concept is being slowly yet steadily fulfilled through the power of serverless computing, which is bound to go through a series of delectable advancements in the years to come. The brewing idea is that the tedious and time-consuming operations of enterprise-scale and modern business workloads get hugely simplified. With the soaring improvisations in the serverless space, the prickling and persisting concerns and challenges of server operations are bound to see drastic decreases in the years to unfurl.

We all know that EDA also plays an important role in serverless environments. Serverless applications are a quite recent phenomenon and they can respond to varying demands artistically and automatically by resource scaling up and down. Serverless applications are generally event-driven. Events trigger application functions to respond accordingly. Thus, the combination of EDA and serverless computing guarantees deeper and decisive automation in IT operations.

Event Streaming and Processing Platforms—IBM Event Streams is an event-streaming platform built on open-source Apache Kafka that helps you build smart applications that can react to events as they happen, making it ideal for mission-critical workloads. This helps to create more engaging customer experiences thanks to access to a wide range of connectors to core systems and restful APIs to extend the reach of your data assets.

2.7   Event-driven microservices

We know that the EDA and MSA patterns hugely simplify the application design, development, deployment, and maintenance tasks. There are some unique properties being associated with each of these architectural styles. Primarily MSA supports synchronous interactions whereas the aspect of asynchronous communication is made possible by EDA.

Now, by skillfully combining these two architectural styles, developers can easily and quickly build distributed, highly scalable and available, fault-tolerant, and extensible systems. These systems can receive, aggregate, enrich, process, and correlate extremely a large amount of event data and messages in real time. Developers can easily extend and enhance these systems by integrating with third-party applications and services through the leverage of middleware solutions. Further on, this strategically sound combination serves to achieve several non-functional requirements (NFRs)/the prominent quality attributes such as scalability, availability, reliability, accessibility, simplicity, maneuverability, security, and sustainability.

Architectural concerns and complexities—These architectural styles also introduce some concerns. There is an explosion of micro-scale services as monolithic and massive applications are being segmented into a pool of microservices in order to be modern in their outputs, offerings, and operations. For ensuring high availability, many instances of a microservice are being prepared and deployed. Thus, even in a relatively small IT environment, there are many microservices and their instances. As told elsewhere, microservices typically fulfills a single business functionality. Microservices are being independently built and deployed. Thus, enterprise-scale business workloads and IT services are comprising a growing set of microservices, which do network calls for purposeful communications and collaborations. Designing and implementation of such distributed systems incur a lot of challenges and complexities. Events have to originate from multiple microservices and their applications and pass through a variety of message-oriented middleware, event processing and storage systems. Defining event-processing workflows is not a straightforward task. With a greater number of system components, the possibility for the occurrence of faults, errors, and failure goes up. The testing and debugging of microservices-centric applications workflows in a microservices become tedious and time-consuming. Software integration, delivery, and deployment get complicated. Further on, system monitoring, measurement, and management become a challenging activity. The other complications are listed below (https://developer.ibm.com/depmodels/microservices/articles/eda-and-microservices-architecture-best-practices/).

1. Asynchronous event processing is quite difficult to implement compared to synchronous processing because of the requirements such as event ordering or sequencing, call-backs, and exception handling.
2. Event messages have to be sequentially received and processed. There should not be any loss or duplication. Event producers and consumers have to be designed to withstand failures, have the ability to replay failed events, and have the deduplication feature.
3. Fulfilling distributed transactions is another worrying factor. Developers have to incorporate custom and complex logic to fulfill rollback and compensation. Microservices are generally spread across several distributed systems.
4. Because of the multiplicity, heterogeneity, and distributed nature of microservices, maintaining data consistency is beset with difficulties. With the widespread usage of NoSQL databases, eventual consistency is being achieved.
5. Event consumers and producers have to evaluate important properties of event brokers, data caches, etc. The aspect of delivery guarantee has to be considered while designing event producing and consuming systems.

Thus, newer concerns and challenges emerge and technocrats are striving hard to surmount them. Reference architecture that outlines the use of architectural patterns, enabling frameworks, services repository, integrated platforms, DevOps, and resiliency tools and setting up a robust and effective governance model are being touted as the way forward to overcome the issues pertaining to modern applications.

Technology choice considerations—As indicated above, there are several technologies and tools such as event brokers, data caches, in-memory data grids, microservices development frameworks, and observability tools to be meticulously chosen for producing event-driven microservices-centric systems. Experts recommend the following aspects to be taken into consideration. The products and platforms have to have some essential and elegant qualities. The chosen product has to inherently support horizontal scalability of individual microservices. For ensuring the need of continuous availability, the clustering feature has to be implemented across primary and secondary cloud centers. The product also has to ensure the system to be fault-tolerant. The other noteworthy features include service error prediction and detection, affected services have to be isolated in order not spread the error to other services of the system, fail fast, quick recovery, etc. The identified technologies have to empower microservices to be configured, customized, and composed. The other factors to be given the thrust are cloud affinity, affordability, manageability, and security.

Event processing topology—In the EDA pattern, processing topology refers to the organization of event producers, consumers, middleware, integration patterns, and topics and queues to provide event processing capability. Integration patterns play a vital role in integrating different event components (source, sink, and intermediaries). For complex event processing, multiple processing topologies can be linked up.

Event processing primarily in two ways. Orchestration leverages a centralized orchestrator to orchestrate the event processing workflow by invoking different components in a pre-defined manner. This ensures deeper visibility and controllability. For payments processing, such a tighter and centralized control is needed. With orchestration, the SAGA pattern can be used. The orchestration method carries a few niggles as well. The orchestration component may induce single point of failure. The system performance may degrade. Choreography, instead of centralization, prefers decentralization for event processing. Events are published into topics and interested services can subscribe to one or more topics. There is no module in the middle to monitor processing flow. However, choreography is not straightforward to implement and maintain.

Deployment topology—In an EDA-MSA, there are many components to be chosen and used. With Kubernetes gaining enormous popularity as the management platform for containerized applications, there are noteworthy automations and accelerations in deploying event-driven microservices-centric applications on Kubernetes clusters. Public cloud services are bringing forth a number of advancements in facilitating appropriate infrastructure modules for running Kubernetes-managed, containerized, and microservices applications. As seen above, the combination of serverless computing and Kubernetes platform promises a myriad of delectable augmentations in the IT operations space. Taking event-driven applications to the market are being speeded up through a host of server-side technologies and tools. Platform solutions, best practices, knowledge guides, deployment patterns, optimized processes, and pioneering products combine well to lessen the cloud infrastructure operations team. Besides automated deployments, automated failover and failback, rollout and rollback, canary and blue-green deployments, externalization of configuration details, etc. are important ingredients for formulating sustainable deployment topology.

Security—With the faster proliferation of microservices and the increased participation of several types of intermediaries in spontaneously uniting different and distributed microservices, the security scenario is bound to change drastically. Security consultants and advisors hence have come out with a series of recommendations for ensuring the unbreakable and impenetrable security for event-driven microservices systems. Authentication and authorization, establishing tighter security for data while in transit, rest and use through strong encryption mechanisms, unearthing and eliminating all kinds of vulnerabilities, security holes, in microservices code, transport-level security, third-party auditing, and scores of security solutions such as firewalls, intrusion detection and prevention, compliance to security standards, employing security patterns and practices are being given the prime importance while formulating the viable security strategy.

Observability—With distributed systems comprising multiple moving components, the attribute of observability is gaining prominence. Generally, observability includes monitoring, logging, tracing, and alerting. Such an overseeing feature comes handy in proactively pinpointing any incoming slide in performance. Security issues can be pre-emptively identified and nullified. Thus, for continuous availability and enhanced reliability, the observability feature widely is insisted. There is each component of the system that should be observable to avoid failures and also to quickly recover from failures. There are tools enabling log monitoring, collection, storage, analytics, and knowledge visualization. Metrics are being defined and values are being carefully captured and evaluated. Thus, system monitoring and management are being activated and automated through a host of powerful tools.

Developers can combine EDA and MSA styles to develop distributed, highly available, fault-tolerant, and high-throughput systems. These systems can process very large amounts of information and can have extreme scalability.

2.8   The emergence of streaming databases

The real complications really rest with database administrators, who are expected to gather, store, and analyze this often-unceasing firehose of bits. However, the faster maturity and stability of streaming databases come as a great solace. Streaming databases are close to new tools like time-series databases or log databases. All are designed to track a series of events and to enable queries that can search and produce statistical profiles of blocks of time. The streaming databases can respond to queries for data and also statistics about the data, generate reports from these queries, and populate all of the dashboards that track what's happening to allow the concerned to make smart and timely decisions about the telemetry.

We have been using SQL databases to store data that typically does not change very often. We have many powerful examples such as ERP, SCM, customer relationship management (CRM), and e-commerce applications that update every few minutes. However, to accommodate continuously streaming data, developers have to add additional code. Developing microservices to process flowing data is definitely tedious and troublesome. And hence the need for streaming databases to handle data streams naturally has gone up in the recent past. Besides, streaming databases facilitate real-time data analytics to extract actionable insights in time out of growing data streams. Further on, streaming databases open up fresh possibilities to visualize and realize modern business applications. Precisely speaking, for setting up and sustaining real-time intelligent enterprises, the role and the responsibility of streaming data technologies and tools are bound to go up considerably. In the subsequent sections, we are to focus on the various aspects of streaming databases.

What is a streaming database?—A streaming database is generally defined as a data store designed to real-time collection, processing, and enriching of data streams. When a datapoint gets created, immediately it gets collected, buffered, and processed to emit out useful and usable information. Unlike the hugely popular SQL databases, a streaming database has to work with continuously pouring data. Primarily event data and messages originating from multiple locations (applications, databases, machines, devices, sensors, etc.) are constantly streamed. Streaming databases then do its specific yet critical role facilitating knowledge discovery and dissemination. This continuously flowing data triggers useful actions. Typically, in the SQL world, queries are formed against data to retrieve required details. Standard databases require human input in the form of queries to generate appropriate responses. For instance, a shopper buys a product in an e-commerce store. This human activity triggers an output in the form of a response. On the other hand, a streaming database receives and processes any data flow on the fly for bringing forth real-time alerts, visualizations, and to emit out actionable insights in time. The query initiates actions in the SQL era. Here, it is the incoming data initiating one or more actions to accomplish various tasks.

There are several types of databases that handle streaming data in real time, including in-memory data grids, in-memory databases, and time-series databases. NoSQL and NewSQL databases are also gaining stream processing capability. In SQL databases, a DB admin load data using an ETL/ELT tool at regular intervals. For advanced use cases, a streaming database sits along with a SQL database. As the volume of data continues to grow and the velocity of data continues to accelerate, some technologies that once relied primarily on batch-oriented databases now rely more heavily on streaming database technologies (e.g., recommendation engines). The figure below vividly illustrates how stream processing systems do the necessary transformations and tricks on data streams. Such a transition and enablement simplify applications to benefit immensely.

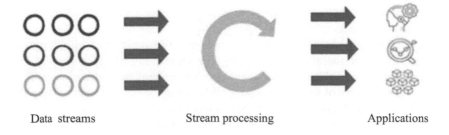

Data streams   Stream processing   Applications

A streaming database collects streaming data in real time for immediate processing or for subsequent batch processing. As told above, streaming database is a recent phenomenon. With the faster proliferation of IoT sensors, devices, systems, and environments, the requirements such as real-time data capture, processing, analytics, knowledge discovery, and dissemination are mandated in order to build and run real-time applications across industry verticals. In short, real-time decision-making and actuation are insisted for fulfilling the goal of customer satisfaction. Even the distant goal of customer delight or ecstasy is also capable of getting accomplished by enterprising business with the faster maturity and stability of streaming databases.

Data streaming involves real-time processing of data from up to thousands of sources such as sensors, financial trading floor transactions, e-commerce purchases, web and mobile applications, social networks, and many more. By aggregating and analyzing these real-time data streams, enterprises can use database streaming to develop intelligence to improve agility, make better-informed decisions, fine-tune operations, improve customer service, and act quickly to take advantage of business opportunity.

2.9 The rise of the event streaming databases

Databases are important ingredients in any digital transformation initiative. The database technology has been steadily improving. Databases are vital for enterprise-grade and mission-critical applications and services. From the inception of SQL databases, there came a number of variants and improvements such as data warehouses, data marts, and cubes. Today we often hear, read, and use NoSQL and NewSQL databases. With the tickling of big data era, we came to know about data lakes. Then there are in-memory databases. Thus, the evolution is definitely noteworthy. Despite all these improvisations, databases still look like static repositories of data. You just send out queries and expect back relevant answers.

But streaming databases bring in an altogether different outlook. There is a paradigm shift in the database technology space. With streaming databases, you can expect instantaneous answer to your question. Continuous processing of streaming data based on pre-defined queries triggers a series of actions simultaneously. Streaming databases are acquiring special significance in the digital world. This database is for solving business problems in conjunction with other IT services and there is a less intervention, involvement, and interpretation from humans. Increasingly business processes are software-defined. Continuous data flowing and processing goes a long way in automating and accelerating a number of business and human activities.

Ride-sharing business conglomerates such as Uber or Ola are a good example. When you order a ride, the entire process gets automated instantly. There is location data of you and the car driver and there are several other decision-enabling datapoints. A variety of such datapoints/variables/parameters/features get collected from different and distributed sources and streamed to ride-sharing software applications. The business-critical data activate several pieces of the software to collaborate and facilitate for people to hail, route, and pay for the ride in a coordinated fashion. This is quite unique and distinct from the traditional database-enabled software applications. Conventionally, taxi operators take and record phone calls from commuters and manage pickups. Such a sequential and time-consuming reservation is not a thing for the digitally empowered world.

Industry verticals are meticulously exploring and expediting flexible and futuristic strategy formation to embrace this next-generation database technology with all the clarity and confidence. For example, event streaming facilitates bank operations automation and orchestration. Above all, real-time data processing and analytics through streaming databases produce timely and trustworthy insights to be shared cross decision-makers, business executives and other stakeholders. Precisely speaking, software libraries are being extensively used to automate complicated business processes. For such an aspiration to be fulfilled elegantly, the database technology has to undergo solid transformation. The arrival of streaming databases is being viewed as a positive movement and moment.

In a database, the data sits there passively. You have to send a query to it. Then only, it acts and reciprocates. With data streams, the data becomes an active component. The arrival of new data triggers queries to be run. This action triggers a series of actions on different pieces of the business software. Business application in association with streaming databases, messaging systems, and data storage components implement the full business process. In short, it is not the query. Instead, the data instigates everything toward the accomplishment of the process.

2.9.1   The advantages of streaming databases

The business sentiments are fast changing. Quick and correct decisions ought to be taken in order to support and sustain the edge earned in the cut-throat competition. Trends and transitions have to be closely watched in order to make immediate inference. Rather than any historic data, current data acquires special significance for stream processing. It is indisputably true that the value of data goes down with time goes by. So, timeliness and trustworthiness of data-driven insights are categorized as the vital ingredients for the intended success of any tactical and stra tegical initiatives and implementations for businesses across the globe. So, instead of waiting, as data arrives, it has to be subjected to suitable investigations. It is a proactive, prompt, and pre-emptive processing. By using a streaming database, data users can ask questions and receive results in real time even as the underlying data changes. There are numerous use cases for this trend-setting technology.

Business leaders and executives see that streaming databases can enable them to do the following:

- Streaming databases can respond to business events reliably
- Real-time notification can be made based on simple and complex events
- Preventive and predictive maintenance of critical infrastructures and assets
- Real-time data analytics toward timely and trustworthy insights
- Can be empowered through AI libraries and frameworks toward advanced and automated analytics

E-commerce companies are keenly analyzing customer transaction data streams to understand what products are selling like hot cakes and what products are not doing fine on the selling side. Analyzing transaction data, which is incidentally continuous, emits out a lot of useful and usable information to retailers to reorient their selling strategies. Inventory and replenishment management activities can be data-driven instead of employing traditional intuition-based decision. Instead of hosting and running many microservices to capture and process streaming data to extract hidden patterns and trends, experts are of the opinion that streaming databases can be an optimal solution for doing analytics on data streams.

Researchers are working overtime in unearthing and popularizing industrial use cases for the domain of streaming databases. Not only for business applications but also for technical computing, experts recommend streaming database to extract actionable insights in time and to plunge into counter measures in time with all the sincerity and sagacity. For example, pharmaceutical and biomedical scientists extensively use streaming databases to monitor results from large-scale clinical studies with the intention of improving drug viability and delivery times. Other prominent use cases are the following:

- *Cybersecurity monitoring*—Cybersecurity solutions monitor constant flows of security-related data through multiple channels/networks. Streaming databases are capable of monitoring the flowing data for abnormalities and generating advance notices and alarms for IT security-enablement solutions to proactively react and prevent any harm to IT resources, applications, and data. Credit card companies and banks can issue real-time fraud alerts if a customer's card or identity is tried to be stolen.
- *Real-time data visualizations*—In the past, business intelligence (BI) and reporting tools had been helping business executives to ponder about the next course of actions to steer businesses in the right direction. Now by integrating BI tools and 360-degree dashboards with streaming databases, it is possible to generate graphs, charts, maps, etc. for critical business processes in real time. Real-time insights empower decision-makers to be vigilant and versatile in their obligations and assignments. Stock investors, market watchers, and brokers can tweak their plans and executions based on the highly volatile market trends and changes.
- *Real-time applications*—Previously, application developers had to join multiple tables and even databases in order to process changing data. This is not an easy task. Software engineers and architects also had to design and develop a variety of microservices to handle complicated instructions to process streaming data with traditional SQL databases. With streaming databases, there is no need for microservices to process data streams. The service development time and costs get removed.

The benefits of streaming databases primarily center around the speed with which data gets captured and analyzed to make sense out of data volumes. With streaming databases, the processing of streaming data gets reduced substantially. Altogether the time complexity toward processing streaming data is halved. Data gets captured, analyzed on the fly, and reported in real time. Such an accelerated analysis of data leads to real-time decisions and actions. The conventional SQL databases fall flat when the data flow rate goes up remarkably. The traditional batch-mode data analytics is not adequate for providing real-time monitoring, analysis, and visualization. With streaming databases, data streams can be processed quickly using simple SQL queries. Streaming data is primarily event data and messages. Events are turning out to be very critical for enterprises to make timely, critical, and enterprise-wise decisions. There are personal, business, and social events emanating from different and distributed sources. Streaming databases can collect and process event data immediately and intelligently and make a timely alert/notification if there is any perceptible deviation. And streaming databases can also execute continuous queries to adroitly process real-time events.

There are noteworthy implications with the arrival of streaming databases. The increasing use of data streams is to drastically disrupt the domain of SQL databases and data warehouses. As reported earlier, event data and messages are the prime streaming data, which get instantaneously processed using streaming databases to emit out actionable insights in time.

2.9.2   Streaming databases: the technical use cases

Streaming data is data that is getting generated continuously by a growing array of data sources. Data is sent as data records simultaneously and also in small sizes. The data sources are many and varied. Software applications, social web applications, IoT devices, and sensors from cloud environments, manufacturing floors, retail stores, airports, hospitals, etc. generate multi-structured and massive quantity of business, machine, sensor, application and infrastructure, operational, transactional and analytical data.

This streaming data needs to be processed sequentially and incrementally on a record-by-record basis or over sliding time windows. Such a stream processing is being performed for a variety of useful purposes such as correlation, aggregation, filtering, sampling, and quick analytics. Such a real-time processing information derived from such analysis gives companies visibility into many aspects of their business and customer activity such as service usage (for metering/billing), server activity, website clicks, and geo-location of devices, people, and physical goods and enables them to respond promptly to emerging situations. For example, businesses can track changes in public sentiment on their brands and products by continuously analyzing social media streams, and respond in a timely fashion as the necessity arises. Technocrats are extensively using streaming databases for a number of reasons.

- *Stream data enrichment*—Event data and messages can be captured and stored in streaming databases, which can suitably enrich streaming data. Enriched and augmented data helps in performing high-quality analytics. Streaming data from IoT devices and sensors can be joined with reference data from a streaming database. This union is going to be more comprehensive and contextually deeper and decisive.

- *Real-time streaming data analytics*—Technical leaders and operators want real-time insights in order to gain the required intelligence in intelligently managing critical infrastructures and assets. Interactive processing is also made possible. This will lead to event-driven enterprises.
- *Event-driven and real-time MSA*—The traditional request and response MSA with synchronous communication will move towards decoupled, non-blocking, asynchronous and adaptive microservices-centric applications. The fields of data fabrics and pipelines are bound to be radically disrupted with streaming databases. Streaming databases can lead to the implementations of a plethora of real-time, event-driven, and service-oriented intelligent applications.

Some streaming databases contribute immensely in reducing data size to bring in huge savings in data storage costs and information retrieval times. This is a kind of data pre-processing. Stream processing replaces a value collected every second with an average computed per day. Thus, a lot of redundant, routine, and repetitive data can be eliminated and such a feature comes handy in dramatically reducing the data size. Thereby data storage costs come down sharply.

Developers can decide and adjust how the data streams are turned into tabular summaries. This is to ensure that the right values are computed and saved while the irrelevant information is ignored. The ability to tune the data pipeline allows streaming databases to handle larger datasets. Traditional databases are also finding a role in streaming applications, but usually as a destination that lies downstream as illustrated above. Thus, there are a number of innovations and disruptions in the streaming database space. By clubbing with traditional databases, a kind of hybrid model is being recommended. Such an integration can be a game-changer for powerful and modern business applications.

For instance, Oracle Streams can be deployed either as a service or as an on-premise installation. This will gather and transform data from a variety of sources and then deposit it with other services that can include their own databases. The message format is designed to be compatible with Apache Kafka. That is, other Kafka applications can benefit immensely. IBM streams enhances the analytical power of the pipeline by integrating with ML libraries. This is compatible with Kafka and can deposit the results in a number of databases.

Streaming databases are enabling stream processing rather than batch processing. That is, the batch-processing of big data is getting switched over to stream processing of Big Data.

2.10 Additional requirements for stream processing

Without an iota of doubt, Apache Kafka has emerged as the de-facto standard for working with events. Kafka offers the abstraction of a durable, immutable, and append-only log. Stream database vendors are incorporating extra features to simplify and streamline working with Kafka. One well-known addition is that stream databases can derive new streams of events from existing ones. Stream processing is a paradigm of programming that exposes a model for working with groups of events as if they were in-memory collections. Most stream processing frameworks offer a directed, acyclic graph API to express these programs. Some frameworks even expose a SQL API to raise the abstraction a bit higher. Kafka truly shines in asynchronous flows.

Stream processing alone is not enough to create an end-to-end application. There is a need for other pieces to be aggregated and used. Data is collected from multiple sources and ingested into Kafka. Then, a stream processor takes over. There are applications insisting for synchronous communication. And hence, the output of stream processor has to be poured into an external database. Applications, then, can query and retrieve relevant results in a synchronous manner. Many organizations are building and using a hybrid model by combining the batch and stream processing approaches by having a real-time layer and a batch layer. Data is first processed by a streaming data platform such as Amazon Kinesis to extract real-time insights and then persisted into a store like S3, where it can be transformed and loaded for a variety of batch-processing applications.

Streaming data processing requires storage and processing layers. The storage layer has to support record ordering and strong consistency to enable fast and replayable reads and writes of data streams. The processing layer is for consuming data from the storage layer, running queries and computations on that data, and then notifying the storage layer to delete data that is no longer needed. These two layers have to be designed to be scalable, available, and reliable.

Streaming platforms have to offer one SQL query language to work with both streams of events (asynchronicity) and point-in-time state (this is synchronous). Event data/message capture, processing, and query serving have to happen in a single cluster in order to ensure high performance and data security.

Further on, the data inside is often split into two tiers. The raw input, called "streams," are immutable, append-only sequences of events. They are meant to be a historical record of what happened and when. The second tier is built from watching the streams and constructing statistical summaries about the events from the streams. For example, it is possible to count how many times a particular event happened per minute or day. Such information helps authorities to consider counter actions with all the confidence. These procured details are then stored in SQL databases. Such an arrangement helps to receive queries to respond. Correct and current information can be pulled from the database toward proceeding with making right conclusions and decisions. Also, with the direct integration with data visualization tools, the captured details can be visually displayed and rendered in multiple formats such as maps, charts, and graphs.

2.11 Processing platforms and infrastructures for event data/message streams

With cloud environments being setup across the globe, the infrastructure requirements for processing data streams and for facilitating streaming applications are being easily fulfilled. Especially, there are hyperscale public cloud centers giving an illusion of infinite compute capability and storage and network capacities. Increasingly, having understood the game-changing use cases of streaming data analytics, streaming platforms, middleware, databases, and applications are being deployed on cloud infrastructures, which are being touted as the most optimized and organized IT infrastructure. The leading cloud service providers offer a variety of solutions and services enabling the era of streaming. The well-known and widely used streaming solutions include Amazon Kinesis, Amazon Managed Streaming for Apache Kafka (Amazon MSK), Apache Flume, Apache Spark Streaming, and Apache Storm.

Amazon Kinesis (https://aws.amazon.com/kinesis/) makes it easy to collect, process, and analyze real-time, streaming data so you can get timely insights and react quickly to new information. Amazon Managed Streaming for Apache Kafka (Amazon MSK https://aws.amazon.com/msk/) is a fully managed service that makes it easy for you to build and run applications that use Apache Kafka to process streaming data.

Amazon Kinesis Data Firehose (https://aws.amazon.com/kinesis/data-firehose/) is the easiest way to reliably load streaming data into data lakes, data stores, and analytics services. It can capture, transform, and deliver streaming data to Amazon S3, Amazon Redshift, Amazon Elasticsearch Service, generic HTTP endpoints, and service providers like Datadog, New Relic, MongoDB, and Splunk.

Azure Stream Analytics—Serverless real-time analytics, from the cloud to the edge (https://azure.microsoft.com/en-in/services/stream-analytics/)—this delivers powerful insights from your streaming data with ease in real time. You can run complex analytics with no need to learn new processing frameworks or provision virtual machines (VMs) or clusters. You can also use the SQL language that is extensible with JavaScript and C# custom code for advanced use cases. This easily enables scenarios like low-latency dashboarding, streaming ETL, and real-time alerting with one-click integration across sources and sinks. You can get guaranteed, "exactly once" event processing with 99.9% availability and built-in recovery capabilities. It is easy to set up a continuous integration and continuous delivery (CI/CD) pipeline and achieve sub-second latencies on most demanding workloads. This platform facilitates bringing real-time insights and analytics capabilities closer to where the data originates. It is possible to enable new scenarios with true hybrid architectures for stream processing and run the same query in the cloud or on the edge. Incorporating ML models to emit out predictive, prescriptive, and personalized insights out of streaming data is made simpler and faster with this streaming analytics platform.

Google Cloud Stream analytics (https://cloud.google.com/solutions/stream-analytics)—Google Cloud's stream analytics solutions make data more organized, useful, and accessible from the instant it is generated. You can ingest, process, and analyze real-time event streams and take business impacting action on high-value, perishable insights. You can leverage an auto-scaling and fully managed streaming infrastructure that solves for variable data volumes, performance tuning, and resource provisioning. It is possible to access native integrations with AI Platform, BigQuery, and other Google Cloud services for rapid and trusted development of intelligent solutions.

IBM Streaming Analytics for IBM Cloud (https://www.ibm.com/in-en/cloud/streaming-analytics) evaluates a broad range of streaming data—unstructured text, video, audio, geospatial and sensor—helping organizations spot opportunities and risks and make decisions in real time.

Kafka Streams (https://kafka.apache.org/documentation/streams/) is a library for building streaming applications, specifically applications that transform input Kafka topics into output Kafka topics (or calls to external services, or updates to databases). Kafka streams, besides distributed and fault-tolerant, directly address a lot of the hard problems in stream processing:

- Event-at-a-time processing (not micro-batch) with millisecond latency
- Stateful processing including distributed joins and aggregations
- A convenient domain-specific language (DSL)
- Windowing with out-of-order data using a DataFlow-like model
- Distributed processing and fault-tolerance with fast failover
- Reprocessing capabilities so you can recalculate output when your code changes
- No-downtime rolling deployments

Kafka streams combine the simplicity of writing and deploying standard Java and Scala applications on the client side with the benefits of Kafka's server-side cluster technology. There are several noteworthy advantages being associated with Kafka streams:

- Is elastic and fault-tolerant
- Can be deployed on containers, virtual machines, and bare metal (BM) servers
- Carries the Kafka security
- Facilitates writing standard Java and Scala applications
- Enables exactly once processing semantics
- Does not insist for separate processing cluster required

By adroitly using stream processing technologies and tools, data streams can be processed, stored, analyzed, and acted upon with all the clarity and confidence. While traditional solutions are built to ingest, process, and structure data before it can be acted upon, streaming data architecture adds the ability to consume, persist to storage, enrich, and analyze data in motion.

2.12   Building real-time applications: the challenges

Real-time enterprises rely upon real-time IT. There is a need for real-time applications. That is, real-time data capture, storage, and processing are demanded. Further on, for arriving at intelligent applications, data analytics has become the core and central aspect of enterprise and cloud IT these days. Real-time and intelligent processing of streaming data are being proclaimed as an important activity for business verticals. Stream processing, therefore, has acquired special significance. We have discussed about EDA and streaming databases, which facilitate the much-needed stream processing. In this section, we are to discuss the prominent and pertinent challenges and concerns being associated with building real-time applications.

Scalability—As told above, log data is continuously flowing and hence real-time analytics of log data is very important for analyzing system performance. The root cause analysis is also being facilitated through log data. With more server machines and connected devices, the log data quantity is bound to escalate. Thus, streaming platforms have to have the scalability feature in order not to lose any log data and to facilitate real-time log analytics to extract actionable insights. Thus, developing scalable streaming applications and running them on elastic infrastructure are insisted to reap the real and originally expressed benefits

Ordering—For streaming applications to attain the required success, streaming data has to be consumed in the correct order. If the ordering is broken, the result may also go awry. When software developers try to debug an issue by looking at an aggregated log view, the ordering is paramount. The data packet ordering may change on its way. The timestamps also may change. Thus, for arriving at correct and competent insights, the ordering is important. For fulfilling the ACID properties, the ordering of event data/messages is prime.

Accessibility and consistency—As told above, data availability and access have to be guaranteed. Further on, data quality and consistency have to be given extra thrust to fulfill the goal of extracting right and relevant data-driven insights. Thereby insights-driven decisions and actions become the new normal. Any data change during its transit or usage has to be proactively identified and rectified.

Fault tolerance—Data flows from different and distributed data sources. Data come in multiple formats. There are different data transmission protocols and formats for data representation, exchange, and persistence. In such a complicated environment, the streaming platforms have to be fault-tolerant in order to guarantee continuous availability. Data durability is insisted these days. Government regulations mandate for keeping up the data for longer period. For enabling comprehensive data analytics, historical data has to be linked up with current data to arrive at game-changing insights.

In summary, to win in the increasingly digitized world, businesses ought to gain the capacity and competency to quickly process digital data. By combining historical and streaming data, enterprising businesses can easily create and deploy event-driven applications with all the reliability, scalability, and availability.

2.13 The convergence of databases and event streams

Popular stream processing technologies increasingly have tables and SQL just like a traditional database has. But stream processing systems serve a different purpose altogether. These technologies are for moving data between different software services. Also, they allow that data to be manipulated as the data flows. They still use the same joins, filters, summarizations, etc., but apply them for data-in-motion. If you run a query, you will not get any answer. However, they run continuously and the output is another event stream.

In a conventional database, the data sits there passively. You have to send a query to get an answer. With event streaming technologies, the data is active. The arrival of new data instigates queries to be run automatically to produce a valid output. That is, the newly arrived data triggers a chain of reactions in the form of activating a series of process components/services, which, when composed, completely automates a business process. The point here is that the trigger is induced by the arrival of the data.

Event data streaming works well for a variety of business operations. However, there are use cases that involve users for initiating, activating, decisioning, etc. Take a B2C e-commerce application such as amazon.in or flipkart.com. Here users have to manually select, click a few buttons, check the shopping cart, etc. Thus, for certain applications, users' involvement is necessary. Users also have to see the dashboard to make some inferences. The stream processing methods could not accomplish this. Therefore, enterprise IT team members and system integrators have to use multiple technologies together to accommodate all kinds of application categories. That is, software engineers would end up bolting technologies such as messaging systems, stream processors, databases, etc. together.

This transition has solidly addressed the question. There are two noteworthy technological shifts. First, stream processors become more database like by replacing the need for a separate database component to serve the results of streaming computations directly into users. Second, databases are becoming more stream-like capable of emitting data from tables as they are getting updated.

KsqlDB is an example of the first category. KsqlDB is a stream processor that can materialize views so that you can query just like a database table. The image below stored in a credit scores table.

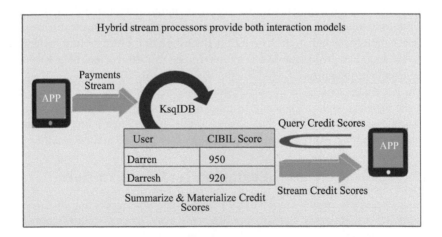

KsqlDB is a stream processor that can materialize views that you can query just like a database table. For example, a stream of payments is transformed into credit scores using a streaming computation and the result of that computation is stored in a credit scores table. The user can then send queries to this table that return specific values or listen to changes via an event stream. This is aptly termed as an event streaming database. KsqlDB is a database that is purpose-built for stream processing applications. It has components to acquire event data from different data sources, store and process them accordingly. Other components are to serve queries against aggregated materializations. Actually, integrating each subsystem together is a difficult task. KsqlDB aims to provide one mental model for doing everything you need. This database primarily depends on Apache Kafka.

The user can then send queries to this table that return specific values, or listen to changes via an event stream. Precisely speaking, technologies like this combine event streaming computations with tables in order to enable users to query and get the answer. These databases are termed as event streaming databases.

The other development is the realization of active databases, which approach the problem from the opposite side. That is, they allow you to create triggers and materialized views that respond to changes made to a database table. These do not have the capability to emit out streams of events. In the recent past, database technologies such as MongoDB, Couchbase and RethinkDB have incorporated the notion of tables that emit event streams when records change. Applications can then react to these streams.

The idea picking up fast is the cool convergence toward a middle ground. That is, they incorporate streams and tables as first-class citizens. These two approaches (active databases and event streaming databases) build on the same three building blocks: queries, tables, and event streams. Active databases are better at queries over tables, but they cannot query event streams. On the other hand, event streaming databases can query both event streams and tables, but the real issue here is that the table-based queries are less advanced when compared with their active database counterparts.

Active databases predominantly suit simple applications or individual microservices that can benefit from an event-based interface to the data. By contrast, event streaming databases typically use Apache Kafka to move data around, making them better suited to microservices or data pipelines. They serve as systems in which event data physically moves from one place to another or creates chains of business logic tied together by these data flows.

Streaming databases approach the problem quite differently. It creates triggers and materialized views to any change being made to a database table. Present day streaming databases gained the capability to emit out streams of events to the outside world. Popular database systems such as MongoDB, Couchbase and RethinkDB have incorporated the notion of tables that emit event streams when records change. Applications can then correctly react to these streams. That is, there is a cool convergence between tables and streams.

2.14   Conclusion

The world generates an unfathomable amount of data every day and the quantity of data getting produced continues to multiply at a staggering rate. However, for any initiative and implementation to support and sustain its journey, data availability, quality and analytics are very vital. However, for beneficially processing and analyzing continuously flowing data, the traditional data processing methods remain inadequate and inefficient. Therefore, enterprise and cloud IT teams move to stream processing, which natively supports real-time data analytics. In the recent past, there are enabling platforms, frameworks, libraries and infrastructures for simplifying and streamlining stream processing. There are simple and complex event processing platforms from the open-source community. There are commercial-grade solutions too. Further on, streaming database solutions are also hitting the market to speed up the process of capturing data streams and to emit out actionable insights in time.

References

[1]   About Event Sourcing, https://www.eventstore.com/blog/what-is-event-sourcing

[2]   ksqlDB example snippets, https://ksqldb.io/examples.html

[3]   What is database streaming?, https://www.qlik.com/us/data-streaming/database-streaming

[4]   Real-Time Data Streaming Databases – Which One Is Right for You?, https://www.theseattledataguy.com/7-real-time-data-streaming-databases-which-one-is-right-for-you/

[5]   What is a Streaming Database? By Peter Wayer, https://venturebeat.com/2021/04/04/what-is-a-streaming-database/

[6]   About Streaming Databases, https://www.upsolver.com/blog/what-is-a-streaming-database

[7]   Streaming Database: An Overview with Use Cases | Hazelcast, https://hazelcast.com/glossary/streaming-database/

Chapter 3

A survey on supervised and unsupervised algorithmic techniques to handle streaming Big Data

R. Saradha[1]

Abstract

The more data an association has, the more troublesome it is to process, store, and break down; however, on the other hand, the more data the association has, the more precise its expectations can be. Too Big Data accompanies big duty. Big Data computing is typically classified into two sorts based on the process necessities, which are Big Data batch computing and Big Data stream computing. Big Data requires military-grade encryption keys to keep data sheltered and private. This is the place data science comes in. Numerous associations, confronted with the issue of having the option to gauge, channel, and dissect data, are going to data science for arrangements—recruiting data researchers, individuals who are authorities in seeming well and good out of a tremendous measure of data. By and large, this implies utilizing measurable models to make calculations to sort, characterize, and process data. In this paper, an audit of different algorithms essential for dealing with such enormous data streams for classification and clustering is given. These algorithms give us different techniques executed to deal with Big Data.

3.1 Introduction

Data mining is the innovation to separate the information from the previous data-bases. It is utilized to investigate and break down the equivalent. The data which is to be mined fluctuates from a little data-set to an enormous data-set for example Big Data [1]. Big Data is huge to such an extent that it does not fit in the funda-mental memory of a solitary machine, and it has to process Big Data by effective algorithms. Current processing has entered the period of Big Data. The gigantic measures of data accessible on the Internet empower PC researchers, physicists, financial specialists, mathematicians, political researchers, bio-informaticists, sociologists, and numerous others to find intriguing properties about individuals,

[1]PG & Research Department of Computer Science, Hindusthan College of Arts and Science, India

things, and their associations. Breaking down data from Twitter, Google, Facebook, Wikipedia, or the Human Genome Project requires the improvement of adaptable stages that can rapidly process enormous scope data. Such systems regularly use enormous quantities of machines in a group or in the cloud to process data in an equal way.

By and large, the size of every photograph is 2 megabytes (MB), this requires 3.6 terabytes (TB) stockpiling each and every day. For sure, as a well-known adage expresses: "words usually can't do a picture justice," the billions of pictures on Flicker are a fortune tank for us to investigate the human culture, get-togethers, open undertakings, debacles, and so on, just in the event that we have the ability to outfit the gigantic measure of data. This is astounding model for Big Data handling, as the data originates from various, heterogeneous, self-governing sources with complex and developing connections, and continues developing. Alongside the above model, the time of Big Data has shown up, every day, 2.5 quintillion bytes of data are made and 90% of the data on the planet today were created inside the previous 2 years [2]. Our capacity for data age has never been so ground-breaking and huge since the time of creation of the data innovation in the mid-nineteenth century. Big Data is unpredictable data set that has the accompanying primary qualities: Volume, Variety, Velocity and Value [3–6]. These make it hard to utilize the current apparatuses to oversee and control [7]. Big Data is the huge measure of data being handled by the data mining condition. As it were, it is the assortment of data sets enormous and complex that it gets hard to process utilizing on hand database the board apparatuses or customary data preparing applications, so data mining devices were utilized. Big Data are tied in with turning unstructured, significant, flawed, complex data into usable data.

Figure 3.1 clarifies the structure of big data which contains four measurements in particular volume, velocity, variety, and veracity [2,3]. Volume alludes the size of the data which fundamentally tells the best way to handle huge versatility databases and high dimensional databases and its preparing needs. Velocity

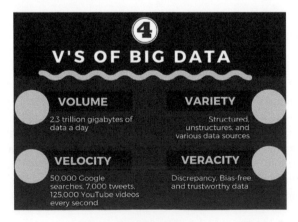

Figure 3.1   4Vs Big Data

characterizes the persistent appearance of data streams from this helpful data are gotten. Besides Big Data has upgraded improved throughput, availability and registering velocity of advanced gadgets which has attached the recovery, procedure, and creation of the data.

Veracity decides the nature of data from different spots. Variety depicts how to convey the various kinds of data, for instance source data incorporates structured conventional social data as well as incorporates semi-structured, semi-structured, and unstructured data, for example, text, sensor data, sound, video, diagram, and a lot more sort. Value is fundamental to get the financial value of various data which shifts altogether. The essential test is to recognize which are significant and the best approach to perform change and the method to be applied to perform data investigation.

3.1.1 What is streaming data?

Streaming data will be data that is produced ceaselessly by a huge number of data sources, which regularly send in the data records all the while, and in little sizes (request of Kilobytes). Streaming data incorporates a wide assortment of data, for example, log records created by clients utilizing your portable or web applications, Internet business buys, in-game player movement, data from informal communities, monetary exchanging floors, or geospatial administrations, and telemetry from associated gadgets or instrumentation in data places.

This data should be prepared successively and steadily on a record-by-record premise or throughout sliding time windows and utilized for a wide assortment of investigation including relationships, accumulations, sifting, and examining. Data got from such investigation gives organizations perceivability into numerous parts of their business and client action, for example,—administration use (for metering/charging), worker action, site clicks, and geo-area of gadgets, individuals, and actual products—and empowers them to react speedily to arising circumstances. For instance, organizations can follow changes in open assumption on their brands and items by persistently investigating online media streams, and react in an opportune style as the need emerges.

3.1.2 Significance of data streams

Stream processing is the key if we want analytics results in real time. By building data streams, we can feed data into analytics tools as soon as it is generated and get near-instant analytics results using platforms like Spark Streaming. Stream processing is useful for tasks like fraud detection.

With expanding volume of the data, it is not, at this point, conceivable to measure the data effectively by utilizing various passes. May be, one can handle a data item at most once. This prompts requirements on the execution of the fundamental algorithms. Subsequently, stream mining algorithms commonly should be planned so the algorithms work with one pass of the data.

Much of the time, there is an inborn temporal component to the stream mining measure. This is on the grounds that the data may advance over the long run. This conduct of data streams is alluded to as fleeting region. Accordingly, a direct variation of one-pass mining algorithms may not be a successful answer for the assignment. Stream mining algorithms should be painstakingly planned with an unmistakable spotlight on the development of the fundamental data.

3.2   Streaming analytics: why and how

Stream processing dissects and performs activities on constant data however the utilization of ceaseless queries. Streaming analytics associates with outside data sources, empowering applications to coordinate certain data into the application stream, or to refresh an outer database with prepared data. Bloor Research expert Philip Howard says stream processing is actually a development of complex event processing (CEP). Both CEP and streaming processing advances empower activity dependent on an investigation of a progression of occasions that have simply occurred. Vital for stream processing is streaming analytics [6]. Streaming analytics is the capacity to continually figure statistical analytics while moving inside the flood of data. Streaming analytics permits the executives, checking, and ongoing analytics of live streaming data.

Streaming analytics includes knowing and following up on occasions occurring in your business out of nowhere. Since streaming analytics happens promptly, organizations should follow up on the analytics data rapidly inside a little open door before the data loses its worth. The data can begin from the Internet of Things (IoT), cell phones, and cell phones like iPads, market data, sensors, Web clickstream, and exchanges. Data that loses its worth outcomes in extra expenses, for example, operational, regulatory, business chances, notoriety harm, possible lawful activity, decrease in usefulness, powerlessness to settle on educated choices, and diminishes an organization's strategic advantage.

3.2.1   Advantages of streaming data

3.2.1.1   Gives deeper insight through data visualization

Visualization of indispensable organization data can assist organizations with dealing with their key presentation markers (KPIs) consistently. KPI data is seen continuously, which delivers a solitary wellspring of reality of ongoing data that can give a helicopter and granular perspective on an organization at some random time. The data can improve deals, decrease costs, recognize mistakes, and give data to respond quicker to dangers to moderate them. Streaming data speeds up dynamic and gives admittance to business measurements and announcing.

3.2.1.2   Stay competitive

Businesses can recognize patterns and benchmarks, foster white papers, use cases, and produce gauges of their organization and industry. This decreases inside and outer dangers and gives familiarity with industry changes. This assists organizations with getting inventive, stay cutthroat, and reinforce their image.

Table 3.1   Traditional data and streaming data

Traditional processing	Stream processing
Data processing is done involving simple calculations	Involves complex operations on multiple input streams
Processing time cannot be predicted	It has a limited processing time
Raw form of data is stored	Summarized form of data is stored
Gives accurate results	Gives mere approximate results
It is a form of offline processing	It is a form real time processing

3.2.2   Difference between streaming data and traditional data

Traditional processing is a sort of disconnected processing that includes straightforward calculations on data when it is being handled. It chiefly stores crude data that is not so much collected and organized. Stream processing is a sort of constant processing where certain tasks are performed on the data at the time it is being made. The tasks can be acted in a chronic or equal way. It additionally permits the clients to inquiry the ceaseless data stream and to decide the conditions in a limited quantity of time when data is gotten. Stream processing additionally performs data investigation, data change, and data total by different strategies. It stores data in a more collected and organized manner. Table 3.1 summarizes the differences between these two.

3.3   Streaming data technologies

3.3.1   Column-oriented databases

A column-oriented DBMS (or columnar database the board framework) is a database the executives' framework (DBMS) that stores data tables by segment rather than by row. Practical utilization of a segment store versus a row store differs little in the relational DBMS world. Both columnar and row databases can utilize traditional database query dialects like SQL to stack data and perform queries. Both row and columnar databases can turn into the spine in a framework to serve data for basic extract, transform, load (ETL), and data perception instruments. However, by storing data in segments rather than rows, the database can more precisely get to the data it needs to answer a query rather than checking and discarding undesirable data in rows.

3.3.2   Schema-less databases

A schema-less database does not require conforming to a rigid composition (database, pattern, data types, tables and so on) that one is required to satisfy through the duration of a framework. They do not enforce data type impediments on singular values pertaining to one single section type and models the business use and not a database pattern, application, or product. It can store structured and unstructured data and wipes out the need to introduce extra layers (ORM layer) to abstract the relational model and uncover it in an item-oriented format.

3.3.3   Hadoop

Hadoop is a popular open-source apparatus for handling Big Data and implemented in MapReduce. It is java-based programming framework which supports large data sets in distributing processing. Hadoop cluster utilizes a master/slave structure. Distributed document framework in Hadoop assists with transferring data in rapid rates. If there should be an occurrence of some hub failure, a distributed document framework permits the framework to proceed with the normal operation. Hadoop has two principles sub-projects to be specific MapReduce and Hadoop Distributed File System.

3.3.4   Hive

Hive: Hive is an ETL (extract, transform, burden) and data warehouse instrument created on the head of the Hadoop-distributed file system. In Hive, tables and databases are created first and then the data is stacked into these tables. Hive as data warehouse is planned uniquely for overseeing and querying just the structured data that is stored in the table.

The fundamental difference in HiveQL and SQL is the Hive query executes on Hadoop's infrastructure rather than the traditional database. The Hive query execution resembles a series of consequently generated Map Reduce occupations

By utilizing Hive, we can accomplish some peculiar usefulness that is not accomplished in the relational database. For an immense measure of data that is in peta-bytes, querying it and getting results in seconds is important, and hive does is very proficient, it processes the query quick and produce results like a flash.

3.4   Algorithms to handle stream data

Numerous applications essentially are moving from being can beyond a question being data-bound. We tend to are seeing large form of large datasets. There are billions of messages and search queries, and an outsized range of tweets and pictures daily, all the same each activity being half-track on the online (by means that of treats) and within the physical world (e.g., through camcorders). Threshold-based techniques, graded cluster, and progressive cluster or on-line cluster are additional relevant to social media analysis. Many on-line threshold-based stream cluster approaches or progressive cluster approaches like mathematician random field, on-line spherical K-means, and condensed clusters are adopted. Progressive approaches square measure appropriate for endlessly generated knowledge grouping by setting a most similarity threshold between the incoming stream and therefore the existing clusters.

3.4.1   Classification algorithms

Big Data is unstructured data that surpasses the processing unpredictability of traditional database frameworks. The data is too big, moves excessively quick, or does not fit the rule restricting behaviour of our database architectures.

This information originates from different, unmistakable, autonomous sources with complex and developing relationships in a Big Data which is continue growing step by step. There are three primary difficulties in Big Data which are data getting to and arithmetic figuring procedures, semantics, and area information for different Big Data applications and the troubles raised by Big Data volumes, distributed data distribution and by perplexing and dynamic characteristics. Big data framework is partitioned into three tiers as appeared in Figure 3.2, to handle the above difficulties.

Tier I which is data accessing and computing focus on data accessing and arithmetic computing procedures. Because a large amount of information is stored at different locations which are growing rapidly day by day, hence for computing distributed large scale of information, we have to consider effective computing-platform like Hadoop.

Data privacy and space information are the Tier II which centres around semantics and area information for different Big Data applications. In informal organization, users are connected with one another that shares their information which are represented by user networks, leaders in each group and social impact demonstrating and so on, therefore for understanding their semantics and application information is important for both low-level data get to and for significant level mining algorithm plans.

Tier III, the big data mining algorithms, revolves around the issues posed by large amounts of data, dispersed data distribution, and mind-boggling and dynamic features. There are three phases in Tier III, as appeared in Figure 3.2, (a) sparse, heterogeneous, uncertain, inadequate and multisource data are pre-processed by data combination procedures; (b) complex and dynamic data are mined after pre-processing; (c) the worldwide information acquired by neighborhood learning and model combination is tried and relevant information is feedback to the pre-processing stage.

The classification method is utilized to settle the above difficulties which group the Big Data according to the format of the data that must be processed, the

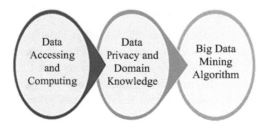

Figure 3.2   Three tiers of Big Data

sort of examination to be applied, the processing procedures at work, and the data sources for the data that the target framework is required to acquire, load, process, break down, and store. Numerous classification methods are utilized dependent on applications chose. Before real classification starts [17], required information is extracted from large measure of data and then arrangement is done. There are two fundamental arrangement methods, supervised and unsupervised.

3.4.2 Supervised methods

Supervised learning is used in the vast majority of practical machine learning applications. Supervised learning is a technique in which you have input variables (*x*) and output variables (*Y*), and you use a methodology to learn the mapping function from the input to the output. *Y* equals *f*(*X*). The goal is to approximate the mapping function so well that you can predict the output variables (*Y*) for new input data (*x*).

The process of algorithm learning from a training dataset is referred to as supervised learning because the process can be compared to a teacher supervising the learning process. We know the correct answers, so the algorithm makes predictions on the training data iteratively and is corrected by the teacher. When the algorithm achieves an acceptable level of learning, the process is terminated. Problems which include arrangement are considered to be cases of a branch of AI called as "supervised learning." In this, the machine is given a "training set" of correctly grouped examples of data in the first stage, and then the algorithm contrived from this "learning" is utilized for the following phase of prediction. The converse of this is "unsupervised learning," which includes characterizing data into categories dependent on some similarity of info parameters in the data.

Supervised data mining procedures are appropriate when we have a particular target value, so we can predict about our data [7]. The targets can have two or more potential results, or even be a ceaseless numeric value. To utilize these techniques, we in a perfect world have a subset of training data (observations and measurement) sets for which this target value is already known. Training data incorporates both the info and desired results.

Regression and classification problems are subsets of supervised learning problems.

3.4.3 Analysis of classification

In machine learning, classification is considered a supervised learning method, referring to a problem of predictive modeling in which a class label is predicted for a given example [8]. Mathematically, it maps a function (*f*) as target, label, or categories from input variables (*X*) to output variables (*Y*). It can be used on structured or unstructured data to predict the class of given data points. For example, spam detection in e-mail service providers, such as "spam" and "not spam," can be a classification problem. The following section summarizes the most common classification problems.

When the output variable is a category, such as "red" or "blue" or "disease," and "no disease," the problem is called a classification problem.

When the output variable is a real value, such as "dollars" or "weight," a regression problem exists.

3.4.4   Analysis of regression

Regression analysis encompasses several machine learning methods for predicting a continuous (y) result variable based on the value of one or more (x) predictor variables [8]. The most important distinction between classification and regression is that classification predicts distinct class labels, like male or female, true or false and spam or not spam. That is why decision trees are used for classification, whereas regression predicts a continuous quantity. Figure 3.3 illustrates how classification categorise a label distinctly. There are frequently overlaps between the two types of machine learning algorithms. Regression models are now widely used in a wide range of fields, such as financial forecasting or prediction, cost estimation, trend analysis, marketing, time series estimation, drug response modelling, and many others.

Recommendation and time series prediction are two common types of problems built on top of classification and regression.

Some well-known supervised machine learning algorithms are [19]:

- Linear regression is used to solve regression problems.
- Random forest is used to solve classification and regression problems.
- Support vector machines are used to solve classification problems.

The target of classification is to examine tremendous data and to build up an accurate description or model for each organized class utilizing the feature present in the data. We utilize that training data to fabricate a model of what a run of the

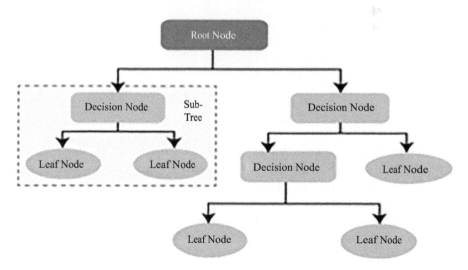

Figure 3.3   Structure of DTs

mill data set resembles when it has one of the various target values. We at that point apply that model to data for which that target value is currently obscure. The algorithm distinguishes the "new" data focuses that coordinate the model of each target value. This model is utilized to characterize test data for which the class descriptions are not known.

3.4.4.1   Decision tree (DT)

A DT is a set of rules used for supervised learning problems along with classification or regression [23]. A choice tree or a classification tree is a tree in which each internal (nonleaf) node is classified with an enter feature. The arcs coming from a node classified with a feature are categorized with each of the possible values of the characteristic. Each leaf of the tree is categorized with a category or a probability distribution over the lessons.

A tree may be "found out" with the aid of splitting the supply set into subsets based on a characteristic cost test. This technique is repeated on every derived subset in a recursive manner referred to as recursive partitioning. The recursion is completed whilst the subset at a node has all the identical value of the goal variable, or when splitting no longer adds fee to the predictions. This system of pinnacle-down induction of decision trees is an instance of a grasping algorithm, and its miles the most common strategy for mastering decision trees.

DTs are an easy approach, and as such has some issues. One of the troubles is the high variance in the resulting models that choice trees produce. In order to relieve this problem, ensemble techniques of selection timber were advanced.

Big Data challenges are developing daily, traditional DT algorithms have a couple of obstacles. First, building a DT is a totally time eating when the dataset is extraordinarily huge. Second, even though parallel computing clusters can be leveraged in DT primarily based classification algorithms, the strategy of information distribution has to be optimized in order so that required statistics for constructing one node is localized and in the meantime the conversation value is minimized.

The disadvantage of DT is that they are prone to over fitting, which means that the model adheres too closely to the idiosyncrasies of the test dataset and performs poorly on a new dataset—that is, the test data. Over fitting DT results in poor general predictive accuracy, also known as generalization accuracy.

3.4.4.2   Support vector machine (SVM)

AI machine learning has the capacity to empower the PC to discover that utilizes algorithm and methods which perform various errands and exercises to give effective learning. Our fundamental issue is that by what method can we speak to complex data and how to reject sham data. Bolster vector machine is a machine learning instrument utilized for order that depends on supervised learning which groups focuses to one of the two disjoint half-spaces. It utilizes nonlinear planning to change over the first data into higher measurement. Its goal is to develop a capacity which will effectively foresee the class to which the new point has a place and the old focuses have a place. In the time of Big Data, the chief reason by and large outrageous edge or segment given that we use a decision breaking point to portray, it could end up more like one part of datasets appeared differently in relation to other people. This happens just if data is structured or direct yet for the most part, we discover data that is unstructured/nonlinear and when dataset is indivisible, then SVM bits are utilized [20].

Customary classification approaches perform pitifully when working straight forwardly due to enormous measure of data; however, SVM can keep away from the issues of speaking to this much data. SVM is the most encouraging method and approach when contrasted with others that characterization draws near. Bolster vector machine balance appropriate and exact enormous measure of data and bargain between classifier multifaceted nature and blunder can be controlled unequivocally. Another advantage of SVMs is that one can plan and utilize an SVM portion for a specific issue that could be applied legitimately to the data without the need for a component extraction process. It is especially significant issues, where tremendous measure of structured data is lost by the component extraction process.

3.4.4.3 Random forest

Breiman (1999) proposed an ensemble learning algorithm in machine learning called random forest, which is a widely used machine learning method with high prediction accuracy. It is made up of a large number of DTs with randomly selected features that are used to build a deterministic forest by averaging their predictions. Furthermore, it is appropriate for dealing with high-dimensionality and multi-collinearity data because the most relevant variables can be chosen from a large number of variables. Figure 3.4 illustrates that how a large group uncorrelated

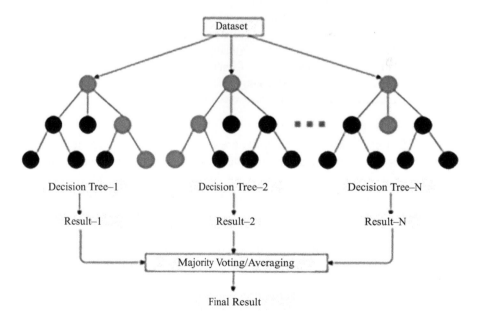

Figure 3.4   A random forest structure considering multiple decision trees

decision trees can produce more accurate and stable results than any of individual decision trees. When we train a random forest for a classification task, we actually train a group of decision trees.

Why does random forest outperform linear regression when it comes to prediction tasks? The assumption of linearity is made by linear regression. This assumption makes the model easy to interpret but is frequently insufficient for prediction. Random decision forests adapt easily to nonlinearities in data and, as a result, tend to predict better than linear regression. Ensemble learning algorithms, in particular, random forests, are well suited for medium to large datasets. Because the number of parameters to be estimated exceeds the number of observations when the number of independent variables exceeds the number of observations, the linear regression, and logistic regression algorithms will not run. Because not all predictor variables are used at the same time, random forest works. Individual DTs are easily interpretable, but this interpretability is lost in random forests due to the aggregated nature of the DTs. Random forests, on the other hand, are frequently much better at prediction tasks. When compared to DTs, the random forest algorithm estimates the error rate more accurately. More specifically, as the number of trees increases, the error rate is mathematically proven to always converge.

- How does it differ from the decision tree?

  A decision tree provides a single path that takes into account all of the features at once. As a result, this may result in deeper trees, causing the model to over fit. A random forest generates a large number of trees with random characteristics; the trees are not very deep. Including an option for ensemble of DTs maximizes efficiency by averaging the results and providing generalized results. While the structure of a decision tree is heavily dependent on the training data and can change dramatically even with a minor change in the training data, the random selection of features provides little deviation in terms of structure change with data change. This can be further reduced by using techniques such as tagging for data selection.

Classifier vs. regressor

Regression and classification algorithms are supervised learning algorithms. Both the algorithms are used for prediction in machine learning and work with the labelled datasets. But the difference between both is how they are used for different machine learning problems. Consider Figure 3.5 given. In classification, the predictions are made by classifying them into different categories. In regression, the system attempts to predict a value for an input based on past data.

- A random forest classifier is used to classify data that has discrete labels.
- For instance, whether or not a patient has cancer, whether or not a person is eligible for a loan, and so on.
- A random forest regressor can only work with data that has a numeric or continuous output and cannot be classified.

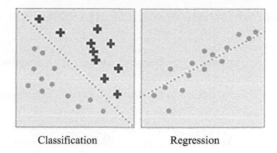

Classification   Regression

Figure 3.5   Classification vs. regression

- For instance, the cost of a house, the amount of milk produced by cows, a company's gross income, and so on.

Despite these benefits, a random forest algorithm has some drawbacks.

- It necessitates a significant amount of computational power as well as resources because it constructs numerous trees and then combines their outputs.
- It also takes a long time to train because it combines many DTs to determine the class.
- It also lacks interpretability due to the ensemble of DTs and fails to determine the significance of each variable.

3.4.5   Unsupervised methods

Clustering is a common application of unsupervised learning. Clustering is the classification of objects or data points that are similar to one another but not to objects in other clusters. Different algorithms for clustering can be used by machine learning engineers and data scientists, with the algorithms themselves falling into different categories based on how they work. Unsupervised learning is the place where you just have input data (*X*) and no comparing yield factors. The objective for unsupervised learning is to demonstrate the underlying structure or appropriation in the data so as to become familiar with the data. These are called unsupervised learning in light of the fact that unlike supervised learning above, there is no right answers and there is no educator. Algorithms are left to their own devices to find and present the intriguing structure with regard to the data. Unsupervised learning issues can be additionally gathered into bunching and affiliation issues.

Clustering: A clustering issue is the place you need to find the inalienable groupings in the data, for example, gathering clients by buying conduct.

Association: An association rule learning issue is the place you need to find decisions that depict enormous bits of your data, for example, individuals that purchase *X* likewise will in general purchase *Y*. Some famous instances of unsupervised learning algorithms are: k-means for clustering issues and a priori algorithm for association rule learning issues.

3.4.5.1   Comparative study of training algorithms

	Decision trees	Neural network	Naïve Bayes	K-Nearest neighbor	Support vector machine
Proposed By	Quinlan	Rosenblatt	Duda and Hurt	Cover and Hart	Vapnik
Accuracy in general	Good	V Good	Average	Good	Excellent
Speed of learning	V.Good	Average	Excellent	Excellent	Average
Speed of classification	Excellent	Excellent	Excellent	Average	Excellent
Tolerance to missing values	V.Good	Average	Excellent	Average	Good
Tolerance to irrelevant attributes	V.Good	Average	Good	Good	Excellent
Tolerance to redundant attributes	Good	Good	Average	Good	V Good
Tolerance to highly inter-dependent attributes	Good	V Good	Average	Average	V Good
Dealing with discrete/binary/continuous attributes	All	Not discrete	Not continuous	All	Not discrete
Tolerance to noise	Good	Good	V Good	Average	Good
Dealing with danger of overfitting	Good	Average	V Good	V Good	Good
Attempts for incremental learning	Good	V Good	Excellent	Excellent	Good
Explanation ability/transparency of knowledge/classification	Excellent	Average	Excellent	Good	Average
Support Multiclassification	Excellent	Naturally extended	Naturally extended	Excellent	Binary classifier

3.4.5.2   Clustering algorithms

Cluster analysis, also known as clustering, is an unsupervised machine learning technique for identifying and grouping-related data points in large datasets with no regard for the end result. It does this by categorizing a collection of objects in such a way that objects in the same category, known as a cluster, are more similar to each other than objects in other groups [8]. It is frequently used as a data analysis technique to identify interesting trends or patterns in data, such as groups of consumers based on their behaviour. Clustering can be used in a wide range of applications, including cyber security, e-commerce, mobile data processing, health analytics, user modeling, and behavioural analytics. Following is a brief discussion and summary of various types of clustering.

3.4.6   Introduction

In the knowledge stream model, the information points will solely be accessed within the order during which they arrive. Random access to the information is not allowed; memory is assumed to be tiny relative to the number of points, then solely a restricted quantity of knowledge may be hold on. In general, algorithms operating on streams are restricted to fairly easy calculations due to the time and area constraints. The challenge facing rule designers is to perform pregnant computation with these restrictions. Some applications naturally generate knowledge streams as critical easy knowledge sets. Astronomers, telecommunications corporations, banks, stock-market analysts, and news organizations, as an example, have immense amounts of information incoming unendingly. In telecommunications, as an example, decision records square measure generated unendingly. Typically, most process is finished by examining a decision record once, when that records square measure archived and not examined once more. As an example, Hernan Cortes et al. report operating with AT&T long distance decision records, consisting of three hundred million records per day for a hundred million customers. There are also applications wherever ancient (non-streaming) knowledge is treated as a stream thanks to performance constraints. For researchers mining medical or selling knowledge, as an example, the degree of information hold on disk is thus giant that it is solely attainable to form one pass (or maybe a really tiny variety of passes) over the information. Analysis on knowledge stream computation includes work on sampling finding quantiles of a stream of points and conniving the L1-difference of two streams. A common sort of knowledge analysis in these applications involves cluster, i.e., partitioning the information set into subsets (clusters) specified members of identical cluster square measure similar and members of distinct clusters square measure dissimilar. Typically, a cluster is characterized by a canonical component or representative called the cluster center. The goal is either to work out cluster centers or to really work out the clustered partition of the information set. This paper cares with the difficult drawback of cluster data incoming within the sort of stream. We offer a replacement cluster rule with theoretical guarantees on its performance. We have a tendency to provide empirical proof of its superiority over the commonly used k-means algorithm. We have a tendency to then adapt our rule to be able to care for knowledge streams and through an experiment demonstrate its superior performance during this context.

3.4.6.1 Streaming data use cases

Streaming knowledge will be used heavily within the producing sector wherever timely and live knowledge must be sent. There is an immense info of things that must be maintained and analyzed at real time and any anomaly or fault ought to be detected right away and corrected. Streaming knowledge is heavily employed in cyber security. If we have got a state of affairs of a Denial-of-Service attack, we would have tens of countless knowledge among a rapid with no means that of obtaining that back. Streaming knowledge is additionally terribly helpful within the care sector. We would like patient's real-time knowledge to be updated into the system's info at each moment. This includes things like rate, pressure level. Therefore, completely different types of algorithms got to be accustomed to trot out these.

Weather is another superb example for the utility of streaming knowledge. Weather are some things that changes multiple times in a very day and things like temperature, wetness, and alternative conditions have to be compelled to be updated in real time to any weathering system information. This may cojointly facilitate the meteorologists to predict any unforeseen circumstances like serious rain, cyclone, etc. and provides a plan on the expected climatical condition within the coming days.

3.4.6.2   Current approaches to managing streaming knowledge and algorithms

K-medoid algorithm

The strategy used here is that the purpose diagrammatic by the cluster may be a representative of the complete cluster.

(i)   Initialize: choose any random k points out of the knowledge points.
(ii)   By using any common distance metric methodology associates every point of the info to the closest medoid.

BJKST algorithmic rule

The BJKST calculation utilizes a collection to stay the examined things. By running Θ (log (1/δ)) free duplicates in equal and returning the mechanism of those yields, the BJKST calculation (ε, δ) approximates the F0-standard of the multiset S.

The essential thought behind the inspecting set up of the BJKST calculation is as per the following:

(i)   Leave B alone a collection that is used to carry tested things, and B = $\varnothing$ initially. The scale of B is O (1/ε2) and simply depends upon the estimation parameter ε.
(ii)   The underlying inspecting chances are one, for instance, the calculation keeps all things seen to this point in B.
(iii) For the purpose, once the set B seems to be full, contract B by discharge regarding things and from that time on the example chance decreases.

K implies calculation

This is a basic nevertheless unbelievable calculation. This strategy segments the knowledge accessible into completely different bunches and also the allotments area unit picked to such associate degree extent that so as to limit the blunders within the teams. The calculation functions as follows.

(i)   Choose associate degree estimation of k that speaks to the number of teams the knowledge is to be isolate into.
(ii)   Assign all the focuses to at least one of the clusters obsessed on the smallest amount separation live.
(iii) The centroids area unit rested obsessed on the present new focuses.
(iv)   If the bunch to that a commentary has been allotted that has modified as lately at that time proceed with steps (ii) and (iii), else stop.

Count Min-Sketch

Check Min-Sketch may be a calculation, wherever the goal is to understand the repeat of normal things, nevertheless we would like extra space for a full table of counters for every and each attainable issue. Instead of simply one hash function, we may employ distinct ones. These hash functions should be pairwise independent. To update a count we has item 'A' with all 'd' hash functions and then increment all indices obtained in this manner. If two hash functions map to the same index, we only increase its cell once. Undeniably, considering the approach that every bunch that we have a tendency to use is considerably a lot of diminutive than the number of stand-out things that we have a tendency to see, it will be essential for quite one issue to possess to a specific territory. The trick is that for the any of most common things, a lot of possible than not, in any occasion one among the hashed regions for that issue can merely have impacts with less basic things. That means keep in mind that territory is going to be typically controlled by that thing. The problem is that thanks to notice the cell that merely has impacts with less customary things. Moreover, henceforth to manage this issue, the incidental calculation was bestowed.

Probe using min of counts: Right after we endeavor to seek out the mean for the thought issue, we glance all told the spots it hashed to and take the base incorporate that we discover in any of them, basic cognitive process that no increasingly realized issue collided with it in those regions. Just in case at any rate one in every of those has recently less normal things, we will get an awfully higher than average count. Since we take the bottom of the total of the watches that we discover, we tend to perceive that we have found the smallest amount influenced count. That is the Count Min-Sketch may be a quite sketch that is terribly helpful for checking a variety of occasions of the foremost standard things we have seen.

STREAM

Stream is an associate degree improvement over the k medoid formula. It achieves a continuing issue approximation in every single pass and a tiny low quantity of area. The formula is as follows:

Algorithm Small-Space(S)

1. Dividing S in disjoint items X1.. X.
2. for every I, notice k centres in Xi. Thereby assignment every purpose in given Xi to its nearest centre.
3. Cluster X' to seek out k centres.

3.5   Semi-supervised algorithms

Machines are capable of learning in a variety of ways. Supervised learning is a machine learning problem that involves learning an input–output mapping function from examples of input–output pairs. Unsupervised learning is the process of discovering patterns in unlabeled data. Semi-supervised learning can be thought of as a cross between supervised and unsupervised learning. When we combine a small amount of labeled data with a large amount of unlabeled data during training, we have a semi-supervised machine learning problem.

Semi-supervised learning (SSL) is a research method that uses a large amount of unlabeled data to improve performance in the presence of limited labeled data.

The majority of traditional SSL methods accept that unlabeled data classes are included in the arrangement of labeled data classes.

Similarly, these techniques do not filter out irrelevant unlabeled examples and use all unlabeled data for training, which is inappropriate in most cases. In this section we discuss about the various semi-supervised machine learning algorithms.

3.5.1   Self-training

Self-training techniques have been used for semi-supervised learning for quite some time. It is a resampling method that labels unlabeled training samples based on the certainty scores and retrains itself with the chosen pseudo-annotated data over and over. This method can also be classified as a self-training strategy.

Figure 3.6 depicts an SSL framework. We follow the proposed algorithm's learning cycle because it is based on self-training. The following steps can be taken to formalize this process. (i) Use labeled data to train a model. (ii) Using the trained model to predict unlabeled data. (iii) Retraining the model using labeled and selected pseudo-labeled data. (iv) Repeat the previous two steps.

In any case, most self-preparation strategies anticipate that labeled and unlabeled data will be produced from the same appropriation. As a result, in real-world situations, a few cases with low probability based on the distribution of the labeled information are likely to be misclassified.

As a result, these incorrect examples lead to even worse outcomes in the next training step. To avoid this problem, we use collection and adjusting techniques to select reliable examples.

3.5.2   Graph-based semi-supervised machine learning

Graph-based SSL algorithms are a significant sub-class of SSL algorithms that have recently received a lot of attention. In this case, one accepts that the data (both labelled and unlabeled) is inserted inside a low-dimensional complex that could be communicated sensibly by a graph. In a weighted chart, each data sample is represented by a vertex, with the loads indicating the proportion of closeness

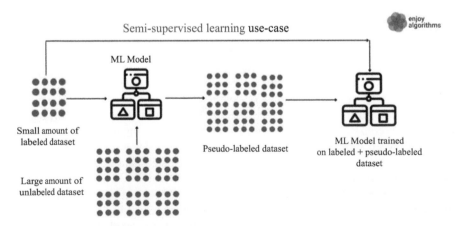

Figure 3.6   Representation of SSL framework

between vertices. As a result, using a graph-based strategy to solve an SSL problem both transductive and inductive graph based SSL methods are used.

A graph must be constructed first, where nodes represent data samples, some of which are labeled while others are not, and edges are associated with a certain weight to reflect each node pair's similarity. In some domains, such as citation networks, there is already an implicit underlying graph. Graph-based methods are thus a natural fit for SSL problems in these domains. Some Inductive graph based reference SSL approaches are Seed supervision and Gaussian Random Fields etc.

This could be completed by attempting to locate the base cut, which directly respects the labels of the information, or by employing Graph Laplacian as a useful penalty.

As previously stated, many data collections of current interest are typically represented by a graph. The Web, for example, is a hyperlinked graph, a social network is a diagram, and communication networks are diagrams, among other things.

Because SSL is based on the fact that a large amount of unlabeled data improve execution, it is critical for SSL algorithms to scale. This is important in a variety of application areas where the ability to deal with large datasets is required.

Many graph-based SSL algorithms can be easily parallelized when compared to other (non-graph-based) SSL algorithms.

In an era when the amount of information available is constantly increasing dramatically, unsupervised data simply cannot wait for those labels to catch up.

Endless real-world situations, such as YouTube videos or website content, appear in this manner. SSL is used in a wide range of applications, from crawlers and content aggregation frameworks to image and speech recognition. The ability of SSL to combine the over fitting and "under fitting" tendencies of supervised and unsupervised learning (individually) results in a model that can perform classification tasks admirably while generalizing, given a small amount of labeled data and a large amount of unlabeled data.

Other than classification tasks, semi-supervised algorithms can be used for a variety of purposes, such as enhanced clustering and anomaly detection. Despite the fact that the field is still relatively new, algorithms are constantly being created and idealized due to the high level of interest in the current advanced scene. Semi-supervised learning is, indeed, machine learning's fate.

3.6   Open challenges in data stream

A data stream could be a period, continuous, ordered (implicitly by time of arrival or expressly by timestamp) sequence of things. It is not possible to regulate the order during which things arrive, neither is it possible to regionally store a stream in its totality. Likewise, queries over. This analysis is partly supported by the Natural Sciences and Engineering analysis Council (NSERC) of North American country.

Streams run unceasingly over an amount of your time and incrementally come back with new results as new information arrive. These area units referred to as long-running, continuous, standing, and chronic queries [9,14]. The distinctive characteristics of information streams and continuous queries dictate the subsequent necessities of information stream management systems:

- the information model and question linguistics should permit order-based and time-based operations (e.g., queries over a five-minute moving window).
- the lack to store a whole stream suggests the use of approximate outline structures, mentioned within the literature as synopses [1] or digests [7]. As a result, queries over the summaries might not come back with precise answers.
- Streaming question plans might not use obstruction operators that have to consume the complete input before any results area unit is created.
- Thanks to performance and storage constraints, backtracking over a knowledge stream is not possible. On-line stream algorithms area unit restricted to creating only one jump over the information.
- Applications that monitor streams in period must react quickly to uncommon information values.
- Long-running queries might encounter changes in system conditions throughout their execution lifetimes (e.g., variable stream rates).
- Shared execution of the many continuous queries is needed to make sure quantifiability

Proposed knowledge stream systems check the abstract design shown in Figure 3.7. Associate degree input monitor could regulate the input rates, may be by dropping packets. Knowledge square measure generally holds on in three partitions: temporary operating storage (e.g., for window queries), outline storage for stream synopses, and static storage for meta-data (e.g., physical location of each source). Long-running queries square measure registered within the question

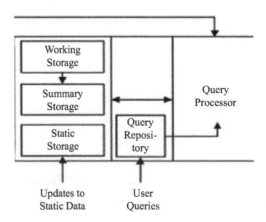

Figure 3.7   Abstract reference architecture of data stream management

repository and placed into teams for shared process, although one-time queries over the current state of the stream may additionally be expose. The query processor communicates with the input monitor and will re-optimize the question plans in response to dynamical input rates. Results square measure streamed to the users or quickly buffered.

In this paper, we tend to review recent add knowledge stream processing, together with knowledge models, question languages, continuous question process, and question optimisation. Related surveys embrace Babcock *et al.* [1] that discusses stream process problems within the context of the STREAM project, and a tutorial by Garofalakis *et al.* [10], that reviews algorithms for knowledge streams. An extended version of this survey [11] includes additional details.

The remainder of this paper surveys necessities of streaming applications, models and query languages for knowledge streams, streaming operators, and question process and optimization.

- Drawing temperature contours on a weather map: Contouring is the process of drawing isopleths. A weather map contains isopleths of different weather parameters (table of common isopleths). For example, maps of forecasted high temperatures have contours of constant temperature, or isotherms (iso-equal; therm-temperature).
- Analyze a stream of recent power usage statistics reported to an influence station (group by location, e.g., town block) and regulate the ability generation rate if necessary.

3.7 Efficiency of clustering algorithms in stream data

It handles streaming data when prior knowledge is not available and maps the clustering problem into a multimodal optimization problem [30]. It introduces a density-based objective function and adopts the fitness proportionate sharing strategy to perform a more effective search for the cluster centers.

Cluster analysis, or clustering, is an unsupervised machine learning task. It involves automatically discovering natural grouping in data. Unlike supervised learning (like predictive modelling), clustering algorithms only interpret the input data and find natural groups or clusters in feature space.

3.8 Findings and recommendations

- Many Department of Energy (DOE) facilities and plan estimates have crucial streaming and steering desires.
- The requirements of DOE and alternative applications have to be compelled to be additional consistently studied to change generalized solutions within the future.
- The advances in sensing technology and computing power that area unit offered nowadays need innovations in streaming algorithms, math, and statistics.

- Prevailing work in algorithms, mathematics, and statistics for streaming systems is not nonetheless mature, with many area units wherever enhancements are required and with several open challenges. There has been an initial analysis in on-line algorithms whose complexness is linear in a variety of information points; however, these algorithms have to be compelled to be refined and changed into usable libraries.
- Addressing streaming challenges would require investigation into existing and new programming models.
- Managing the end-to-end advancement is crucial to make sure innovations from streaming information.

Recommendations
- There is a desire for analysis into on-line algorithms that use concepts like sampling and sketches to support streaming and scale back their time quality. Metrics to assess the pertinency and quality of those algorithms are required.
- Machine learning algorithms together with deep learning, graph analytics, and dimension reduction have to be compelled to be extended to a broader vary of DOE applications [39,40]. Their price and implementation must be evaluated for practicality and performance.
- Develop capabilities and QoS metrics to gauge the end-to-end workflows in information streaming to address the usability, robustness, and performance wants of streaming applications.
- Develop advanced methodologies to permit for composition and management of stream process pipelines.
- Investigate and develop planning policies and algorithms that change stream process at the same time with batch jobs and/or the co-scheduling of distributed resources. Equally policies and algorithms to support interactive stream process are required.
- Explore existing and rising information streaming technologies (e.g., Spark, Heron) in high performance computing (HPC) facilities and develop solutions that change them to be integrated with existing software system stacks and infrastructure.
- Identify community best practices and drive generalization across science wants by developing common libraries.

3.9   Conclusion

As a result of challenges and opportunities given by the knowledge technology revolution, massive information streaming analytics have emerged because of the new frontier of competition and innovation. The International Organisations working with the United Nations agency, seize the chance of massive information streaming analytics which are supplied with insights for sturdy (creating|deciding| higher cognitive process) in time period thereby making them to own a position over their competitor. In this report, we saw the distinctive administered arrangement procedures on the period of Big Data. Both procedures are more qualified than the other for various applications [41,43]. We likewise expressed a table demonstrating the points of interest and weaknesses of the diverse characterization methods. These procedures can be utilized to sort out a wide range of client needs. Every method has an alternate precision, speed, and indicators. The study shows that the arrangement exactness of SVM algorithm was better than DT algorithm which likewise gives preferable arrangement datasets over DT algorithm.

References

[1]   R. Saradha, A study on data science methodologies and analytics, *Journal of Computer Science and Artificial Intelligence*, 64, 2020, 222.

[2]   X. Francis, "On the Origin(s) and Development of the Term \Big Data"_ Francis X, 2012.

[3]   V.N. Inukollu, S. Arsi, and S.R. Eavuri, Security issues associated with big data in cloud computing, *International Journal of Network Security & Its Applications*, 6(3), 2014, 45.

[4]   U. Matzat and U.-D. Reips, Mining "Big Data" using Big Data services, International Journal of Internet Science, 9(1), 2014, 1–8.

[5]   M. Ghesmoune and H. Azzag, *State-of-the-art on Clustering Data Streams*, New York, NY: Springer, December 2016.

[6]   H. Chen, Business intelligence and analytics: from big data to big impact, *MIS Quarterly*, 36, 2012, 1165–1188.

[7]   I.A.T. Hashema, I. Yaqooba, N.B. Anuara, S. Mokhtara, A. Gania and S.U. Khanb, The rise of "big data" on cloud computing: review and open research issues, *Information Systems*, 47, 2014, 98–115.

[8]   K. Udommanetanakit, T. Rakthanmanon and K. Waiyamai, E-stream: evolution-based technique for stream clustering, in: *ADMA*, 2007, pp. 605–615.

[9]   Y. Piao, H.W. Park, C.H. Jin and K.H. Ryu, Ensemble method for classification of high-dimensional data, in: *2014 International Conference on Big Data and Smart Computing (BIGCOMP)*, 2014, IEEE, pp. 245–249, 978-1-4799-3919-0/14.

[10] G.C. Fox, L. Ramakrishnan and S. Jha, Stream 2015 Final Report, 2015, Available: 32. https://doi.org/10.13140/RG.2.1.3907.2240

[11] S. Kulkarni, N. Bhagat, M. Fu, et al., Twitter heron: stream processing at scale, in: *Proceedings of the 2015 ACM SIGMOD International Conference on Management of Data*, 2015, ACM, pp. 239–250.

[12] N. Singh, N. Garg, and V. Mittal, Data – insights, motivation and challenges, *International Journal of Scientific & Engineering Research*, 4(12), 2013, 2172, ISSN 2229-5518 2013.

[13] S. Robak, B. Franczyk and M. Robak, Research problems associated with big data utilization in logistics and supply chains design and management, *Computer Science and Information Systems*, 3, 2014, 245–249, doi:10.15439/2014F472

[14]   C.L. Philip Chen and C.-Y. Zhang, Data-intensive applications, challenges, techniques and technologies: a survey on Big Data, *Information Sciences*, 275, 2014, 314–347.

[15]   X. Wu, X. Zhu, G.-Q. Wu and W. Ding, Data mining with big data, *Transactions on Knowledge and Data Engineering*, 26(1), 2014, 97–107.

[16]   D. Wang, X. Liu and M. Wang, A DT-SVM strategy for stock futures prediction with Big Data, in: *16th International Conference on Computational Science and Engineering*, 2013, IEEE, 978-0-76955096-1/13.

[17]   G. Kesavaraj and S. Sukumaran, A study on classification techniques in data mining, in: *4th ICCCNT Tiruchengode*, India, July 4–6, 2013, IEEE.

[18]   S. Suthaharan, *Big Data Classification: Problems and Challenges in Network Intrusion Prediction with Machine Learning*, Department of Computer Science, University of North Carolina at Greensboro, Greensboro, NC, USA, 2012.

[19]   S.B. Kotsiantis, Supervised machine learning: a review of classification techniques, *Informatica*, 31, 2007, 249–268.

[20]   H. Yu, J. Yang and J. Han, Classifying large data sets using SVMs with hierarchical clusters, in: *SIGKDD '03* Washington, DC, 2003, ACM, 1581137370/ 03/0008.

[21]   V. Yenkar and M. Bartere, Review on data mining with Big Data, *International Journal of Computer Science and Mobile Computing*, 3(4), 2014, 97–102.

[22]   G. H. Mohammed and A.L. Zamil, The application of semantic-based classification on Big Data, in: *International Conference on Information and Communication Systems (ICICS)*, 2014, IEEE, 978-1-4799-30234/14.

[23]   W. Dai and J. Wei, A MapReduce implementation of C4.5 decision tree algorithm, *International Journal of Database Theory and Application*, 7, 2014, 49–60.

[24]   http://www-01.ibm.com/software/data/bigdata/, 2012, IBM.

[25]   F. Li and S. Nath, Scalable data summarization on Big Data, *Distributed and Parallel Databases*, 15, 2014, 313–314.

[26]   United Nations Global Pulse, 2012, Big Data for Development Challenges & Opportunities, May 2012.

[27]   McKinsey Global Institute, 2011, Big Data: The Next Frontier for Innovation, Competition, and Productivity, May 2011.

[28]   S. Joseph, E.A. Jasmin and S. Chandran, Stream computing: opportunities and challenges in smart grid, *Procedia Technology*, 21, 2015, 49–53.

[29]   J.D. Deng, Outline detection energy data streams using incremental and kernel PCA algorithms, in: *2016 IEEE 16th International Conference on Data Mining Workshops*, 2016, pp. 390–397.

[30]   Y.-H. Lu and Y. Huang, Mining data streams using clustering, in: *2005 International Conference on Machine Learning and Cybernetics*, Guangzhou, China, vol. 4, 2005, pp. 2079–2083, doi:10.1109/ ICMLC.2005.1527288.

[31] A. Ara and A. Ara, Case study: integrating IoT, streaming analytics and machine learning to improve intelligent diabetes management system, in: *2017 International Conference on Energy, Communication, Data Analytics and Soft Computing* (*ICECDS*), Chennai, 2017, pp. 3179–3182, doi: 10.1109/ICECDS.2017.8390043.

[32] M. Pechenizkiy, Predictive analytics on evolving data streams anticipating and adapting to changes in known and unknown contexts, in: *2015 International Conference on High Performance Computing & Simulation* (*HPCS*), *Amsterdam*, 2015, pp. 658–659, doi: 10.1109/HPCSim.2015. 7237112.

[33] H. Isah, T. Abughofa, S. Mahfuz, D. Ajerla, F. Zulkernine and S. Khan, A survey of distributed data stream processing frameworks, *IEEE Access*, 7, 2019, 154300–154316, doi: 10.1109/ACCESS.2019.2946884.

[34] "Spark", Available: http://spark.apache.org/

[35] M. Zaharia, M. Chowdhury, T. Das, et al., Resilient distributed datasets: a fault-tolerant abstraction for in-memory cluster computing, in: Presented as part of the *9th USENIX Symposium on Networked Systems Design and Implementation* (*NSDI 12*). San Jose, CA: USENIX, 2012, pp. 15–28, Available: https://www.usenix.org/conference/nsdi12/technical-sessions/ presentation/zaharia

[36] A. S. S. Software, Available: http://storm.apache.org/

[37] T.D. Yogita, Clustering techniques for streaming data—a survey, in: *2013 IEEE 3rd International Advance Computing Conference* (*IACC*), 2013, IEEE, pp. 951–956.

[38] J. Han, J. Pei and M. Kamber, *Data Mining: Concepts and Techniques,* Amsterdam: Elsevier, 2011.

[39] S.F. Ardabili, A. Mosavi, P. Ghamisi, *et al.*, Covid-19 outbreak prediction with machine learning, *Algorithms,* 13(10), 2020, 249.

[40] A. Essien, I. Petrounias, P. Sampaio and S. Sampaio, Improving urban traffic speed prediction using data source fusion and deep learning, in: *2019 IEEE International Conference on Big Data and Smart Computing* (*BigComp*), 2019, IEEE, pp. 1–8.

[41] I.H. Sarker, Machine learning: algorithms, real-world applications and research directions, *SN Computer Science*, 2, 2021, 160, https://doi.org/10. 1007/s42979-021-00592-x

[42] H. Zikang, Y. Yong, Y. Guofeng and Z. Xinyu, Sentiment analysis of agricultural product ecommerce review data based on deep learning, in: *2020 International Conference on Internet of Things and Intelligent Applications* (*ITIA*),2020, IEEE, pp. 1–7.

[43] C. Shorten, T.M. Khoshgoftaar and B. Furht, Deep learning applications for Covid-19, *Journal of Big Data,* 8(1), 2021, 1–54.

Chapter 4

Sentiment analysis on streaming data using parallel computing

Jishnu Saurav Mittapalli[1], Jainav Amit Mutha[2] and R. Maheswari[1]

Abstract

Today as everything has become online and everyone has the chance to voice their opinion. Every opinion is important for the success of the company. Therefore, every company has started giving more and more important to this sentiment analysis, thereby making sentiment analysis a huge field in itself and a hot research topic in the field of natural language processing and linguistic communication. As more and more people are having access to the Internet, the Internet is filled with opinions about products, which has led to the data explosion and big data. And as we have to now do the analysis of this large amount of data, we have to find out some mechanism to make this process of analysis faster and more efficient. Parallel computing comes to the rescue in this case. Parallel computing has been a topic of research for a lot of years now. We can use this in the field of sentiment analysis as well. This is what is done in this work. The various ways in which sentiment analysis can be done using parallel computing are compared in terms of efficiency and time taken to compute. Streaming data has become the trend today as data is continuously being added to the Internet. So performing sentiment analysis on streaming data is much more helpful using parallel computing.

4.1 Introduction

A situation, event or product-based feeling is known as a sentiment. From the 1990s itself, this field of sentiment analysis had come into research. It is basically the analysis of this sentiment from the text, words or speech given by a human being. In this case, finding out whether a given text is positive or negative is considered as sentiment analysis. This can be done from a single sentence, a paragraph or even a full document. This is very important in business today as the Internet is

[1]School of Computer Science and Engineering, Vellore Institute of Technology, India
[2]School of Electronics Engineering, Vellore Institute of Technology, India

so fast, a single negative comment can spread like wildfire spoiling the entire reputation and sales of a product [1]. Not just that understanding people's emotions is very important for companies as customer satisfaction is very important for any company but the company's team cannot sit and read all the comments from every user and this is where sentiment analysis comes into the picture. The sentiment analysis model can read and separate out all the negative comments and give us results so that the company can do the necessary to rectify the problems faced by the customers, change what they do not like and understand their expectations. If the computer understands the emotions of the user from the text itself, the companies can understand their customers' requirements easily from surveys conducted on online platforms and other ways. And as there is a lot of data to be processed in this way, a very efficient and fast model is required. Parallel computing has in recent times become a really important topic in the field of research due to the huge increase in data available. The transition of computers from having single cores to ones with more than one core and ones with GPUs itself proves that parallelism is a far better solution for the purpose of increasing the computation speed. This is one of the main reasons GPUs have become really important in recent times. They improve the performance at a really low price itself. Therefore, making the usage of supercomputing to everyone possible. In today's world, the Internet has so many opinions, reviews which are all data [2].

In this particular work, we aim at surveying the concept of parallelism using GPUs for the purpose of sentiment analysis. Finding out/designing parallel algorithms to use on a GPU might be a herculean task. So we compare the various algorithms that are currently being used in the field of sentiment analysis. In this work, we survey the concept of parallel computing and especially GPU computing. I would like to show how this new technology would help the future of sentiment analysis. Parallel computing is one of the best ways in which efficiency can be increased. We discuss major algorithms and differences between the various algorithms and which ones are suitable for use on a GPU.

4.2   Related works

Junchao Dong *et al.*, in their paper, "A Commodity Review Sentiment Analysis Based on BERT-convolutional neural network (CNN) Model," have in detail helped understand the use of CNN for sentiment analysis, and they have included that in comparison with bidirectional encoder representations from transformers (BERT) and CNN models their BERT CNN model had an elevation of 14.4% and 17% [3].

Azamat Serek *et al.*, in their paper, "Distributed sentiment analysis of an agglutinative language via Spark by applying machine learning methods," have given the methods to use machine learning for the purpose of sentiment analysis, using spark for the purpose of distributed computing [4].

Eugene Ch'ng *et al.*, in their paper, "Real-time GPU-accelerated social media sentiment processing and visualization," have given how GPUs can be used to increment or accelerate sentiment processing [5].

Santosh Shivaji Kolekar *et al.*, in their paper, "S. S. Kolekar and H. K. Khanuja, "Sentiment Analysis using Deep Learning on GPU," have given ways to perform sentiment analysis using deep learning and have got a training accuracy of 98% [6].

Mirco Ravanelli, Titouan Parcollet, Yoshua Bengio and their tea, in their paper "The Pytorch-Kaldi Speech Recognition Toolkit," have given details about a micro framework Kaldi built on PyTorch used for the purpose of using GPU for computation [7].

S. S. Kolekar and H. K. Khanuja and their team in their paper, "Sentiment Analysis using Deep Learning on GPU," have given us information on how we can use deep learning on GPUs for the purpose of sentiment analysis [8].

A. Ugarte and their team in their paper "QMSpy: An Integrated Modular and Scalable Platform for Quantitative Metagenomics in Pyspark" have given a very innovative approach towards using pyspark [9].

D. Goularas and S. Kamis and their team in their paper "Evaluation of Deep Learning Techniques in Sentiment Analysis from Twitter Data" have given the various ways in which deep learning methods can be used for sentiment analysis and compared between the various methods [10].

A. Serek, A. Issabek, and A. Bogdanchikov and their team in their paper, "Distributed Sentiment Analysis of an Agglutinative Language via Spark by Applying Machine Learning Methods," have given an approach to use apache spark for the purpose of sentiment analysis using spark [11].

Z. Gao, A. Feng, X. Song, and X. Wu in their paper, "Target-Dependent Sentiment Classification with BERT," have helped us understand sentiment classification using the BERT model [12].

S. Parui, A. K. Roshan Bajiya, D. Samanta, and N. Chakravorty, in their paper, "Emotion Recognition from EEG Signal using XGBoost Algorithm," have used the XGBoost algorithm to accelerate.

4.3   Methodology

In this work, the various ways of performing sentiment analysis parallelly are compared. Each of the methods that have been used is explained in this section. Predictions can be made on streaming data as we get data continuously and the API can continuously make predictions as we are parallel computing.

4.3.1   Logistic regression (machine learning)

Logistic regression is the method of machine learning which basically at the core of the model uses the sigmoid function. Logistic regression is an algorithm used in machine learning for the purpose of classification that can be used to observe and classify a particular observation into a discrete set of divisions. Logistic regression can be used for solving problems like classifying, online bank transactions as not fraud or fraud, classifying e-mails as not spam or spam or it could even be used to classify tumors as benign or malignant. Logistic sigmoid functions are used to

```
5   predictions = lrModel.transform(val_df)
6   eval()
```

CPU times: user 78.7 ms, sys: 18 ms, total: 96.7 ms
Wall time: 6 min 13s

Figure 4.1   Machine learning on CPU training time

Positive 😜
CPU times: user 31.3 ms, sys: 4.01 ms, total: 35.3 ms
Wall time: 334 ms

Figure 4.2   Machine learning on GPU prediction time

return probability values that help us classify the observations. Logistic regression is basically linear regression but logistic regression uses a complex cost function rather than a basic linear function. Basically, the cost function gives a result between 0 and 1.

So, here we used this sigmoid function for the purpose of classifying sentences into positive or negative, we have run this model on both CPUs and GPUs. As shown in Figure 4.1, this algorithm is trained on a CPU and the same algorithm is trained on a GPU as you can see in Figure 4.2. It can be seen that machine learning algorithms work better on CPUs than on GPUs [15].

4.3.2   BERT model (deep learning)

For the purpose of classifying text into positive and negative using deep learning, we use the BERT model. BERT model is basically BERT. It is basically a deep learning technique based on transformers that have been developed by Google primarily for natural language processing [16]. Jacob Devlin and his colleagues created and published it in 2018. Google has been using this to better understand searches from 2019 [14]. So, this model has been used to classify sentiments and we have used it on both CPU and GPU for the purpose of comparison, as can be seen in Figures 4.3 and 4.4.

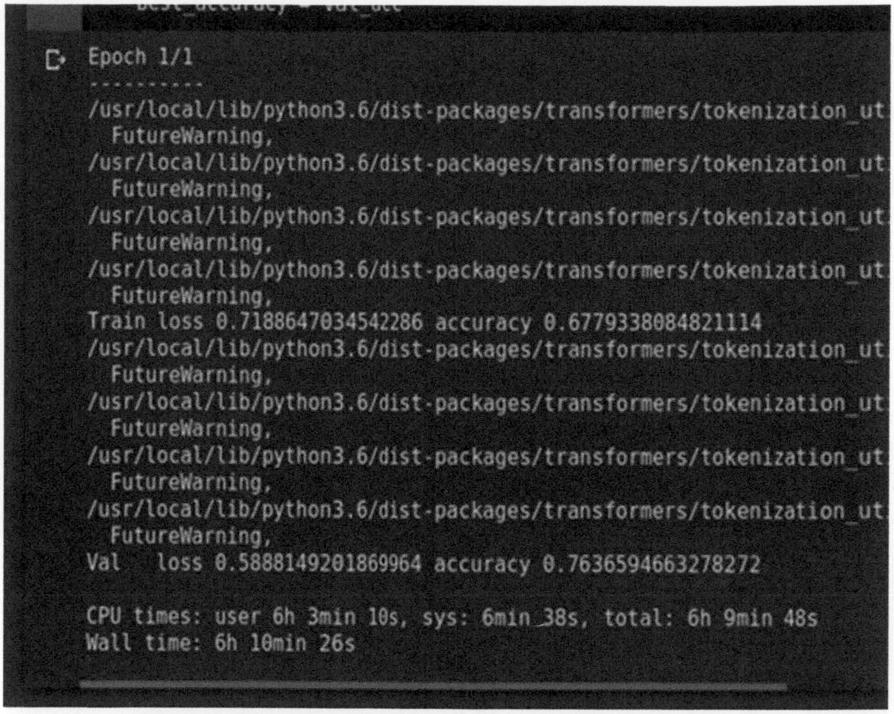

```
best_accuracy = val_acc

Epoch 1/1
----------
/usr/local/lib/python3.6/dist-packages/transformers/tokenization_ut
  FutureWarning,
/usr/local/lib/python3.6/dist-packages/transformers/tokenization_ut
  FutureWarning,
/usr/local/lib/python3.6/dist-packages/transformers/tokenization_ut
  FutureWarning,
/usr/local/lib/python3.6/dist-packages/transformers/tokenization_ut
  FutureWarning,
Train loss 0.7188647034542286 accuracy 0.67793380884821114
/usr/local/lib/python3.6/dist-packages/transformers/tokenization_ut
  FutureWarning,
/usr/local/lib/python3.6/dist-packages/transformers/tokenization_ut
  FutureWarning,
/usr/local/lib/python3.6/dist-packages/transformers/tokenization_ut
  FutureWarning,
/usr/local/lib/python3.6/dist-packages/transformers/tokenization_ut
  FutureWarning,
Val   loss 0.5888149201869964 accuracy 0.7636594663278272

CPU times: user 6h 3min 10s, sys: 6min 38s, total: 6h 9min 48s
Wall time: 6h 10min 26s
```

Figure 4.3   Deep learning on CPU training time

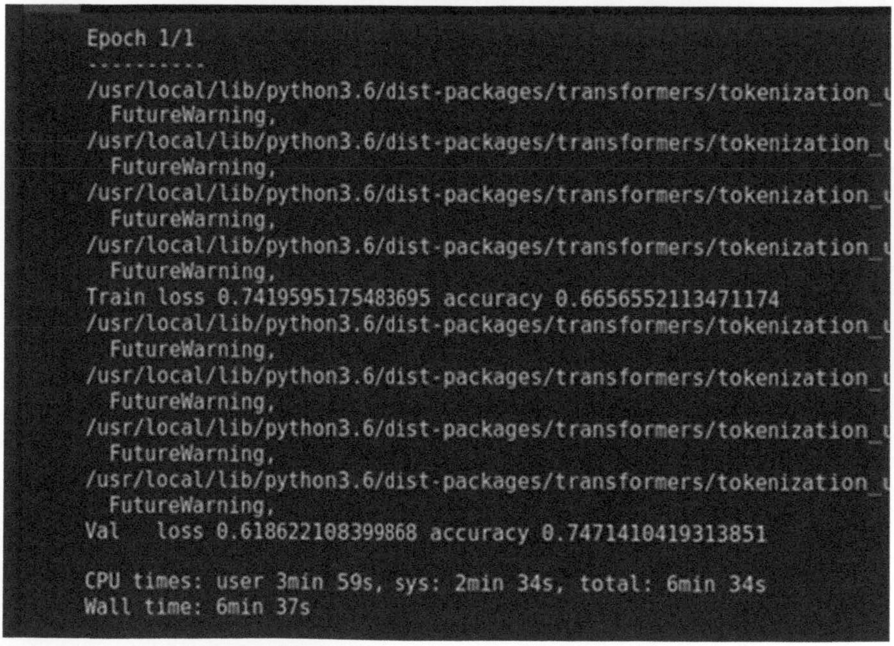

```
Epoch 1/1
----------
/usr/local/lib/python3.6/dist-packages/transformers/tokenization_u
  FutureWarning,
/usr/local/lib/python3.6/dist-packages/transformers/tokenization_u
  FutureWarning,
/usr/local/lib/python3.6/dist-packages/transformers/tokenization_u
  FutureWarning,
/usr/local/lib/python3.6/dist-packages/transformers/tokenization_u
  FutureWarning,
Train loss 0.7419595175483695 accuracy 0.66566552113471174
/usr/local/lib/python3.6/dist-packages/transformers/tokenization_u
  FutureWarning,
/usr/local/lib/python3.6/dist-packages/transformers/tokenization_u
  FutureWarning,
/usr/local/lib/python3.6/dist-packages/transformers/tokenization_u
  FutureWarning,
Val   loss 0.618622108399868 accuracy 0.7471410419313851

CPU times: user 3min 59s, sys: 2min 34s, total: 6min 34s
Wall time: 6min 37s
```

Figure 4.4   Deep learning on GPU training time

As we can see, GPU works far better for deep learning when compared to CPU.

4.3.3   RNN using LSTM

RNN or recurrent neural networks is basically a generalization of a normal neural network. Recurrent neural networks are repeating in nature; they repeat the same function after every input based on the previous computation [17]. Once the output is produced, it is saved and is sent again into the RNN. While making a decision, the current input and the previous output are considered. So we have used this with long short-term memory or LSTM to compare parallel and without parallel as shown in Figures 4.5 and 4.6.

4.3.4   XGboost

XGBoost is a gradient boosting algorithm supporting open source libraries that supports C++, Python, Julia, R, Java, Scala, etc. It works on all operating systems and it also works on Hadoop, spark, and flink as well as on single cored machines [13]. We have used this as well for comparing parallel and non-parallel computing for sentiment analysis as you can see in Figures 4.7 and 4.8.

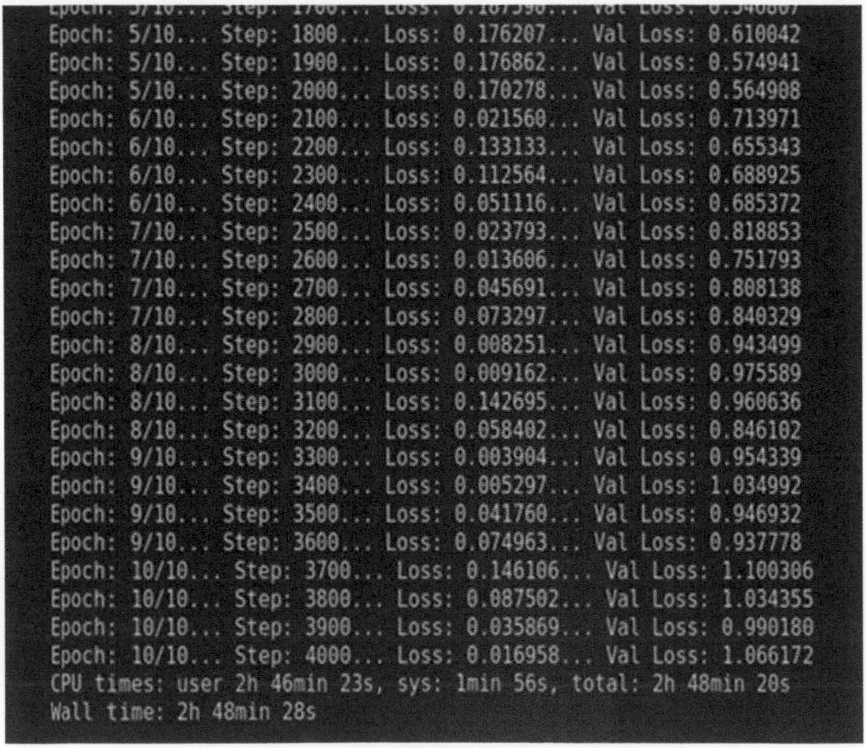

```
Epoch: 5/10... Step: 1700... Loss: 0.107590... Val Loss: 0.540007
Epoch: 5/10... Step: 1800... Loss: 0.176207... Val Loss: 0.610042
Epoch: 5/10... Step: 1900... Loss: 0.176862... Val Loss: 0.574941
Epoch: 5/10... Step: 2000... Loss: 0.170278... Val Loss: 0.564908
Epoch: 6/10... Step: 2100... Loss: 0.021560... Val Loss: 0.713971
Epoch: 6/10... Step: 2200... Loss: 0.133133... Val Loss: 0.655343
Epoch: 6/10... Step: 2300... Loss: 0.112564... Val Loss: 0.688925
Epoch: 6/10... Step: 2400... Loss: 0.051116... Val Loss: 0.685372
Epoch: 7/10... Step: 2500... Loss: 0.023793... Val Loss: 0.818853
Epoch: 7/10... Step: 2600... Loss: 0.013606... Val Loss: 0.751793
Epoch: 7/10... Step: 2700... Loss: 0.045691... Val Loss: 0.808138
Epoch: 7/10... Step: 2800... Loss: 0.073297... Val Loss: 0.840329
Epoch: 8/10... Step: 2900... Loss: 0.008251... Val Loss: 0.943499
Epoch: 8/10... Step: 3000... Loss: 0.009162... Val Loss: 0.975589
Epoch: 8/10... Step: 3100... Loss: 0.142695... Val Loss: 0.960636
Epoch: 8/10... Step: 3200... Loss: 0.058402... Val Loss: 0.846102
Epoch: 9/10... Step: 3300... Loss: 0.003904... Val Loss: 0.954339
Epoch: 9/10... Step: 3400... Loss: 0.005297... Val Loss: 1.034992
Epoch: 9/10... Step: 3500... Loss: 0.041760... Val Loss: 0.946932
Epoch: 9/10... Step: 3600... Loss: 0.074963... Val Loss: 0.937778
Epoch: 10/10... Step: 3700... Loss: 0.146106... Val Loss: 1.100306
Epoch: 10/10... Step: 3800... Loss: 0.087502... Val Loss: 1.034355
Epoch: 10/10... Step: 3900... Loss: 0.035869... Val Loss: 0.990180
Epoch: 10/10... Step: 4000... Loss: 0.016958... Val Loss: 1.066172
CPU times: user 2h 46min 23s, sys: 1min 56s, total: 2h 48min 20s
Wall time: 2h 48min 28s
```

Figure 4.5   RNN using LSTM on CPU training time

```
Epoch: 7/10... Step: 2500... Loss: 0.008187... Val Loss: 0.949137
Epoch: 7/10... Step: 2600... Loss: 0.027354... Val Loss: 0.904230
Epoch: 7/10... Step: 2700... Loss: 0.002338... Val Loss: 0.962811
Epoch: 7/10... Step: 2800... Loss: 0.014689... Val Loss: 0.939297
Epoch: 8/10... Step: 2900... Loss: 0.002627... Val Loss: 1.067186
Epoch: 8/10... Step: 3000... Loss: 0.003665... Val Loss: 1.058642
Epoch: 8/10... Step: 3100... Loss: 0.005205... Val Loss: 1.048160
Epoch: 8/10... Step: 3200... Loss: 0.048207... Val Loss: 1.016735
Epoch: 9/10... Step: 3300... Loss: 0.002330... Val Loss: 1.154703
Epoch: 9/10... Step: 3400... Loss: 0.003946... Val Loss: 1.264812
Epoch: 9/10... Step: 3500... Loss: 0.005112... Val Loss: 1.073769
Epoch: 9/10... Step: 3600... Loss: 0.039553... Val Loss: 1.142276
Epoch: 10/10... Step: 3700... Loss: 0.000554... Val Loss: 1.189018
Epoch: 10/10... Step: 3800... Loss: 0.022010... Val Loss: 1.052656
Epoch: 10/10... Step: 3900... Loss: 0.001211... Val Loss: 1.149897
Epoch: 10/10... Step: 4000... Loss: 0.001633... Val Loss: 1.184924
CPU times: user 3min 3s, sys: 57.5 s, total: 4min
Wall time: 4min 2s
```

Figure 4.6   RNN using LSTM on GPU training time

```
5   xgb=model_bow.predict_proba(x_valid_bow)
6   xgb
```

```
CPU times: user 4 min 2s, sys: 0 ns, total: 4 min 2 s
Wall time: 4 min 12 s
```

Figure 4.7   XGBoost training time GPU

```
[998]    valid_0's binary_logloss: 0.237594
[999]    valid_0's binary_logloss: 0.233471
[1000]   valid_0's binary_logloss: 0.23548
CPU times: user 30 min 40 sec, sys: 110 ms, total: 30 mins 40sec
Wall time: 30 min 49 sec
```

```
1   print("accuracy: {}".format(accuracy_score(y_valid, 1*(bst.predic
```

```
accuracy: 0.8443228026274633
```

Figure 4.8   XGBoost training time CPU

4.4   Results and discussion

All the techniques have been compared and have been tabulated in Tables 4.1, 4.2, 4.3, and 4.4. As we can see, series computing is more suited for machine learning while parallel computing is more suitable for deep learning.

Table 4.1   Logistic regression CPU vs. GPU

Attribute	CPU	GPU
Training time	6 min 13 sec	39 min
Prediction time	334 ms	5.6 min
Accuracy	78.36%	79%

Table 4.2   BERT model CPU vs. GPU

Attribute	CPU	GPU
Training time	6 h 10 min 26 s	6 min 37 s
Prediction time	529 ms	22.2 ms
Accuracy	74.492%	0.72842

Table 4.3   RNN using LSTM CPU vs. GPU

Attribute	CPU	GPU
Training time	2 h 48 min 28 s	4 min 2 s
Prediction time	68 ms	12.1 ms
Accuracy	77.8%	79.0%

Table 4.4   Gradient boosting – XGBoost vs. LightGBM

Attribute	GPU	CPU
Training time	4 min 12 s	30 min 49 s
Accuracy	57.80%	84.43%

4.5   Future scope

Advances in this field have been continuing, and new works are coming up in a persistent and widespread manner. Sentiment analysis can be used for better user experience, and as a result of this, many companies are investing a lot in this field. Much more advances can be made on the accuracy of the sentiment report, and these techniques can be applied in various places as technological advancements are made. Specific places where progress can be made are like understanding the emotion of children/infants – this might be a very challenging task to accomplish as we will be having mostly visuals and less audio to be dealt with for the analytical purpose. Also, more libraries can be developed in python for better use of GPUs and these existing ones should be used in a more widespread way. Apart from this, many people are still not comfortable in using GPUs as they are not familiar with these technologies and so, as deep learning and machine learning are today's most researched fields in the field of computer science, the use of GPUs will become compulsory and very much necessary in the future. Also in the future, other modes of parallel processing like spark and Hadoop can be explored for the purpose of sentiment analysis.

4.6   Conclusion

I would like to conclude by saying that both using parallel and non-parallel have their own advantages and disadvantages. They have to be situationally used depending on the requirements of our project. For example, advantages of CPU include when we use machine learning easy integration with other frameworks while GPU parallel processing is useful as it makes the process of training really fast. Deep learning suits best with GPU architecture rather than CPU architecture due to its batch processing and the ratio of computation to data is very high. Logistic regression like linear algorithms are best suited for CPU as there are less tasks to be done and data shuffling is more. The modern techniques of RNN with LSTM also gave great performance and accuracy with GPU and relatively poor performance in CPU. The different gradient boosting algorithm gives good performance for one scenario whereas gives good accuracy in some other. Sentiment analysis based on Twitter – social media data is carried out and positive and negative sentiments of the Twitter data were found. Since, we are using parallel computing, performing sentiment analysis on streaming data becomes easy.

References

[1]   J.S. Mittapalli, A. Jaiswal and R. Selvamani, "Advances in sentiment analysis—an overview", *JRAR* 2021:8(1):887–898.
[2]   C. Navarro, H. Nancy and L. Mateu. "A survey on parallel computing and its applications in data-parallel problems using GPU architectures",

Communications in Computational Physics, 2013;15:285–329, doi:10.4208/cicp.110113.010813a.

[3]   J. Dong, F. He, Y. Guo and H. Zhang, "A commodity review sentiment analysis based on BERT-CNN model", in: *2020 5th International Conference on Computer and Communication Systems (ICCCS)*, Shanghai, China, 2020, pp. 143–147, doi:10.1109/ICCCS49078.2020.9118434.

[4]   A. Serek, A. Issabek and A. Bogdanchikov, "Distributed sentiment analysis of an agglutinative language via Spark by applying machine learning methods", in: *2019 15th International Conference on Electronics, Computer and Computation (ICECCO)*, Abuja, Nigeria, 2019, pp. 1–4, doi:10.1109/ICECCO48375.2019.9043264.

[5]   E. Ch'ng, Z. Chen and S. See, "Real-time GPU-accelerated social media sentiment processing and visualization", in: *2017 IEEE/ACM 21st International Symposium on Distributed Simulation and Real Time Applications (DS-RT)*, Rome, 2017, pp. 1–4, doi:10.1109/DISTRA.2017.8167690.

[6]   S.S. Kolekar and H.K. Khanuja, "Sentiment analysis using deep learning on GPU", in: *2018 IEEE Punecon*, Pune, India, 2018, pp. 1–5, doi:10.1109/PUNECON.2018.8745401.

[7]   M. Ravanelli, T. Parcollet and Y. Bengio, "The pytorch-kaldi speech recognition toolkit", in: *ICASSP 2019 – 2019 IEEE International Conference on Acoustics, Speech and Signal Processing (ICASSP)*, Brighton, UK, 2019, pp. 6465–6469, doi:10.1109/ICASSP.2019.8683713.

[8]   S.S. Kolekar and H.K. Khanuja, "Sentiment analysis using deep learning on GPU", in: *2018 IEEE Punecon*, Pune, India, 2018, pp. 1–5, doi:10.1109/PUNECON.2018.8745401.

[9]   A. Ugarte, M. Quang-Dao, B.H. Ho, et al., "QMSpy: an integrated modular and scalable platform for quantitative metagenomics in Pyspark", in: *2019 IEEE-RIVF International Conference on Computing and Communication Technologies (RIVF)*, Danang, Vietnam, 2019, pp. 1–6, doi:10.1109/RIVF.2019.8713709.

[10]   D. Goularas and S. Kamis, "Evaluation of deep learning techniques in sentiment analysis from Twitter data", in: *2019 International Conference on Deep Learning and Machine Learning in Emerging Applications (Deep-ML)*, Istanbul, Turkey, 2019, pp. 12–17, doi:10.1109/Deep-ML.2019.00011.

[11]   A. Serek, A. Issabek and A. Bogdanchikov, "Distributed sentiment analysis of an agglutinative language via Spark by applying machine learning methods", in: *2019 15th International Conference on Electronics, Computer and Computation (ICECCO)*, Abuja, Nigeria, 2019, pp. 1–4, doi:10.1109/ICECCO48375.2019.9043264.

[12]   Z. Gao, A. Feng, X. Song and X. Wu, "Target-dependent sentiment classification with BERT", *IEEE Access*, 2019;7:154290–154299, doi:10.1109/ACCESS.2019.2946594.

[13]   S. Parui, A.K. Roshan Bajiya, D. Samanta and N. Chakravorty, "Emotion recognition from EEG signal using XGBoost algorithm", in: *2019 IEEE 16th*

India Council International Conference (INDICON), Rajkot, India, 2019, pp. 1–4, doi:10.1109/INDICON47234.2019.9028978.

[14]   Z. Gao, A. Feng, X. Song and X. Wu, "Target-dependent sentiment classification with BERT", *IEEE Access*, 2019;7:154290–154299, doi:10.1109/ACCESS.2019.2946594.

[15]   F. Alzamzami, M. Hoda and A.E. Saddik, "Light gradient boosting machine for general sentiment classification on short texts: a comparative evaluation", *IEEE Access*, 2020;8:101840–101858, doi:10.1109/ACCESS.2020.2997330.

[16]   A. Aslam, U. Qamar, P. Saqib, R. Ayesha and A. Qadeer, "A novel framework for sentiment analysis using deep learning", in: *2020 22nd International Conference on Advanced Communication Technology (ICACT)*, Phoenix Park, PyeongChang, Korea (South), 2020, pp. 525–529, doi:10.23919/ICACT48636.2020.9061247.

[17]   J. Gao, R. Yao, H. Lai and T. Chang, "Sentiment analysis with CNNs built on LSTM on tourists comments", in: *2019 IEEE Eurasia Conference on Biomedical Engineering, Healthcare and Sustainability (ECBIOS)*, Okinawa, Japan, 2019, pp. 108–111, doi:10.1109/ECBIOS.2019.8807844.

Chapter 5

Fog and edge computing paradigms for emergency vehicle movement in smart city

A.P. Jyothi[1] and S. Usha[2]

Abstract

At the point when things are associated with the cloud to deal with their information in a brought together manner, a few difficulties become basic. It does not generally bode well to move all the information to the cloud and there are a few situations where reaction time is basic. In those cases, conveying computational limit is the arrangement, and there are two fundamental methods of doing that utilizing edge or fog figuring.

This book chapter discusses introduction, background study, overview, comparison, benefits, use cases, challenges, future of edge, and fog compute model along with a case study of streaming analytics in big data for emergency vehicles movement in smart city traffic management and conclusion.

Controlling traffic signal in favor of emergency vehicles like ambulances is the need of the hour with an increase in the number of COVID cases. It will help the patients reach hospitals in time and save their lives. A case study based on signal-free movement of the emergency vehicles by using fog and edge computing paradigms with streaming analytics in big data is explored in this book chapter.

5.1 Exordium

At the point when we talk about the Internet of Things (IoT), we frequently believe that the lone conceivable design is that of numerous gadgets spread all throughout the planet and associated with the cloud in a practically mystical manner. Yet, when we center on the mechanical world, things get muddled.

Regularly the machines we associate move massive measures of data, and moving the entirety of that data to the cloud is trying from multiple points of view. Yet, the most noticeably terrible thing is that by and large, regardless of addressing the test, we do not get what we need. At the end of the day, get a reaction adequately quick to give esteem with the data gathered.

[1]Department of Computer Science and Engineering, Ramaiah University of Applied Sciences, India
[2]Department of CSE, RRCE, VTU, India

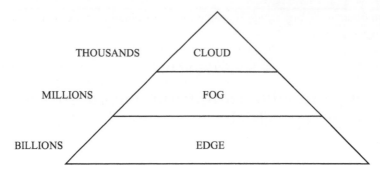

Figure 5.1   Edge, Fog and Cloud Computing paradigms

In this way, the worldview of associating things to the cloud to appreciate an enormous brought together information is not generally the answer. This is the framework wherein Edge and Fog figuring start to be examined. Fundamentally, the distinction between the two is unpretentious. Since in the two cases we talk about disseminating the processing competence, Figure 5.1 shows the Edge, Fog and Cloud Computing ideal models.

5.2   Baseline survey

Gartner characterized Edge registering in their glossary as follows: "Edge computing is part of a distributed computing topology where information processing is located close to the edge, where things and people produce or consume that information" [5]. Rather than depending on a data center that can be a large number of miles away for capacity and handling, edge registering brings information stockpiling and computing near to the gadget that create and gather the information. Closeness is fundamental for applications that require continuous information for their activities and extremely low idleness. Also, by handling information locally, associations can set aside hard cash by decreasing the information volume to be moved and processed in cloud servers [6]. Organizations that have embraced cloud-based answers for carry out numerous business cycles may have understood that the necessary data transfer capacity brings about greater expenses than anticipated.

A regular model is a camcorder associated with the Internet that sends live photos from a public square around there or an application that monitors health equipment in a health facility utilizing a few sensors and IoT gadgets. A solitary camcorder can rapidly send the created information over a set of connections. Nonetheless, when numerous camcorders all the while communicate live chronicles, numerous issues can emerge. In addition to the fact that latency affects quality, it even increases bandwidth expenses.

Edge processing is multiplying because of the quick and developing organization of IoT gadgets, which produce tremendous measures of information during their activities. These gadgets interface with the Internet straightforwardly or through doors to communicate information to the cloud or get directions from the cloud worker.

As indicated by IDC's conjecture for 2019, "in any event 40% of the information created by IoT gadgets would be stored, processed and analyzed at the edge of the organization" [7]. The incompetence of cloud-based data dispensation solution for latency-sensitive edge applications has led to the design of some solutions deployed at the network's edge. These solution include micro data centers, cloudlets and fog compute-based solution [6,8].

Cisco Systems characterized Fog figuring as: "Fog Computing is a highly virtualized platform that provides compute, storage, and networking services between end devices and traditional Cloud Computing Data Centers, typically, but not exclusively located at the edge of the network" [9].

The previous writing on Fog processing and edge registering portrayed the two standards reciprocally. For the two innovations, IoT information preparing is done near the information sources prior to being moved to a cloud server. With edge figuring, information is regularly prepared in edge gadgets and afterward sent to fog hubs or cloud workers utilizing edge passages, which have more impressive correspondence capacities than edge gadgets. With fog registering, the information are investigated and prepared in a fog hub at the local network's edge.

The open Fog consortium (openFogconsortium.org), which is presently important for the Industrial Internet Consortium (IIC), uncovers that edge figuring is frequently erroneously called fog processing. Its reference engineering for fog registering, delivered in February 2017, certifies that: (I) Fog hubs are coordinated progressively, with a three-level design, despite the fact that n-levels can be utilized for explicit situations, and (ii) Fog processing gives calculation, systems administration, stockpiling, and control anyplace from cloud to IoT and detecting gadgets, while edge figuring gives restricted compute assets at the edge [10].

Its first level, close to the edge of the set-up, ordinarily includes getting information from edge gadgets, normalizing information, and controlling sensors and actuators. The subsequent level includes the filter, compress, and alteration of data. The third level is the place where the total of information and the change of that information into knowledge happen.

Fog hubs address the foundation of the fog figuring framework. They can be actual gadgets like gateways, switches, servers, routers, or programming parts like virtual machines and cloudlets associated with edge gadgets and access organizations to give them information stockpiling and registering assets. For instance, Cisco network gadgets like switches, switches, and unified computing system (UCS) servers could fill in as Fog hubs. These servers incorporate figuring equipment, virtualization support, switching fabric, and management software. Associations can create and improve their IoT applications in the cloud to at long last send them in Fog hubs or cloud workers [11].

The Fog registering layer lies between the edge layer, where the end gadgets dwell, and the cloud processing layer, where limitless computing power and storage are available. Fog hubs can work in an independent mode or can be designed to work in a bunch to offer the assistance to their clients [12].

Fog hub can be conveyed anywhere within a group of connections: on a manufacturing plant, close by a railway track line, in a means of transport, etc. as indicated by Cisco. Its execution is portrayed in [13] and its engineering plan and execution are examined in [14].

Eva Marín Tordera *et al.* [15] focused on recognizing the fundamental usefulness of a Fog hub and the related chances and difficulties. They summed up and thought about the ideas and the exercises gained from the execution of cutting edge fog processing advancements.

Also, they showed how a combined meaning of fog hubs could rise out of an applied structure. Moreover, they examined a portion of the open issues and difficulties that emerge when fog hubs uncover conceptual and virtualized perspectives on their actual assets to the upper layers in a fog cloud situation. There is nearly unanimity in the writing that Fog processing is not intended to supplant distributed computing, yet rather it is an expansion. Many distributed computing advancements, like virtualization, additionally apply to fog registering [16].

Streaming analytics for IoT applications [51] discusses about Analytical Tasks in Continuous Data Streams.

Besides, information processing should be possible on a solitary fog hub or co-operating numerous hubs. At the point when more processing power is required, extra fog hubs may be sent, improving the versatility and giving the flexibility needed by numerous undertaking applications.

5.3   Overview

5.3.1   Edge computing

We allude to Edge figuring when the information gathered or handled remains on the gadget that has made the sensor readings, or on the IoT Gateway. On the off chance that we add information handling facility now, it is with regard to Edge processing. It is helpful when the information should change practices identified with the real-time operation of the machines.

5.3.2   Fog computing

When computing is conveyed and we leave the information handling limit in the local network where the gadget associated with the sensor is found, it is the point at which we talk about fog processing. Regularly the utilization of this information centers on definition changes between orders relegated to production lines or other use cases that do not suggest a response as quick as the edge, yet that an extremely low idleness on a lot of data is as yet critical. Figure 5.2 shows an overview of edge-fog-cloud continuum.

5.3.3   Stream analytics

Streaming analytics is the processing and analyzing of records facts constantly instead of in batches. Generally, streaming analytics is beneficial for the kinds of data sources that ship records in small sizes (frequently in kilobytes), in a

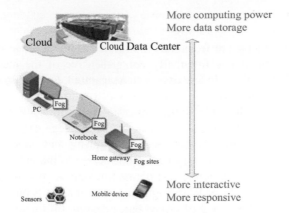

More computing power
More data storage

More interactive
More responsive

Figure 5.2   Overview of Edge-Fog-Cloud continuum

Incident —→ Incident Queuing —→ Stream Analytics —→ Storage, staging
Creation & Stream Ingestion   & Accomplishment

Figure 5.3   Stream analytics

continuous flow as the records is generated. Figure 5.3 indicates streaming analytics. Streaming analytics can also additionally encompass an extensive kind of data sources, which includes telemetry from related devices, log documents generated through clients the usage of Internet applications, ecommerce transactions, or data from social networks or geospatial services. It is frequently used for actual-time aggregation and correlation, filtering, or sampling.

Data historically is moved in batches. Batch processing technique processes big volumes of records on the equal time, with lengthy durations of latency. For example, a technique can be run each 24 h. While this may be an efficient way to deal with big volumes of records, it does not work with time-sensitive records that have intended to be streamed, due to the fact that records may be stale by the point it's processed.

5.3.4   Optimization of streaming analytics

When organizations are gathering records to the track of masses of heaps or may be hundreds of thousands of activities in step with second, truly big datasets are the result. Traditional structures can take days to supply insights from records at this scale. To generate actual-time actions, you want actual-time records processing and analysis. This may be finished with the proper records-streaming platform and infrastructure. Stream analytics constructed on Google Cloud merchandize and services, for example, allow organizations to ingest, process, and examine records streams in actual time.

5.4 Analogy

Edge and fog processing are frequently utilized conversely. Edge processing is a more pervasive term and is frequently comprehensive of the ideas driving fog figuring as one firm system. In any case, when separated, Fog registering was made to go with edge systems and fill in as an extra structural layer to give improved preparing abilities that the edge alone cannot generally do.

It cannot exist without edge registering, while the edge can exist without fog. There are numerous similitude between fog figuring and edge processing, for example, that the two of them carry processing nearer to the information source.

Notwithstanding, the principle distinction between the two is the place where the processing is taking place. With fog processing, insight is pushed down to the local area network (LAN) level of organization design. Information is prepared in an IoT passage or fog hub.

With edge figuring, insight is pushed straightforwardly into gadgets like programmable automation controllers (PACs). Therefore, further developed degrees of handling, investigation and AI are conceivable in fog versus the edge.

Figure 5.4 shows side by side perspective of edge and fog models. Edge runs explicit applications in a fixed rationale area and gives an immediate transmission administration without information examination. Fog works with edge to

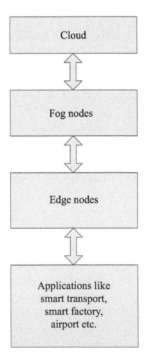

Figure 5.4   Edge vs. Fog computing

run applications in a multi-facet design that decouples and networks the equipment and programming capacities, considering arranging/reconfiguring for various applications while performing shrewd transmission administrations with processing/stockpiling/correspondence abilities along the cloud to things continuum.

5.5 Benefits

IoT sensors gather crude information as it were. This information should be crunched into something usable for the end client, regardless of whether that is a worker or a completely independent machine, and it should be crunched rapidly so organizations and associations can stay serious in the midst of the continuous fourth industrial revolution.

Cloud data centers can crunch this information, obviously, and they are a solid answer for organizations and associations with lower-volume organizations, however as we have recently talked about, the cloud alone has become an inefficient computing paradigm for some multiplex business and authoritative cycles with a flat out need for almost immediate reaction times.

Setting up an edge figuring design includes finding servers, normally alluded to as edge servers, nearer to the information producing IoT sensors. These local servers are running the applications that crunch this information and give client arranged bits of knowledge. Thus, less information goes to the cloud, and organizations get a good deal on information transfer and improve reaction times.

Furthermore, albeit a portion of this prepared information can be put away at the edge, a lot of it is being sent back to the cloud for perpetual capacity, however recall, this is being done after the crude information has been handled by edge servers.

Along these lines, you are successfully sending just significant information back to the cloud rather than a perpetual stream of crude information, which costs more to move and makes an ascent in latency.

The essential advantage of both edge figuring and fog registering ideal models is the capacity to store and deal with information quicker, making constant applications basic to business activities more productive. Prior to the approach of edge and fog processing, an application utilizing a surveillance camera needed to invoke a cloud-based support to perform facial detection, which brings about high idleness.

With an edge or fog processing-based arrangement, an edge server or gateway would run the assistance locally. Applications like self-driving vehicles, virtual and expanded reality, and shrewd transportation frameworks require quick handling and reaction.

The Benefits of Streaming Analytics are

- *Data representation*: Watching out for the main organization data can assist associations with dealing with their key exhibition markers consistently. Streaming information can be observed progressively permitting organizations to realize what is happening at each and every second.

- *Business bits of knowledge*: It very well may be utilized in network protection, to mechanize identification and reaction to the actual danger.
- *Increased seriousness*: Organizations hoping to acquire an upper hand can utilize streaming information to perceive patterns and set benchmarks quicker. This way they can dominate their rivals who are as yet utilizing the drowsy interaction of group examination.
- *Cutting preventable misfortunes*: With the assistance of streaming investigation, we can forestall or possibly diminish the harm of occurrences like security breaks, fabricating issues, client beat, stock trade emergencies, and web-based media emergency.
- *Analyzing routine business activities*: Streaming investigation offers associations a chance to ingest and acquire a moment understanding from the ongoing information that is pouring in.

5.6   Use cases

5.6.1   *Self-ruling automobiles*

All together for automobiles to work productively, they need a lot of machine intelligence working in the vicinity and constantly in real-time. Independent automobiles are among the most capricious edge devices as on today, persistently giving response to changing conditions and building an enormous number of estimations reliably.

Artificial intelligence (AI) philosophy is used to authentic circumstances that ought to react, without depending upon accessibility or the cloud for increasing computation capability. Edge computing supports self-administering vehicles to perform artificial intelligence at the edge, making sure that the most insignificant probable latency is reduced.

In autonomous vehicles, we think that, all computations are going on locally, inside the real vehicle and fog may not be useful to free vehicle applications. Regardless, as governments and advancement providers continue making clever traffic establishments, it will get useful for structure to interface directly with free vehicles. Local data centers can be sent nearby traffic establishment to assist manage these associations. Particular vehicles will continue performing operational estimations locally (i.e., at the Edge), at any rate-related system may make a cross section association, giving area organization to different vehicles and gathering information from them in the Fog, giving more unequivocal setting to the individual vehicles subject to the aggregate traffic data.

Self-administering platooning of truck convoy is as shown in Figure 5.5, will likely be one of the fundamental use cases for independent vehicles. Here, a social affair of truck travels not a long way behind one another in a band, saving fuel costs and lessening stop up. With edge figuring, it will be doable to take out the necessity for drivers in regardless of trucks from the front one, considering the way that the trucks will really need to talk with each other with very low inaction.

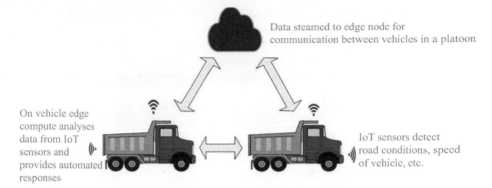

Figure 5.5 Autonomous platooning of truck convoys

5.6.2 Distant monitoring of resources in the oil and gas manufacturing

Oil and gas resources ought to be carefully checked. In any case, oil and gas plants are routinely in far off territories. Edge figuring engages real-time analytics with processing much closer to the asset, meaning there is less reliance on good quality connectivity to a centralised cloud.

5.6.3 Intelligent grid

Edge enlisting will be a middle development in more wide determination of keen cross sections and can help grant endeavors to improved level which promptly manage their energy consumption. Sensors and IoT contraptions related to edge phase underway lines, firms, and work environments are used to screen power use and separate their usage constantly.

5.6.4 Prognostic upkeep

Manufacturers require having the alternative way to explore and recognize a change in their design lines before a mistake occurs. Edge enrolling will assure this by taking care of information close to the device, which helps IoT sensors to screen device affluence with low delays and carry out assessment consistently.

5.6.5 In-centre patient noticing

Clinical consideration has a couple of edge openings. Examination devices with its characteristic data from devices ought to be taken care by an invulnerable cloud. This poses safety threat for clinical consideration providers. An edge can manage infor-mation locally to keep up the information security. Edge moreover enable correct time admonitions to doctors of abnormal patient trends or behaviors (in the course of examination/AI), and arrangement of 360-degree see patient records for diagnosis.

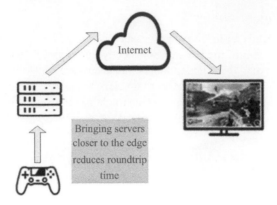

Figure 5.6   Cloud gaming

5.6.6   *Virtualized radio networks and 5G (vRAN)*

Managers look for virtualize segments of their flexible associations (vRAN), so that cost and versatility benefits is fetched. This hardware has to do intricate processing with a less latency. Directors require edge servers to facilitate virtualizing their RAN near to the cell tower.

5.6.7   *Cloud gaming*

Figure 5.6 depicts the process involved in cloud gaming. It streams a live feed of the game clearly to devices that are extremely reliant on delay. These associations are expecting to manufacture edge servers near to players to diminish inactivity, providing a totally receptive with striking playing practice.

5.6.8   *Content conveyance*

By caching content – for instance music, video, website – at the edge, improvement to content deliverance with improvisation to great extent. Delay can be lessened drastically. The companies that provide the content want to fit content delivery networks considerably to the edge, so as to guarantee versatility and design according to requirement on the set of connections depending upon customer travel claims.

5.6.9   *Traffic supervision*

Edge preparing can allow town traffic control. Examples of this comprise upgrading transport rate of recurrence given variations in requirements, control the opening and shutting of additional ways, and, in future, regulating self-administering vehicle streams. With edge enlisting, there is no convincing motivation to move gigantic volumes of traffic data to the fused cloud, there by lessening the charge of bandwidth and latency.

5.6.10   Intelligent homes

Shrewd home depends on IoT contraptions assembling and getting ready information from within the region of the house. Consistently this record is dispatched off a centralized remote server, where it is arranged and taken care of. Utilizing edge figuring, passing on the administration and extra room close to the shrewd home, backhaul and roundtrip time is lessened, and receptive data might be set up at the edge. For instance, the period taken for voice-based associate gadgets may be a lot speedier.

5.6.11   Intelligent transportation management

Intelligent transportation, especially management of traffic, is a perfect claim for Edge compute technology. By applying calculated wisdom locally, on the real traffic hardware, disused or "noisy" information can be lessened at the edge. This basically diminishes the proportion of information that ought to be sent over the network, decreasing operating and storage costs. In addition, considering the way that sensor data is dealt with at the edge, pieces of information are able to be settled without achieving net torpidity, by being sure that traffic structure can act in response to changes in busy time gridlock circumstances with the most diminished likely delay.

So where does the fog come in? For some smart cities, traffic system may be related with cell associations or through a Wi-Fi organization. In these cases, micro-data centers can be used locally, nearby cell zeniths or Wi-Fi switches, to perform assessment on the absolute traffic data from various edge center points (controllers, signs, and common sensors). Implementation as a "local cloud," these data centers are deployed within the LAN, and so they are well thought-out to be a component of "the Fog."

5.6.12   Trade and commercial networking

In the present, hardware organizations possess the edge. Before data reaches the cloud, it passes on network hardware contacts data first. Business network operators can misuse their immediacy to the data source and impact the fog, passing on local data centers uses nearby switches and other association equipment to separate solitary switch and overall association execution. This engages network managers to force downwards the quantity of data on the path to the cloud, decreasing the load on the association and cloud applications. Besides, both plan to apply machine learning to improve channel assurance and conform to variations in the association scene.

Improvements in edge figuring developments have given a choice rather than discovering a data center with each switch or association nexus. For gear makers, the real switches are edge contraptions. Edge subject matter experts (programming models) can be passed on changes to research switch execution locally. This wipes out the need to co-discover laborer models with switches, as the genuine switches are powered enough to do multifaceted assessment. This is ultimate for far off or various zones where co-discovering a data center might not be likely. Edge experts can be passed on and controlled indirectly, and need not bother with extra hardware to help them.

5.6.13   *Elegant metering for utilities*

Shrewd meters are among the most inevitable edge gadgets sent on the planet today. Astonishing meters produce goliath volumes of information, which makes a test for application structures performing appraisal in the cloud. To diminish a touch of the strain accomplished by high information rates, a fog game-plan could be to send local data centers along with other devices managing multiple smart meters and channel information from them in a focal region, inside the LAN.

A more fruitful method for managing this surge of sensor information, regardless, is measure information at the Edge, filtering information on the confirmed smart meter. This is more helpful several reasons. From the outset, by arranging information at the edge, excess or immaterial, "noisy" information can be disengaged at the source. This recommends essentially relevant information is passed on over the local network, completely decreasing required data transmission and reducing (or taking out) the need for extra storage at the transformer level. Moreover, there are cash saving advantages, as there is no persuading inspiration to introduce and administer extra IT infrastructure in the field, the compute and memory existing on the smart meter, itself, is adequate. Considering everything, smart meters utilizing edge computing can be fortified and controlled distantly, anyway fog blueprints may require hardware updates by field administrators.

5.6.14   *Fleet management*

Logistics service providers impact IoT telematics data to recognize amazing fleet management operations. Drivers rely upon vehicle-to-vehicle correspondence similarly as information from backend control apexes to make better decisions. Spaces of low accessibility and sign strength are confined similarly as the speed and volume of data that can be imparted among vehicles and backend cloud associations.

With the presence of self-overseeing vehicle developments that rely upon continuous estimation and data assessment limits, fleet traders will search for compelling strategies for network transmission to intensify the value capacity of naval force telematics data for vehicles going to far away regions.

By drawing in estimation capacities proximity of naval force vehicles, shippers can decrease the impact of communication dead zones as the data will not be expected to send directly back to united cloud data centers. Suitable vehicle-to-vehicle correspondence will enable worked with traffic streams between naval forces organizations, as AI-engaged sensor structures passed on at the association edges will confer astute examination information instead of unrefined data relying upon the circumstance.

5.6.15   *Predictive upkeep*

The manufacturing industry enthusiastically relies upon the show and uptime of modernized machines. In 2006, the cost of amassing individual time in the vehicle business was evaluated at $1.3 million consistently. Following 10 years, the rising financial endeavor toward vehicle technologies and the creating usefulness in the market make abrupt assistance impedances all the more exorbitant in various huge degrees.

5.7 Issues

With edge figuring, IoT sensors can screen machine prosperity and perceive signs of time-sensitive help issues persistently. The data is analyzed on the manufacturing premises and examination results are moved to united cloud data centers for uncovering or further assessment.

Researching anomalies can allow the workforce to perform therapeutic measures or perceptive help earlier, before the issue uplifts and affects the creation line. Analyzing the main machine prosperity estimations can allow relationship to draw out the significant presence of collecting machines. As a result, creating affiliations can cut down the cost of upkeep, improve operational ampleness of the machines, and recognize better yield on assets.

Voice assistance technologies like Amazon Echo, Google Home, and Apple Siri, among others, are stretching the boundaries of AI. The rapidly creating client development parcel requires advanced AI getting ready and low-dormancy response time to pass on fruitful correspondences with end-customers.

Particularly for use cases that incorporate AI voice assistant capabilities, the advancement needs go past computational power and data transmission speed. The drawn out achievement of voice help depends upon consumer privacy and data security limits of the advancement. Tricky individual information is a jackpot for underground cybercrime rings and potential association shortcomings in voice assist structures with introducing amazing security and assurance threats to end-customers. To address this test, venders, for instance, Amazon are updating their AI limits and passing on the development closer to the edge, so that voice data does not need to get across the association. Amazon is obviously endeavoring to cultivate its own AI chip for the Amazon Echo contraptions.

Inescapability of edge figuring in the voice help section will hold identical importance for large business customers as agents working in the field or on the collecting line will really need to get to and examine significant information without interrupting manual work exercises.

The accompanying difficulties are to be tended to:

- The IoT/edge and fog arrangements are still new and right now going through revolutionary turn of events.
- It is consistently important to characterize which information is given in the cloud and which information stays in the edge and fog.
- Storage, CPU, and cost limits in the Edge/Fog.
- Modeling in one spot – execution and circulation in a few areas.
- Standards for distributed arrangements are not yet adequately accessible

5.8   Future

According to the Gartner Hype Cycle 2017, edge handling is drawing closer to the tip of inflate prospect and will most likely show up at the Plateau of Productivity in 2–5 years. Thinking about the advancing assessment and enhancements in AI and 5G organization progressions, and the rising solicitations of splendid present day IoT applications, Edge Computing may show up at advancement faster than expected.

Despite the data improvement and existing association limitations, propels like 5G accessibility and Artificial Intelligence are getting ready for edge handling. 5G will help send figuring capacities closer to the insightful edge of the association as passed on cell towers. The development will be prepared for more noticeable data amassing and dealing with while simultaneously keeping up fast data transmission among vehicles and correspondence towers.

Man-made consciousness will also work with wise unique capacities logically, allowing vehicles to react faster than individuals in light of abrupt changes in busy time gridlock streams. Fog figuring can really be considered as a strategy for offering sorts of help even more rapidly, yet likewise as a technique for bypassing the more broad web, whose rates are by and large subject to carriers.

Google and Facebook are among a couple of associations exploring setting up substitute strategies for web access, for instance, inflatable and robots to avoid network bottlenecks. Nonetheless, more humble affiliations may make a Fog out of whatever contraptions are as of now around to develop ever closer relationship with measure resources.

There will doubtlessly still be a spot for more consolidated and amassed disseminated figuring, anyway it seems, by all accounts, to be that as sensors move into more things and data creates at a goliath rate, another approach to manage working with the applications will be required. Fog enlisting, which could imaginatively utilize existing devices, could be the right method to manage working with a huge new plan of uses.

In any case, the advancement to the edge does not decrease the meaning of the center. Out of the blue, it suggests that the data center ought to be a more grounded center for developing figuring designing. Information Week benefactor Kevin Casey actually made that the cloud has not actually diminished laborer bargains, as one may some way or another expect. Cross variety preparing models, gigantic data and IoT have added to laborer requirements that may be moving, yet are not really dying down as specific experts had expected.

The IoT is a material platform to presumably the best issues isolating the cloud and the Fog (like bandwidth, which could provoke a crossbreed cloudiness cloud model) as affiliations attempt to change their undertaking grade worker ranch needs with assistance for extending edge network advancement. Fog preparing handles a huge issue in circulated processing, specifically, decreasing the prerequisite for bandwidth by not sending all of information over cloud channels, and rather amassing it at specific ways. This sort of flowed method cuts down costs and improves efficiencies. Even more oddly, it is single direction to manage dealing with the emerging thought of IoT.

Fog enrolling loosens up the conveyed figuring perspective to the edge of the association to address applications and organizations that do not fit the perspective of the cloud due to particular and system limitation including:

- Applications that require low and unsurprising idleness
- Geographically dispersed applications
- Fast versatile applications
- Large-scale circulated control frameworks

Tech beasts like IBM are the central purpose behind Fog enlisting, and interface their plan to IoT. Today, there might be many related contraptions in an office or worker ranch, anyway a few years that number could explode to thousands or a few thousands, all related and granting. By far most of the buzz around Fog has a close relationship with IoT.

The way that everything from vehicles to indoor controllers is gaining web information suggests that quick customer end enrolling and correspondence may after a short time be a higher need than ever. A more basic gander at Fog handling shows that it is connected to tolerating decisions as close to the data as could truly be anticipated. Hadoop and other enormous data game plans have started the example to convey getting ready close to the data's region. Fog preparing is connected to doing similarly for a greater degree. You need decisions to be taken as close to where the data is created and keep it from showing up at the cloud. Simply significant data should travel appropriated processing associations.

There are reasonable advantages to using fog handling. All things needed is an essential plan (or various responses for) to train models and send them to particularly smoothed out and low resource concentrated execution engines that can be helpfully embedded in devices, mobile phones and smart hubs/gateways.

To achieve this even handed, cloudiness enlisting is best done through AI models that get arranged on a little piece of the data on the cloud. After a model is seen as good, by then it is pushed to the devices. Estimations like decision trees or some cushy reasoning or even a significant conviction association can be used locally on a contraption to make a decision that is more affordable than setting up a system in the cloud that prerequisite to oversee unrefined data from a large number of devices.

5.9 A case study of streaming analytics in big data for emergency vehicles movement in smart city traffic management

5.9.1 Introduction

Web of Things (IoT) contraptions are commonly furnished with various sensors, going from accelerometers and spinners to closeness, light, and encompassing sensors, similarly as mouthpieces and cameras. For splendid metropolitan territories, these contraptions are geographically passed on and can convey an amazing proportion of data that addresses a test for getting, regulating, taking care of and looking at these data inside a responsive satisfactory time.

In particular, separating IoT data streams makes region information for some IoT applications in keen metropolitan networks to interface successfully with their occupants and improve the city execution and lessen operational costs. Regardless, this is a non-insignificant cooperation since we need an absolutely new IoT designing that is prepared for performing streaming sensible tasks running in relating to give ideal assessed and accurate results.

5.9.2 Proposed work

This context-oriented investigation proposes a design that joins the edge-Fog cloud continuum to help streaming assessment for boosting the potential pieces of information from IoT data streams with respect to Emergency vehicles advancement in Smart City Traffic Management as per the proposed model of Figure 5.7. An IoT designing is proposed reliant upon a streaming examination determined construction that is particularly significant for joining IoT contraptions using the edge-Fog cloud continuum.

Streaming examination is used to give more huge level information about IoT data streams at the edge, the cloudiness or the cloud. The fact of the matter is to create new pieces of information as mentioned by an IoT application to address the requests: "What's happening in actuality?" (streaming descriptive analytics); "why is it happening?" (streaming diagnostic analytics); and "what will happen?" (streaming predictive analytics).

5.9.3 Methodology

An IoT planning is proposed dependent on a streaming assessment reasonable development that is especially valuable for combining IoT contraptions utilizing the edge-Fog cloud continuum. Figure 5.7 shows some keen assignments that might be needed for supporting an IoT application. Attracting reasonable undertakings are

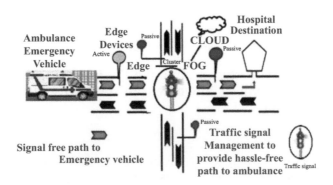

Figure 5.7   Proposed model for the emergency vehicles movement in smart city traffic management

performed at the edge; diagnostic legitimate assignments performed at the shadiness; predictive wise errands performed at the cloud. The coherent undertakings have various degrees of intricacy and require a reasonable information life-cycle to help different techniques for calculation going from information cleaning and information mix errands that require an energetic stream of information, to additional stunning assignments like information contextualization and information diagram assignments that require assembled information streams for time-fragile outcomes.

Streaming practical assessment might be performed at the edge, the fog and the cloud; notwithstanding, we expect that they will much more reliably be executed at the edge since (i) IoT information streams have small volume at the edge and (ii) different IoT applications will keep information away from being moved to a cloud considering wellbeing and costs concerns.

Streaming decisive assessment can be executed close or a long way from an IoT gadget, reliant upon where it is more possible to introduce normally surprising computational assets. Streaming unequivocal consistent undertakings are normally kept up by a couple on-line assessments, stream gathering calculations, unrehearsed solicitations, and unlimited requests.

Fog and cloud assets are should have been utilized to perform streaming definite appraisal since they give assessment, gathering and gas pedal assets that are more fitting than edge focus focuses to play out the streaming undertakings. Fog and scattered figuring can improve the exactness and lessen the computational multi-layered plan of the mechanized undertakings in close consistent.

The following tools and platforms were used for software Stream Processing & Analytics.

5.9.3.1 Data Flow Editor

Cisco Kinetic Dataflow Editor: This is a feature in EFM that can be used to customize, modify, and manage data flows with a graphical layout. It also offers a convenient interface to create and debug data flows.

5.9.3.2 Parser

JSON parser: JSON objects are mainly exchanged between the computational nodes in our system. Therefore, the parser is used to encode the data structures to JSON strings and decode them back to dictionary, list, tuple, Boolean, or other numerical data types.

5.9.3.3 Stream ML library

Scikit-Multiflow: It offers main packages to assist the users with handling and learning from their data streams such as stream generators, learning methods, change detectors, and evaluation methods.

5.9.3.4 Processing library

Python: For dealing with structured incoming data streams and detecting different data patterns, we have developed the algorithms to take action when the events happen. A variety of built-in Python libraries, such as numpy and scipy, were used to develop our algorithms.

Figure 5.8 shows the implementation philosophy of the Edge-Fog-Cloud engineering as per the proposed model of Figure 5.7 comparing to the emergency vehicles development in Smart City Traffic Management and streaming investigation assignments of Figure 5.9. The streaming information is created at the edge gadgets like sensors to detect and refresh the edge hubs when the vehicle shows up. It is then shipped off the edge hub where the Raspberry pi is utilized for processing, to do expressive examination of streaming information. Indicative investigation is performed at the Fog hub with workers for traffic light

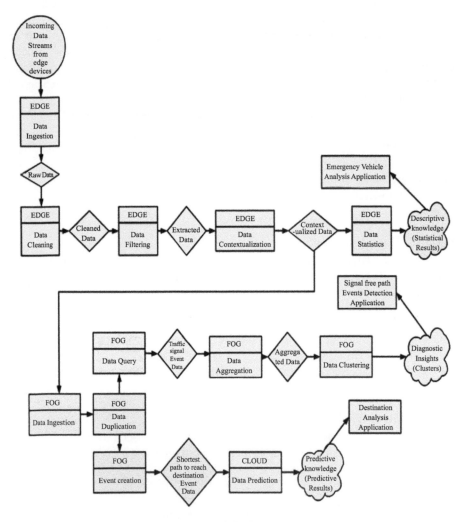

Figure 5.8   Implementation of the Edge-Fog-Cloud architecture

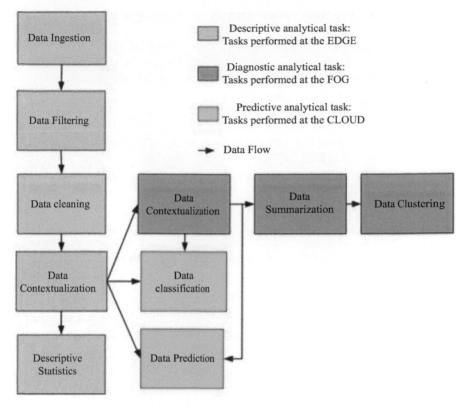

Figure 5.9   Overview of streaming analytics

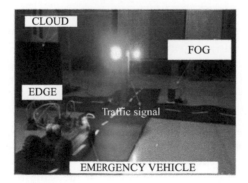

Figure 5.10   Green signal for emergency vehicle signal-free movement

Figure 5.11   Emergency vehicle circuitry

calculations at the junctions or circles by utilizing the idea of bunching which together would permit the crisis vehicle to move openly at signals. Further prescient investigation can likewise be brought out by associating Fog hubs through a door to the cloud.

5.9.4   Results

Figure 5.10 shows the output obtained for signal free movement of the emergency vehicle. Figure 5.11 shows the circuitry used in the emergency vehicle.

5.10   Conclusions

Future sensible courses of action will not simply be operated on the machine or in the Cloud. Taking everything into account, Edge and Fog architectures will dynamically transform into the proper answer.

Mix courses of action of genuine entryways Edge, Fog and cloud stages are used which is a functional sort of executing keen game plans close to the machine or structure while simultaneously using figuring resources in the cloud.

Future reasonable blueprints would not just be worked on the machine or in the Cloud. Considering everything, Edge and Fog developments will progressively change into the fitting arrangement. Blend strategies of real doorways Edge, Fog and cloud stages are utilized which is a practical kind of executing sharp approaches near the machine or construction while at the same time utilizing figuring assets in the cloud.

The case study considered in this book chapter on streaming analytics in big data for emergency vehicles movement in smart city traffic management would have been different if the traditional data processing is used instead of streaming data analytics using fog and edge computing, as streaming analytics framework plays an important role in generating better results with respect to increased speed of computation. It results in improved performance for other real-time applications along with reducing the operational cost.

References

[1] N. Hassan, S. Gillani, E. Ahmed, I. Yaqoob and M. Imran, The role of edge computing in the Internet of Things, *IEEE Communications Magazine*, 99, 2018, 1–6.

[2] M. Liu, F.R. Yu, Y. Teng, V.C. Leung and M. Song, Distributed resource allocation in blockchain-based video streaming systems with mobile edge computing, *IEEE Transactions on Wireless Communications*, 18(1), 2019, 695–708.

[3] E. Ahmed, A. Akhunzada, M. Whaiduzzaman, A. Gani, S.H. Ab Hamid and R. Buyya, Network-centric performance analysis of runtime application migration in mobile cloud computing, *Simulation Modelling Practice and Theory*, 50, 2015, 42–56.

[4] P. Pace, G. Aloi, R. Gravina, G. Caliciuri, G. Fortino and A. Liotta, An edge-based architecture to support efficient applications for healthcare industry 4.0, *IEEE Transactions on Industrial Informatics*, 15(1), 2019, 481–489.

[5] Gartner Glossary. Available online: https://www.gartner.com/en/information-technology/glossary/edge-computing.

[6] M. Satyanarayanan, P. Simoens, Y. Xiao, *et al.*, Edge analytics in the Internet of Things, *IEEE Pervasive Computing*, 14, 2015, 24–31.

[7] IDC.com, IDC FutureScape: Worldwide Internet of Things 2017 Predictions, 2016. Available online: https://www.idc.com/research/viewtoc.jsp?containerId=US40755816

[8] M. Satyanarayanan, P. Bahl, R. Cáceres and N. Davies, The case for vm-based cloudlets in mobile computing, *IEEE Pervasive Computing*, 8, 2009, 14–23.

[9] F. Bonomi, R. Milito, J. Zhu and S. Addepalli, Fog computing and its role in the Internet of Things, in: *Proceedings of the First Edition of the MCC Workshop on Mobile Cloud Computing, MCC '12*, Helsinki, Finland, 13–17 August 2012, New York, NY: ACM, 2012, pp. 13–16.

[10] OpenFog Consortium Architecture Working Group, OpenFog Reference Architecture for Fog Computing. Available online https://www.iiconsortium.org/pdf/OpenFog_Reference_Architecture_2_09_17.pdf.

[11] Cisco.com. Cisco Fog Computing Solutions: Unleash the Power of the Internet of Things. 2015. Available online: https://www.cisco.com/c/dam/en_us/solutions/trends/iot/docs/computing-solutions.pdf

[12] M. Iorga, L. Feldman, R. Barton, M.J. Martin, N.S. Goren and C. Mahmoudi, Fog Computing Conceptual Model. Available online: https://www.nist.gov/publications/fog-computing-conceptual-model.

[13]   M. Yannuzzi, F. van Lingen, A. Jain, et al, A new era for cities with fog computing, *IEEE Internet Computing*, 21, 2017, 54–67.

[14]   M.R. Anawar, S. Wang, M.A. Zia, A.K. Jadoon, U. Akram and S. Raza, Fog computing—an overview of big IoT data analytics, *Wireless Communications and Mobile Computing*, 2018, 2018, 1–22. [CrossRef]

[15]   E.M. Tordera, X. Masip-Bruin, J. Garcia-Alminana, *et al.*, What Is a Fog Node A Tutorial on Current Concepts towards a Common Definition. arXiv 2016, arXiv:1611.09193.

[16]   D. Roca, J.V. Quiroga, M. Valero and M. Nemirovsky, Fog function virtualization—a flexible solution for IoT applications, in: *Proceedings of the 2017 Second International Conference on Fog and Mobile Edge Computing (FMEC)*, Valencia, Spain, 8–11 May 2017, pp. 74–80.

[17]   F. Bonomi, R. Milito, J. Zhu and S. Addepalli, Fog computing and its role in the internet of things, in: *Proceedings of the first Edition of the MCC Workshop on Mobile Cloud Computing*, New York, NY: ACM, 2012, pp. 13–16.

[18]   T.H. Luan, L. Gao, Z. Li, Y. Xiang, G. Wei and L. Sun, Fog Computing: Focusing on Mobile Users at the edge. arXiv:1502.01815v3.

[19]   E. Ahmed, A. Ahmed, I. Yaqoob, *et al*, Bringing computation closer toward the user network: is edge computing the solution? *IEEE Communications Magazine*, 55(11), 2017, 138–144.

[20]   P. Mell and T. Grance, The Nist Definition of Cloud Computing, 2011. Available online: http://csrc.nist.gov/publications/nistpubs/800-145/SP800-145.pdf (Accessed on 23 July 2018).

[21]   A.P. Jyothi and S. Usha, MSoC: multi-scale optimized clustering for energy preservation in wireless sensor network, *Wireless Personal Communication*, 105, 2019, 1309–1328. https://doi.org/10.1007/s11277-019-06146-y

[22]   I. Yaqoob, E. Ahmed, A. Gani, S. Mokhtar and M. Imran, Heterogeneity-aware task allocation in mobile ad hoc cloud, *IEEE Access,* 5, 2017, 1779–1795.

[23]   P. Wang, C. Yao, Z. Zheng, G. Sun and L. Song, Joint task assignment, transmission and computing resource allocation in multi-layer mobile edge computing systems, *IEEE Internet of Things Journal*, 6, 2019, 2872–2884.

[24]   Y. Sahni, J. Cao and L. Yang, Data-aware task allocation for achieving low latency in collaborative edge computing, *IEEE Internet of Things Journal*, 6(2), 2019, 3512–3524.

[25]   J. Ren, Y. He, G. Huang, G. Yu, Y. Cai and Z. Zhang, An edge-computing based architecture for mobile augmented reality, *IEEE Network*, 33(4), 2019, 162–169.

[26]   Z. Ning, X. Kong, F. Xia, W. Hou and X. Wang, Green and sustainable cloud of things: enabling collaborative edge computing, *IEEE Communications Magazine*, 57(1), 2019, 72–78.

[27]   W. Li, Z. Chen, X. Gao, W. Liu and J. Wang, Multi-model framework for indoor localization under mobile edge computing environment, *IEEE Internet of Things Journal*, 6, 2019, 4844–4853.

[28] A.P Jyothi and S. Usha, Interstellar-based topology control scheme for optimal clustering performance in wireless sensor network, *International Journal of Communication Systems*, 33(8), 2020, pp. 1–16, doi: 10.1002/dac.4350

[29] M. Satyanarayanan, How we created edge computing, *Nature Electronics*, 2(1), 2019, 42.

[30] E. Ahmed, I. Yaqoob, I.A.T. Hashem, *et al.*, The role of big data analytics in the internet of things, *Computer Networks,* 129, 2017, 459–471.

[31] H. Khelifi, S. Luo, B. Nour, *et al.*, Bringing deep learning at the edge of information-centric internet of things, *IEEE Communications Letters*, 23(1), 2019, 52–55.

[32] A.P. Jyothi and S. Usha, CFCLP – a novel clustering framework based on combinatorial approach and linear programming in WSN, in: *2nd International Conference on Computing and Communications Technologies (ICCCT)*, Chennai, 2017, pp. 49–54, doi:10.1109/ICCT2.2017.7972237

[33] A. Ferdowsi, U. Challita and W. Saad, Deep learning for reliable mobile edge analytics in intelligent transportation systems: an overview, *IEEE Vehicular Technology Magazine*, 14(1), 2019, 62–70.

[34] B. Han, S. Wong, C. Mannweiler, M.R. Crippa and H.D. Schotten, Context-awareness enhances 5G multi-access edge computing reliability, *IEEE Access*, 7, 2019, 21290–21299.

[35] H. Cao and M. Wachowicz, An edge-fog-cloud architecture of streaming analytics for Internet of Things applications, *Sensors*, 19(16), 2019, 3594, doi:10.3390/s19163594

[36] M. Aazam and E.-N. Huh, E-hamc: leveraging fog computing for emergency alert service, in: *2015 IEEE International Conference on Pervasive Computing and Communication Workshops (PerCom Workshops)*, IEEE, New York, NY, 2015, pp. 518–523.

[37] M.A. Al Faruque and K. Vatanparvar, Energy management-as-a-service over fog computing platform, *IEEE Internet of Things Journal*, 3(2), 2016, 161–169.

[38] C. Lin and J. Yang, Cost-efficient deployment of fog computing systems at logistics centers in industry 4.0, *IEEE Transactions on Industrial Informatics*, 14(10), 2018, 4603–4611.

[39] R. Iqbal, T.A. Butt, M.O. Shafique, M.W.A. Talib and T. Umer, Context-aware data-driven intelligent framework for fog infrastructures in internet of vehicles, *IEEE Access*, 6, 2018, 58182–58194.

[40] J. He, J. Wei, K. Chen, Z. Tang, Y. Zhou and Y. Zhang, Multitier fog computing with large-scale iot data analytics for smart cities, *IEEE Internet of Things Journal,* 5(2), 2018, 677–686.

[41] S.K. Datta, C. Bonnet and J. Haerri, Fog computing architecture to enable consumer centric internet of things services, in: *International Symposium on Consumer Electronics (ISCE)*, IEEE, New York, NY, 2015, pp. 1–2.

[42] M. Aazam and E.-N. Huh, Fog computing and smart gateway based communication for cloud of things, in: *International Conference on Future Internet of Things and Cloud*, IEEE, New York, NY, 2014, pp. 464–470.

[43]   J. Preden, J. Kaugerand, E. Suurjaak, S. Astapov, L. Motus and R. Pahtma, Data to decision: pushing situational information needs to the edge of the network, in: *Cognitive Methods in Situation Awareness and Decision Support* (*CogSIMA*), 2015, pp. 158–164.

[44]   L. Yin, J. Luo and H. Luo, Tasks scheduling and resource allocation in fog computing based on containers for smart manufacturing, *IEEE Transactions on Industrial Informatics*, 14(10), 2018, 4712–4721.

[45]   B. Jia, H. Hu, Y. Zeng, T. Xu and Y. Yang, Double-matching resource allocation strategy in fog computing networks based on cost efficiency, *Journal of Communications and Networks*, 20(3), 2018, 237–246.

[46]   L. Gu, D. Zeng, S. Guo, A. Barnawi and Y. Xiang, Cost efficient resource management in fog computing supported medical cyber-physical system, *IEEE Transactions on Emerging Topics in Computing*, 5(1), 2017, 108–119.

[47]   M. A. Hassan, M. Xiao, Q. Wei and S. Chen, Help your mobile applications with fog computing, in: *12th Annual International Conference on Sensing, Communication, and Networking Workshops* (*SECON Workshops*), IEEE, New York, NY, 2015, pp. 1–6.

[48]   K. Hong, D. Lillethun, U. Ramachandran, B. Ottenwalder and B. Koldehofe, Mobile fog: a programming model for large-scale applications on the Internet of Things, in: *Proceedings of the Second ACM SIGCOMM Workshop on Mobile Cloud Computing – MCC 13*, ACM, 2013, pp. 15–20.

[49]   F. Bonomi, R. Milito, P. Natarajan and J. Zhu, Fog computing: a platform for internet of things and analytics, in: *Big Data and Internet of Things: A Roadmap for Smart Environments*, Springer, New York, NY, 2014, pp. 169–186.

[50]   M. Aazam and E.-N. Huh, Fog computing micro datacenter based dynamic resource estimation and pricing model for IoT, in: *2015 IEEE 29th International Conference on Advanced Information Networking and Applications*, IEEE, New York, NY, 2015, pp. 687–694. doi:10.1109/aina.2015.254.

[51]   H. Cao, and M. Wachowicz, An edge-fog-cloud architecture of streaming analytics for Internet of Things applications, *Sensors (Basel, Switzerland)*, 19(16), 2019, 3594, doi:10.3390/s19163594

Chapter 6

Real-time stream processing on IoT data for real-world use cases

Pethuru Raj[1], J. Akilandeswari[2] and M. Marimuthu[3]

Abstract

It is indisputably clear that real-time stream processing of IoT data can result in a series of personal, professional, and social use cases. In this chapter, we have explained how real-time processing of IoT data may lead to a series of real-world premium services and applications across industry verticals including manufacturing.

Databases have been an extremely important part of application development, irrespective of how they store data. They follow a paradigm where data is passively stored, waiting for commands from an external part to read or modify the data. Basically, these applications are CRUD based with business logic added on top of a process run by humans through a user interface (UI). A problem with these CRUD style applications is that they commonly lead to an infrastructure with lots of ad hoc solutions using messaging systems, ETL products and other techniques for integrating applications in order to pass data between them. Often code is written for specific integrations, and all this causes a mess of interconnections between applications in an organization.

It is better to move away from relying on humans working through a UI to a platform that is able to trigger actions and react on things happening in software. The solution leverages events and event streams. They represent a new paradigm where a system is built to support a flow of data through the business and reacting in real-time to the events occurring. The core idea is that an event stream is a true record of what has happened. Any system or application can read the stream in real time and react on each event. This compares with a central nervous system but for a software defined company, a digital organization needs the software equivalent to a nervous system for connecting all its systems, applications, and processes.

For this to work, we have to treat the streams of everything that is happening within an organization as data and enable continuous queries that process this data.

[1]Edge AI Division, Reliance Jio Platforms Ltd., Bangalore, India
[2]Department of Information Technology, Sona College of Technology, India
[3]Department of CSE, Sona College of Technology, India

In a traditional database, the data sits passively and an application or a user issues queries to retrieve data. In stream processing, this is inverted. Data is an active and continuous stream of events and queries are passive, reacting to and processing the events in the stream as they arrive. Basically, this is a combination of data storage and processing in real time. This is a fundamental change in how applications are built.

Other experts however believe that there are benefits to using more types of messages besides events. With only events available, they are also used to indirectly request something to happen in another service. This often increases the coupling between services and can create a very entangled choreography. Therefore, besides events, there is a need for two other types of messages: Commands, which represent an intent to change something, and Queries to fulfill a need for information.

6.1   About stream processing

Stream processing is a big data technology. It is used to query continuous data stream and detect conditions, quickly, within a small time period from the time of receiving the data. The detection time period varies from few milliseconds to minutes. For example, with stream processing, you can receive an alert when the temperature has reached the freezing point, querying data streams coming from a temperature sensor.

Why is stream processing needed?: Big data established the value of insights derived from processing data. Such insights are not all created equal. Some insights are more valuable shortly after it has happened with the value diminishes very fast with time. Stream processing enables such scenarios, providing insights faster, often within milliseconds to seconds from the trigger. Following are some of the secondary reasons for using stream processing.

Reasons 1: Some data naturally comes as a never-ending stream of events. To do batch processing, you need to store it, stop data collection at some time and processes the data. Then you have to do the next batch and then worry about aggregating across multiple batches. In contrast, streaming handles never-ending data streams gracefully and naturally. You can detect patterns, inspect results, look at multiple levels of focus, and also easily look at data from multiple streams simultaneously.

Stream processing naturally fit with time series data and detecting patterns over time. For example, if you are trying to detect the length of a web session in a never-ending stream (this is an example of trying to detect a sequence). It is very hard to do it with batches as some session will fall into two batches. Stream processing can handle this easily. If you take a step back and consider, the most continuous data series are time series data: traffic sensors, health sensors, transaction logs, activity logs, etc. Almost all IoT data are time series data. Hence, it makes sense to use a programming model that fits naturally.

Reason 2: Batch processing lets the data build up and try to process them at once while stream processing process data as they come in hence spread the processing over time. Hence, stream processing can work with a lot less hardware than batch processing. Furthermore, stream processing also enables approximate query processing via systematic load shedding. Hence, stream processing fits naturally into use cases where approximate answers are sufficient.

Reason 3: Sometimes data is huge and it is not even possible to store it. Stream processing let you handle large fire horse style data and retain only useful bits.

Reason 4: Finally, there are a lot of streaming data available (e.g., customer transactions, activities, website visits) and they will grow faster with IoT use cases (all kind of sensors). Streaming is a much more natural model to think about and program those use cases.

However, stream processing is also not a tool for all use cases. One good rule of thumb is that if processing needs multiple passes through full data or have random access (think a graph data set) then it is tricky with streaming. One big missing use case in streaming is machine learning algorithms to train models. On the other hand, if processing can be done with a single pass over the data or has temporal locality (processing tend to access recent data), then it is a good fit for streaming.

How to do stream processing?: If you want to build an App that handles streaming data and takes real-time decisions, you can either use a tool or build it yourself. The answer depends on how much complexity you plan to handle, how much you want to scale, how much reliability and fault tolerance you need, etc. If you want to build the App yourself, place events in a message broker topic (e.g., ActiveMQ, RabbitMQ, or Kafka), write code to receive events from topics in the broker (they become your stream) and then publish results back to the broker. Such a code is called an actor. However, instead of coding the above scenario from scratch, you can use a stream processing framework to save time. An event stream processor lets you write logic for each actor, wire the actors up, and hook up the edges to the data source(s). You can either send events directly to the stream processor or send them via a broker.

An event stream processor will do the hard work by collecting data, delivering it to each actor, making sure they run in the right order, collecting results, scaling if the load is high, and handling failures. Among examples are Storm, Flink, and Samza. Since 2016, a new idea called Streaming SQL has emerged. We call a language that enables users to write SQL like queries to query streaming data as a "Streaming SQL" language. There are many streaming SQL languages on the rise. With Streaming SQL languages, developers can rapidly incorporate streaming queries into their apps. By 2018, most of the Stream processors support processing data via a Streaming SQL language.

Let us understand how SQL is mapped to streams. A stream is a table data in the move. Think of a never-ending table where new data appears as the time goes. A stream is such a table. One record or a row in a stream is called an event. But, it has a schema, and behave just like a database row.

The first thing to understand about SQL streams is that it replaces tables with streams. When you write SQL queries, you query data stored in a database. Yet, when you write a Streaming SQL query, you write them on data that is now as well as the data that will come in the future. Hence, streaming SQL queries never ends. Is it a problem? No, it works because the output of those queries is streams.

The event will be placed in output streams once the event matched and output events are available right away.

A stream represents all events that can come through a logical channel and it never ends. For example, if we have a temperature sensor in boiler we can represent the output from the sensors as a stream. However, classical SQL ingest data stored in a database table, processes them, and writes them to a database table. Instead, Above query will ingest a stream of data as they come in and produce a stream of data as output. For example, let us assume that there are events in the boiler stream once every 10 min. The filter query will produce an event in the result stream immediately when an event matches the filter.

So you can build your App as follows. You send events to stream processor by either sending directly or by via a broker. Then you can write the streaming part of the App using "Streaming SQL." Finally, you configure the Stream processor to act on the results. This is done by invoking a service when Stream Processor triggers or by publishing events to a broker topic and listening to the topic.

WSO2 Stream Processor (WSO2 SP) can ingest data from Kafka, HTTP requests, message brokers, and you can query data stream using a "Streaming SQL" language. WSO2 SP is open source under Apache license. With just two commodity servers, it can provide high availability and can handle 100K+ TPS throughput. It can scale up to millions of TPS on top of Kafka and supports multi-data center deployments.

Who is using stream processing?: In general, stream processing is useful in use cases where we can detect a problem and we have a reasonable response to improve the outcome. Also, it plays a key role in a data-driven organization. Following are some of the use cases.

- Algorithmic trading, stock market surveillance
- Smart patient care
- Monitoring a production line
- Supply chain optimizations
- Intrusion, surveillance, and fraud detection (e.g., Uber)
- Most smart device applications: smart car, smart home, etc.
- Smart grid (e.g., load prediction and outlier plug detection)
- Traffic monitoring, geofencing, vehicle, and wildlife tracking, e.g., TFL London Transport Management System
- Sports analytics: augment sports with real-time analytics
- Context-aware promotions and advertising
- Computer system and network monitoring
- Predictive maintenance
- Geospatial data processing

6.2   About event-driven architecture (EDA)

EDAs comprise complex business processes interconnected with streams of events. These are often online service use cases and also backend processes such as billing, fulfillment, or fraud detection, which may need to be decoupled from the frontend where users click buttons and expect things to happen. The event-driven model provides many benefits: it decouples dependencies between services, provides some level of pluggability to the architecture, enables services to evolve independently, etc.

EDAs are being used to build business-critical systems. Also there are articles explaining the value of turning databases "inside out" and on treating event streams as a "source of truth." There are write-ups on how to apply patterns, including event collaboration, event sourcing and CQRS for building microservices and event-oriented architectures. Such systems typically use Apache Kafka as the foundation. Kafka is like a central data plane that holds shared events and keeps services in sync. Its distributed cluster technology provides availability, resiliency, and performance properties that strengthen the architecture, leaving the programmer to simply write and deploy client applications that will run load balanced and be highly available.

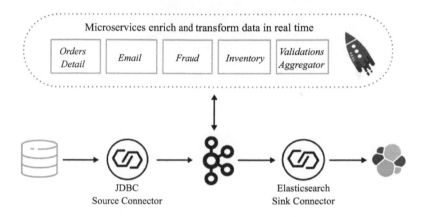

In this example, the system centers on an Orders Service which exposes a REST interface to POST and GET Orders. Posting an Order creates an event in Kafka that is recorded in the topic orders. This is picked up by three different validation engines (fraud service, inventory service and order details service), which validate the order in parallel, emitting a PASS or FAIL based on whether each validation succeeds.

The result of each validation is pushed through a separate topic, Order Validations, so that we retain the single writer status of the Orders Service —> Orders Topic. The results of the various validation checks are aggregated in the Validation Aggregator Service, which then moves the order to a Validated or Failed state, based on the combined result.

To allow users to GET any order, the Orders Service creates a queryable materialized view (embedded inside the Orders Service), using a state store in each instance of the service, so that any Order can be requested historically. Note also that the Orders Service can be scaled out over a number of nodes, in which case GET requests must be routed to the correct node to get a certain key. This is handled automatically using the interactive queries functionality in Kafka Streams.

The Orders Service also includes a blocking HTTP GET so that clients can read their own writes. In this way, we bridge the synchronous, blocking paradigm of a RESTful interface with the asynchronous, non-blocking processing performed server side. There is a simple service that sends e-mails, and another that collates orders and makes them available in a search index using Elasticsearch. Finally, Confluent KSQL is running with persistent queries to enrich streams and to also check for fraudulent behavior. Here is a diagram of the microservices and the related Kafka topics:

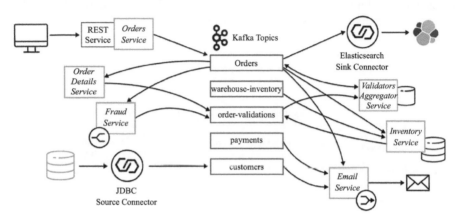

Persist events: You will persist events into Kafka by producing records that represent customer orders. An event is simply a thing that happened or occurred. An event in a business is some fact that occurred, such as a sale, an invoice, a trade, and a customer experience, and it is the source of truth. In event-oriented architectures, events are first-class citizens that constantly push data into applications. Client applications can then react to these streams of events in real time and decide what to do next.

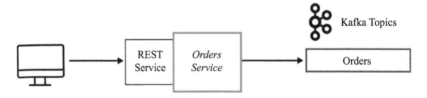

Event-driven applications: You will let the order event itself trigger a service. In such an event-driven design, an event stream is the inter-service communication that leads to less coupling and queries, enables services to cross deployment boundaries, and avoids synchronous execution. In contrast, service-based architectures are often designed to be request driven, in which services send commands to other services to tell them what to do, await a response or send queries to get the resulting state.

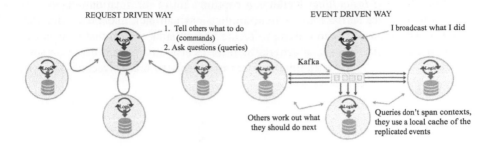

Enriching streams with joins: You will write a service that enriches the streaming order information by joining it with streaming payment information and data from a customer database. Many stream processing applications in practice are coded as streaming joins. For example, applications backing an online shop might need to access multiple updating database tables (e.g., sales prices, inventory, customer information) in order to enrich a new data record (e.g., customer transaction) with context information. In these scenarios, you may need to perform table lookups at very large scale and with a low processing latency.

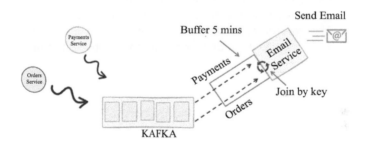

A popular pattern is to make the information in the databases available in Kafka through the so-called change data capture (CDC), together with Kafka's Connect API to pull in the data from the database. Once the data is in Kafka, client applications can perform very fast and efficient joins of such tables and streams, rather than requiring the application to make a query to a remote database over the network for each record.

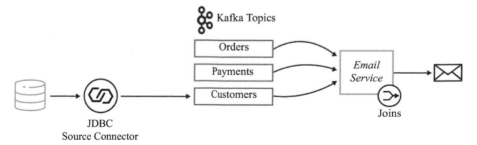

Filtering and branching: Kafka can capture a lot of information related to an event into a single Kafka topic. Client applications can then manipulate that data based on some user-defined criteria to create new streams of data that they can act on. You can define one set of criteria to filter records in a stream based on some criteria. Then you will define another set of criteria to branch records into two different streams.

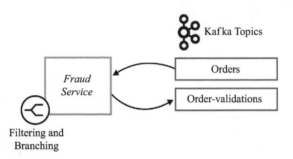

Stateful operations: You can create a session window to define five-minute windows for processing. You can combine current record values with previous record values using aggregations. They are stateful operations because they maintain data during processing. Oftentimes, these are combined with windowing capabilities in order to run computations in real time over a window of time. Additionally, you will use a stateful operation to collapse duplicate records in a stream.

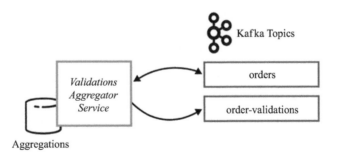

State stores: You will create a state store which is a disk-resident hash table held inside the API for the client application. The state store can be used within stream processing applications to store and query data, an important capability when implementing stateful operations. It can be used to remember recently received input records, to track rolling aggregates, to de-duplicate input records, etc.

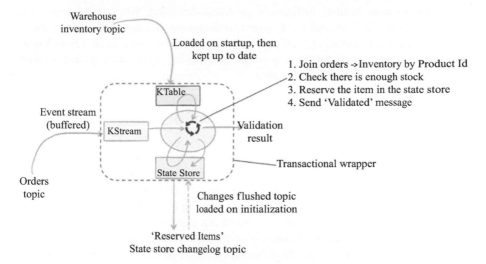

A state store is also backed by a Kafka topic and comes with all the Kafka guarantees. Consequently, other applications can also interactively query another application's state store. Querying state stores is always read-only to guarantee that the underlying state stores will never be mutated out of band (i.e., you cannot add new entries).

6.3   Enrichment with KSQL

Confluent KSQL is the streaming SQL engine that enables real-time data processing against Apache Kafka. It provides an easy-to-use, yet powerful interactive SQL interface for stream processing on Kafka, without requiring you to write code in a programming language such as Java or Python. KSQL is scalable, elastic, fault tolerant, and able to support a wide range of streaming operations, including data filtering, transformations, aggregations, joins, windowing, and sessionization. In this exercise, you will create one persistent query that enriches the orders stream with customer information. You will create another persistent query that detects fraudulent behavior by counting the number of orders in a given window.

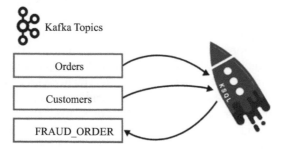

In summary, EDAs comprise complex business processes interconnected with streams of events. These are often online service uses cases and also backend processes such as billing, fulfillment or fraud detection, which may need to be decoupled from the frontend where users click buttons and expect things to happen. The event-driven model provides many benefits: it decouples dependencies between services, provides some level of pluggability to the architecture, enables services to evolve independently, etc.

6.4   Stream processing of IoT data

Today, with the rise of IoT and smart devices, we are generating data at an unprecedented speed. With distributed computing, data is generated somewhere and processed somewhere else. Sensors or UI on devices capture some data (manual or automated) as an event and send it to some other unit for processing. This happens continuously. These events may be processed at a fixed rate or in bursts, resulting in a stream of events. This process is known as an Event Stream. In most scenarios, these events are generated at a very high speed (seconds or even milliseconds). So, we need to process these event streams at the same or higher processing rate.

6.5   The role of Apache Kafka

Today, Apache Kafka provides a distributed stream processing engine, Kafka-Streams. In this series of articles, we will first try to cover:

1.   Kafka and its use cases.
2.   Kafka API and Kafka Streams API.
3.   Setting up a single node Kafka-Cluster.
4.   Processing GPS events for real-time analysis of online and offline vehicles.

The first three parts introduce you to concepts and terminologies related to Kafka and real-time stream processing.

Apache Kafka: This is an open-source distributed stream processing platform. We can describe Kafka as a collection of files, filled with messages that are distributed across multiple machines. Most of Kafka analogies revolve around tying these various individual logs together, routing messages from producers to consumers reliably, replicating for fault tolerance, and handling failure gracefully. Its architecture inherits more from storage systems like HDFS, HBase, or Cassandra than it does from traditional messaging systems that implement JMS or AMQP. The underlying abstraction is a partitioned log, essentially a set of append-only files spread over several machines. This encourages sequential access patterns. A Kafka cluster is a distributed system that spreads data over many machines both for fault tolerance and for linear scale-out.

Kafka has quickly evolved from a messaging system to a fully-fledged streaming platform with the following attributes:

1. Scalable.
2. Fault-tolerant.
3. Publish-subscribe messaging system.
4. Higher throughput compared with most messaging systems.

6.6 Kafka's capabilities as a streaming platform

1. *Publish and subscribe to streams of records*: We already have many messaging systems. Why do we need one more? At the heart of Kafka lies the humble, immutable commit log, and from there you can subscribe to it, and publish data to any number of systems or real-time applications. Unlike messaging queues, Kafka is a highly scalable, fault-tolerant distributed system.

   Kafka has stronger ordering guarantees than a traditional messaging system. A traditional queue retains records in order on the server, and if multiple consumers consume from the queue, the server hands out records in the order they are stored. However, although the server hands out records in order, the records are delivered asynchronously to consumers, so they may arrive out of order to different consumers. Kafka does this more efficiently. Kafka can provide both ordering guarantees and load balancing over a pool of consumer processes.

2. *Store streams of records in a fault-tolerant durable way*: In Kafka, data is written to disk in a fault-tolerant way using replication of data. Kafka allows producers to wait for acknowledgment for completion, and a write is not considered complete until it is fully replicated and guaranteed to persist even if the server written to fails. Kafka will perform the same whether you have 50 KB or 50 TB of persistent data on the server. As a result, we can think of Kafka as a kind of special purpose distributed file system dedicated to high-performance, low-latency commit log storage, replication, and propagation.

3. *Process streams of records as they occur*: A streaming platform would not be complete without the ability to manipulate data as it arrives. The Streams API within Apache Kafka is a powerful, lightweight library that allows for on-the-fly processing. In Kafka, a stream processor is anything that takes continual streams of data from input topics, performs some processing on this input, and produces continual streams of data to output topics. For example, a retail application might take input streams of sales and shipments and output a stream of reorders and price adjustments computed off this data. Simple processing can be done directly using the producer and consumer APIs. For more complex transformations, Kafka provides a fully integrated Streams API.

6.7   Concepts in Apache Kafka

- Kafka is run as a cluster on one or more servers that can span multiple data centers.
- The Kafka cluster stores streams of records in categories called topics.
- Each record consists of a key, a value, and a timestamp.

Kafka use cases: Kafka is used in two broad classes of applications. It can build real-time streaming data pipelines that reliably move data between systems and applications. It can also be used to build real-time streaming applications that transform or react to streams of od data.

Some use cases for these include:

- Messaging.
- Real-time website activity tracking.
- Metrics.
- Log aggregation.
- Stream processing.
- Event sourcing.
- Commit log.

6.8   Stream processing by Apache spark streaming

The demand for stream processing is increasing a lot these days. The reason is that often, processing big volumes of data is not enough. Data has to be processed fast so that a firm can react to changing business conditions in real-time. Stream processing is the real-time processing of data continuously and concurrently. Apache Spark is an open-source, general-purpose, lightning fast cluster computing system. It provides a high-level API that works with, for example, Java, Scala, Python and R. Apache Spark is a tool for running Spark applications. Spark is 100 times faster than doing big data on Hadoop and ten times faster than accessing data from disk. Spark also provides interactive processing, graph processing, in-memory processing, and batch processing of data with very fast speed, ease of use, and a standard interface.

Spark is not only a big data processing engine. It is a framework that provides a distributed environment to process data. This means we can perform any type of task using Spark. To see its performance, let us take an example of factorial. Calculating the factorial for a very large number is always cumbersome in any programming language. CPU will take much time to complete the calculation. Here is a factorial function.

6.9   Using tail recursion in Scala

```
def factorial(num: BigInt): BigInt = {
def factImp(num: BigInt, fact: BigInt): BigInt = {
if (num == 0) fact
else
factImp(num - 1, num * fact)
}
factImp(num, 1)
}
```

The time taken by above code to find the factorial of 200,000 on my machine (Quad Core Intel i5) was about 20 s.

6.10   Factorial function using Spark

```
def factorialUsingSpark(num: BigInt): BigInt = {
if (num == 0) BigInt(1)
else {
val list = (BigInt(1) to num).toList
sc.parallelize(list).reduce(_ * _)
}
}
```

The time taken by Spark to find the factorial of 200,000 on the same machine was only 5 s, which is almost 4× faster than using Scala alone. Computation do depends on hardware of system but at least it gives us an idea how spark efficiently processes complex computations. A lot of players on the market have built successful MapReduce workflows to daily process terabytes of historical data. But who wants to wait 24 h to get updated analytics? This introduces you to the Lambda Architecture designed to take advantages of both batch and streaming processing methods. So we will leverage fast access to historical data with real-time streaming data using Apache Spark (Core, SQL, Streaming), Apache Parquet, Twitter Stream, etc. Clear code plus intuitive demo are also included! Apache Hadoop's rich history started in ~2002. Hadoop was created by Doug Cutting, the creator of Apache Lucene, a widely used text search library.

As a result, a lot of customers implemented **successful** Hadoop-based M/R pipelines which are operating today. I have at least a few great examples from real life:

- Oozie-orchestrated workflow operates daily and processes up to 150 TB to generate analytics
- Bash managed workflow runs daily and processes up to 8 TB to generate analytics

Business realities have changed, so now making decisions faster is more valuable. In addition to that, technologies have evolved too. Kafka, Storm, Trident, Samza, Spark, Flink, Parquet, Avro, Cloud providers, etc. are known buzzwords that are widely adopted both by engineers and businesses. As a result, modern Hadoop-based M/R pipeline (with Kafka, modern binary format such as Avro and data warehouse, i.e. in this case Amazon Redshift, used for ad-hoc queries) might look in the following way:

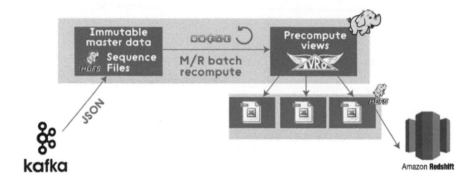

That looks quite ok, but it is still a traditional batch processing with all the known drawbacks, main of them is stale data for end-users since batch processing usually takes a lot of time to complete while new data is constantly entering into a system.

6.11   Lambda architecture

Nathan Marz came up with the term Lambda Architecture for generic, scalable, and fault-tolerant data processing architecture. It is data-processing architecture designed to handle massive quantities of data by taking advantage of *both* batch and stream processing methods.

Layers: Here's how it looks, from a high-level perspective:

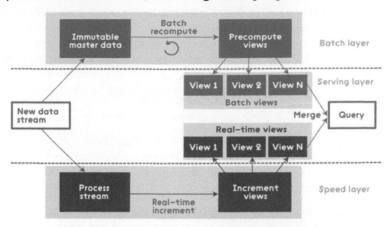

All data entering the system is dispatched to both the batch layer and the speed layer for processing. The batch layer manages the master dataset (an immutable, append-only set of raw data) and pre-computes the batch views. The serving layer indexes the batch views so that they can be queried in ad hoc with low-latency. The speed layer deals with recent data only. Any incoming query has to be answered by merging results from batch views and real-time views. A lot of engineers think that Lambda Architecture is all about these layers and defined data flow, but Nathan Marz puts a focus on other important aspects like:

- think distributed
- avoid incremental architecture
- force data immutability
- create re-computation algorithms

6.12 Relevance of data

$$query = function(batch\ view,\ real\ time\ view)$$
$$real\ time\ view = function(real\ time\ view,\ new\ data)$$
$$batch\ view = function(all\ data)$$

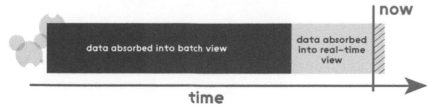

As it was mentioned earlier, any incoming query has to be answered by merging results from batch views and real-time views, so those views need to be mergeable. One point to notice here, a real-time view is a function of a previous real-time view and delta of new data so that an incremental algorithm can be used there. A batch view is a function of all data, so a re-computation algorithm should be used there. Usually, there are a few main trade-offs we need to address

- Full re-computation vs. partial re-computation
  - o   in some cases, it is worth using Bloom filters to avoid complete re-computation

- Re-computational algorithms vs. incremental algorithms
  - o   there is a big temptation to use incremental algorithms, but according to a guideline we have to use re-computational algorithms even if it makes it harder to achieve the same result

- Additive algorithms vs. approximation algorithms
  - o   Lambda Architecture works well with additive algorithms. Thus this is another case we need to consider using approximation algorithms, for instance, HyperLogLog for a count-distinct problem, etc.

Implementation: There are many ways of implementing Lambda Architecture as it is quite agnostic about underlying solutions for each of the layers. Each layer requires specific features of underlying implementation that might help to make a better choice and avoid overkill decisions

- *Batch layer*: write-once, bulk read many times
- *Serving layer*: random read, no random write; batch computation and batch write
- *Speed layer*: random read, random write; incremental computation

For instance, one of the implementations (using Kafka, Apache Hadoop, Voldemort, Twitter Storm, Cassandra) might look as follows:

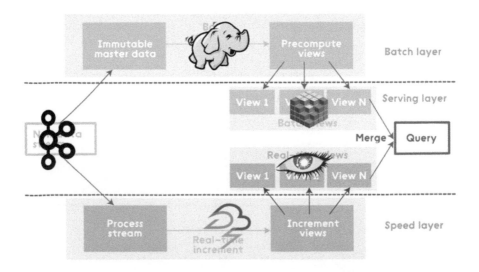

6.13   Apache Spark

Apache Spark can be considered as an integrated solution for processing on all Lambda Architecture layers. It contains Spark Core that includes high-level API and an optimized engine that supports general execution graphs, Spark SQL for SQL and structured data processing, and Spark Streaming that enables scalable, high-throughput, fault-tolerant stream processing of live data streams. Definitely, batch processing using Spark might be quite expensive and might not fit for all scenarios and data volumes, but, other than that, it is a decent match for Lambda Architecture implementation.

Sample application: Let us create a sample application with some shortcuts to demonstrate Lambda Architecture. The main goal is to provide hashtags statistics used in the #morningatlohika tweets all time till today + **right now**.

Batch view: For simplicity, imagine that our master dataset contains all the tweets since the beginning of times. In addition, we have implemented a batch processing that created a batch view needed for our business goal, so we have one batch view pre-calculated that contains statistics for all hashtags used along with #morningatlohika:

```
apache – 6
architecture – 12
aws – 3
java – 4
jeeconf – 7
lambda – 6
morningatlohika – 15
simpleworkflow – 14
spark – 5
```

Numbers are quite easy to remember as I just used a number of letters in the appropriate hashtags for simplicity.

Real-time view: Imagine that someone is tweeting right now when application is up and running.

"Cool blog post by @tmatyashovsky about #lambda #architecture using #apache #spark at #morningatlohika"

In this case, an appropriate real-time view should contain the following hashtags and their statistics (just 1 in our case as corresponding hashtags were used just once):

```
apache – 1
architecture – 1
lambda – 1
morningatlohika – 1
spark – 1
```

6.14   Query

When an end-user query comes in order to give a real-time answer about overall hashtags statistics, we simply need to merge batch view with the real-time view. So output should look as follows (appropriate hashtags have their statistics incremented by one):

apache – 7
architecture – 13
aws – 3
java – 4
jeeconf – 7
lambda – 7
morningatlohika – 16
simpleworkflow – 14
spark – 6

Scenario: Simplified steps of demo scenario are the following:

- Create batch view (.parquet) via Apache Spark
- Cache batch view in Apache Spark
- Start streaming application connected to Twitter
- Focus on real-time #morningatlohika tweets
- Build incremental real-time views
- Query, i.e., merge batch and real-time views on a fly

Spark streaming architecture is pure micro-batch architecture.

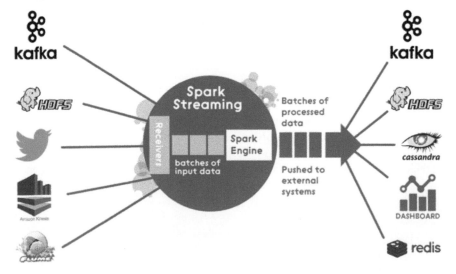

So for a streaming application, I was using DStream connected to Twitter using TwitterUtils:

```
JavaDStream<Status> twitterStatuses = TwitterUtils.createStream(javaStreamingContext,
                        createTwitterAuthorization(),
                        new String[]{twitterFilterText});
```

On each micro-batch (using configurable batch interval), I was performing a calculation of hashtags statistics in new tweets and updating the state of a real-time view using updateStateByKey() stateful transformation. For simplicity, a real-time view is stored in memory using a temp table. Query service reflects merging of batch and real-time views represented by DataFrame explicitly via code:

```
DataFrame realTimeView = streamingService.getRealTimeView();
DataFrame batchView = servingService.getBatchView();
DataFrame mergedView = realTimeView.unionAll(batchView)
                .groupBy(realTimeView.col(HASH_TAG.getValue()))
                .sum(COUNT.getValue())
                .orderBy(HASH_TAG.getValue());
List<Row> merged = mergedView.collectAsList();
return merged.stream()
        .map(row -> new HashTagCount(row.getString(0), row.getLong(1)))
            .collect(Collectors.toList());
```

Using the simplified approach, the real-life Hadoop-based M/R pipeline mentioned at the beginning might be enhanced with Apache Spark and look in the following way:

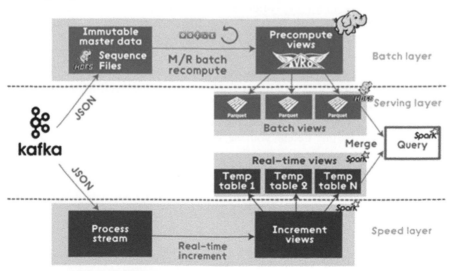

As it was mentioned earlier Lambda Architecture has its pros and cons, and as a result supporters and opponents. Some of them say that a batch view and real-time views have a lot of duplicate logic as, eventually, they need to create mergeable views from a query perspective. So they created a Kappa Architecture - simplification of Lambda Architecture. A Kappa Architecture system is the architecture with the batch processing system removed. To replace batch processing, data is simply fed through the streaming system quickly:

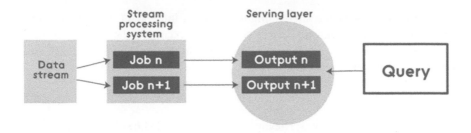

But even in this scenario, there is a place for Apache Spark in Kappa Architecture too, for instance for a stream processing system:

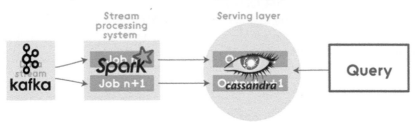

Kappa Architecture is a software architecture pattern. Rather than using a relational DB like SQL or a key-value store like Cassandra, the canonical data store in a Kappa Architecture system is an append-only immutable log. From the log, data is streamed through a computational system and fed into auxiliary stores for serving.

Kappa Architecture is a simplification of Lambda Architecture. A Kappa Architecture system is like a Lambda Architecture system with the batch processing system removed. To replace batch processing, data is simply fed through the streaming system quickly. Kappa Architecture revolutionizes database migrations and reorganizations: just delete your serving layer database and populate a new copy from the canonical store! Since there is no batch processing layer, only one set of code needs to be maintained.

Chapter 7

Rapid response system for road accidents using streaming sensor data analytics

*V. Sai Mahesh[1], Sangam Rajat Sajeev[1], V.V.S. Bharadwaj[1]
and R. Maheswari[1]*

Abstract

Every year, approximately 1.35 million deaths occur due to car accidents across the globe. There are about 1 in 106 chances of an average person dying in a car accident. Even though India mostly relies on traveling by road transport, it is the least safe mode in the country right now. This work aims to prevent loss of life by providing a rapid response system for road accidents. Many people lose their lives to road transport accidents. Most of these deaths occur due to the patient not reaching a hospital on time or ambulances not reaching them on time. A large number of these fatalities can be prevented by medical help reaching them in the immediate and crucial amount of time after the accident. Currently, the victims depend on another human contacting the helpline number to request assistance. This situation can be improved by developing a more efficient system through automation. This work focuses on designing an automatic rapid response system for such cases, which uses various sensors to detect whether the vehicle has met with an accident (or even is in flames) and sends the location of the vehicle to the nearest fire station and hospital. All of this, including the choice of the fire station and hospital, is automated. Most of these sensors are inexpensive and some are even already found in the vehicles of today. Hence, multiple lives of accident victims can be saved through the proper implementation of this work.

7.1 Introduction

According to the World Health Organization (WHO), every year the lives of approximately 1.35 million people are cut short as a result of a road traffic crash. A further number of about 50 million more people are afflicted with non-fatal injuries, a large percentage of them resulting in disabilities. If there is a system in place which can help alert the hospitals and other services in time, a big percentage of

[1]School of Computer Science and Engineering, Vellore Institute of Technology, India

these deaths could be avoided [1]. Hence, the importance to develop such a system that could alert the nearby hospital and the fire station in time is significant. The proposed system is capable of detecting sudden deceleration, hike in temperature which helps to understand if there is a fire and also the orientation of the vehicle. The system makes use of a temperature sensor, 3-axis accelerometer, Wi-Fi Module, and GPS module. The temperature sensor helps to understand if there is a fire caused. Generally, the maximum cabin temperatures in a road transport vehicle are between 40°C and 76°C [2]. The 3-axis accelerometer aids to find if there is sudden deceleration. The 3-axis accelerometer also helps to find the orientation of the vehicle which in turn supports understanding if the vehicle has toppled or is not in the proper orientation. Orientation of the vehicle is helpful as it denotes whether the vehicle is on its normal axis or if it has toppled over [3]. It has been found that during a collision accident, the deceleration may range anywhere between 6 g and 12 g [4,5]. The location is tracked with the GPS module and the collected data and uploaded with the help of a Wi-Fi module. The data collected is constantly sent to the cloud where the collected data is compared with the threshold. If the threshold is crossed the system is alarmed and a message is sent to the nearest fire station and hospital. The system detects the closest hospital and fire station and sends the location of the incident. Currently, no efficient rapid response systems are being used. A few systems are being proposed but have not been implemented in real life due to many drawbacks. Car manufacturers like Tesla are trying to implement such features in their vehicles. This system can help to identify people who need immediate assistance when they are affected by a major accident. When any of the three parameters are fulfilled, the system will detect that case as an accident. As stated above, the three thresholds are temperature, accelerometer, and GPS module. If the temperature is above a certain value, and the deceleration is above a certain value, it will be considered an accident. Then the GPS sends the location of the vehicle to the nearest hospitals and fire stations. Cloud computing has become such an integral part of the average human's everyday life in the twenty-first century that it is hard to imagine the situation and working of most of the industries without its existence. It is an important component of the Future Internet [6]. Cloud computing service allows for on-demand availability of computation resources for any application. The computational resources allocation for a specific application can be fine-tuned to fit exactly right. This ensures that the usage of these computational resources is efficient and effective, allowing for ease of access and an economic solution for distributed systems. In an Internet of Things (IoT) system, the use of cloud computing is especially apparent due to the low computational power of the onboard chips on the embedded devices and the ability of these devices to communicate effectively with one another and with the Internet [7]. The system proposed makes use of cloud computing to calculate the state of the vehicle and the nearest stations. MQTT protocol (Message Queuing Telemetry Transport) is a network protocol that operates with the backbone of publish–subscribe methodology. It is a lightweight protocol that allows for faster transmission of small and important data, which is relatively cost-effective when compared to alternatives and is well suited for IoT applications than techniques such as RESTful services

[8]. This system can be used in cities, towns, and even highways, both national and state. A GPS-based map system has also been integrated to identify hospitals and fire stations nearby. Speed is a crucial factor when dealing with road accidents. Many lives can be saved when the emergency services arrive on time to the accident spot, even if it is by mere minutes faster than the traditional methods [9].

7.2 Literature survey

IoT devices are rapidly increasing in usage in the real world, for purposes such as monitoring and analyzing a continuous stream of data. In their work, Lakshmana Phaneendra *et al.* explained the usage of IoT to achieve an efficient and smart emergency response system for fire hazards in a Smart City system [10]. This system is vital to achieving the complete functioning of the Smart City system, which combines the functionality of multiple organizations working in tandem with each other to improve the lifestyle of the citizens in the said city. Certain proposed systems plan to revolutionize how first responders on the scene of a fire receive the information on the fire, making use of the critical and up-to-date information provided by the IoT systems present at the scene. This eliminates problems such as insufficient communication networks and terrible lag in the said information exchange. To this end, ESP-32 Wi-Fi module, MQ-5 Smoke detection sensor, flame detection sensor, volatile gas sensor, and GPS module are used. The sensors, once a hazard is detected, gather the information and send an alert to the nearest department with the location of the incident. The entire system is managed through the MQTT protocol to improve the speed and reliability of the system. Sahriar Habib *et al.* [11] have also made use of the MQ-5 Smoke detection sensor and volatile gas sensor in their work to develop an IoT-based accident detection and emergency response system.

Another proposed system discusses the method to build a better IoT system that can detect fire emergencies [12]. This is useful as temperature detection is a major part of detecting accidents and understanding the intensity of that particular accident. In the system proposed in this work, a temperature sensor has been incorporated for the same reason. This work by Noorbasha Johnsaida *et al.* talks about an IoT flame detection system that uses a GPS to locate the position of the accident. The materials that have been used in this work are a flame sensor, the raspberry pi module, a GPS module, and a cloud service called Twilio. Twilio helps to send messages to the concerned authorities about the fire, its intensity, and its location on the GPS. This system can fight many dangers that are associated with fire; examples include forest fires, household fires, accidents that cause huge fire explosions, and many more. This can also be used as an evacuation system, as the authorities will be informed when the accident happens, so they can contact the police or some other authority to evacuate the premises immediately.

An article featured by "Bridgera," by Joydeep Misra, mainly focuses on the many ways that IoT can be used to help various public and private sectors that directly are in contact with a huge number of people. Some of the mentioned sectors are Fire

Department and Hospital EMTs (emergency medical technicians), both of these demographics are targets of the study regarding the system proposed in this work. This chapter has also some case studies where IoT has helped the police departments.

Fire departments are some of the sectors which will benefit hugely from IoT usage. IoT can be used to detect fires quickly, estimate their potency and send the required equipment, with the added capability of even predicting some fires. EMTs, or ambulance services in a few countries, similar to the fire department, gain a lot from the usage of IoT smart systems. These ambulances can be equipped with certain sensors that detect any mishaps in close proximity, allowing them to rush to the site of the incident immediately. The police department is another department that can benefit a lot from the use of IoT smart systems. The police can use IoT in many different ways, from speeding vehicles, park ticket fines to stopping major crimes that can happen.

The research paper by M.M. Ullah Rathore *et al.* [13] deals with the various ways in which IoT can be helpful in the medical sector. As discussed previously, IoT has a myriad of uses in sectors like the fire department, ambulance services, and also the police department. In this paper, the focus is on a more crucial service, the medical service. IoT smart systems can help the medical service in many ways, for example, monitoring patients' heartbeat, pulse, oxygen saturation levels, and much more. These can also be used for much more complex and important tasks, such as analysis of a patient's condition in real-time, etc. This task is very complex, as it is not simple to read data, check if it is above or below a certain limit, and inform the authorities if it is. This task involves much more complexity, and IoT can do this with the right equipment and training. So IoT in the medical sector is a very huge step towards better treatment, care of the patient, and it can also help the doctors, nurses, and staff to monitor more patients at the same time. The number can range from 10s to 100s, and even thousands. Hence, IoT in the medical field is a very important stride.

Cloud computing has become an integral part of man's daily life and is being used in every major industrial sector to improve efficiency and a system proposed by L.D. De Paolis deals with the collection of data via ThingsBoard platform and usage of Spark Streaming framework for cluster computing with the intent of performing data analytics via cloud computing [14]. Due to the wide and easy availability of small and low-cost sensors, many new designs of systems that can monitor the required parameters in real-time have sprung up in various fields. This includes certain fields like the service sector, agriculture sector, industrial sector, commercial sector, etc. For example, in the agriculture sector, real-time monitoring of the soil can lead to better automation of irrigation systems [15]. Care must be taken to ensure that the data obtained from these sensors is reliable as it can have major ramifications. In the work of Vincenzo Di Lecce, an urban wastewater monitoring system using real-time monitoring is described [16]. In this use case, there must be measures in place to ensure unreliable data is filtered out from reliable data in order to perform analysis. Through the usage of the concept of IoT, these systems can be interconnected to form a larger macro network to allow for large-scale interoperability. A stream aggregation approach enables the aggregation of sensors into groups [17]. These systems can have an array of uses in a vast number of fields – including clinical and environmental use cases. In particular, this system delves deeper into the usage of sensors to collect data and perform streaming analytics on biomedical data regarding the breath of patients suffering from respiratory diseases. This real-time monitoring of the data lets the doctors be warned at the right moment in the case of an anomaly. The work of Klemen Kenda *et al.* also describes and highlights the importance of interconnection of various data sources and proper segregation of data to realize the maximum potential of streaming analytics [18].

Finally, even with the usage of all the right tools such as cloud computing, smart sensors, and reliability verification, the result of any real-world application depends on a single crucial part – decision making. The incorporation of these tools helps to improve the quality of the decision made at the endpoint, especially in emergency systems using IoT technology [19].

7.3   Existing works

In today's world, no real form of rapid response system exists. Systems have been proposed to help in accident prevention by utilizing techniques such as increasing driver awareness and passive automatic detection systems [20]. But the chance for an accident to occur is never nil and hence preparations must be made to deal with the aftermath. The closest existing system is the emergency helpline provided for all emergency services such as hospitals, fire stations, and police stations. This implementation works with the user contacting the emergency service required via usually a phone call. As this involves human intervention in order to request emergency services, there are often chances of help not arriving in time to prevent a catastrophe. There are also chances of some users misusing the helpline to waste precious time which could be used more productively. Hence, proper automation in the form of sensor automation can be crucial in achieving better response times, with the usage of "smart sensors," which have the capabilities of both sensing and transmitting [21]. A few related theoretical works published by authors provide other alternatives to these services for fire hazards and medical applications. Existing works speak about expanding the horizon by combining a few systems, such as collision detection and pollution monitoring systems, to provide a compound system that is more cost-effective than its parts [22]. Most of these works make use of the concept of detecting anomalies in the data collected in order to respond [23]. But the task of doing so is a herculean one when dealing with large amounts of data without proper parameters for anomaly detection. Others include providing a manual method of notifying the authorities without relying on the phone network in the case of a crisis [24].

7.4   Proposed system

To combat the issues and drawbacks with the existing system of helpline stated above, a new and improved system is proposed, which makes use of concepts of the

IoT to achieve greater automation and faster response in a severe situation. In this system, the aim is to streamline the help and response in case of a vehicular accident using the MQTT protocol. To do this, the system makes use of sensors embedded in the vehicle to measure the tilt, acceleration, and temperature of the vehicle. When a predefined critical event occurs through the measurement of these sensors, a signal is sent via the MQTT network which includes the sensor measurements and the GPS location of the vehicle. This signal is then processed and sent to the hospital and fire station which are nearest to the site of the incident. Using this, these emergency stations are alerted and the rapid response teams are deployed as soon as possible.

7.4.1   Flow chart of proposed model

The complete flow structure of the rapid response system is provided in Figure 7.1 and comprises the flow of the data and services in the entire system. The flow begins at the base level in the form of the vehicle. The sensors present in the vehicle collect the various required data which is read and sent to the cloud server for analysis. Next, conditional statements are used to check whether the vehicle has met with a collision accident or a fire accident. In case of either being true, the program locates the nearest hospital and fire station to the site of the accident and notifies the rapid response teams stationed at these stations, while simultaneously notifying the user of the location of the hospital and the fire station chosen and that the help is on its way. Finally, the system is reset to start reading the sensor data once the crisis has been dealt with. In the case of neither of the accident conditions being true, the system continues to monitor the vehicles associated with the system.

7.4.2   Proposed architecture diagram

Figure 7.2 is the architecture module of the proposed system. It contains two main microcontrollers, one to be used for the alarms that need to sound when an accident takes place. The other is to be used for the main system in the car and has a temperature sensor, an accelerometer, and a GPS module. Both the microcontrollers are connected to Wi-Fi modules, to send and receive signals from one to the other. The sensors have pre-set threshold values, that continuously keep reading the real-time values of the vehicle, when the values are above, then a signal is sent through the Wi-Fi module to the other sensor placed in each police station and fire station in the city. The GPS module helps to identify the nearest police station and fire station.

As the alarm is sounded, the authorities in the police station and the fire station are alerted, and they move to the location. This is a very simple way of identifying the accident, as this process does not involve any tedious calculations, phone calls, etc. Since most of the accident cases that take place on highways are reported by human beings, there is always a delay in making the phone call, giving the exact location, and much more formalities. Through this process, confirmation can be obtained that this human delay is eliminated, as the

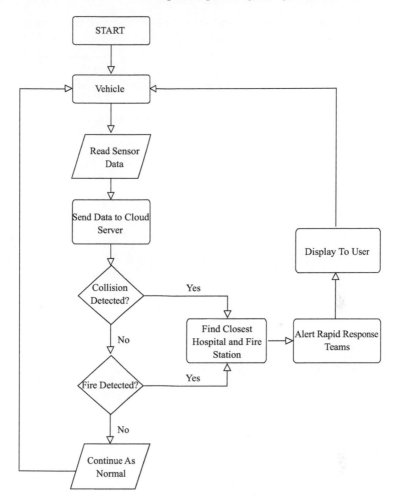

Figure 7.1   Flow chart

information of the accident, such as location, is already revealed. Factors such as speed and temperature also give the authorities some idea of the intensity of the accident that has taken place, so officers can react accordingly. So, in short, this system has increased the speed at which many authorities respond to accident cases. In the absence of this system, it takes significantly longer when compared to instances with the system.

7.5   Working modules

The proposed system consists of multiple modules that it incorporates. A comprehensive list of the modules present in the system follows.

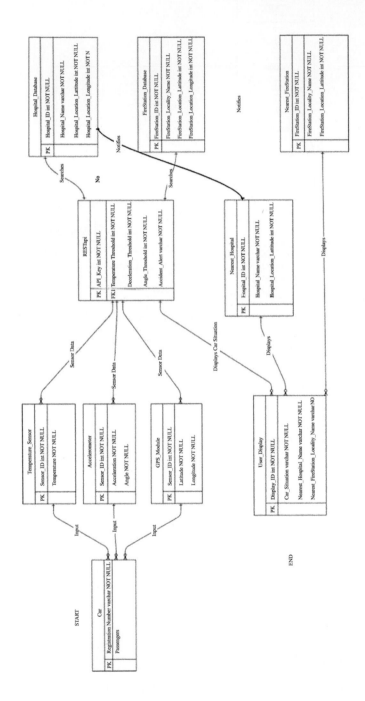

Figure 7.2 Block diagram of rapid response system

7.5.1   Hardware

7.5.1.1   Temperature sensor

The system makes use of a TMP36 temperature sensor, as shown in Figure 7.3. The sensor helps in keeping a track of the overall temperature of the vehicle. The output of the sensor is in the form of analog values, which are proportional to the ambient temperature. The range of the values of temperature which the sensor can detect is −40 to 150°C. It uses a solid-state technique to determine the temperature. In solid-state technique, the sensor utilizes a topology of resistors and transistors in a particular arrangement and is made as a single IC. The output produced is proportional to absolute temperature (PTAT) over a given range of temperatures.

7.5.1.2   Accelerometer sensor

The 3-axis accelerometer, shown in Figure 7.4, helps in measuring two the acceleration of the vehicle and also helps understand the orientation of the vehicle, which is crucial in determining if the vehicle has met with an accident. It is available in the form of a kit consisting of a G selection Shunt, a 2-pin header, and a 5-pin male header. The accelerometer can figure out the angle by which it is tilted with respect to the ground or earth, by measuring the acceleration due to gravity. The acceleration of the vehicle can be measured by the sensor by sensing the amount of dynamic acceleration. The 3-axis accelerometer module has an MMA7361 which operates in two selectable modes, which are ± 1.5 g and 6 g.

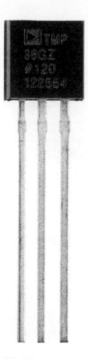

Figure 7.3   TMP36 temperature sensor

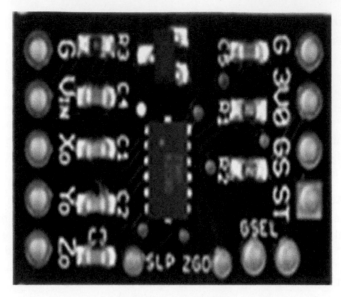

Figure 7.4   3-Axis accelerometer module

Figure 7.5   NEO-6M GPS module

7.5.1.3   GPS module

The NEO-6M GPS module in Figure 7.5 can be used to find the location coordinates of the vehicle. The module has an editable Universal asynchronous receiver–transmitter (UART) interface for the purpose of serial communication. The default UART(TTL) baud rate is 9,600. The GPS signal is right-hand-circular-polarized (RHCP). Hence, the design of the GPS antenna is different from the normal whip

Figure 7.6   ESP8266 Wi-Fi module

antennas used for linear polarized signals. The patch antenna is the most popular antenna type used for this purpose. They are flat, normally have a metal and ceramic body, and are mounted on a metal base plate. Since these sensors have very high accuracy it can even be used indoors, for example, in a parking lot.

7.5.1.4   Wi-Fi module

The ESP8266 Wi-Fi module in Figure 7.6 is a self-contained System on a Chip (SoC) with an integrated TCP/IP protocol stack that can help connect any micro-controller to Wi-Fi. ESP8266 has the capability of hosting an entire application or offloading all Wi-Fi networking functions from another application processor. They are pre-programmed with an AT command set firmware, which enables the user to directly connect it to an Arduino device and get almost the same Wi-Fi abilities that are offered by a Wi-Fi shield. Hence, the ESP8266 can be used to connect the Arduino to the cloud.

7.5.1.5   Arduino Uno R3

Arduino Uno R3 is a microcontroller board based on AVR microcontroller Atmega328. It is used to control and sense the external devices connected to it. In the proposed system, the temperature sensor, accelerometer, and other sensors are connected to the Arduino which acts as the brain of the electronic devices.

7.5.2   Software

7.5.2.1   Node-Red software

Node-Red software allows simulation of the overall design and implementation of the proposed system. The system takes the inputs from the sensors embedded in the vehicle in the form of text input to make the simulation more accessible. The output segment of the simulation presents the information available at both the server-side and the emergency stations side. The main flow consisting of the basic logic and the dashboard capabilities is shown in Figure 7.7 while the flow describing the world map display is depicted in Figure 7.8.

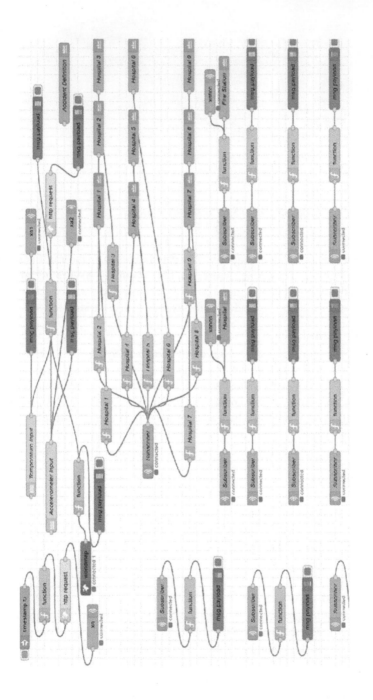

Figure 7.7 Node-Red flow of rapid response system

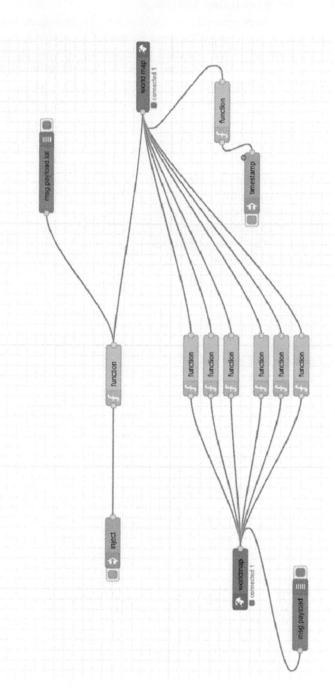

Figure 7.8 World map flow

7.5.2.2 Python programming language

Python language is used to program the API which receives the request from the flow and sends a response to the designated node in case of an accident. A micro web framework by the name of "Flask" is used to design the API which captures and responds to the requests sent by the rest of the system, such as the sensors in the vehicle. A personal computer is used to simulate a pseudo-cloud machine storing the API.

7.6   Pseudocode

7.6.1   Combining inputs

DEFINE temperature, acceleration, location
IF message.topic IS temperature:
    SET temperature AS message.payload
ELSE IF message.topic IS acceleration:
    SET acceleration AS message.payload
ELSE IF message.topic IS location:
    SET location AS message.payload
COMBINE temperature, acceleration, location AS sensordata
RETURN sensordata

7.6.2   API

CAPTURE request FROM vehicle
ASSIGN acceleration, temperature, location
IF acceleration > threshold OR temperature > threshold:
    SET accident TO "true"
CAPTURE request FROM system
IF accident IS "true":
    RETURN location, accident

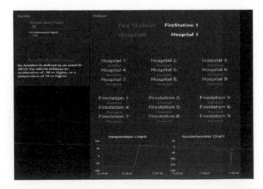

Figure 7.9   Case 1 – collision – dashboard

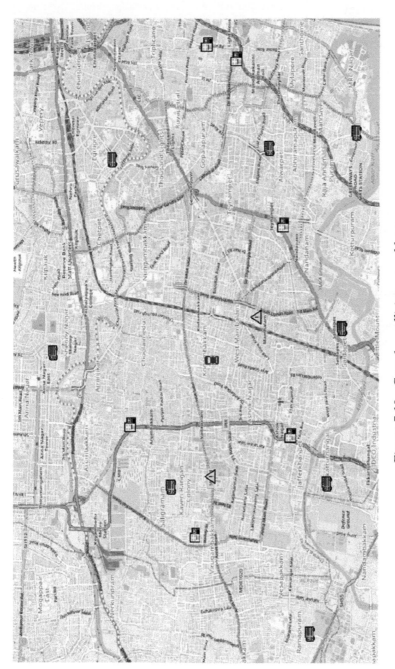

Figure 7.10   Case 1 – collision – world map

7.6.3   *Receiving output from the API and parsing*

7.6.3.1   Hospital

DEFINE hospitals
ASSIGN location
IF accident IS "true":
    CALCULATE distance (location, hospitals)
    FIND MIN OF distance (location, hospitals)
    RETURN MIN

7.6.3.2   Fire station

DEFINE firestations
ASSIGN location
IF accident IS "true":
    CALCULATE distance (location, firestations)
    FIND MIN OF distance (location, firestations)
    RETURN MIN

7.7   Results/output

In the following test cases, the temperature of 70°C in the cabin and the deceleration of 30 m/s^2 are assumed to be the threshold parameters to simulate the occurrence of an accident.

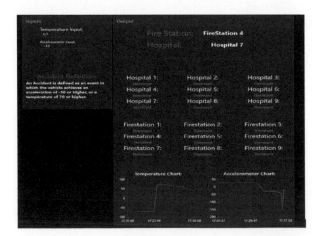

Figure 7.11   Case 2 – fire – dashboard

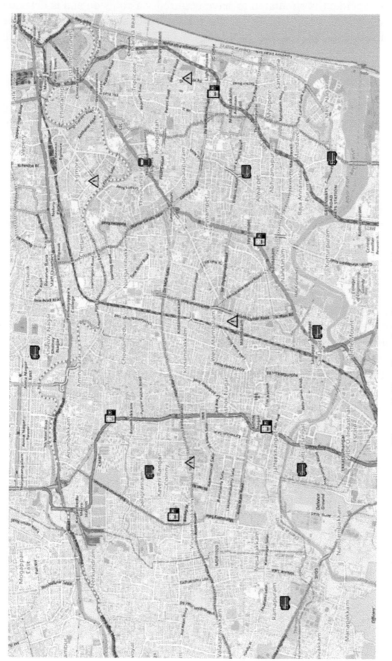

Figure 7.12 Case 2 – fire – world map

7.7.1   Case 1 (accident via collision)

In this case, an accident is simulated to have occurred via collision and is detected using the acceleration of the vehicle via the accelerometer sensor. The state of the dashboard, in this case, is depicted in Figure 7.9, and the state of the world map display is depicted in Figure 7.10.

7.7.2   Case 2 (accident via fire)

In this case, an accident is simulated to have occurred via fire and is detected using the temperature of the vehicle via the temperature sensor. The state of the dashboard, in this case, is depicted in Figure 7.11, and the state of the world map display is depicted in Figure 7.12.

7.7.3   Case 3 (no accident)

In this case, the simulation does not consist of an accident and the system continues to work normally and monitor the vehicles. The state of the dashboard, in this case, is depicted in Figure 7.13, and the state of the world map display is depicted in Figure 7.14.

7.7.4   Case 4 (accident via fire and collision)

In this case, an accident is simulated to have occurred via both collision and a resultant fire and is detected using the acceleration of the vehicle via the accelerometer sensor and the temperature via the temperature sensor. The state of the dashboard, in this case, is depicted in Figure 7.15, and the state of the world map display is depicted in Figure 7.16.

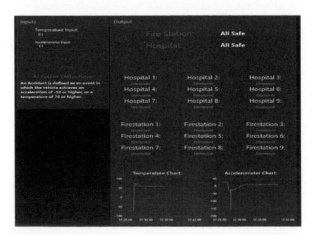

Figure 7.13   Case 3 – no accident – dashboard

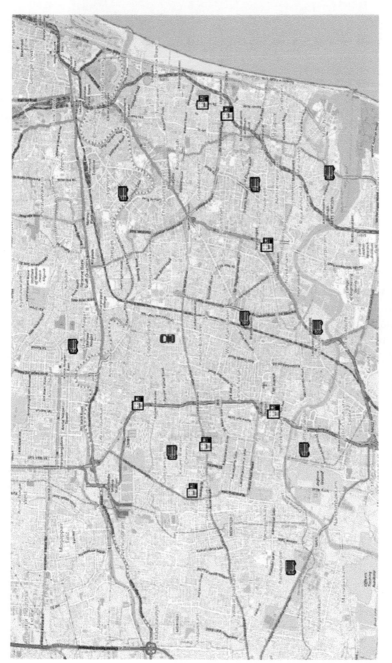

Figure 7.14   Case 3 – no accident – world map

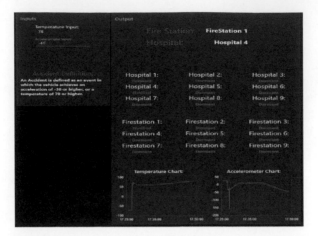

Figure 7.15   Case 4 – fire and collision – dashboard

7.8   Conclusion and future scope

In conclusion to this work, automation and IoT have a big role to play in many parts of human lives, and also a major role in saving said lives. Making clever use of it can open up many avenues and scope for future development. The system which has been proposed has the potential to be a major lifesaver, especially due to the high fatality numbers in vehicular accidents.

In the future, this system can be developed to an even more encompassing level, where it can take into account various other indications of accidents, such as smoke in the cabin, gas leakages, etc. as demonstrated by existing works in the field [25]. A system that would allow similar automation in case of fire accidents in homes can also be incorporated. This would be massively helpful for saving and providing medical care to senior citizens who might be living alone and may not be able to manually call for help. This could also help in the case of any person being rendered unable to call for help as well.

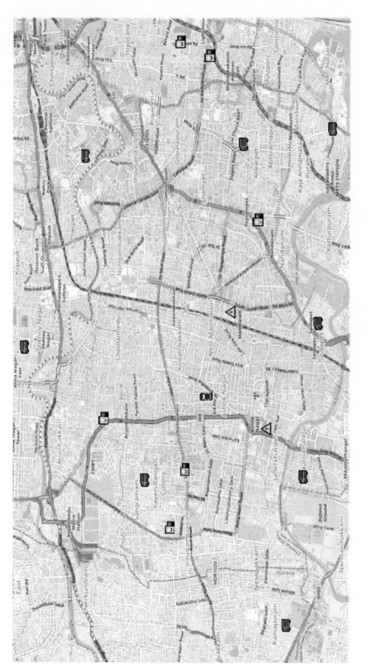

Figure 7.16   Case 4 – fire and collision – world map

References

[1]   E. Nasr, E. Kfoury and D. Khoury, "An IoT approach to vehicle accident detection, reporting, and navigation," in: *2016 IEEE International Multidisciplinary Conference on Engineering Technology* (*IMCET*), 2016, pp. 231–236.

[2]   A. Grundstein, V. Meentemeyer and J. Dowd, "Maximum vehicle car temperatures under different meteorological conditions," *International Journal of Biometeorology*, 53, 2009, 255–261, doi:10.1007/s00484-009-0211-x.

[3]   P.S. Akshay Keshwatkar, V.V. Smitha and R. John Williams, "Sensor based automated accident tracking system," *International Journal of Advanced Research in Computer Science Engineering and Information Technology*, 2, 2014, 43–49.

[4]   D. Covaciu and D.S. Dima, "Solutions for acceleration measurement in vehicle crash tests," *IOP Conference Series: Materials Science and Engineering*, 252, 2017, 012007.

[5]   V. Choksi, K. Nandaniya and M.B. Potdar, "Microcontroller based collision detection and warning system," *International Journal of Advanced Research in Electrical, Electronics and Instrumentation Engineering*, 3, 2014, 9565–9570.

[6]   A. Botta, W. de Donato, V. Persico and A. Pescapé, "Integration of cloud computing and Internet of Things: a survey, future generation computer systems (2015)," *Future Generation Computer Systems*, 56, 2016, 684–700, http://dx.doi.org/10.1016/j.future.2015.09.021

[7]   M. Aktas, M. Hassanalieragh, B. Kantarci, *et al.*, "Health monitoring and management using Internet-of-Things (IoT) sensing with cloud-based processing: opportunities and challenges," in: *IEEE International Conference on Services Computing*, June 2015, pp. 285–292.

[8]   R.K. Kodali and S. Sahu, "MQTT based vehicle accident detection and alert system," in: *2017 3rd International Conference on Applied and Theoretical Computing and Communication Technology* (*iCATccT*), 2017, pp. 186–189.

[9]   S. Sharma and S. Sebastian, "IoT based car accident detection and notification algorithm for general road accidents," *International Journal of Electrical and Computer Engineering (IJECE)*, 9(5), 2019, 4020–4026.

[10] L.P. Maguluri, T. Srinivasarao, M. Syamala, R. Ragupathy and N.J. Nalini, "Efficient smart emergency response system for fire hazards using IoT," *International Journal of Advanced Computer Science and Applications (IJACSA)*, 9(1), 2018, 314.

[11] S. Habib, Z. Afnan, S. Chowdhury, S. Chowdhury and A. Mohsin, "Design and development of IoT based accident detection and emergency response system," in: *CCIOT 2020: Proceedings of the 2020 5th International Conference on Cloud Computing and Internet of Things*, 2020, New York, NY: ACM. 10.13140/RG.2.2.20276.27523.

[12] N. Johnsaida, L.V. Rahul and T. Shalini, "IOT based smart fire emergency response system," *International Journal of Advance Research and Development*, 3(2), 2018, 93–96.

[13] M.M.U. Rathore, A. Ahmad, A. Paul and J. Wan, "Real-time medical emergency response system: exploiting IoT and Big Data for public health," *Journal of Medical Systems*, 40(12), 2016, 283.

[14] L.T. De Paolis, V. De Luca and R. Paiano, "Sensor data collection and analytics with thingsboard and spark streaming," in: *2018 IEEE Workshop on Environmental, Energy, and Structural Monitoring Systems (EESMS)*, 2018.

[15] R.K. Kodali and B.S. Sarjerao, "A low cost smart irrigation system using MQTT protocol," in: *2017 IEEE Region 10 Symposium (TENSYMP)*, 2017, pp. 1–5.

[16] C. Guaragnella, V.D. Lecce, D. Petruzzelli, *et al.*, "Real-time monitoring system for urban wastewater," in: *IEEE Workshop on Environmental, Energy, and Structural Monitoring Systems (EESMS)*, July 2017, pp. 1–5.

[17] S. Henning and W. Hasselbring, "Scalable and reliable multi-dimensional sensor data aggregation in data streaming architectures," *Data-Enabled Discovery and Applications*, 4, 2020, 5.

[18] K. Kenda, B. Kazic, E. Novak and D. Mladenic, "Streaming data fusion for the Internet of Things," *Sensors (Basel, Switzerland)*, 19(8), 2019, 1955.

[19] S. Valliappan, P. Sivakumar and V. Ananthanarayanan. "Efficient real-time decision making using streaming data analytics in IoT environment," in *ICANI-2018*, 2019, 10.1007/978-981-13-2673-8_19.

[20] K. Poorani, A. Sharmila, G. Sujithra, *et al.*, "IOT based live streaming of vehicle, position accident prevention and detection system," *International Journal of Recent Trends in Engineering and Research*, 9, 2017, 4020.

[21] S. Middelhoek and A. Hoogerwerf, "Smart sensors: when and where?" *Sensors and Actuators*, 8(1), 1985, 39–48.

[22] M.A. Rakhonde, S.A. Khoje and R.D. Komati, "Vehicle collision detection and avoidance with pollution monitoring system using IoT," in: *2018 IEEE Global Conference on Wireless Computing and Networking (GCWCN)*, 2018, pp. 75–79.

[23] S. Ahmad and P. Scott, Real-Time Anomaly Detection for Streaming Analytics, *arXiv:1607.02480v1 [cs.AI]*, Jul 2016.

[24] P. Raut and V. Sachdev, "Car accident notification system based on Internet of Things," *International Journal of Computer Applications (0975-8887)*, 107(17), 2014, 29–31.

[25] Dhanlakshmi and S.L. Ezil, "Instance vehicle monitoring and tracking with Internet of Things using Arduino," *International Journal on Smart Sensing and Intelligent Systems*, 10, 2017, pp. 123–135.

Chapter 8

Applying streaming analytics methods on edge and fog device clusters

T. Subha[1], R. Ranjana[2], S. Usha[3], P. Pavithra[2] and Advaith Krishna[2]

Abstract

IoT consists of millions of devices that range from voice assistants to smart meter, in store beacons, any touchable devices, etc., and these IoT devices are flooding the world. A study report says that it is expected to touch around 75 billion IoT devices by 2025. Huge amounts of data are being collected from all these devices and the problem is what to do with this data and how to analyse the data? The two possible solutions are edge computing and fog computing. Both the technologies leverage the computing capabilities to the local network. So that it is easy to carry out the heavy computation tasks locally within the network and this image is equal to the work carried out in cloud. Data can be processed in a fog node or in the IoT gateway which is located within the LAN in fog computing. Data can be processed in sensor or on any device itself in edge computing without transferring the data to anywhere. In such a way, the streaming analytics platform helps to build a model that helps to collect and analyse the data to infer the useful findings within an IoT device. Our proposed chapter will outline the contribution of edge and fog computing in streaming analytics or frameworks.

8.1 Introduction

Computing in today's world has revolutionized to a greater extent, bringing in flexibility and ease of use in many engineering and non-engineering domains. Edge and fog computing are the recent trends in computing which have found various applications across the globe. Similarly, data analytics has also changed the way businesses are functioning and progressing, as lots of insights into data is gained by applying analytics. Stream analytics, specifically used for analyzing data streams,

[1]Department of Computational Intelligence, SRM Institute of Science and Technology, India
[2]Department of Information Technology, Sri Sairam Engineering College, India
[3]Department of Computer Science and Engineering, Rajarajeshwari College of Engineering, India

is proving useful across real-time applications. This chapter aims to address how edge computing and fog computing paradigms are useful in data stream analytics. The various methods and techniques used for the same. The challenges encountered in terms of deployment and the scope are also discussed.

8.1.1   Introduction to Edge computing

Edge computing has changed the way several of devices around the world handle, process, and deliver data. Edge-computing systems are being driven by the rapid growth of devices that are connected through Internet and their applications that demand processing on real time.

Edge computing refers to the data processing at the network's periphery, or edge. That is computations and relevant data storage are kept near to the devices, rather than placing them in a remote server. This will greatly reduce the overhead involved in data transmission.

Edge computing and cloud computing work well together. The cloud manages the network, while edge computing ensures service continuity.

The edge device is given the responsibility of handling and distributing data storage, control and data transmission proximal to the end user. Edge computing has gained prominence due to the expansion of Internet of Things (IoT) devices that connect to the internet to either get or store data to the cloud. As a result, deploying edge computing in a network improves the network in a variety of ways. Edge computing, according to Gartner, is: "a part of a distributed computing topology in which information processing is located close to the edge – where things and people produce or consume that information." In the case of cloud and IoT services, edge computing is a term that defines technologies that allow computations or services to take place at the network's periphery, on both downstream and upstream data [1]. The term "edge" refers to any device that is placed user and cloud servers (Figure 8.1).

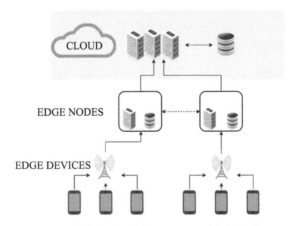

Figure 8.1   Sample representation of edge computing

8.1.2   Introduction to fog computing

Fog computing is an emerging technology that provides the benefits of cloud computing to devices' periphery for faster data analytics. As a result, fog computing is being used to enable a new set of services and the associated applications that need localized and timely decision making. Fog computing has characteristics like location edge deployment, location consciousness and a large number of nodes that are geographically dispersed, as well as heterogeneity, which enables greater mobility, lower latency, and real-time interaction [2]. Fog computing has a de-centralized structure that falls somewhere between the cloud and data producing devices. This adaptable structure allows users to place resources, such as applications and the data they generate, in logical locations to improve performance. The adaptable structure intends to locate basic analytic services at the network's periphery, closer to where they are required. Data will travel a shorter distance across the network as a result of this, resulting in improved performance and network efficiency. Fog computing is an excellent solution for latency-sensitive IoT applications. Several researchers and organizations have defined fog computing from a variety of perspectives, despite the fact that the term was first coined by Cisco. The Open Fog Consortium defines fog computing as "a system-level horizontal architecture that distributes computing, storage, control, and networking resources and services anywhere along the continuum from Cloud to Things" (Figure 8.2).

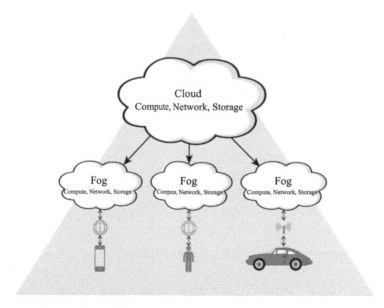

Figure 8.2   Schematic representation of fog computing

8.2   Stream analytics in edge and fog computing

8.2.1   *What is edge analytics?*

Edge analytics is a method of collecting and analyzing data. It avoids the waiting time needed for the data to be sent and returned from a server after processing. This involves performing automated analytical computations on the devices like a sensor or a switch. Edge analytics had become popular in recent years due to the advent of IoT and the connected devices. Edge analytics, in contrast to traditional analytics models, emphasizes speed and decentralization, and thus ignores traditional methods for collecting large amounts of data [3]. It is inextricably linked to the prominence that IoT has gained and is also seen as a viable future technology.

Because of technology like 5G networks, with the advancement of the Internet and web connectivity, edge analytics has become a more practical concept. It has evolved in part as a result of the demands of IoT networks for quick response times and data analytics. Other connected devices, such as smart technology, would be ineffective if their data analysis process as a whole consisted of forwarding information back to the central location, where it will be processed and returned. Edge analytics, on the other hand, increases the efficiency of the process by performing the majority of the on-site examination, only sending the most important data back to a central server, typically in a nearby connected network switch or device.

8.2.2   *Analytics in fog computing*

By diversifying cloud capabilities to the network's edge, fog computing brings analytics to the source of the data. This enables instantaneous action and real-time processing. Instead of sending copious amount of raw data to the cloud, only alerts and exceptions are sent back by the fog system, which sorts and indexes the data locally [4].

The Internet of Everything (IoE) has paved the way for a slew of applications with a high data rate in real time that necessitate a novel technique that we refer to as "fog."

Fog analytics will necessitate a network architecture that is adaptable with a few elements in the cloud, for example, policy, and data processing functions that operate in real time moves to the edge. Data that is not as time-sensitive can still be stored and for the long term, it was analyzed in the cloud.

8.3   Edge computing and its applications

There are numerous reasons why data should be processed and analyzed at the edge. This reduces the need for communication between client and server that are distributed at remote places, resulting in lower latency. Here are some of the innovative applications of edge computing [5].

8.3.1 Smart cities

Without edge computing technology, smart cities will be nothing more than a pipe dream. Edge computing devices collect data in order to perform basic processing tasks, which is the core of smart city development. Autonomous vehicles in smart cities are changing the quality of life of people in metropolitan cities [6]. However, the futuristic cities must change in infrastructure to handle and accommodate the various gadgets that collect and process data for the smart edge applications.

8.3.2 Manufacturing with edge

Edge computing enables industrial machinery to make decisions without the need for human intervention. The decentralized design helps save time and money. Edge computing developed the architecture for machine learning networks, so robotics-driven manufacturing is also possible.

8.3.3 Healthcare

Edge computing in healthcare aims to improve connectivity between machine-to-machine and machine-to-human interaction. With IoT devices capable of delivering massive amounts of patient-generated health data (PGHD), healthcare providers could gain continuous access to vital data about their patients rather than interacting with limited data. Devices can be used to collect and process data during disease diagnosis and treatment. Medical data as it is a sensitive data has many regulatory measures in place when it comes to sharing and each country have defined their own measures for the same. However, augmented with techniques like blockchain, edge, could provide a better solution [7].

8.3.4 AI virtual assistant

Edge computing eliminates the need for artificial intelligence virtual assistants to send processing and data requests to a centralized server. They can instead distribute the load across multiple edge data centers while still performing some computations locally. By incorporating edge computing architecture into their systems, organizations can improve overall performance and reduce inactivity. The proliferation of localized data servers for Cloud Computing has made it easier for services to expand their network reach and position themselves to get the most out of their data assets.

8.3.5 Augmented reality devices

When augmented reality (AR) is used in a variety of tasks, it provides the industry with numerous opportunities to save time and money. The most significant impediment to widespread mobile AR adoption is that current devices still have scope for improvement for better computational and visual

performance. In order to accommodate the demand for the real-time requirements of AR, the Edge Computing architecture of AR applications will offload
the computationally intensive algorithms to a high-end PC through a locally
connected network [8]. Wearable AR devices like glasses and headsets are
sometimes used to achieve this effect, but most clients have first seen AR on
their phone screens. Devices are expected to process visual information continuously and join pre-rendered visual components as part of the AR innovation.
This visual data would otherwise be sent back to a cluster of Cloud servers,
where the digital components could be added before being sent back to the
device, if edge computing were not used.

8.4 Use cases for edge computing

8.4.1 AR gadgets

Although most people are more familiar with the term virtual reality, AR is more
recent and has more realistic applications. AR adds digital components to
real-world environments rather than creating an entirely virtual world. Wearable
AR devices such as glasses and headphones are often used to achieve this effect,
but the majority of consumers have had their first AR experience on their smartphone screens. AR has been used by someone who has played games like Pokemon
GO or used a Snapchat or Instagram filter.

AR technology necessitates devices processing visual data in real time and
incorporating pre-rendered visual elements. Without edge computing, this visual
data will have to be sent back to centralized cloud servers for the digital elements to
be applied before being sent back to the user. This setup will eventually result in a
lot of latency. Edge computing enables IoT devices to immediately composite AR
displays, enabling users to look anywhere they want to take in new AR data without
having to wait for them to load [9].

8.4.2 Hospitals

Edge computing brings exciting new possibilities for providing patient care to the
healthcare sector, which has long struggled to incorporate the latest IT solutions.
Instead of interacting with sluggish and incomplete databases, healthcare professionals will theoretically have real-time access to vital information about their
patients thanks to IoT devices capable of providing massive quantities of PGHD.
Medical devices may also be designed to collect and process data as part of the
diagnosis or treatment process.

Edge computing has the potential to revolutionize the delivery of healthcare to
hard-to-reach rural areas. Patients in these areas are often several miles from the
closest health facility, and even though they are seen on-site by a healthcare
practitioner, they do not have access to critical medical records. Edge computing
allows computers to collect, store, and distribute data in real time, and also use their
processing capabilities to make treatment recommendations.

8.4.3   Self-driving cars

Although self-driving cars are unlikely to take over the roads anytime soon, the automotive industry has already invested billions of dollars in research and development [10]. These vehicles would need to collect and analyses large quantities of data about their environment, directions, and weather conditions in order to function safely, not to mention communicate with other vehicles on the road. They will also have to communicate with local municipal networks and feed data back to manufacturers to monitor utilization and maintenance warnings.

Unfortunately, this influx of data will be mixed in with the traffic generated by cellular phones, computers, and a variety of other connected devices. If manufacturers do not implement new computing technologies, bandwidth constraints would be unavoidable as a result of the increased number of vehicles collecting and transmitting data. It is one thing for an office machine to experience awkward lag while connecting to a network; it is another thing entirely for a self-driving vehicle to experience lag when travelling at 65 mph on a freeway.

8.5   Edge computing platform for stream analytics

Stream processing, which allows the processing and analysis of events or streams of events in real-time, is one of the technologies that is increasingly being used to support data processing and analytics from the edge to the core. In fact, stream processing serves a dual purpose in edge data processing. It can be used to build low-latency data ingestion applications, data collection, and processing at the edge from streaming IoT sources, and data streaming to a centralized system for long-term storage and analysis. While much of the analytics done at the edge entails diagnostic analysis, such as filtering and monitoring, as well as real-time metric and measurement analysis, According to data from 451 Research, Edge-based IoT analytics workloads are becoming more sophisticated, with a shift away from rules-based actions and toward AI and machine learning.

While the massive amounts of data and compute power required to train machine learning models make them unsuitable for edge computing, inference – or applying the trained models to new data – is a perfect fit for data as it is generated. Anomaly detection models, in particular, can be pushed down and executed directly on edge devices to generate warnings that elicit immediate action, while the data that triggers the alerts can also be sent to central data processing locations for further review.

8.5.1   Edge and fog analytics platforms

This section describes the major framework or platforms available for edge and fog analytics.

AWS Greengrass – is a framework that has the following specific key components. They are

1. Lambda functions – known as anonymous functions, the role of these functions is to create response whenever a local event happens in an edge device.
2. Inference from machine learning – this makes learning easier for greengrass as amazon cloud site is used for learning.
3. IoT core – used to restrict data transmission within the same network, by using the core authentication engine.

Moreover, any change in the local databases is synchronized with the cloud. Since the usage of lambda functions guarantees minimal response time and local processing, offline services can also be provided. The lambda functions can be coded specific to a device and application and hence overall development cost can be minimized.

Cisco Fog Director – is specifically used to manage IoT analytics applications based on Fog. It has a good amount of APIs that is supported by a web programming interface for easy management. The major parameters of this model are:

1. hassle free integration and rapid adaptability
2. round the clock IOT application monitoring
3. excellent service management
4. Ad hoc debugging and assistance

Hence, it provides an analytics solution that is capable of providing operational efficiency and enhanced application performance.

Cisco IOx – it is an edge analytics platform predominantly based on CISCO IOx framework and Fog director. It provides the following services for edge development.

1. Managing the lifecycle of IOT applications
2. Providing platform as a service
3. Used to deploy docker containers
4. VPN and IPsec
5. Aligned with IOx client tool

Foghorn – Foghorn is a promising venture in edge analytics. The objective is to provide data analytics on streams, proximal to the end user. Basically it is suited for closed loop edge solutions. It can be easily deployed in varied devices. The features that are provided by Foghorn are:

- Data can be gathered from local sensors
- Unique operational technology
- Local machine learning
- Processing for domain-specific language
- Cloud independent monitoring
- Easy to maintain the deployed instance
- Consumes less bandwidth

Crosser – provides an edge analytics solution framework that can be integrated with any of the IoT application with less effort. It has a robust built in module for orchestration. It has the facility to gather data from sensors and transfer the same to other on premise or remote devices for further processing. It has the following additional capabilities:

- Generation of meta data
- Data cleaning
- Anomaly and outlier detection
- Notification services
- Low bandwidth consumption
- Cloud independent
- Optimal network cost

Swim.ai – specifically built for distributed analytic applications, it uses machine learning for processing real time edge analytics. The processing engine is built using the convolutional neural networks for analyzing the IoT stream data. It has the capacity to train itself from the gathered edge data. So it does the following with minimum effort:

- Predicting events
- System management
- Proactive failure management
- Identifying patterns in activities

Macchina.io – is a solution framework that can effectively manage on premises and cloud based resources as it provides edge analytics software with remote management and monitoring. Based on the JavaScript engine, it has robust communication for IOT applications. The major advantage of using this is that there is no lock-in with hardware, robust software framework and reduced deployment cost. The additional advantage is that remote access to edge devices is made possible through web interfaces and mobile applications.

EdgeX Foundry – is a plug and play software platform that is independent of the platform and is open source framework. It is interoperable and collaborative based on Linux operating system. Cloud independence is achieved through IP specific and non-IP-specific micro services. The key features provided are:

- Data orchestration
- Management of edge data
- System management at the edge
- Edge analytics

Edgent – is an application platform incubated as open source Apache product. Therefore, different edge devices are used for building EDGENT. It acts as a robust

Table 8.1   Comparison of various edge software

Software	Machine learning	Cloud agnostic	Open source	Core IoT support
Greengrass	√	X	X	√
Cisco fog detector	X	X	X	√
Cisco IOx	X	√	X	√
Foghorn	√	√	X	√
Crosser.io	√	X	X	X
Swim.ai	√	X	X	X
Macchina.io	X	X	X	√
EdgeX Foundry	X	√	√	√
Edgent	X	√	√	√

back end for an edge application. Communication within edgent is done using various types of message services like

- MQTT
- IBM Watson IOT
- HTTP
- JDBC
- KAFKA

Edgent is also capable of linking with stream analytics solution like Storm, Flink, SAMZA, and IBM streams. Edgent uses connectors to interface with other entities. A comparison among edge software and analytics is shown in Table 8.1.

8.6   Applications of edge computing

8.6.1   Self-driving cars

When a driverless car suddenly sees a person crossing, it must almost instantaneously take the decision of stopping the vehicle. The decision however could not be delayed by contacting the server and waiting for a response. Edge technology comes as an optimal solution for such use cases where quick response is definitely needed.

8.6.2   In hospitals

Monitoring of vital health parameters for patients, who are critically disabled due to illness, heavily relies upon wearable devices. These devices can monitor the vital patients sign and alter the healthcare personnel or the caretaker as when it is required. Here again the decision making should not be delayed and must be taken immediately. Any delay in a fraction of second can also cause the life of a patient. Hence, edge computing is an ideal choice.

8.6.3   In cloud gaming

Cloud gaming is the most preferred mode of gaming wherein live status of the game is updated to each user. If a user experiences delay in getting updates, then probably he may lose interest and quality of experience. So gaming software have taken up edge computing to avoid the latency experienced in conventional methods [11].

8.6.4   In the management of traffic

Edge computing can help cities handle traffic more efficiently. Optimizing bus frequency in response to demand variability, controlling the opening and closing of extra lanes, and, in the future, managing automated car flows are all examples of this. Edge computing eliminates the need to transmit voluminous data to a central server and hence the delay of transmission and the cost for infrastructure and bandwidth are averted.

8.6.5   In smart homes

IoT systems capture and process data from all over the house in smart homes. This information is often transmitted to a centralized remote server, where it is processed and stored. However, there are issues with the current architecture in terms of

- cost
- latency
- security

As data is processed at the edge devices, the transmission time is reduced in the smart home application. On similar lines, the response of virtual assistant devices will also be quick.

8.7   Challenges in implementing stream analytics for edge computing

Even though edge computing has a lot of potential, however, several of the features and methods needs to be standardized and defined. This will enhance more adoption of edge computing and will increase its applications. The following are the minor issues that need to be addresses while building an edge application [12].

Naming: varied applications are run in an Edge device and each of them have their own method and structure. In edge computing, naming is important to identify the device and then only it is possible to communicate with them. But presently there are no standards for providing a naming convention in edge. This creates confusion while working with edge devices and the protocols that are used with edge computing.

Programmability: edge computing has a heterogeneous architecture. As a result, the runtime and programming language are distinct from those found in other established architectures. This makes programming for edge devices a cumbersome task. Comparing with cloud, the cloud users can write and deploy code in a specific language. Transparency is also more in Cloud.

Edge device management: edge device management is not easy because of

- functionalities that are complex
- demand for scalability
- highly heterogeneous architecture
- security
- performance of the infrastructure

Edge orchestration is expected to have self-reliant recovery methods to reduce the need for manual correction. As it is designed, the edge devices are expected to move and collect and process data. Managing the devices while they are mobile produces problems that are to be addressed.

8.8   Fog computing and stream analytics

Exploring IoT data streams provided by smart applications requires converting data analytics for optimistic business decisions. This will also be used for developing new infrastructure and create new ways of urban governance. The most frequently used sensors in IOT devices are

- proximity sensors
- light sensors
- microphones
- camera
- gyroscopes
- accelerometers
- temperature
- humidity

These devices will be geographically spread in smart cities and can produce a vast amount of data, making it hard to manage, capture, process, and analyze such data in a well-timed manner. In a smart city environment, effective communication is made possible with the residents by analyzing the IoT data streams and thereby obtaining location data and improved efficiency, and lowered costs [13]. This is a hard task and needs a new IoT architecture that can execute streaming analytical tasks in parallel and can deliver reliable results in real time. Although there are several issues in moving IOT analytics to cloud, most of the previous research have focused on that.

IoT implementations pose new technical challenges. First, the decision to deploy applications like smart city with the existing cloud architecture, as the smart city has components that are static and dynamic. The alternate architectural solutions involving a combination of edge-fog-cloud can also be considered.

Second, the present data cycles offer low latency and the same is expected while managing IoT applications that perform the analytics. Using the alternate architecture, the entire smart city infrastructure can be built to work on a single analytical system.

The edge-fog-cloud setup can be used as new architectural solution that will eventually provide a better integration of IoT devices and their analytics [14].

Most of the analytics in IoT data are in its primitive stage and requires processing of varied inputs at different time frames. Having observed that it is very obvious that IoT analytics and their possible effects are gaining focus in recent research literature only.

Analyzing large volumes of incoming IoT data streams is difficult. Many different types of architectures that use stream processing, micro, and batch processing are reported in the literature. While choosing an IoT architecture, the most important consideration is to strike a balance between the two basic performance metrics namely throughput and delay. In order to get a balance of these two metrics, IoT streams are generally moved to the cloud for storage and later taken up in batches for analytic processing.

Experiments have shown that batch processing yields better results when large data volume needs to processed, as in case of IoT analytics and also constrained by throughput and latency. The Hadoop MapReduce framework does exactly the same. It distributes data over cheap commodity cluster of servers and is efficient for batch processing tasks.

Spark is another example of a system that is capable of batch processing with data that are geographically distributed. IoT data streams can also be handled as micro batch buffers when performance improvement is needed. However, spark can limit the size of the processing batch and order the tasks irrespective of their arrival time. But this will result in latency due to the time spent by the data stream in the pipeline waiting for tis turn to be processed.

Stream-oriented systems, on the other hand, generally provide good response for time critical tasks; however, they tend to incur heavy processing costs. The cost of dealing with continuous data stream like that of IoT is also high. Data is seldom put to rest in stream-oriented processing architectures. The idea is to decrease the time spent by the data in the data pipeline before it gets processed. The three common frameworks that are based on stream processing are [15]:

- Storm
- Samza
- Flink

Any IoT architecture solution is expected to provide better analytics application and device integration. These solutions are seeing a shift in their basic structure. As IoT data streams arrive to a computational node, several algorithms are used to get value from it. But such an extraction of valuable data from a stream in not an easy task, given that the devices are mobile and data does not come continuously from a single location. The streaming algorithms need to function under time and storage constraints. However, few successful IOT data streams frameworks are Massive Online Analysis (MOA), Scalable Advanced Massive Online Analysis (SAMOA), and skit-multiflow.

IOT framework can get benefitted from an integrated solution based on edge, fog, and cloud computing. This integrated framework is capable of processing and handling IoT data streams. The data streams can be analyzed and visualized for better decision making [16,17].

Such an integrated framework supports an analytics anywhere architecture [16]. This framework works in an asynchronous way with data streams and makes maintenance easy and more scalable.

8.9   Characteristics of fog computing for analytics

Recently applications are being moved from cloud to fog and this makes the different IoT applications and services get a new dimension and hence the following features of fog computing analytics have emerged. They are listed below:

1. *Cognitive analytics*: fog-based analytics tends to improve client response and has a better edge in data handling than the cloud. As the applications are at the end devices, this proximity produces better customer relation [18].
2. *Distributed environment*: fog computing relies on virtualized resources for proving storage, computation, and network. It has different nodes and sensors with varied functionalities that are distributed geographically [19].
3. *Low latency service*: many of today's applications like smart TVs and online gaming apps have latency bound requirement at the edge of the core network [20]. There are also certain time critical applications that also require real-time interaction with fog edge sensors. Hence, fog applications are expected to provide low latency and capability for real-time processing.
4. *Mobility*: is an added advantage of fog, as it helps mobile devices to interact directly using software-defined networking (SDN) protocols, thereby the host and location identities are decoupled. Fog is also found to be beneficial in applications involving large-scale sensors.
5. *Interoperability*: for example, mobile gateways and wireless access protocols can be used as fog nodes. Also Fog nodes must be able to work along with varied operating environments to provide predictive analytics based on stream data.

Fog computing architecture

Fog computing plays a major role in industrial IoT applications as it helps to analyse huge amounts of data from multiple IoT devices. Generally, the fog computing architecture consists of data plane and control plane. They are elaborated as below:

Data plane: The fog data plane will control and monitor:

- Control of bandwidth
- Caching at edge
- Management of data centers
- Data transmission between devices

Control plane: The fog control plane will handle the following:

- Status of network devices
- Storage management
- Session control
- Stream analytics
- IoT-based real-time data processing

A sample architecture for fog stream analytics is proposed and this model was being inspired and derived from the cloud streaming model. There are six layers divided based on their functionalities and are discussed as under:

- An application layer that frames the objectives and holds the logic of the fog computing service.
- Processing layer: it handles the processing tasks required by the application. Examples of such stream engines are Storm, Flink, and Streaming. Basically, built for cloud, these processing engines will be efficient for Fog too.
- Data layer: handles the storage of data in terms of files, databases, caches, warehouses, and datalakes. Many NoSQL databases designed for handling Big Data analytics can be used for fog servers, However, they require an additional management for local networks too.
- Resource management layer needs to address the issues of resource utilization, allocation, and energy management of devices.
- Virtualization layer manages the virtualized hardware resources like computing, storage, and network. In addition, it needs to provide the interfaces required for data caching, sensing, and mobility.
- Physical layer of a fog system has heterogeneous and hierarchal architecture with varied devices.

8.10 Challenges in adopting edge computing for IoT analytics

Edge computing presents management challenges that data centers and cloud computing do not. Spreading mission-critical applications and data to the edge poses scale and performance challenges, requiring edge environments to function efficiently and reliably regardless of the number of instances introduced. Each implementation of Edge computing poses its own set of problems [21]. They do, however, share the following characteristics to varying degrees.

1. Performance: monitoring and management of edge performance. This needs monitoring data transfer from the customer to the edge and vice versa and the movement of data from the edge to the cloud server.
2. Control: When there is a problem with the network or its down, edge locations go dark, posing challenges in managing physical approach, controlling IT

hardware, taking care of the environment (power and cooling), tracking devices, assessing, isolating, as well as resolving problems.

3. Scale: Multiple monitors are required at each remote edge location to gain a better understanding of the health and status of each IT component, encompassing everything from physical approach to power and cooling to servers as well as network equipment.
4. Security: Control aspects, as well as all aspects of access, threat, and data security.
5. Heterogeneity: The applications, services, and infrastructure involved are varied and lead to decentralized control and management. Such fragmented control may incur high costs and need expert resources.
6. Organization: Controlling edge in the exact same manner that a traditional data center is controlled, with distinct teams in charge of various "slices" of the infrastructure, results in a lot of inefficiencies in terms of support, skills, resources, costs, and the availability of the business are all factors to consider.

8.11   Challenges in adopting fog computing

1. Privacy: When there are numerous networks involved, privacy concerns are always present. Due to the fact that fog computing relies on wireless technology; network privacy is a major concern.
2. Security: Fog computing security issues arise as a result of the large number of devices linked to fog nodes and at various gateways.
3. Authentication issues: Because these services are provided on a large scale, authentication is one of the most troublesome aspects of fog computing. Fog service providers can include a wide range of entities, including end users, cloud service providers, and Internet service providers.
4. Energy consumption: Fog computing consumes a lot of energy because there are so many fog nodes in the fog environment that they all need energy to work [22].
5. Fog servers: Fog servers should be placed correctly in order to provide the best possible service. Before putting the fog node in place, the company should analyze the demand and work that it does. This will help to lower the maintenance costs.

8.12   Conclusion

Cloud computing had paved way for edge and fog computing that are evolving in a faster pace in today's World. IoT applications are also becoming common, making smarter devices, and thereby providing room for analytics in personal and social context. The usage of IoT is seen in a wide range of domains from smart cities, smart agriculture to smart waste management. This chapter had outlined a brief introduction to both edge and fog computing, highlighting the applications of both. The chapter also discusses the integration frameworks required for IoT analytics in edge and fog computing. Finally, the challenge that needs to be faced is also elaborated.

References

[1] A. Filali, A. Abouaomar, S. Cherkaoui, A. Kobbane and M. Guizani, "Multi-access edge computing: a survey," *IEEE Access*, vol. 8, pp. 197017–197046, 2020, doi: 10.1109/ACCESS.2020.3034136.

[2] P. Habibi, M. Farhoudi, S. Kazemian, S. Khorsandi and A. Leon-Garcia, "Fog computing: a comprehensive architectural survey," *IEEE Access*, vol. 8, pp. 69105–69133, 2020, doi: 10.1109/ACCESS.2020.2983253

[3] A. Majeed, "Efficient edge analytics in Internet-of-Things (IoT)," in: *2017 IEEE 7th Annual Computing and Communication Workshop and Conference (CCWC)*, 2017, pp. 1–4, doi: 10.1109/CCWC.2017.7868458.

[4] N.M. Gonzalez, W.A. Goya, R. de Fatima Pereira, *et al.*, "Fog computing: data analytics and cloud distributed processing on the network edges," in: *2016 35th International Conference of the Chilean Computer Science Society (SCCC)*, 2016, pp. 1–9, doi: 10.1109/SCCC.2016.7836028.

[5] K. Cao, Y. Liu, G. Meng and Q. Sun, "An overview on edge computing research," *IEEE Access*, vol. 8, pp. 85714–85728, 2020, doi: 10.1109/ACCESS.2020.2991734.

[6] L. Kuang, T. Gong, S. OuYang, H. Gao and S. Deng, "Offloading decision methods for multiple users with structured tasks in edge computing for smart cities," *Future Generation Computer Systems*, vol. 105, pp. 717–729, 2020.

[7] P. Dong, Z. Ning, M.S. Obaidat, *et al.*, "Edge computing based healthcare systems: enabling decentralized health monitoring in Internet of Medical Things," *IEEE Network*, vol. 34, no. 5, pp. 254–261, September/October 2020, doi:10.1109/MNET.011.1900636.

[8] S. Sukhmani, M. Sadeghi, M. Erol-Kantarci and A. El Saddik, "Edge caching and computing in 5G for mobile AR/VR and tactile Internet," *IEEE MultiMedia*, vol. 26, no. 1, pp. 21–30, 2019, doi: 10.1109/MMUL.2018.2879591.

[9] X. Hou, Y. Lu and S. Dey, "Wireless VR/AR with edge/cloud computing," in: *2017 26th International Conference on Computer Communication and Networks (ICCCN)*, 2017, pp. 1–8, doi: 10.1109/ICCCN.2017.8038375.

[10] S. Liu, L. Liu, J. Tang, B. Yu, Y. Wang and W. Shi, "Edge computing for autonomous driving: opportunities and challenges," *Proceedings of the IEEE*, vol. 107, no. 8, pp. 1697–1716, 2019, doi:10.1109/JPROC.2019.2915983.

[11] X. Zhang, H. Chen, Z. Yangchao, *et al.*, "Improving cloud gaming experience through mobile edge computing," *IEEE Wireless Communications*, vol. 26, no. 4, pp. 178–183, 2019, doi:10.1109/MWC.2019.1800440.

[12] S. Dey, A. Mukherjee, H.S. Paul and A. Pal, "Challenges of using edge devices in IoT computation grids," in: *2013 International Conference on Parallel and Distributed Systems*, 2013, pp. 564–569, doi: 10.1109/ICPADS.2013.101.

[13]   H. Hong, P. Tsai, A. Cheng, M.Y.S. Uddin, N. Venkatasubramanian and C. Hsu, "Supporting Internet-of-Things analytics in a fog computing platform," in: *2017 IEEE International Conference on Cloud Computing Technology and Science* (*CloudCom*), 2017, pp. 138–145, doi: 10.1109/CloudCom. 2017.45.

[14]   R.S. Sanketh, Y. MohanaRoopa and P.V.N. Reddy, "A survey of fog computing: fundamental, architecture, applications and challenges," in: *2019 Third International Conference on I-SMAC* (*IoT in Social, Mobile, Analytics and Cloud*) (*I-SMAC*), 2019, pp. 512–516, doi: 10.1109/I-SMAC47947.2019.9032645.

[15]   H. Isah, T. Abughofa, S. Mahfuz, D. Ajerla, F. Zulkernine and S. Khan, "A survey of distributed data stream processing frameworks," *IEEE Access*, vol. 7, pp. 154300–154316, 2019, doi: 10.1109/ACCESS.2019.2946884.

[16]   H. Cao and M. Wachowicz, "Analytics everywhere for streaming IoT data," in: *2019 Sixth International Conference on Internet of Things: Systems, Management and Security* (*IOTSMS*), 2019, pp. 18–25, doi: 10.1109/ IOTSMS48152.2019.8939171.

[17]   J. Ren, H. Guo, C. Xu and Y. Zhang, "Serving at the edge: a scalable IoT architecture based on transparent computing," *IEEE Network*, vol. 31, no. 5, pp. 96–105, 2017, doi: 10.1109/MNET.2017.1700030.

[18]   M. Chiang and T. Zhang, "Fog and IoT: an overview of research opportunities," *IEEE Internet of Things Journal*, vol. 3, no. 6, pp. 854–864, 2016.

[19]   F. Bonomi, R. Milito, P. Natarajan and J. Zhu, "Fog computing: a platform for internet of things and analytics," *Studies in Computational Intelligence*, vol. 546, pp. 169–186, 2014.

[20]   P. More, "Review of implementing fog computing," *International Journal of Research in Engineering and Technology*, vol. 4, no. 6, pp. 335–338, 2015.

[21]   W. Shi, J. Cao, Q. Zhang, Y. Li and L. Xu, "Edge computing: vision and challenges," *IEEE Internet of Things Journal*, vol. 3, no. 5, pp. 637–646, 2016, doi:10.1109/JIOT.2016.2579198.

[22]   F. Haouari, R. Faraj and J.M. AlJa'am, "Fog computing potentials, applications, and challenges," in: *2018 International Conference on Computer and Applications* (*ICCA*), 2018, pp. 399–406, doi: 10.1109/COMAPP. 2018.8460182.

Chapter 9

Delineating IoT streaming analytics

Pethuru Raj[1] and Jaspher Willsie Kathrine[2]

Abstract

With the massive surge in the number of developed and deployed IoT devices and sensors in mission-critical environments such as smart homes, hospitals, hotels, warehouses, retail stores, railway stations, ports, etc., the speed, size, scope and structure of IoT data is evolving fast. In this chapter, we specifically focused on capturing, cleaning and crunching IoT streaming data in real time to extract actionable insights for producing real-time and real-world IT and business services and applications.

Streaming data has become an important component of worldwide business houses. The enterprise data architecture has to take this trend into account in order to be futuristic and flexible. Due to the exponential growth of Internet of Things (IoT) devices and sensors, enterprises are keenly strategizing afresh to accommodate IoT data. Typically, IoT data and other data sources such as web applications, security logs, and device interactions are streaming data. Meticulously receiving and subjecting streaming data deftly and quickly to make sense/money out of it are being seen as a viable activity for any enterprise to keep up its edge over its competitors. Analysis of streaming data gives a huge understanding into timely and trustworthy insights for enterprises. Decision-makers and other senior management people can take both tactical and strategically sound decisions with all the clarity and confidence.

In this chapter, we are going to dig deeper in order to explain how all sorts of IoT streaming data can be subjected to a variety of studies with the intention of emitting out actionable insights. Also, how the knowledge discovered gets disseminated to participating and contributing IoT devices to exhibit a kind of adaptive behavior. Also, the insights extracted can be supplied to senior management

[1]Edge AI Division, Reliance Jio Platforms, Bangalore, India
[2]Department of Computer Science and Engineering, Karunya Institute of Technology and Sciences, India

people to visualize and realize next-generation cognitive IoT products, solutions, and services.

9.1   Introduction

Streaming technologies are gaining the prominence as the amount of streaming data getting produced is growing exponentially. The number of distributed and different sources for streaming data is growing rapidly. Especially, with the onslaught of IoT devices and sensors, the streaming data sources go up sharply. Therefore, to capture, cleanse, and crunch streaming data, the industry is betting on a variety of powerful and pioneering streaming technologies. Thus, in the recent past, there is a faster adoption and adaption of streaming technologies and tools. Streaming platforms, frameworks, accelerators, appliances, specialized engines, processes, practices, and patterns for making sense out of streaming data are flourishing with the overwhelming support of product and tool vendors. Research labs, academic institutions, IT organizations, and business houses are keenly investing their time, treasure, and talent in procuring the right expertise, education, and experience in skillfully tackling the surge in streaming data beneficially. Intelligence squeezed out of data comes handy for start-ups, business behemoths, citizen-friendly governments, and customer-centric organizations, service providers, etc. for adequately and adroitly planning and preparing for fresh possibilities and opportunities.

9.2   The emergence of sophisticated IoT systems, applications, and environments

A variety of business workloads, integrated platforms, and server farms have been worked upon. That is, server machines and user machines besides software applications are the prime components of the IT world. Now, electronics, equipment, instruments, machineries, robots and other resource-intensive devices in the everyday environments are parts in the mainstream computing. That is, software applications are being deployed and run on these everyday devices, which are increasingly instrumented to be interconnected and intellectual. There are smartphones, wearables, and other input/output (I/O) devices to interact with software applications running on servers and resource-intensive devices. Thus, IoT devices are being enabled to serve as web and mobile servers. IoT sensors turn out to be data generators. Precisely speaking, IoT devices and sensors have become an important ingredient in the expanding IT world. With these improvisations, IoT devices-enabled edge/fog computing started to flourish these days. With the deployment of billions of IoT devices and sensors across sensitive and mission-critical environments, there is a huge amount of multi-structured data, which has to be methodically analysed to extract actionable insights in time. Thus, the domain of IoT data analytics is gaining prominence.

9.3 The key layers in IoT architecture

There are different layers and levels in the IoT architecture as explained below:

o *IoT devices* – In this layer, there are IoT devices and sensors in a plenty for collecting environmental and device data. Due to the unprecedented adoption of miniaturization technologies, Miniscule, disappearing yet indispensable IoT elements are getting produced and deployed across. Sensors have the inherent capability to form ad hoc networks dynamically to share their distinct capabilities and data. The prime idea behind the grand success of the IoT paradigm is that the IoT phenomenon could convert commonly found and cheap articles in our daily locations into digitized artifacts systematically. That is, all kinds of electrical, mechanical and physical systems in our hotels, homes, hospitals, etc. are digitized through the smart application of digitization and edge technologies. In short, the IoT paradigm represents scores of pioneering and pathbreaking technologies and tools to transition ordinary things into digital objects, which generate a lot of digital data. Now, with the faster stability of data transmission protocols, IoT sensor and device data gets transmitted to nearby IoT gateways/buses/brokers and any other middleware.

o *Network/gateway layer* – The bridge between IoT device layer and the Cloud layer is this network/gateway layer. This layer acts as the middleware for performing data aggregation/intermediation/enrichment/transformation. There are networking facilities such as LAN/WAN/the Internet to take IoT data from the IoT gateway to cloud-based data analytics platform. Further on, there are lightweight protocols (MQTT, AMQP, COAP, and HTTP) to establish the much-needed communication between IoT gateway and cloud-based servers.

o *Cloud layer* – This represents software-defined cloud environments. There are integrated analytics platforms (big, fast, and streaming data) and artificial intelligence (AI) libraries for knowledge discovery in time. Further on, there are data lakes, and other data stores (SQL, NoSQL, and distributed SQL). Data handling, storage, processing, and analytics are fully accomplished in this layer.

o *Process layer* – The final layer of the IoT analytics architecture is the process layer. This layer is for hosting of different processes, which use the knowledge discovered in the previous layer.

Man-generated data is only 15% and the remaining data gets generated by machines and devices. Thus, for enabling networks, systems, IoT devices and environments to be smart in their operations, outputs and offerings, IoT data has to be subjected to a variety of investigations in order to squeeze out actionable insights in time.

IoT protocols – there are IoT-specific protocols to enable connectivity and data integration.

✓ *Message queuing telemetry transport (MQTT)* – MQTT is a lightweight protocol which fully subscribes to the well-known publish/subscribe architecture.

MQTT broker is the core aspect of this protocol. A small code footprint and minimal network bandwidth in connecting IoT devices with MQTT. MQTT is used in several business domains including manufacturing, automotive, oil and gas and telecommunications. Every IoT device/client/producer includes a subject name while publishing data to the broker. Topics carry the routing information to reach the broker unambiguously. Each IoT device/client/consumer which requires communication such as messages, subscribes to a particular topic and the broker delivers all messages with the matching topic to the consumer.

✓ *Constrained application protocol (CoAP)* – This is a specialized web transfer protocol for use with constrained devices and networks. The CoAP protocol is designed to seamlessly map to existing web protocols such as HTTP. The CoAP protocol provides simple resources discovery, maintains key concepts, and security on the web such as uniform resource identifiers, methods, and media types. It is based on RESTful architecture. All the API calls GET, PUT, POST, DELETE data are possible via URL in the CoAP protocol. CoAP enables IoT device interactions and is used for applications such as machine-to-machine (M2M) applications like building automation and smart energy.

✓ *Advanced messaging queuing protocol (AMQP)* – AMQP is a message-oriented middleware and is an open standard application layer protocol. AMQP supports routing which includes point-to-point and publish-and-subscribe, message orientation, queuing, reliability, and security

✓ *Hypertext transfer protocol (HTTP)* – HTTP is an application-layer protocol. HTTP is used for transmitting hypermedia documents. HTTP protocol was designed for communication between web browsers and web applications, which, in turn, use a collection of web services to be business-critical. HTTP is a standard with well-defined constraints. Most of our everyday interactions on the Internet are powered by HTTP communication protocol.

✓ *Representational state transfer (REST)* – REST is *not* a standard or a specification. REST is the architectural style mostly considered for distributed hypermedia systems. The attributes of a RESTful architecture make it ideal for large interconnected systems like the internet.

✓ *Data distribution service (DDS)* – DDS is a standard applied for real-time IoT analytics since it is scalable and provides high-performance M2M communication. It can be deployed both in low footprint devices and on the cloud system as well.

Thus, IoT devices, sensors, and actuators are the most prominent data collectors. IoT gateways contribute as IoT data aggregators and forwarders. There are IoT devices-specific communication and data transport protocols in plenty. Let us throw some light on the vital ingredients of any IoT architecture.

Edge devices – Collectively IoT devices can output a massive amount of multi-structured data continuously. IoT data usually comes from IoT devices directly or from the attached sensors and actuators. We have an array if multifaceted sensors for monitoring and measuring a variety of useful data like temperature, pressure, presence, gas, humidity, illumination, electricity consumption, cameras, speed-ometer, air quality, motion, and many more. Once the data is acquired from a sensor on a device, there is a need to be able to transmit this data to our nearby or remote cloud storage appliances and to compute machines for storing and processing it at scale. Besides a secure channel between the ground-level IoT devices and cloud servers for ensuring safe data passage, there is a need for competent and integrated data analytics platforms to capture and process of millions of device records per second. If we do not process data as it comes along, we may lose a lot of data-driven value. Besides the core processing, there is a need to filter, enrich, translate, query, aggregate, and route data.

Device data can follow a fixed schema or change frequently. Also, it can be scarce, numeric, or binary. For filtering out redundant and routine data at the source in order not to eat into precious network resources, IoT edge gateways that can handle any data type are being recommended. There are a few open-source solutions such as Apache NiFi, which can comfortably handle more number of devices with masses of data points. Device data is often numeric and hence requires conversions. We may not have the full information about the device data till we start testing it. For example, a reading can be taken from a light and proximity sensor which will be decimal data or whole numbers ranging between 1 and 64,000. This means it is necessary to find out the range of data value. Then, we can build an AVRO schema to ensure data range accuracy. This can let us to query that data on the device in MiNiFi (https://nifi.apache.org/minifi/index.html) or in Apache Calcite (https://calcite.apache.org/) using Apache NiFi at the router or gateway level. The edge devices, Apache NiFi have to be able to receive any types of data like large sets of numbers, large strings, JSON, images, and unstructured data.

Edge processing – This type of proximate processing of IoT edge devices and sensors is gaining prominence. Instead of sending all IoT data to one or more faraway cloud environments to be stocked and processed, local processing is preferred due to some critical requirements such as low latency, bandwidth saving, and data security. Also, real-time data capture, processing, and analytics to arrive at actionable insights in time are being facilitated through edge computing. The Apache NiFi software library installed in edge gateways brings in necessary corrections on edge device data to make it right and relevant to businesses and people. Appropriate alert conditions can be embedded in order to trigger real-time alerts and actions. Doing data collection, cleansing and crunching locally is the new normal with the ready availability of lightweight and lithe software and hardware solutions. To enable more powerful transformations and enrichment, there are competent dataflow management solutions (MiNiFi) that can run on edge devices. Typically, for enabling the much-needed edge processing, one or more servers are being put up in a corner place of manufacturing floors, buildings or campuses. These servers host NiFi server software. Such a setup accomplishes powerful transformation, rule processing, queries, alerting conditions and machine learning classifications and analytics.

Transportation options – The edge data has to be sent to another machine. In between them, there is a need to leverage an IoT middleware solution such as a dataflow management engine. This engine is for the aggregation of data from heterogeneous devices. This then forwards captured data streams to cloud environments (nearby edge clouds, or private/public clouds) for further granular processing and analytics. For transport needs, there are a few tested and tried options. The first is to use MiNiFi's HTTPS transport, which can be used among any IoT middleware. A detailed description of this process is explained in this page (https://www.freecodecamp.org/news/building-an-iiot-system-using-apache-nifi-mqtt-and-raspberry-pi-ce1d6ed565bc/). This ensures secure, fast, and robust transport of device data with full data provenance and lineage and without loss.

The other option is to allow MiNiFi to send data streams via MQTT, which is a fast and open-messaging protocol. Here is an easy-to-understand and use tutorial (https://www.baeldung.com/iot-data-pipeline-mqtt-nifi). The last option is to use MiniFi to send messages directly to Apache Kafka, which supplies a durable queue to store IoT data and allows many consumers to subscribe and receive IoT event data and messages. The best approach is to use MiniFi's S2SHTTPS transport to take IoT data to an Apache NiFi cluster. This process can do more conversation, routing, filtering, aggregating, and cleaning before routing it to a stream processing framework through Apache Kafka. This gives the much-needed flexibility and scalability. Let us digress a bit to throw some light on the IoT architecture.

Streaming data – In the IoT era, the device and sensor ecosystems are growing rapidly. Through their purpose-driven interactions, the variety, velocity, viscosity, virtuosity, and volume of data getting generated and collected are changing fast. Especially IoT data gets generated continuously in large quantity. Therefore, IoT data has to be streamed to target environments such as data storage and analytics platforms to make sense and money out of IoT data. There are also requirements to manage streaming data with the traditional big or batch data. But unlike traditional batch-based data flows, where data is loaded on a scheduled basis (i.e., hourly, daily, or monthly), streaming data flows are quite different.

1. Streaming data is time sensitive and the value is bound to go down with time.
2. Streaming data is typically large in volume.
3. The long-term value of streaming data is not great.

9.4   Delineating streaming analytics

Doing analytics on streaming data using state-of-the-art platform solutions and analytical methods is to bring a bevy of business and technical advantages. Streaming analytics enables you to access, analyze, and act on both historical and streaming data emanating from IoT devices. It helps in determining if there is any issue relating to hardware devices and software systems in specific environments such as manufacturing floors and preventing any future problem.

In any environment, which is stuffed with a number of purpose-specific and agnostic equipment, you want to proactively and preemptively spot and pinpoint any deviation or problem before it becomes a big and irreparable issue. Equipment failure can be fully avoided through such real-time and continuous analytics on equipment and environment data, which is a prime example for streaming data. Predictive maintenance of mission-critical assets is a popular use case for streaming analytics. If there is any threshold break-in on any noteworthy aspect and artifact, then the power of streaming analytics can be realized. With streaming analytics, it is possible to prevent certain events from happening in the first place. You can also predict and detect value-adding business events the moment they occur. This goes a long way in minimizing any business risk. Also, real-time analytics on data streams brings forth a variety of fresh possibilities for existing problems and to visualize and realize fresh opportunities in the form of premium products, solutions and services.

Another point to be noted is that with the emergence of high-performance computing, it is possible to do real-time analytics on big data also. Previously it takes minutes and hours to finish a big data analytics activity. Now, we have physical and virtual supercomputers to remarkably speed up the analytics activity. As told above, due to the faster proliferation of IoT sensors, connected assets, networked embedded systems, cyber physical systems (CPSs), ambient intelligence (AmI) products, sentient materials, consumer electronics, cloudified ICT infrastructures, digital twins, and smart objects, the era of big and fast data has finally dawned. It is therefore important to consider ways and means of tackling them beneficially for businesses as well as societies. With streaming real-time analytics, the following benefits can be reaped:

- Streaming analytics can capture, process, detect, and pinpoint anything important on event data and messages.
- This can work on data coming from different and distributed sources.
- Using prediction capability, streaming analytics can respond to events preemptively and proactively.
- Quickly take decisions and initiate appropriate actions without human intervention and interpretation.
- Spot tactical as well as strategically sound patters and insights to speed up digital transformation.

Precisely speaking, as vividly illustrated in the below figure, streaming analytics enables the real-time detection and articulation of actionable patterns and insights of streaming data. The knowledge discovered gets distributed to actuation and production systems to readily and rewardingly initiate correct actions.

IoT brings a whole new world of data and this insists for streaming analytics in order to bring in deeper automation as shown in Figure 9.1. IoT devices, systems, and applications in association with their streaming analytics can bring forth real digital transformation. There are operational difficulties like a large stream of massive data and security issues. Further on, data has to be made available for use at scale. These practical challenges can be solved to a major extent by employing streaming analytics tools.

Detect patterns & act on real-time insights

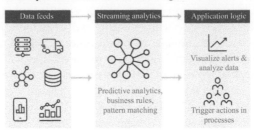

Figure 9.1　Streaming analytics

9.5　Demystifying stream processing

Data that is continuously generated is termed as streaming data. The data generation speed is also on the higher side. A well-known streaming data source is a stream of logs that record events as they happen. When a user clicks on a hyperlink in a web site, it generates an event. When temperature goes above the threshold value, a temperature sensor sends out an event message. There are connected devices, IoT sensors, event-driven microservices, business workloads, software infrastructures, IT infrastructure modules, etc. emitting out a variety of data, which gets streamed to nearby or faraway data analytics platforms.

　　Once upon a time, server machines, desktops, and laptops were connected. But today, all kinds of consumer electronics, smartphones, medical instruments, defense equipment, information appliances, industrial machineries, robots, drones, smartphones, etc. are getting integrated with one another and also with remotely held business applications, IT services, databases, etc. through the Internet communication infrastructure. It is projected that the future Internet will be comprising trillions of digitized entities, billions of electronics devices, and millions of microservices. Digitized entities/elements are being realized through the smart application of edge and digitization technologies on all kinds of physical, mechanical and electrical systems in our everyday environments. The IoT paradigm, therefore, represents the future Internet comprising digitally empowered things. The concept of CPSs is similar to the IoT concept and CPS is all about empowering physical systems at the ground level with the integration of remotely held software services and databases. That is, cloud-integrated physical systems can exhibit certain intelligence in their workings. Digital Twins is also a related topic of study and research. Mission-critical physical systems such as rockets, satellites, medical instruments, equipment, machineries, and robots are having their digital/virtual/cyber versions/representations running in faraway cloud environments. Such a formation goes a long way in expertly building, safeguarding, and sustaining the corresponding ground-level physical entities.

With such a huge number of digital articles and artifacts joining with the already Internet-enabled devices, the variety of streaming data getting generated is bound to go up remarkably. The end-user and edge devices are unceasingly generating thousands or millions of records. This is being touted as a data stream comprising structured, semi-structured and unstructured data. There are multiple data representation, exchange, and persistence formats. JSON and XML are prominent among them. A single streaming data source can generate massive amounts of event data/message per minute. In its raw form, event data is very complicated to work with as it does not have a proper schema and structure. So, using SQL-like query languages to play around with such event data streams is beset with difficulties. Therefore, data needs to be pre-processed. All kinds of basic transitions and transformations have to be performed on raw streaming data to bring in a kind of structure and semblance to that data before it gets properly processed and analyzed.

The rising complexity of stream processing – A streaming data architecture specifies the various software components that enable data ingestion and processing. The architecture has to accommodate the right mechanism to ingest and process large volumes of streaming data emanating from multiple sources. The traditional solutions do batch processing while a streaming data architecture captures and crunches data immediately. That is, it does real-time data analytics to create insights in time. As data value goes down with time, data has to be consumed and analyzed quickly to bring forth actionable insights. In other words, even if it is big data, real-time data analytics is being insisted.

Streaming architectures need to take the unique characteristics of data streams into account. The data volume of streams can be massive (ranging from terabytes to petabytes). Also, data can be semi-structured. Streaming analytics requires a lot of pre-processing before embarking on deeper and decisive analytics on data streams. Stream processing is a complex process and hence the role and responsibility of data and solution architects are greater. He or she has to look into different technologies and tools to arrive at an end-to-end architecture.

Batch processing vs. stream processing – Batch processing mainly focuses on historical data as shown in Figure 9.2. Data warehouses are vital for this processing and the macro-level batch processing architecture is given in Figure 9.2.

Extraction, transformation and loading (ETL) tools help to get and transform data in order to simplify and streamline data loading. Data processing happens on batches of data. A batch of data will be queried by a user or on a regular basis by a software program. For an example, every organization stores sales data in its warehouse. If the user requires to query a data for analysis, the parameters are passed to clearly define the required portion of the information, like:

Product: leather strap
Sales region: Northern California
Time-period: 1st quarter of 2020

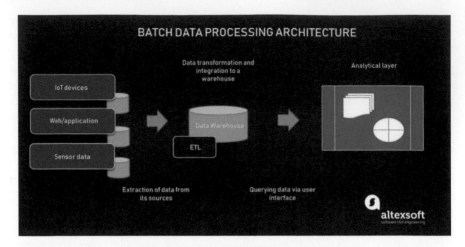

Figure 9.2   Batch data architecture

Based on the parameters, the system understands which data to fetch from storage. Batch processing includes processing of high volume of data in a batch but within a specific time span. Batch processing is also a technique where large volume of data are all processed at once. In batch processing, delays can occur due to the time duration between the time data appears in the storage layer and at the time analytics is done by the reporting tools. But this latency is not an issue with batch processing.

Also if there is a need to analyze the correlation between SaaS license renewals and customer support tickets, there needs to be an interaction of the CRM system with one of the ticketing system. If that interaction happens once a day rather than the second, a ticket is resolved, it does not make much of a difference.

In micro-batch processing, the batch processes are run on much smaller accumulations of data. These smaller size data are of typically less than a minute's worth of data. Hence the data that is available can be considered as near real-time data. In practice, the difference between micro-batching and stream processing is very minimal. When the need is very fresh data, micro-batch processing is used but it does not necessarily mean real-time. Since the time taken to run a batch processing analysis may need an hour or a day to run when there is no need to know what happened in the last few seconds. Hence, in situations like the case of a large e-commerce service provider which makes a major change to its user interface, the analysts would like to know how this change has affected the purchasing behavior and which is required almost immediately. Also any dip in the conversion rates could result in huge losses. Here, a minute's delay is seen as a big issue. Thus, leveraging micro-batch processing in this situation is touted as a good choice.

In short, a certain amount of raw data is piled up before running an ETL job as pictorially represented below.

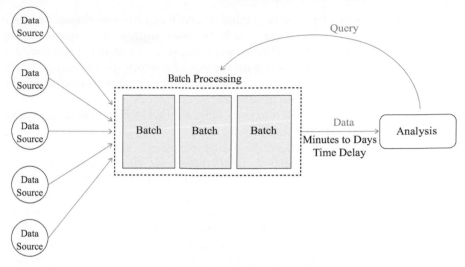

Batch processing is preferred if data freshness is not a big issue, if you are working on big data and running a complex algorithm that needs the full dataset and if you are joining tables in relational databases.

Stream processing – This processing typically deals with *data streams*. A data stream is a constant flow of data with high frequency. As we all know, the relevance and the value of streaming data are bound to go down with time. Therefore, without waiting a bit, data getting streamed from different and distributed data sources has to be processed immediately. This is a prime example for real-time analytics and insights. Transactional and operational data are the prime example for streamed data. With the faster proliferation of IoT edge devices and sensors, cloud-based business workloads and IT services, the amount of streaming data goes up considerably.

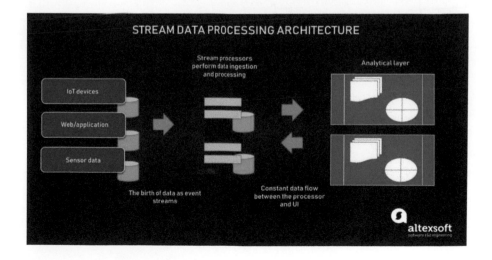

Since data streams have no beginning or end, they cannot be fragmented into batches. So, storing data in a temporary or persistent storage and subjecting it for knowledge discovery and dissemination are being seen as a barrier. Therefore, the way forward is to process data while on the move for information extraction. Data in real time such as streaming data are analyzed by streaming processes. In stream processing, data size is unknown in advance. Stream processor takes few seconds or milliseconds to process data. Stream processing are used to analyze or serve data as close as possible to when the data is gathered.

Data freshness is very crucial for online inference in machine learning, real-time advertising, or fraud detection. In all these cases, there is a need for data-driven systems that need to make a split-second decision like the advertisement to serve and many other immediate needs. Stream processing does to quickly access the data, performs our calculations and reaches a result. In short, in stream processing, data is processed as soon as it arrives in the processing system. Data generated reaches the system immediately in most of the cases. This would be typically in sub-second timeframes and this enables the end-user to get the results in real time. These operations would not be stateful, or would only be able to store a 'small' state.

Hybrid processing – This is to leverage both batch and stream processing in certain situations. The high-level architecture diagram below vividly illustrates how the both processes happen together. The event processor/event stream processing (ESP) captures and processes event data streams and from there, an analytical engine

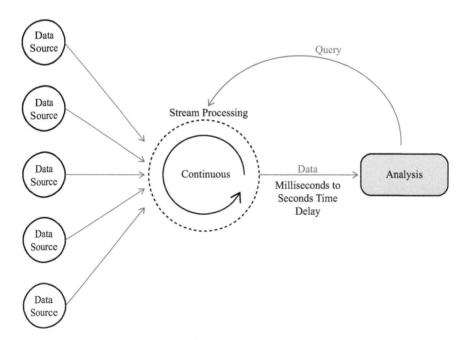

Figure 9.3   Stream processing

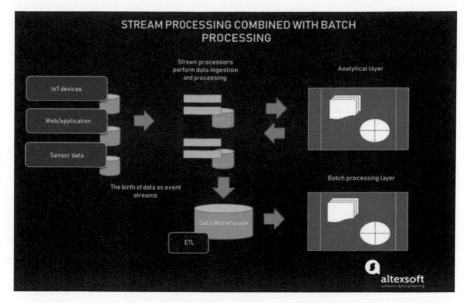

Figure 9.4   Stream processing combined with batch processing

takes over. On the other side, transformed and enriched event data get deposited in data warehouse in order to facilitate big data analytics through batch processing.

ESP is the process of taking action on a series of data points that originate from any digitized system, which is continuously creating event data. The term "event" denotes each data point in the system and "stream" refers to a series of event data. This series of events are referred to as streaming data or data streams. A variety of actions can be performed on those event data/message. The actions include aggregations such as summation, mean, median, and standard deviation, analytics for predicting future events based on patterns and trends exposed by data streams, transformations such as data formats and transmission protocols, enrichment such as adding encryption, metadata, and context details, and ingestion such as inserting data into a target datastore.

In short, batch processing is to take required actions on a large set of static data ("data at rest"), while ESP is taking appropriate action on a constant flow of data ("data in motion"). ESP is for extracting real-time insights, which, in turn, enable the visualization and realization of real-time applications.

9.6   The IoT stream processing

In the past, ETL tools were used to transfer data from data sources/relational databases into data warehouse. BI tools were used to do data analytics. There are data/knowledge visualization tools in plenty. The data was structured and hence could be accommodated in rows and columns. The real challenge is to accommodate semi-structured and unstructured data. In the IoT era, device and sensor

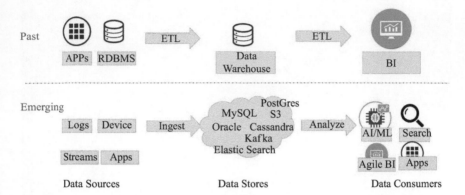

Figure 9.5 *Evolution of data in motion*

data are abounding and making sense/money out of IoT digital data is being presented as a huge challenge. The other challenge is the speed and scalability of processing.

About IoT data pipeline – A data pipeline is any set of processes designed for two things:

1. To define what data to collect, where and how.
2. To extract, transform, combine, validate, and load the data for further analysis and visualization.

The architecture consists of six basic layers:

✓ Data ingestion layer
✓ Data collection layer
✓ Data pre-processing layer
✓ Data storage layer
✓ Data query layer
✓ Data visualization layer

Data ingestion layer – This involves procuring event data/message from different and distributed sources (IoT devices and sensors, business applications, mobile and web applications, IT infrastructure modules' logs, etc.) and transferring the data into a data store for further processing.

Data can be streamed in real time or ingested in batches. The process of bringing data into data processing system is termed as ingestion. For real-time data ingestion, once the data arrives, it gets ingested immediately. If it is being done in batches, then data items are at a periodic interval of time ingested in some chunks.

Data ingestion can be asynchronous, uninterrupted, in real time, batched, or in any mixture thereof. There exist many data ingestion tools and technologies to collect raw data from different sources and to upload them to a *single source*.

9.7   Data ingestion tools

Apache Flume, Apache Kafka, and Apache NiFi are some regularly used data ingestion tools.

- *Apache Flume* – Apache Flume is a reliable and distributed system for collecting and moving huge quantities of log data. The architecture of Apache Flume is simple and flexible based on streaming data flows. Apache Flume is mainly used to collect log data present in log files from web servers and aggregating it into HDFS which can be used for further analysis.
- *Apache Kafka* – Apache Kafka is an open-source distributed event streaming platform for high-performance streaming analytics, data integration data pipelines and mission-critical applications.
- *Apache NiFi* – Apache NiFi provides provisions for powerful and scalable directed graphs of data routing, transformation, and system mediation logic. The flow of data between systems is automated using NiFi.

There are many other data ingestion tools in the market. Check this page https://www.predictiveanalyticstoday.com/data-ingestion-tools for more information.

9.8   Data transport/collection layer

This transport layer concerns getting data from any location to any other. The key component in data transport are the message brokers. The main job of a message broker is to decipher a message from a sender's protocol to that of a receiver and also to transform messages before transmitting the messages. Apache Kafka is a high-throughput distributed messaging system for fault-tolerant, consistent, durable message collection, and delivery.

Streams of records or topics are published by Kafka producers. These records are the once to which the consumers subscribe. The streams of records are kept and processed as they are produced. Some broad classes of applications that used Kafka are the following:

- Real-time streaming data pipelines *between* systems or applications
- Real-time streaming applications that *transform* streams of data
- Real-time streaming applications that *react* to streams of data

When compared with simpler messaging systems such as ZeroMQ (https://zeromq.org/), RabbitMQ (https://www.rabbitmq.com/), Kafka guarantees better throughput, integrated partitioning, and fault tolerance. These characteristics makes it suitable for large-scale message handling. Kafka can handle everything from commit logs, to website activity tracking, to stream processing.

AWS Kinesis (https://aws.amazon.com/kinesis/) is a real-time and cloud-based data processing platform. It can handle widely varying amounts of ingest data in a scalable and simplified manner. It ingests, buffers, and processes streaming data in real time. Solace PubSub+ Event Broker (https://solace.com/) – the unified event broker technology can be used as a purpose-built hardware, a run-anywhere software and as a managed service that can be used together to stream events across a distributed enterprise.

- *Direct ingestion from MQTT broker* – This is to ingest data right away from the MQTT broker and directing it to the multiple required destinations. To use direct ingestion from MQTT broker, the data flow pipeline has to be designed by using different Apache NiFi processors.
- *By using StreamSets data collector edge* – To perform fast data ingestion and light transformations, StreamSets data collector can be used. The designing the pipelines for streaming, batch and change data capture (CDC) in can be performed in minutes. This process includes starting the CDC operations so as to keep the data fresh and protected also to monitor the data in flight and to handle the data drift with completely instrumented pipelines. StreamSets Data Collector Edge (SDC Edge) is a lightweight execution agent without a UI that runs pipelines on edge devices with limited resources. SDC Edge reads data from an edge device or to accept data from another pipeline and then can then act on that data to manipulate an edge device.

9.9   Data pre-processing layer

The collected data is not going to be straightaway ready to be queried and analyzed. There are works such as data formats have to be translated to be suitable for the target environment. There are multiple data representation, exchange and persistence formats. A number of pre-processing activities to be performed on the data. Data or message enrichment is one important aspect not to be taken lightly. The type of data pre-processing differs between batch and stream data types. In real-time stream processing for analytics, there exists three steps.

- *Transformation* – As noted down above, IoT device data has to be converted in order to facilitate the data streams to speed up and simplify deeper and decisive data analytics.
- *Data enrichment* – This is acquiring special mention. IoT data has to accordingly enriched by combining with other data in order to simplify and speed up the task of knowledge extraction. To improve data visibility, data security, and data analysis options, it is mandatory for IoT data to be integrated with non-IoT data. The diagram below clearly illustrates what we just read.

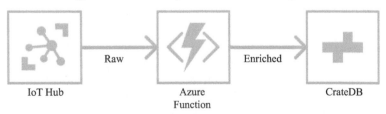

IoT Hub   Azure   CrateDB
                          Function

- *Storing data* – This is used to store the data at the required storage location.

9.10   Data storage/management layer

In this big data era, Apache Hadoop and Apache Spark are well-known data processing and storage frameworks. A framework that can process big data sets across
clusters is named as Hadoop. Sqoop is a part of Hadoop that moves relational data
into HDFS. Queries on HDFS are run on a SQL-like interface called Hive. For
machine learning purposes, Mahout is used. Besides using HDFS for file storage,
Hadoop is capable of using S3 buckets or Azure blobs as input.

Spark is faster than Hadoop because Spark has the in-memory data processing
capacity. Spark supports SQL queries. Files to HDFS are red and written by
Hadoop. Spark is used to process data in RAM using the notion of resilient distributed dataset (RDD). Spark can work in stand-alone mode or in combination
with a Hadoop cluster which acts as the data source or in unification with Mesos.
The Mesos master replaces the Spark master or YARN for scheduling purposes.

Spark is built on Spark Core, the engine that drives the scheduling, optimizations, and RDD abstraction. Spark Core connects Spark with a variety of filesys-
tems such as HDFS, S3, RDBMs, or Elasticsearch. There are several libraries
including Spark SQL, which allows you to run SQL-like commands on distributed
data sets. There are additional libraries such as MLLib for machine learning,
GraphX for graph problems, and streaming which allows for the input of continually streaming log data. There are SQL, NoSQL, and distributed SQL databases
in order to store big data and to facilitate fetching data when queried.

InfluxDB time series databases – The rapid instrumentation of the physical
world with the IoT devices, networks, systems, and environments has led to an
explosion of time-stamped data. Time series databases serve constructively here for
bringing forth the much-anticipated digital transformation. Time series database
(https://www.influxdata.com/) is handled by InfluxDB which includes complex
logic or business rules over massive and fast-growing data sets. InfluxDB also
gives the advantage for a variety of ingestion methods which includes the capability
to attach tags to different data points. InfluxDB is an essential time series toolkit
with dashboards, queries, tasks, and agents all in one place.

Time series data provides significant value to organizations because it enables
them to analyze important real-time and historical metrics. *InfluxDB* is purpose-
built to handle the massive volumes and countless sources of time-stamped data
produced by sensors, applications, and infrastructure.

9.11   Data/knowledge visualization layer

When data gets transitioned into information and into knowledge, there is a need
for report-generation, visual dashboards, and other visualization tools capable of
providing 360° view. Business executives and other decision-makers depend
greatly on the knowledge extrapolated and exposed in order to ponder about next-
course of actions with all the clarity and confidence. Developing insights and
bringing forth conclusions to steer enterprises in the right direction are the need of

the hour. Data scientists need visualization tools to clearly articulate and disseminate any knowledge discovered to their masters, marketers, and consumers.

Time series visualization and analytics give the much-needed ability to envisage the time series data and spot trends to track variations over time and to generate forecasts. Queries on time series data can be performed with results as graphs in dashboards covering different types of visualization, like gauges, line graphs, maps, charts, and tables. There are easy-to-use monitoring and visualization tools available in the market. Grafana (https://grafana.com/) is to compose observability dashboards with the whole lot from Prometheus & Graphite metrics, to logs and application data to power plants and beehives. Grafana is a popular tool for visualization which can be used to monitor real-time data from different data sources. It has plugins that could be used to connect different tools/databases such as ElasticSearch and influxdb. Since it supports many databases, we can query the database table from Grafana itself. This could be a very useful feature while monitoring real-time data such as manufacturing IoT data.

Grafana provides a dashboard where we can add panels for the graphs we want to visualize. Each panel holds a graph of a specific type. To make Grafana dynamic, there are variables in Grafana. These variables appear as dropdown lists at the top of the dashboard and accordingly one can change the query dynamically with the help of these variables. One can also set alerts in Grafana which can be very useful for monitoring changes in the data. Grafana was originally built for performance and system monitoring but it also supports more than 40 data sources and 16 apps directly.

The prime components of a streaming architecture – A flexible and futuristic streaming architecture must include these four key modules.

The message broker/stream processor – This module takes data from different and distributed event producers, translates it into a standard message format (this is a pre-processing activity), and streams it without any break. Event receivers can then listen in and consume the event messages passed on by the broker. The early prominent message brokers include RabbitMQ (https://www.rabbitmq.com/) and Apache ActiveMQ (https://activemq.apache.org/). There are other message-oriented middleware (MoM) products. Later on, we came across hyper-performant messaging platforms such as Kafka (https://kafka.apache.org/), which is a promising and widely used stream processing engine. Because of Kafka's ability to run concurrent processing and move large amounts of data quickly, it is used for big data streams, like Netflix's big data ingestion platform.

There are cloud-based stream processors. The most popular one is AWS Kinesis (https://aws.amazon.com/kinesis/). The macro-level stream processing architecture is given below.

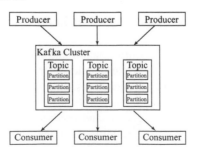

Batch and real-time ETL tools – This is a prime ingredient of a streaming data architecture. As described above, data stream elements have to be transformed before the data stream can be queried and analysed by SQL-like tools. ETL tools play a vital role here. There are data integration/virtualization platforms connecting many data sources with event processor. Also, ETL tools fetch events from message queues and apply the query to generate a result. They often perform additional joins and transformations on aggregations on the data. The result can be an action, an API call, an alert, a visualization, or forming a new data stream. Some examples of open-source ETL tools for streaming data are given below.

- Apache spark streaming (https://spark.apache.org/streaming/) is a scalable and fault-tolerant stream processing system that supports both batch and streaming workloads. The extension of the core Spark API is spark streaming and it allows data engineers and data scientists to process real-time data from various sources including Kafka, Flume, and Amazon Kinesis. The processed data can be pushed out to file systems like live dashboards and databases.

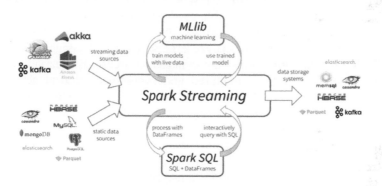

- *Apache Storm* (https://storm.apache.org/) is a distributed real-time computation system. Apache Storm makes it easy to process unbounded streams of data in a reliable way. This is for real-time processing what Hadoop did for batch processing. Apache Storm has many use cases: real-time analytics, online machine learning, continuous computation, distributed RPC, ETL, etc. Apache Storm is really fast. The Apache Storm has been benchmark clocked at processing over a million tuples per second per node. The queuing and database technologies can be integrated by the Apache Storm. The streams of data are consumed by Apache Storm and the streams are processed in arbitrarily complex ways by repartitioning the streams between each stage of the computation.
- *WSO2 streaming integrator* (https://wso2.com/integration/streaming-integrator/) allows implementation of streaming ETL, CDC, and can process large files and real-time APIs. Event-driven architectures can be connected and realized with distributed streaming systems such as Kafka, Amazon SQS, and more.

All the tools are capable of listening to message streams, processing the data and saving it to storage. The stream processors like Spark and WSO2 provide a SQL syntax for querying and manipulating the data. But most operations need to be coded in Java or Scala.

Apache Kafka can be integrated with Apache Hive, a warehousing solution, and Hadoop for batch processing of the stored data. Apache Kafka can also be used with Apache Spark which is a big data processing engine. Stream processing can also be performed with tools such as Storm and Flink for distributed stream processing, and mixed types of data processing. Both can also be used as an ETL tool or a batch processor combined into Hadoop.

Data analytics/serverless query engine – There are many streaming data analytics platforms. Here are a few.

- *Amazon Athena* (https://aws.amazon.com/athena/) is an interactive query service that makes it easy to examine data in Amazon S3 using standard SQL. Since Athena is serverless, there is no infrastructure to manage. It involves loading data in Amazon S3, identify the schema, and perform querying using standard SQL. Results are delivered within seconds. There is no need for complex ETL jobs to arrange the data for analysis in Athena. This makes it easy for anyone with SQL skills to quickly analyze large-scale datasets. Usage of Athena is easy.
- With *AWS Redshift* (https://aws.amazon.com/redshift), querying and combination of exabytes of structured and semi-structured data across the data warehouse, operational database, and data lake using standard SQL are possible. Redshift enables easy saving of the results of the queries back to the S3 data lake using open formats, like Apache Parquet. This is done so that additional analytics from other analytics services like Amazon EMR, Amazon Athena, and Amazon SageMaker can be performed.
- *Amazon Kinesis Data Firehose* (https://aws.amazon.com/kinesis/data-firehose/) is the easiest way to reliably load streaming data into data stores, data lakes, and analytics services. Amazon Kinesis Data Firehose can capture, transform, and deliver streaming data to Amazon S3, Amazon Redshift, Amazon Elasticsearch Service, generic HTTP endpoints, and service providers like New Relic, MongoDB, Splunk, and Datadog. The Amazon Kinesis can be used to batch, compress, transform, and encrypt the data streams before performing loading, minimization of the storage used and for improving security.
- *Kafka Connect* (https://docs.confluent.io/platform/current/connect/index.html) is a tool used for scalable and reliable streaming data with other data systems. Kafka Connect makes it easy to define connectors that move large data sets into and out of Kafka. Entire databases can be ingested using Kafka Connect or metrics can be collected from all the application servers into Kafka which ensures low latency data availability for stream processing. To deliver data Kafka topics into secondary indexes like Elasticsearch or into batch systems such as Hadoop for offline analysis an export connector can be used.
- *Elastic Enterprise Search* (https://www.elastic.co/enterprise-search) is a free tool to bring search experiences quickly, and to scale them seamlessly. Kafka

Connect can be used to stream topics directly into Elasticsearch. Elasticsearch mappings with correct data types are created automatically by using Avro data format and a schema registry. This assists in performing rapid text search or analytics within Elasticsearch.

- *The Apache Cassandra database* (https://cassandra.apache.org/) is the correct choice for purposes of scalability and high availability without any compromise in performance. The characteristics of linear scalability and proven fault-tolerance on commodity hardware or cloud infrastructure makes this the perfect platform for mission-critical data. Replication across multiple datacenters and providing lower latency for users is the best of Cassandra's database. Kafka streams can be processed and persisted to a Cassandra cluster. Another Kafka instance can be implemented that receives a stream of variations from Cassandra and serves them to applications for real-time decision-making.

Streaming data storage – Here are a few options for storing streaming data. There are databases and data warehouses. SQL-based analytics is possible with such data storage solutions. Message brokers and queues are also emerging as a persistent data storage option. These are inherently dynamic and there is no need to structure data into tables. In the recent past, especially with the impending big data era, data lakes emerge as the most preferred data storage solution. The most flexible and inexpensive option for storing event data is done by a data lake.

Many companies are adopting a full-stack approach rather than relying on patching together multiple open-source technologies. The modern data platform is primarily built on business-centric value chains rather than IT-centric processes. In the recent times, the complexity of traditional architecture is abstracted into a single self-service platform that turns event streams into actionable insights.

9.12   IoT streaming analytics: the benefits

With the explosion of IoT devices, the days of creating and streaming IoT data have started to flourish. The cool convergence of information, communication, and operational technologies (ICT and OT) has laid down a stimulating platform for producing a large amount of semi-structured and structured streaming data. As we discussed earlier, data is turning out to be a strategically sound asset for governments, business behemoths, and service organizations. It is not wise to throw any perceptible data away. Instead, every bit of data (internal as well as external) has to be meticulously garnered, stored, and processed in a methodical manner. For fulfilling this goal, enterprise and Cloud IT teams have to have appropriate infrastructure modules, platforms, middleware solutions, applications in place to do the justice for any data streamed. As indicated above, the major part of these streams are event data or messages. Thus, with the faster proliferation of connected electronics, CPSs, digitized entities and assets, composable microservices, digital twins, and the IoT sensors, there is a surging popularity for stream processing. Capturing and subjecting data streams into a timely and tantalizing investigations are bound to unravel a variety of insights. Stream processing has become an important ingredient for business houses to gain data-driven insights and accomplish insights-driven things.

With big data, stream processing provides several benefits as enunciated below.

- *It deals with never-ending streams of events*: Some data is natively structured and streamlined to be streamed across. Batch processing tools, if applied to data streams, have to temporarily stop the stream of event data, capture, and batch them to produce batches of data and then do the processing on that batches to arrive at useful conclusions. The size of a batch can be reduced and increased. Apache Spark supports micro-batching. But, in the case of stream processing, one or many data streams may get combined to derive context-aware and applicable insights in time. Stream processing can disentangle useful information on streaming data without any stoppage. Any perceptible deviation or anomaly can be inferred quickly so that proactive and pre-emptive counter measures can be considered and put in place immediately.
- Real-time processing – Batch processing traditionally consumes a lot of time to conclude something useful. But the stream processing capability can unearth viable insights in real time. Real-time and intelligent services and applications can be visualized and realized through stream processing. It is possible with the latest innovations in chipsets and hyperconverged infrastructures (HCIs)/ appliances, it is possible to speed up the analytics process. It is also possible to accelerate the analytics activity with high-performance database systems. Still, the real-time data analytics can be natively obtained through stream processing.
- *Detecting patterns in time-series data* – As inscribed above, stream processing is the continuous processing of data streams. Such a set up simplifies detecting patterns over time. This helps in arriving at some tactical as well as strategical insights. The continuity plays an important role. In the case of batch processing, the aspect of continuity goes away and thereby enterprises may miss some timely trends and opportunities. Stream processing may open up fresh possibilities. Batch processing actually breaks data into batches. Thereby some critical information can be messed up resulting in losses for companies.
- *Easy data scalability* – Big data needs high-end data processing capability. Parallel processing or distributed processing is required for batch processing. This puts a lot of load and strain on IT resources. Modern stream processing middleware solutions can handle gigabytes of data per second. This can work well if there are sudden spike in data being produced and consumed.

9.13   The industrial applications of IoT stream processing

Real-time streaming data analytics is being vociferously used across many industry verticals including cybersecurity, financial services, retail, manufacturing, the energy industry, healthcare, etc.

- Healthcare – The medical electronics field is growing rapidly. There are multiple healthcare instruments catering to different needs, monitoring, and scanning solutions in plenty. That is, IoT devices and sensors are being deployed in hospitals and clinics. Multifaceted sensors are being leveraged to fulfill a variety of medical needs and these sensors can form localized, ad hoc, dynamic, and purpose-specific sensor networks to accomplish bigger and better things for healthcare service providers, patients, nurses, doctors, surgeons, and other experts in the medical field. Further on, there are a number of software solutions for enabling a variety of healthcare tasks. Patient, asset, and human resource management software are being insisted in order to arrive at digitally transformed healthcare facilities. Healthcare data analytics is another serious business gaining prominence for giving advanced diagnoses and medication. The accumulation of devices, sensors, actuators, and other digitization and edge technologies and tools has led to the generation and transmission of a lot of useful and usable data continuously. Real-time monitoring of health-conditions, clinical risk-assessment, client-state analysis, and alerts are some of the use cases of IoT streaming data.
- Streaming data analytics for smart manufacturing – There are business use cases of real-time analytics performed on streaming data. Almost all manufacturers have embedded intelligent sensors in devices in their production line and supply chain. Analyzing the data from these sensors in real time allows a manufacturer to spot and pinpoint problems and correct them before a product leaves the production line. Production and efficiency of operations is improved.
- In cybersecurity uses, streaming analytics can promptly identify anomalous behavior and doubtful activities and flag them for instant investigation. Instead of remediating after the occurrence of a problem, the attack can be stopped before it can do any damage.
- In the hospitality industry, a real-time analytics of the reservations can be performed by using streaming analytics. Spotting a location that has high availability in the late afternoon, the chain could act (by texting or emailing special promotions to frequent guests, for example) to fill those empty rooms that night. In many cases, companies use real-time streaming analytics to complement information derived from other applications, such as transaction processing. Ponder a global airline that can process thousands of reservation businesses per second. Real-time analytics can optimize income opportunities by finding out which routes have a surplus of seats that need to be filled.
- Smart transportations – It is important to keep vehicles on the road by predicting their maintenance needs. There is an utmost necessity to streamline logistics using real-time data and alerts. This can be achieved by monitoring performance, optimizing delivery routes, and quickly responding to delays or issues as they occur. Thus, real-time streaming analytics comes handy in easing up traffic congestion thereby enabling the smooth flow of vehicles on the road. Traffic prediction, congestion avoidance, and pinpointing problematic locations are being facilitated through streaming data analytics capability.

- Smart retail – Customer experience is very important for retail store owners to sustain the loyalty earned. To search for fresh avenues toward heightened revenue streams is an important thing for retailers. Retail stores are being decorated with a variety of IoT devices, systems and networks. Robots and drones are acquiring special significance in such shopping and serious locations. Applying advanced streaming analytics techniques on different and distributed IoT device data enables precise inventory management, and most importantly enhancing the consumer's shopping experience. There are newer possibilities and fresh opportunities for achieving retail operations improvement
- Smart buildings – Homes, apartments, malls and condominiums, warehouses, manufacturing floors, airports and other critical and crowded places are being stuffed with a lot of purpose-agnostic and generic IoT sensors and devices. When IoT data gets fed into streaming analytics platforms, a variety of real-time and real-world insights get extracted and exposed. For example, for setting up and sustaining smart buildings, the knowledge discovered and disseminated goes a long way in aptly personalizing and automating building's heating and cooling. The aspect of room utilization efficiency gets a solid boost. Structural monitoring is being advanced through streaming data analytics. IoT data stream analysis ensures smart protection and alert systems improvement.
- Smart agriculture – Multifaceted IoT sensors and actuators are being deployed in cultivated areas to have minute monitoring of everything that happens there. The leverage of real-time streaming analytics on all the data captured and transmitted by ground-level IoT sensors is bound to produce real-time actionable insights, which can be used by farmers or actuators to plunge into the best course of actions with all the clarity and confidence. Farmers can gain a lot of useful insights such as soil moisture and nutrients. Controlling water usage for plant growth to get better outcomes is also achieved with the advancements in streaming data analytics.
- Finance – Without an iota of doubt, the finance industry is a hugely dynamic one. Transaction processing, market/currency state monitoring, investment insights, etc. are some of the real-time analytics on financial, insurance, investors, and bank data.
- Automated IT operations – Information and communication technologies are indispensable not only for business houses but also for common people these days. Therefore, IT investments by enterprises and establishments are growing steadily. Besides the capital costs, IT operational costs are rising. Bringing in advanced automations into IT monitoring, measurement, management, and maintenance is definitely advantageous for enterprise and Cloud IT teams. Capturing all kinds of IT data and applying sophisticated streaming analytics methods on it throws a lot of actionable insights in time. Thus, data-driven insights and insights-driven decisions and actions have become the new normal in the IT industry.
- Logistics – Logistics companies track trucks and cars on the road with IoT sensors. They are able to see which vehicles will arrive on time, or ahead of, or

behind schedule. They can observe vehicle proximity and reroute a vehicle if another vehicle in the area suffers a breakdown. All of this is facilitated with IoT devices and sensors attached to vehicles that are monitored in real time. The savings can mount up. For refrigerated trucks alone, the late fee for one load of cargo can be $500.

9.14 Streaming analytics – best practices

Every day, machines and men generate data at unprecedented speeds. The tips below help to formulate a viable streaming analytics strategy. The following scenarios definitely mandate for leveraging the streaming analytics process.

- Social applications such as Facebook, Twitter, and LinkedIn generate tremendous number of tweets, posts, comments, updates, etc. every minute. Millions of email messages are being sent per minute.
- Bank and E-commerce transactions are happening in millions per minute
- Hospitals, especially intensive care units (ICUs), generate thousands of alerts per minute.
- Travel reservations are being done in millions per minute across the world.
- Credit card usage and stock investments are also seeing millions of data points.

Taking all sources of data generation together, there are 2.5 quintillion bytes of data created each day. Further on, with the accumulation of IoT devices and services, data volumes are to skyrocket in quantity. Data is turning out to be a critical asset for any enterprising business to be intrinsically competitive and customer-centric. Whether it is an internal data or external data, every data point cannot be discarded. Instead, every bit of data has to be meticulously collected, cleansed, and crunched to visualize and realize real digital transformations. Streaming analytics play a very vital role in transitioning raw data to information and to insights. With more data sources and applications joining in the mainstream computing, highly resilient streaming analytics infrastructure is needed. Further on, any streaming analytics platform solution has to have the extensibility to get readily integrated with third-party data sources, business workloads, and IT services. These help to arrive at real-time decisions or to take immediate actions regarding customer service, security or fraud prevention, product recommendations, or automated chat or voice response.

Data analytics has become the core and central activity for all business functions. It is not only for data scientists and business analysts. Sales and marketing, finance, and customer service executives also have to involve themselves in data analytics to be right and relevant to their consumers and clients. Thus, doing data analytics has to be sharply simplified by incorporating additional automated tools such as data integration/virtualization and visualization so that non-technical people can also benefit immensely out of data analytics. Streaming analytics guarantee real-time insights to consistently support event-driven digital transformation requirements. There are three ways in which streaming analytics solutions can be deployed and leveraged.

The do-it-yourself (DIY) on-premises approach – First, companies need a big real estate with electricity and cooling facilities to house and maintain all hetero-geneous compute servers, storage appliances and networking components. Other prominent ingredients include cybersecurity solutions. Further on, the company IT team has to install, configure, operate, and use above-mentioned IT infrastructure modules. The critical software infrastructure is none other than the streaming ana-lytics platform. This approach involves heavy capital and operational costs to run the show successfully. With more data and use loads in the subsequent days, the on-premise data/cloud center machines have to scale up or out in an automated manner to fulfill highly varying workloads. With constantly changing business sentiments and newer digital technologies, this secluded and secure setup may face the heat.

The home-grown and open-source cloud approach – We have off-premise, online and on-demand public cloud centers across the globe. That is, the necessary compute, storage and network infrastructure modules are available for a fee. Now, these cloud centers already have installed all kinds of streaming analytics platforms (open source as well as commercial-grade solutions) on their infrastructures. The widely reported challenge here is to establish the much-needed integration to have a competent streaming analytics solution. Another worry here is that the platform runs on one or more public cloud service provider environments. However, the data gets originated from different and distributed sources. Also, data scientists and business analysts may feel certain performance degradation when the analytics platform is hosted and run in a faraway cloud environment.

A dedicated streaming analytics cloud approach – Having understood the business needs and technological challenges, experts are of the opinion to have a dedicated streaming analytics cloud approach. High-performance and real-time analytics on data streams is also being insisted. Also, the data ingestion rate has to be on the higher side.

Thus, dedicated streaming analytics cloud solutions are capable of fulfilling these unique business and technical requirements.

IBM Streaming Analytics (https://www.ibm.com/in-en/cloud/streaming-ana-lytics) provides solution to the challenges of setting up and using streaming analytics by providing an easy-to-use cloud-based stream processing service.

The solution provides connection to the streaming data source and the target systems and is also configured to execute data processing or any ana-lytic operations to be done while the data is in transit.

The streaming analytics service can analyze millions of events per sec-ond, enabling sub-millisecond response times and lead to instant decision making. Very high data rates can be handled by IBM Streaming Analytics. Using IBM Streams, any business can collect, analyze, monitor, and correlate data on a real-time basis from the data sources.

IBM Streams is designed for enterprise deployment. IBM Streams includes a complete set of accelerators and templates to assist businesses. For example, IBM can provide one accelerator to assist financial markets and recognize patterns in high-volume transaction and can deploy another accelerator to help telecom companies to analyze millions of call data records every second. Streams is designed to mix easily with an enterprise's data warehouses, data lakes, and big data platforms. By utilizing IBM Watson speech-to-text capabilities in real time, Streams translates spoken words to text. This further enables data to be analyzed for further understandings. Where ever voice-based interactions are required, the speech-to-text service can be used. Hence, it is suitable for transcribing media files, mobile experiences, voice control of embedded systems, converting sounds to text and call center transcriptions. The latest version of the IBM Streaming Analytics service on IBM Cloud has been rebuilt to run in Docker containers, instead of bare virtual machines, and it uses Kubernetes for container orchestration.

9.15   The future of streaming data architecture

Streaming data architecture is in constant flux. The following three trends are being anticipated.

- The emergence of platforms that decouple storage and compute – The exponential growth of streaming data is impacting data warehouse solutions badly. So, there is a movement towards data lakes, which turn out to be a cheap persistence option for storing large volumes of event data.
- Table modeling to schema less development – Data consumers want to run an interactive and iterative process. Lengthy table modeling, schema detection and metadata extraction are a real burden.
- Automation of data plumbing – Organizations are abhorrent of spending precious data engineering time on data plumbing. Instead, organizations can focus on things that add real value. Therefore, data teams prefer full-stack platforms that reduce time-to-value, over tailored home-grown solutions.

9.16   Conclusion

The digital age has dawned and hence enterprises and people are offered a wealth of new capabilities to drastically advance their operations, outputs and offerings. The days of manually updating database tables are gone. Today's digital systems are inherently capable of capturing the minutiae of user interactions with apps, connected devices and digital systems. With the drastic and decisive improvements, it is easier and faster to operationalize data to prepare it for deeper analytics leveraging integrated data analytics platforms and AI algorithms.

With digital data being generated at a tremendous pace, developers and analysts have a broad range of possibilities when it comes to operationalizing data and preparing it for analytics and machine learning.

The fundamental question to ask when planning out on the data architecture is to identify whether to go for batch or stream processing. In this chapter, the concentration is on stream processing of IoT data. With the rapid growth of the IoT devices and sensors, data volumes have increased substantially. Therefore, a suite of engineering advancements has led to scores of new ways for collecting, processing, and analyzing data. Therefore, real-time collection and analytics on data streams are seeing the grandiose reality. Advanced stream processors facilitate fast computation and concurrent work with multiple data streams.

Chapter 10

Describing the IoT data analytics methods and platforms

Pethuru Raj[1] and P. Vijayakumar[2]

Abstract

As explained in the beginning of this book, the overwhelming leverage of miniaturization, digitization, distribution, consumerization (mobility), consolidation, centralization and industrialization (cloud), compartmentalization (virtualization and containerization), and deeper connectivity technologies has a number of trendsetting and transformational implications on IT as well as businesses across the globe. Edge or fog computing through cloudlets and micro clouds is another potential phenomenon for next-generation IT. There will be a cool convergence in forming and firming up hyper-converged cloud environments to host and deliver smarter and sophisticated applications for the total humanity.

All these advancements are bound to bring forth a number of distinct outputs and opportunities. The principal one among them is the enormous growth in data generation. Further on, there are greater variability, viscosity, and virtuosity in data scope, structure, and speed. That is, with the continuous growth of value-adding data sources and resources, the amount of data getting generated, captured, transmitted, and stored is tremendously huge. As data is turning out to be a strategic asset for any organization to be decisive, distinctive and disciplined in its operations, offerings, and outputs, a host of competent technologies, tips, and tools are being unearthed to smartly stock and subject all incoming and stored data to a variety of deeper investigations to gain actionable insights in time.

Especially extracting and extrapolating knowledge out of data heaps in time goes a long way in empowering every kind of enterprises and endeavors to be exceptionally efficient and effective in their deals, deeds, and deliveries. In this chapter, we would like to dig deeper and dwell at length on the various analytical approaches, frameworks, algorithms, platforms, engines, and methods for squeezing out value-adding and venerable insights out of IoT data.

[1]Edge AI Division, Reliance Jio Platforms Ltd., Bangalore, India
[2]Department of ECE, Tech Park, SRM IST (Formerly known as SRM University), India

10.1   Introduction

Leading market watchers, analysts, and researchers have clearly indicated that the data getting generated is doubling every 2 years. There are several noteworthy developments being given as the principal reason for such a monumental and massive growth of decision-enabling data. Deeper and extreme connectivity technologies and topologies supplemented by service-enablement standards are the most crucial advancements and articulations creating a cascading and chiller effect on our enterprises. Business strategies and enterprise architectures of various business behemoths across the globe are being adequately reconsidered and remedied to be synched up varying peoples' expectations.

Newer data sources and resources are emerging and evolving, edge/fog technologies are empowering every concrete and casually found object to be computational, communicative, sensitive, perceptive, decisive, and responsive, all kinds of physical, mechanical, electrical, and electronics systems are being functionally enabled through a seamless integration with cyber applications and services to be smartly participative and contributive, every sort of digital assistants (personal as well as professional) are equipped with smart software to be context-aware and people-centric, every commonly found, cheap, and casual article in our working, wandering and walking environments are becoming digitized artifacts signaling their valiant and salient entry into the mainstream computing arena, clouds are being positioned as the core and central IT infrastructure for hosting IT and business workloads, databases and warehouses, data marts and cubes, integrated platforms, millions of web, and social sites.

Further on, every noticeable event, transaction, interaction, collaboration, corroboration, correlation, request & reply, etc. are being expectantly captured and persisted in storage appliances and arrays for real-time as well as posterior investigations. Ordinary objects are being readily digitized to be extraordinary in their actions and reactions. These then are capable of getting interconnected with one another in the vicinity and with remote ones and hence they are laying out a stimulating and sparkling foundation for sophisticated networks that are simply going to be creatively autonomic, event-driven, mission-critical, software-defined, and service-oriented. In a nutshell, the realization of extremely connected and service-enabled digital objects and machines in our midst generates big, fast, and streaming data, which is typically multi-structured, massive in volume, and mesmerizing in variety, velocity and value. Precisely speaking, the IoT data is going to be big but the real challenge is to capture, clean up, ingest, and process them immediately to bring forth real-time insights. In the following sections, we are to throw more light on big data platforms and infrastructures.

As widely experienced, data is the fountainhead of information and knowledge that can be wisely used to bigger and better things. For the dreamt knowledge era, data is being carefully collected, cleansed, classified, clustered, and conformed. This end-to-end process is being portrayed as the most sought-after one for fulfilling the long-standing goals of data-driven insights and insights-driven decisions. That is, the final destination is none other than crafting and using actionable insights in time. Big data storage solutions are feverishly prevalent and paramount these days. The most respectable activity on big data is to do synchronized and systematic analytics to rightly and readily emit big insights. Big data analytics frameworks primarily comprising data processing and storage modules, toolsets, distributed and centralized publish-subscribe engines, drivers, and adaptors are made available by open source as well as commercial-grade solution vendors. Due to the extreme complicity and complexity induced by multiplicity and hetero-geneity of big data, enabling big data analytics (BDA) products and procedures are being derived and released platform, product, and tool vendors to do BDA easily and quickly.

10.2 The steps towards knowledge discovery and dissemination

Next-generation systems are expected to be elegantly and extremely sensitive and responsive to be highly relevant for people in their daily decisions, deals, and deeds. Apart from embedding a variety of real-world features inside, modern IT systems need to be adequately enabled through external systems and data-driven insights in order to be proactively and perceptively reactive. The renowned examples include smart energy grids, automatic financial trading, homeland security, logistics, and production control. For example, in a smart grid scenario, the timely detection of a deviation between the energy consumption and the energy production can lead to the instantaneous deployment of an intelligent demand response system. For such kinds of real-time applications, incoming data streams of low-level information arriving from different and distributed sources and sensors at high rates need to be programmatically subjected to purpose-specific processing, mining, and analysis in real time in order to identify more complex situations. Thus, knowledge discovery for cognitive businesses relies upon competent data and event stream processing engines.

With the faster maturity and stability of the IoT paradigm, there are fresh challenges as well as opportunities for both business executives and IT teams (enterprise and cloud). The first and foremost is the precise capture, storage, and analysis of massive collections of data. Because of large volumes of poly-structured data, the following IT requirements are being insisted for enabling data analytics:

- Highly optimized and organized IT infrastructures (compute, storage and net-work) for transmitting, storing, and processing large volumes of data published at a high speed.
- Data security while in transit, rest, and usage.
- Robust and resilient mining, processing and analysis algorithms, processes, and patterns.
- Highly synchronized platforms for faster data virtualization and ingestion, pioneering data analytics, and knowledge visualization.

- With the projected trillions of digitized objects and billions of connected devices, the data, user, and analytics loads on IT infrastructures are hugely variable and hence load-aware infrastructures are insisted.
- Data and application integration standards and middleware with diverse sensors, devices, networks, and systems.
- Data archival, backup, and recovery plus access control are very important for the big, fast, streaming IoT data world.

The following are the key phases for extracting and exposing insights from data heaps gleaned from multiple sources.

1. *Aggregate* from multiple data sources through data integration and virtualization tools.
2. *Pre-process* and transform captured data to be compatible with the target environments.
3. *Ingest and store* the cleansed and polished data in memory as well as in disk-based databases. There are in-memory data grids (IMDGs), in-memory databases, clustered, parallel, analytical and distributed SQL databases, NoSQL and NewSQL (distributed SQL) databases, etc. in order to efficiently stock IoT data.
4. *Investigate* for extracting actionable insights leveraging competent statistical, machine-learning, mathematical and data mining algorithms, complex queries, and renowned methods such as searching, scanning, filtering, slicing, and dicing. There are a plenty of programming, query, and script languages in plenty to code specific analytics requirements and run.
5. *Visualize* the knowledge generated via portals, dashboards, consoles, report-generation tools, maps, charts, graphs, etc. in different devices (smartphones, wearables, tablets, etc.)
6. *Actuate the knowledge extracted* – Decision-makers can go ahead with appropriate plan and smart execution with all the clarity and confidence gained from the knowledge discovered and disseminated.

It is indisputably clear that data leads to insights, which in turn productively and pragmatically participate and pamper individuals, innovators, and institutions in their enterprising journey.

The rewarding repercussions of the data explosion – The exponential growth of disparate data has brought in several challenges as well as advantages for business establishments and enterprise IT teams. Here is a list of strategically significant implications of multi-structured, multi-sourced, and massive volumes of data.

1. Novel analytical competencies (prognostic, predictive, prescriptive, and personalized analytics).
2. To have and sustain repositories comprising insights-driven business and IT services.
3. To dynamically craft and compose smarter applications out of those containerized, composable, configurable, and portable services by purpose-specific service integration and orchestration tools.

In short, it is all about fulfilling the smarter planet vision skillfully by realizing context-aware, connected, and cognitive applications through the leverage of versatile and resilient technologies and tools. The growing number of software services (business and IT) getting stored and continuously refined in private as well as public repositories is another booster for the increasingly software-driven and defined world. Thus new analytical thinking and types are constantly emerging to enable every kind of industry domains to be inspiringly insightful in their operations and offerings. These are bound to expeditiously mature and stabilize to become the new normal amongst us. The ultimate goal of transforming data to information and to knowledge is being facilitated through the power of data analytics and artificial intelligence (AI) algorithms. In other chapters, we have discussed the nitty-gritty of AI along its libraries, frameworks, use cases, and advancements. In this chapter, we restrict to big, fast and streaming data analytics. Let us start the arduous journey with a brief on big data analytics. As enunciated elsewhere, the overwhelming adoption of digitization and digitalization technologies and tools has resulted in realizing tremendous amount of data. If unattended, we may miss out the knowledge embodied in datasets.

10.3   Expounding the need for IoT data analytics

The traditional business intelligence (BI) capability for structured business data for extracting tactical as well as strategic business-centric insights is no more efficient and sufficient. There is, therefore, an insistence for comprehensive yet cognitive analytics to be performed on all kinds of value-adding, insights-generating, and decision-enabling data emanating from different and geographically distributed sources, which are incidentally on the rise, to spit out rewarding insights in time. The IoT data volumes are exponentially growing whereas the prominent data processing formats include batch/ad hoc, interactive, iterative, and real-time processing. The widely available Hadoop implementations have accentuated the realization of big insights via batch data processing. However, in the recent past, there is a clarion call for interactive processing on multi-structured data to craft and carve out real-time insights. Especially with the massive volumes of fast IoT data, the extraction of real-time insights is going to be a game-changing affair.

On the other hand, the cloud-enabled IT optimization has been a new revelation and revolution for the impending era of cloud-based analytics. Forming edge clouds are the latest buzzword in the fast-expanding cloud landscape and hence, the aspect of edge analytics is gaining a surging popularity for real-time analytics. That is, analytics happens not at the faraway cloud servers instead at the proximate edge devices so that the security of data is ensured and the scarce network bandwidth gets saved.

The key drivers for IoT data analytics – Lately, there are a number of interesting things happening simultaneously. The emergence of smart sensors and actuators in large numbers with generic as well as specific capabilities, the grand revelation of cutting-edge technologies, the information and communication technologies (ICT) infrastructure optimization and organization through cloud technologies and tools, the process excellence through rationalization and synchronization, the commendable improvements in the connectivity technologies and topologies, the pace at which smarter environments (smarter homes, hospitals, hotels, etc.) being realized and accepted across, etc. are the widely discussed and discoursed transitions in business and IT landscapes. There are market analysis and research reports proclaiming that there will be millions of software applications, billions of connected devices and trillions of digitized entities by the year 2020. These revolutionary and evolutionary advancements clearly are bound to lead to the accumulation of massive amount of multi-structured and sourced IoT data. The reality is that data is simply pouring in from different sources at varying speeds, structures, sizes, and scopes. The ultimate value out of data-driven insights and insights-driven decisions seems to be tantalizingly transformational for any small, medium and large enterprises across the globe.

On the infrastructure front, technologically advanced server, storage, and network infrastructures are being put in place for next-generation data analytics. Data collection, cleansing, and ingestion are speeded up through a variety of data connectors, drivers, adapters, and other middleware solutions. The conventional ETL tools are also being leveraged to establish an adaptive linkage with an array of home-grown, packaged, and enterprise-class business applications. Specialized storage appliances and networks are being readied to duly persist and protect incoming and even processed data. Further on, there are standards-compliant data virtualization and visualization tools coming up fast for contributing immensely toward the requirement of knowledge engineering and exposition. Having considered the short as well as long-term significance of systematic and sagacious data analytics for strategically enhancing the business efficiency and value, the open-source community as well as commercial-grade product vendors across the globe have come out with a few solid and succulent advancements in their analytical solutions and services to smartly streamline and speed up the process of knowledge discovery and dissemination.

The need now is to have an end-to-end and converged data analytics platform for performing purposeful and pioneering analytics on all kinds of IoT data at different layers and levels in order to conceptualize and concretize scores of state-of-the-art and sophisticated systems for the envisioned smarter planet. In other words, highly modular IoT data analytics platforms and infrastructures collectively lay a stimulating and sustainable foundation for deriving and deploying a growing collection of people-centric and situation-aware applications to be delivered as publicly discoverable, network accessible, composable, and unobtrusively deliverable services. That is, for the ensuing smarter world, the rewarding and resplendent roles and responsibilities of highly competent and cognitive IoT data analytics solutions and services cannot be taken lightly. In the following sections, we would like to insist on the urgent necessity for hyper-converged and hybrid IoT data analytics platforms (can run on edge clouds as well as on traditional clouds) for building and sustaining path-breaking applications and services that are more tuned and tipped for people empowerment.

The key sources of IoT data – There are pioneering technologies and tools being unearthed with a passion for sustainably empowering the IT contributions toward business automation and acceleration. This continuous stream of technological advancements is resulting in fresh possibilities and opportunities for businesses that in turn vouch for enhanced care, choice, comfort, and convenience for customers and consumers. The noteworthy implications out of all these transformations are that the number of data sources goes up considerably and the amount of data being generated and garnered is also exponentially growing. The principal contributors to the heightened data collection are listed below.

- Sentient materials/smart objects/digitized entities through deeper and edge technologies (nano and micro-scale sensors, actuators, codes, chips, controllers, specks, smart dust, tags, stickers, LED, etc.).
- Miniaturized, connected, resource-constrained, and embedded devices and machines.
- Ambient sensing, vision, and perception technologies.
- Social media and knowledge sharing sites.
- Consumerization (mobiles, handhelds, and wearables).
- Centralization, commoditization, and industrialization (cloud computing).
- Compartmentalization (virtualization and containerization).
- Communication (ambient, autonomic, and unified).
- Integrations such as device-to-device (D2D), device-to-cloud (D2C), cloud-to-cloud (C2C), device-to-edge cloud, etc.
- Technical and scientific experimentation data.
- Operational, transactional, and interactions data.

Let us digress into various data analytics methods.

10.4   Describing big data analytics (BDA)

Big data represents huge volumes of data in petabytes, exabytes, and zettabytes in near future. As we move around the globe, we leave a trail of data behind us. B2C and C2C e-commerce systems and B2B e-business transactions, online ticketing and payments, web 1.0 (simple web), web 2.0 (social web), web 3.0 (semantic web), web 4.0 (smart web), still and dynamic images, etc. are the prominent and dominant sources for data. Sensors and actuators are deployed in plenty in specific environments for context-awareness and for enabling the occupants and owners of the environments with a new set of hitherto unforeseen services. In short, every kind of integration, interaction, orchestration, automation, acceleration, augmentation, and operation produces streams of decision-enabling data to be plucked and put into transactional and analytical data stores for initiating analytics and mining activities. Every tangible entity in the world is interconnected purposefully and programmatically. Hence, the data generation sources and resources are bound to grow ceaselessly resulting in heaps and hordes of data.

We have already discussed the fundamental and fulsome changes happening in the IT and business domains. The growing aspect of service-enablement of applications, platforms, infrastructures (servers, storages, and network solutions), and even everyday devices besides the varying yet versatile connectivity methods has laid down a strong and stimulating foundation for big interactions, transactions, hyper-automation, and insights. The tremendous rise in the data collection along with all the complications has instinctively captivated both business and IT leaders and luminaries to act accordingly and adeptly to make sense out of huge and fast-growing data volumes. This is an impending and data-driven opportunity for national governments, corporates, cities, and organizations to gain big data analytics capability. This is the beginning of the much-discussed and discoursed big data computing discipline.

This paradigm is getting formalized with the collaboration among product vendors, service organizations, independent software producers, system integrators, cloud service providers (CSPs), academics, and research labs. Having understood the strategic significance, all the different stakeholders have come together in complete unison in building and sustaining easy-to-grasp and use techniques, synchronized platforms, elastic infrastructures, integrated processes, best practices, design patterns, and key metrics to make this new discipline pervasive and persuasive. Today the acceptance and activation levels of big data computing are consistently on the climb. This phenomenon is to be highly impactful and insightful for business organizations to confidently traverse in the right route if it is taken seriously. The continuous unearthing of prickling issues, data science methods, and incredible solutions are the good indicators for the shining and strategic big data phenomenon.

The future of business definitely belongs to those enterprises that swiftly embrace the big data analytics movement and use it strategically to their own advantages. It is pointed out that business leaders and other decision-makers, who are smart enough to adopt a flexible and futuristic big data strategy, can take their businesses toward greater heights. Successful companies are already extending the value of classic and conventional analytics by integrating cutting-edge big data technologies and outsmarting their competitors. There are several forecasts, exhortations, expositions, and trends on the discipline of big data analytics. Market research and analyst groups have come out with positive reports and briefings, detailing its key drivers and differentiators, the future of this brewing idea, its market value, the revenue potentials and application domains, the fresh avenues and areas for fresh revenues, the needs for its sustainability, etc.

10.5   BDA platforms and solutions

With the continued accumulation of IoT devices and sensors, big data becomes the new normal. Big data represents massive amounts of multi-structured data that are not stored in the relational form in traditional enterprise-scale databases. There are NoSQL and distributed SQL databases for storing big data. These new-generation database systems are typically based on symmetric multiprocessing (SMP) and massive parallel processing (MPP) techniques. These are being framed in order to store, aggregate, filter, mine, and analyze big data efficiently. The following are the general characteristics of big data:

- Data storage is defined in the order of petabytes, exabytes, etc. in volume to the current storage limits (gigabytes and terabytes).
- There can be multiple structures (structured, semi-structured, and less-structured) for big data.
- Multiple types of data sources (sensors, machines, mobiles, social sites, etc.) and resources for big data.
- Data is time-sensitive (near real-time as well as real-time). That means big data consists of data collected with relevance to the time zones so that time-sensitive insights can be extracted.

Thus, big data has created a number of rightful repercussions for businesses and hence big data has gained a prominent place. The evolving IT strategy of enterprising businesses across the world centers around big data. There are enterprise data warehouses, analytical platforms, in-memory appliances, etc. Data warehousing delivers deep operational insights with advanced in-database analytics. There are data analytics appliances in the market to simplify big data analytics. IBM Analytics solutions architecturally integrate database, server, and storage into a single, purpose-built, easy-to-manage system. Then SAP HANA is an exemplary platform for efficient big data analytics. Platform vendors are conveniently tied up with infrastructure vendors especially cloud service providers (CSPs) to take analytics to the cloud so that the goal of analytics as a service (AaaS) sees a neat and nice reality sooner than later. There are multiple startups with innovative product offerings to speed up and simplify the complex part of big data analysis. We also have a number of data analytics platforms such as Apache Hadoop and Apache Spark (https://spark.apache.org/).

10.6 Big data analytics in healthcare

Enterprises can understand and gain the value of big data analytics based on the number of value-added use cases and how some of the hitherto hard-to-solve problems can be easily tackled with the help of big data analytics. Every enterprise is mandated to grow with the help of analytics. As elucidated before, with big data, big analytics is the norm for businesses to realize big insights. Several domains are eagerly enhancing their IT capability to have embedded analytics and there are several reports eulogizing the elegance of big data analytics.

The healthcare industry has been a late adopter of technology when compared to other industries such as banking, retail, and insurance. As per the trendsetting McKinsey report on big data from June 2011, if US healthcare organizations could use big data creatively and effectively to drive efficiency and quality, the potential saving could be more than $300 billion every year.

- Patient monitoring: inpatient, outpatient, emergency visits and ICU – Everything is becoming digitized. With rapid progress in technology, sensors are embedded in weighing scales, blood glucose devices, wheelchairs, patient beds, X-ray machines, etc. Digitized devices generate large streams of data in real-time that can provide insights into patient's health and behavior. If this data is captured, it can be put to use to improve the accuracy of information and enable practitioners to better utilize limited provider resources. It will also significantly enhance patient experience at a health care facility by providing proactive risk monitoring, improved quality of care and personalized attention. Big data can enable complex event processing (CEP) by providing real-time insights to doctors and nurses in the control room.

- Preventive care for ACO – One of the key accountable care (ACO) goals is to provide preventive care. Disease identification and risk stratification are very crucial to business function. Managing real-time feeds coming in from health information exchange (HIE), pharmacists, providers and payers will deliver key information to apply risk stratification and predictive modeling techniques. In the past, companies were limited to historical claims and HRA/survey data but with HIE, the data availability for health analytics has fully changed. Big data tools can significantly enhance the speed of processing and data mining.

- Epidemiology – Through health information exchange (HIE), most of the providers, payers, and pharmacists will be connected through networks in the near future. These networks will facilitate the sharing of data to better enable hospitals and health agencies to track disease outbreaks, patterns, and trends in health issues across a geographic region or across the world allowing determination of source and containment plans.

- Patient care quality and program analysis – With the exponential growth of data and the need to gain insight from information, comes the challenge to process the voluminous variety of information to produce useful metrics and key performance indicators (KPIs) that can improve patient care quality. Big data tools and techniques make it easy processing terabytes and petabytes of data to provide deep analytic capabilities.

In a similar line, with the leverage of the innumerable advancements being accomplished and articulated in the multifaceted discipline of big data analytics, myriad industry segments are jumping into the big data bandwagon in order to make themselves ready to acquire superior competencies especially in anticipation, ideation, implementation, and improvisation of premium and path-breaking services and solutions for the world market. Big data analytics brings forth fresh ways for businesses and governments to analyze a vast amount of unstructured data (streaming as well as stored) to be highly relevant to their customers and constituencies.

10.7   Machine data analytics by Splunk

All our IT applications, platforms, and infrastructures generate a lot of data every millisecond of every day. With more devices and machines in and around us, the amount of machine data is exponentially growing. However, machine data provides useful insights when methodically collected and crunched. The most valuable insights include a definitive record of users' transactions, customer behavior, sensor activity, machine operations, security threats, fraudulent, and fake actions. Machine data hold critical insights useful across the enterprise.

- Monitor end-to-end transactions for online businesses providing 24×7 operations.
- Understand customer experience, behavior and usage of services in real time.
- Fulfill internal service level agreements (SLAs) and monitor service provider agreements.
- Identify spot trends and sentiment analysis on social platforms.
- Map and visualize threat scenario behavior patterns to improve security posture.

Making use of machine data is beset with challenges. It is a difficult proposition to process and analyze machine data by simply following traditional data management and analytics methods. Another challenge is to do the analytics in an interactive fashion in order to bring forth real-time insights. Machine data is generated by a multitude of disparate sources and hence, correlating meaningful events across these is definitely not an easy task to do. The data is unstructured and difficult to fit into a predefined schema. Machine data is of high volume and is majorly time-series data. Hence, there is a valid insistence for novelty-filled approaches for their effective management and analysis. The most valuable insights from machine data are often needed in real time. Traditional business intelligence, data warehouse or IT analytics solutions are simply not designed and engineered for this class of high-volume, dynamic, and poly-structured data.

As indicated in the beginning, machine-generated data is more voluminous than man-generated data. Thus, without an iota of doubt, machine data analytics is occupying a more significant portion in big data analytics. Machine data is being produced $24 \times 7 \times 365$ by nearly every kind of software application and electronic devices. The software applications, server farms, network devices, storage and security appliances, sensors attached to machines, browsers, cameras, and various other systems deployed to support various business operations are continuously generating data relating to their status, situations, any noteworthy events, and activities. Machine data can be found in a variety of formats such as application log files, call detail records (CDRs), user profiles, key performance indicators (KPIs), and clickstream data associated with user web interactions, data files, system configuration files, alerts, and tickets. Machine data is generated by both machine-to-machine (M2M) as well as human-to-machine (H2M) interactions. Nowadays are machines are being empowered by remotely held cloud-based services. So the strengths, sizes, scopes, and speeds of machine interactions and collaborations are on the growth trajectory.

Outside of the traditional IT infrastructure, every controller and processor-based system including HVAC controllers, smart meters, toasters, drones, GPS devices, actuators and robots, manufacturing systems, and RFID tags and consumer-oriented systems such as medical instruments, personal gadgets and gizmos, aircrafts, scientific experiments, and automobiles that contain embedded devices are continuously generating machine data. As the device ecosystem is growing, the list of participating and contributing devices is constantly growing.

With the solid growth of mobiles, wearables, portables, implantables, nomadic and fixed devices, etc., the amount of machine data has grown up exponentially. Accordingly, the IT infrastructure complexity has gone up remarkably in order to host, manage, and deliver machine-centric applications, services, and data. As organizations open up for the brewing trend of "bring your own devices (BYODs)," the enterprise IT team is tasked with several complicated activities.

The goal here is to aggregate, parse, and to visualize machine data to spot trends, and act accordingly. By monitoring and analyzing data emitted by a deluge of diverse, distributed and decentralized devices, there are opportunities galore. Someone wrote that sensors are the eyes and ears of future applications. Environmental monitoring sensors in remote and rough places bring forth the right and relevant knowledge about their operating environments in real-time. The arrival of advanced algorithms for enabling sensor data fusion leads to develop situation-aware applications. With machine data analytics in place, any kind of performance degradation of machines can be identified in real-time and corrective actions can be initiated with full knowledge and confidence. Security and surveillance cameras pump in still images and video data that in turn help analysts and security experts to preemptively stop any kind of undesirable intrusions. Firefighting can become smart with the utilization of machine data analytics. Log analytics is all that is expected to realize preventive maintenance for mission-critical machines.

The much-needed end-to-end visibility, analytics, and real-time intelligence across all of their applications, platforms, and IT infrastructures enable business enterprises to achieve required service levels, manage costs, mitigate security risks, demonstrate and maintain compliance and gain new insights to drive better business decisions and actions. Machine data provides a definitive and time-stamped record of current and historical activity and events within and outside an organization, including application and system performance, user activity, system configuration changes, electronic transaction records, security alerts, error messages, and device locations. Machine data in a typical enterprise is generated in a multitude of formats and structures, as each software application or hardware device records and creates machine data associated with their specific use. Machine data also varies among vendors and even within the same vendor across product types, families, and models.

There are a number of newer use cases being formulated with the pioneering improvements in smart sensors, their ad-hoc and purpose-specific network formation capability, data collection, consolidation, correlation, and corroboration, knowledge discovery and dissemination, information visualization, etc. Splunk (www.splunk.com) is a data analytics company specializing in extracting actionable insights out of diverse, distributed, and decentralized data. Some real-world customer examples include

- E-Commerce – A typical e-commerce site serving thousands of users a day will generate gigabytes of machine data which can be used to provide significant insights into IT infrastructure and business operations.

The Expedia group (https://www.expediagroup.com/home/default.aspx) uses Splunk to avoid website outages by monitoring server and application health and performance. Today, around 3,000 users at Expedia use Splunk to gain real-time visibility on tens of terabytes of unstructured, time-sensitive machine data (from not only their IT infrastructure but also from online bookings, deal analysis, and coupon use).

• Software as a Service (SaaS) – Salesforce.com uses Splunk to mine the large quantities of data generated from its entire technology stack. It has >500 users of Splunk dashboards from IT users monitoring customer experience to product managers performing analytics on services like "Chatter." With Splunk, Salesforce Developer Community (SFDC) claims to have taken application troubleshooting for 100,000 customers to the next level.

• Digital publishing – NPR (https://www.npr.org/) uses Splunk to gain insights of their digital asset infrastructure, to monitor, and troubleshoot their end-to-end asset delivery infrastructure, to measure program popularity and views by the device, to reconcile royalty payments for digital rights and to measure abandonment rates and more.

Splunk Enterprise is the leading platform for collecting, analyzing, and visualizing machine data. It provides a unified way to organize and extract real-time insights from massive amounts of machine data from virtually any source. This includes data from websites, business applications, social media platforms, application servers, hypervisors, sensors, and traditional databases. Once our data is in Splunk, we can search, monitor, report, and analyze it, no matter how unstructured, large or diverse it may be. Splunk software gives us a real-time understanding of what is happening and a deep analysis of what has happened, driving new levels of visibility and insight. This is called operational intelligence.

10.8   Real-time and streaming analytics

When the data size is massive, generally it is being subjected to batch and historical processing techniques to extract all kinds of hidden intelligence. However, on the other hand, there are fast and streaming data, which are relatively small in size but widely vary in structure and speed. There are open source and commercial-grade platforms emerging and evolving for undertaking real-time and streaming analytics on fast and streaming data. Lately, there is a cry for doing immediate and interactive analytics not only on fast data but also on big data to emit out insights in time. With the grand availability of exemplary solutions such as SAP HANA, the days of accomplishing real-time analytics on big data are not too far away.

All these advancements do not imply that the fully matured and stabilized business intelligence (BI) and data warehousing (DW) solutions are going away. But there is a telling need to complement them with newer technologies for storing and analyzing fast and streaming IoT data. The era of real-time and streaming analytics is steadily arriving and there are a number of use cases being unearthed mandating real-time and streaming analytics capabilities for any organization to grow fast. There are well-known use cases such as full-text indexing, recommendation systems (e.g., Netflix* movie recommendations), log analysis, computing web indexes, and data mining. These are the well-known processes that can be allowed to run for extended periods of time. The high-level architecture for real-time processing is given below.

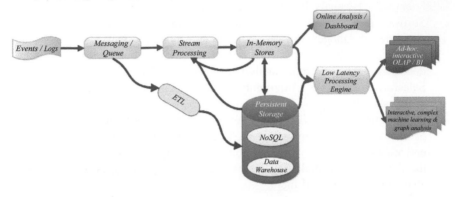

Operational analytics (OA) is a kind of real-time analytics that provides enhanced visibility into business processes, events, and operations as they are happening. The practice of OA is succulently enabled by special technologies that can handle machine data, sensor data, event streams, and other forms of streaming data and big data. OA solutions can also correlate and analyze data collected from multiple sources in various latencies (from batch to real time) to realize and reveal actionable information. Organizations can act on extracted knowledge by sending an appropriate alert notification to the correct manager in time, updating a management dashboard, offering an incentive to a churning customer, adjusting machinery, or preventing fraud.

Majorly Apache Hadoop and MapReduce (MR) technologies have been in the forefront of big data analytics. However, this parallelization framework was primarily designed for big data storage, data management, statistical analysis, and statistical association between various data sources using distributed computing and batch processing. However, today's environment demands all of the above plus real-time analytics. Very recently, Apache Spark and Storm frameworks (https://storm.apache.org/) are drawing an extensive attention and attraction for real-time analytics. Spark use cases include stream processing (e.g., credit card fraud detection), sensor data processing and real-time querying of data for analytics. There are powerful data processing frameworks such as Apache Flink (https://flink.apache.org/) and Apache Samza (http://samza.apache.org/).

There are research works on automating and advancing several tasks through the Spark paradigm. For example, there is a master thesis depicting and describing a valid use case "Real-Time Anomaly Detection in Water Distribution Networks using Spark Streaming." Andrew Psaltis has worked on and presented his findings through a PowerPoint file with the title "Exploring Clickstream Analytics with Kafka, Spark Streaming, and WebSockets." VoltDB people have focused on the scalability and performance aspects of the Spark framework. Reactive applications are a special kind of next-generation applications getting readily developed, deployed, and delivered via the Spark programming model. Performing fast and interactive analytics over Hadoop data with Spark is getting accelerated. OA is increasingly accomplished through the smart leverage of Spark. The widely discoursed use case of insider threat detection is quickly realized through the deftness of Spark. Another research paper explains how Spark comes handy in soft and real-time GPRS traffic analysis for commercial M2M communications. Thus, there is a grandiose concentration by worldwide industry researchers and academic professors in taking the notion of data analytics to the next level with the impressive and influential contributions from Spark.

Similarly doing real-time analytics on streaming data gains immense momentum. Spark can do streaming analytics. On the commercial side, IBM streams analytics (https://www.ibm.com/in-en/cloud/streaming-analytics) is a highly synchronized and syndicated engine for streaming analytics. IBM streaming analytics for IBM Cloud evaluates a broad range of streaming data – unstructured text, video, audio, geospatial, and sensor – helping organizations spot opportunities and risks and make decisions in real time. There are other vendors bringing forth competent and compatible solutions for easing up real-time and streaming analytics. There are so many other ways and means of speeding up the process of real-time analytics. In-memory and in-database analytics are being touted as the most sensible and logical way forward for real-time and streaming analytics. There are supercomputers, purpose-specific appliances, hyperconverged infrastructures (HCIs), clusters, grids and other parallel computers to achieve real-time analytics.

Upsolver (https://www.upsolver.com/data-lake-platform) revolutionizes the way you work with cloud data. By providing a self-service, high-speed compute layer between your data lake and the analytics tools of your choice, Upsolver automates menial data pipeline work, so you can focus on developing analytics and real-time applications.

10.9   The emergence of Edge Clouds for real-time insights

With the runaway success of the pioneering digitization and edge computing technologies and tools, every tangible thing in our daily environments is becoming digitized/smart/sentient object. It is foreseen that everyone in this world will have a smartphone. Every unique asset and artifact (physical, mechanical, electrical, and electronics) in our daily lives is systematically enabled through edge/fog technologies. Ultimately our everyday environments are to be decked with a variety of smart sensors and actuators to fulfill the prime goals of precision-centric context-awareness and activity recognition. There will be deeper and decisive interactions among enabled objects, devices and humans in the days ahead. Further on, the cloud-based cyber applications will have a salivating role in empowering physical items in the ground.

In today's digitally connected society, the large volumes of multi-structured data getting generated through the interactions and collaborations of different and distributed digital elements, smartphones, social media, satellite telemetry, and imagery lead to various new analytical competencies such as social media analytics and sentiment analytics for people empowerment. The prickling challenge is how efficiently and effectively subject captured and cleansed data to various specific investigations to extract real-time intelligence.

There is a new paradigm of fog or edge computing vigorously and rigorously capturing the imagination of IoT professionals these days. That is, the real-time and relatively small-scale processing is shifted to edge devices instead of aggregating and transmitting device data to faraway cloud servers to squeeze out insights. Localized and personalized decisions are essential in certain scenarios and hence the fast-evolving concept of fog computing is being gleefully received. The edge devices are dynamically discovered and linked through body, personal, and local area networks to form ad-hoc edge clouds to accelerate and accentuate edge analytics. With the exponential explosion of connected things, devices, and services, it is understandable that the decentralized networking is the best way forward as it has the inherent potential to reduce infrastructure and maintenance costs. Decentralization guarantees increased robustness by removing single points of failure. By shifting from centralized to decentralized processing, devices at the edges gain greater autonomy to become the core and central point of transactions toward enhanced productivity and value for owners and users.

The public cloud idea typically represents the online, off-premise, and on-demand computing whereas the fog computing is for proximity computing. Of course, there are private and hybrid clouds that use dynamically changing clusters of commodity server machines for data processing and logic execution. But the fog computing paradigm extends the computing to the network of edge devices. The fog vision was conceived and aptly concretized in order to comprehensively attend some specific use cases for the smarter computing era. There are specific applications such as gaming and video conferencing mandating very low and predictable latency. Then there are geo-distributed applications (smarter traffic, grid, etc., pipeline monitoring, environmental monitoring and management through the sensor and actuator networks, etc.). Further on, mobility applications such as connect cars and transports are pitching for the fog paradigm. The next logical step is to have hybrid environments by seamlessly and spontaneously integrating edge and traditional cloud environments for availing advanced and aggregated analytics.

10.10   Deep diving and digging into edge analytics

Devices are increasingly instrumented and interconnected to be expressly adaptive, assistive, articulative, and capable of accomplishing smarter actuation. In other words, edge devices are gradually and glowingly joining in the mainstream computing. That is, they are capable of data capture and processing toward knowledge discovery. Precisely speaking, devices are inherently empowered to perform the transition of data to information and to intelligence. Typically, there are three prominent levels in which usable intelligence can be generated.

The first level is that every participating and contributing device is capable of processing the data it gathers. For example, in a smarter home environment, every type of articles and artifacts such as refrigerators, electrical switches, consumer electronics, media players, machines, instruments, utensils, wares, and equipment could process their data and take decisions as per the situation warrants.

The second level covers the so-called gateways and data-aggregation devices. The other probable nomenclature includes hubs, brokers, middleware, adapters, etc. As we all know that there are bountiful resource-constrained and networked embedded systems in our everyday environments to take care of everyday needs of people. Further on, the maturity and stability of digitization, distribution, and decentralization technologies lead to a massive number of digitized/sentient/smart objects (these are originally ordinary stuff and are enabled to be computational, communicative, sensitive, responsive, perceptive, etc., by various edge and fog technologies such as sensors, actuators, tags, motes, speckles, chips, controllers, stickers, codes, LEDs, etc.). The relevance of gateways and other intermediaries is being felt here as these individual entities need to be clubbed together to get consolidated and composite data to enable the gateways to indulge in analyzing to arrive at insights.

The final level is the cloud-based analytics. That is, edge devices individually and/or through the above-mentioned gateways can connect and integrate with cloud-based analytical platforms and applications so that compact and specialized analytics. The innovations in edge and gateway devices are bringing forth sophisticated algorithms and it is cost-effective to store and analyze granular data at edge devices. With the pervasiveness of network infrastructures, the edge-to-cloud movement is laying a stimulating and sparkling foundation for higher-end analytics at cloud servers. Let us discuss a couple of use cases in the subsequent sections.

The emerging trend of in-memory computing can be a game-changing phenomenon for carving out real-time insights. Cloud-based MQTT, XMPP, and other RESTful servers are being used to capture and store data from different and distributed sensors and instruments. And from there, analytics engine or any other specific systems such as context aggregator and decider can comfortably proceed for producing insights. The idea is for performing historical and comprehensive analytics at the cloud, which is affordable, all-encompassing, and elastic. That is, all the gleaned data have to be sent across to powerful cloud environments for embarking on predictive, prescriptive, and posterior analytics.

10.11   The renowned edge analytics use cases

- Smart water system – This is a specialized system wherein smart sensors for measuring water and flow levels and water quality are the prominent entities deployed on water tanks, reservoirs, and water pipes. This local IoT system comprising multi-faceted sensors is connected to the faraway cloud applications and data sources via the public Internet through a local IoT gateway device. These sensors emit events periodically and report observations such as the water level in the tank, quality parameters such as total dissolved solids, chlorine content, temperature, and the volume of water flow. The sensor data can be processed by the gateway device and the results can be immediately communicated to actuators at the ground level in order to go ahead with the clean-up operations. The sensor data also can be transmitted to cloud systems in order to have comprehensive analytics. But for real-time systems, edge analytics is the best course of action.

- Smarter grid – This has been one of the widely quoted use cases as the energy optimization has been the universal goal for the nations across the globe. The smart grid application may run on network edge devices such as smart meters and micro-grids. Based on the brewing energy demand, the power availability and the lowest price, these devices automatically switch to alternative energies like solar and the wind. Gateways at the edge capture, store, and process the data generated by grid sensors and devices and accordingly issue control commands to the actuators to proceed with the decisions made. Edge analytics devices also filter the data to be consumed locally and send the rest to faraway powerful systems for coordinated and compact analysis to generate tactical as well as strategic insights, reports, maps, charts, graphs, etc. to be disseminated into and displayed by knowledge visualization tools and dashboards.

- Smarter homes and buildings – Edge analytics enables localized monitoring and decision-enablement in time. One or more edge devices in the neighborhood are purposefully forming ad hoc clouds in order to accomplish coordinated processing. The trend is clearly tending toward decentralized decision-making with all the household consumer electronics, utensils, and monitoring systems such as air conditioning, elevators, security, and surveillance cameras are getting instrumented and interconnected to share their capabilities with one another seamlessly and spontaneously. There is a spurt in deploying a growing array of sensors and actuators for monitoring, measuring, management, and maintenance purposes within homes and buildings. Temperature, humidity, gas, fire, presence, and pressure levels are being minutely monitored by these sensors and the data captured are systematically combined to form reliable and holistic measurements. The local gateway devices are then leveraged to process and take decisions in time. That is, insights-driven actuators can plunge into appropriate actions with all the intrinsic clarity and confidence. Automated energy management through continuous observations and actions is a well-known edge analytics application.

Similarly other important junctions, eating joints, auditoriums, battlefields, airports, railway stations, entertainment plazas, educational institutions, manufacturing plants and floors, warehouses, theaters, etc. are going to be technologically stuffed, saturated, and sandwiched to be smarter in their operations and offerings. The security, safety, emergency, concierge services are going to be very common, casual and cheap through edge clouds and analytics.

- Smarter retailing – The shopping experience for shoppers at hypermarkets and malls is going to be unique with recently attained edge processing and knowledge delivery capabilities. For example, designing and delivering location and context-based services to users, implementing augmenting reality, improving the overall shopping experience, or dealing with secured online payment are going to be the technology-sponsored features and facilities.

- Self-maintaining trains – Sensor monitoring on a train's ball-bearing can detect heat levels, allowing applications to send an automatic alert to the train operator to stop the train at next station for emergency maintenance and avoid potential derailment.
- Smarter mines – In lifesaving air vents scenario, sensors on vents monitor air conditions flowing in and out of mines and automatically change air-flow if conditions become dangerous to miners.
- Device integration – It is going to be the connected era. Devices are getting integrated with one another in the vicinity as well as with remote ones. The device connectivity enables interactions and coordination resulting in a lot of data to be meticulously captured and methodically investigated to derive actionable insights. Today every industry segment is blessed with a number of differently enabled devices. The faster maturity and stability of edge/fog computing along with innumerable connected devices have laid down a stimulating and scintillating foundation for venturing into hitherto unexplored avenues for aggregating fresh revenues for investors, entrepreneurs, startup companies, and established business houses and behemoths.
- Smarter traffic systems – Traffic lights are becoming very prominent and pervasive in urban areas for enabling pedestrians as well as vehicle drivers. There are high-fidelity video cameras in plenty along the roads, expressways, tunnels, etc. in order to activate and accelerate a variety of real-time tasks for pedestrians, traffic police, and vehicle drivers. Wireless access points like WiFi, 3G, 4G, road-side units, and smart traffic lights are deployed along the roads. Vehicles-to-vehicle, vehicle-to-access points, and access points-to-access points interactions enrich the application of this scenario.

All kinds of connected vehicles and transport systems need actionable insights in time to derive and deliver a rich set of context-aware services. Safety is an important factor for car and road users and there are additional temporal as well as spatial services being worked out. With driverless cars under intense development and testing, insights-driven decisions, and knowledge-centric actions are very vital for next-generation transports.

The impending need is to have smarter traffic systems in order to fulfill the unique goals behind the smarter traffic. This system has to be deployed at each intersection within the city areas and they can be networked with one another to have hooked up with centralized control and analytics systems. It also has to be equipped with a variety of sensors to measure the distance and the speed of approaching vehicles from every direction. The other requirements include detecting the presence of pedestrians and cyclists crossing the street or road in order to proactively issue "slow down" warnings to incoming vehicles and instantaneously modifying its own cycle to prevent collisions. Besides ensuring utmost safety and the free flow of traffic, all kinds of traffic data need to be captured and stocked in order to do specific analytics to accurately predict and prescribe the ways and means of substantially improving the traffic system. Ambulances need to get a way out through traffic-free open lanes in the midst of chaotic and cruel traffic.

The noteworthy factor here is that the smarter traffic system has to learn, decide, and act instantaneously in order to avert any kind of accidents. That is, the real-time reaction is the crucial need and hence, the concept of edge clouds out of edge devices for collaboratively collecting different data and processing them instantaneously to spit out insights is gaining widespread and overwhelming momentum. Another point here is that data flows in streams. Thus, all kinds of discreet/simple, as well as complex events, need to be precisely and perfectly captured and combined to be subjected into a bevy of investigations to complete appropriate actions. The whole process has to be initiated at the earliest through a powerful and pioneering knowledge discovery and dissemination platform to avoid any kind of losses for people and properties. Here collecting and sending data to remote cloud servers to arrive at competent decisions are found inappropriate for real-time and low-latency applications. However, the edge data can be aggregated and transmitted to powerful cloud servers casually in batches to have historical diagnostic and deterministic analytics at the later point in time.

10.12   The architectural components of the smarter traffic system

1. As articulated above, as far as physical components are concerned, a smarter traffic system has to include traffic lights, sensors, and actuators within its jurisdictional region so that the reaction time is on the order of <10 ms.
2. A miniaturized orchestration platform is an overseeing software solution, which has to be a part and parcel of the system. This module is greatly obligated to orchestrate and manage all the other software modules of the system effectively. It has to be policy-aware. That is, well-intended policies can be established easily and enforced accordingly towards effective governance.
3. A centralized decision-enabling module is another noteworthy one for garnering data from all the deployed traffic lights and pushing the decisions to individual traffic lights through a messaging bus, which is another mandatory software solution for enabling data transmission on both directions.

There can be multiple smarter traffic systems from different providers tied up with different networking and communication service providers. All these deviations and deficiencies need to be addressed systematically in order to accomplish edge analytics. Thus, any edge analytics software solution has to take multiple scenarios and factors into consideration in order to be right and relevant for realizing real-time applications such as smarter traffic. Such systems are capable of taking lightning-fast yet correct decisions which are turning out to be essential for the projected smarter world. A hybrid version of traditional and edge analytics is vividly illustrated in the figure below.

10.13   The technological components of the hybrid IoT analytics platform

Most edge devices exchange data and send the information to centralized control, storage, and analytical systems at private or public cloud. But the businesses expect more deft and decisive services quickly and hence edge devices individually as well as collectively are more often empowered to arrive at actionable insights instantaneously through local and proximate processing. At the edge, there can be a litany of sensors and actuators (cyber-physical systems, connected devices, robots, consumer electronics, autonomous agents, intelligent machines, etc.). It is going to be a grand cluster of resource-constrained as well as computationally powerful entities. To have pragmatic edge analytics, it is prudent and paramount to smartly leverage a combination of promising and proven technological solutions.

With machines communicating one another in the vicinity as well with remote ones through personal, local, and wide area networks, there came a number of newer applications such as home, building, and industry automation systems. The domains of telematics and telemetry have grown significantly since then. There are a few popular messaging protocols enabling the capture and communication of device data and event messages to their respective destinations. All these tectonic technological advancements gel well in building and deploying sophisticated situation-aware applications.

Extensible messaging and presence protocol (XMPP) is one of the popular communication protocols providing additional security features such as secure communication and authentication of end users. XMPP can be used for the unified communication of messaging, presence information and file transfer. XMPP brings up a number of applications such as sensor-enabled monitoring and management of systems and even environments.

Complex event processing (CEP) – Relational databases (DBs) are mainly designed to collect and store data. As far as the analysis aspect is concerned, DB is extensively used for aggregating and filtering data, searching for unique patterns and arriving at high-level summary information. However, the analysis happens off-line. But any standards-compliant CEP engine is capable of receiving incoming streams of messages and runs them through a set of predefined and continuous queries to produce hidden patterns, usable associations and tips in time.

CEP is the key technology for processing volumes of low-level events and transforming them into higher-level and composite events for visualization and automated response. For example, CEP is being used to detect any suspicious credit card usage by monitoring credit card activity as it occurs. It can perform time-series analysis and trending over streams of events and it can correlate a stream of real-time information with stored and historical data, such as new credit card activity with customer information from a CRM system.

With the focus is turning toward edge analytics, the CEP technology is being tweaked to be used in edge devices apart from being taken to high-end cloud servers. As indicated previously, with our everyday environments are stuffed with innumerable sensors, the scale of messages emanating is going to be tremendously large. The brewing need here is how to smartly partition the CEP query execution across the edge devices and even the cloud. Transmitting data to the off-premise cloud is beset with data privacy, locality, and security issues besides wasting the precious network bandwidth. However, considering the limited capacities and capabilities of edge devices for proper analytics, a kind of lighter version of CEP engine is being implemented to speed up the process of knowledge discovery out of large-scale event messages. The control flow is as follows. Sensor and actuator data being generated are gleaned to be routed through an edge/fog data aggregator.

10.14 The key capabilities of next-generation IoT data analytics platforms

IoT data analytics not only for making sense out of IoT data to empower everyday devices (physical, mechanical, electrical, and electronics) to be intelligent in their operations and outputs but also enable end-users and knowledge workers to benefit immensely in their everyday occupations and obligations. There are IoT application enablement platforms (AEPs) and gateways in plenty but there are a lot of recently expressed needs to build and sustain highly competent IoT data analytics platforms in order to exploit IoT data efficiently and effectively. These end-to-end analytical platforms are slated to connect, extract, preprocess, analyze, and mine data from a large number of sensors, actuators, transactional and operational systems, engineered systems, etc. Typically, operational and information technologies (OT & IT) systems are transitioning from the systems of records to the systems of engagements due to the incredible fact that new-generation systems are intrinsically empowered to have purposeful collaboration, correlation, and corroboration with one another and with faraway services too. Data virtualization, integration, capture, cleansing, and ingestion into data storage and file systems are the other tasks accomplished through a host of publish–subscribe servers, the tweaked ETL tools, and a litany of connectors, adaptors, etc. Finally, the proposed platforms have to have a seamless integration with different report-generation tools, dashboards, consoles, and other visualization platforms to disseminate and display what is extracted in multiple preferred forms and formats.

The figure below clearly articulates the trends and transitions happening in the data analytics space. Originally it was batch processing on big data but the direction and the destination are to do real-time processing of big data to generate real-time insights. The IoT data volume is tremendously huge and there is an insistence for instantaneous extraction of intelligence to enable timely decision-making. To benefit out of IoT data, interactive processing is being recommended. This is the reason for the emergence of competent solutions for real-time IoT analytics.

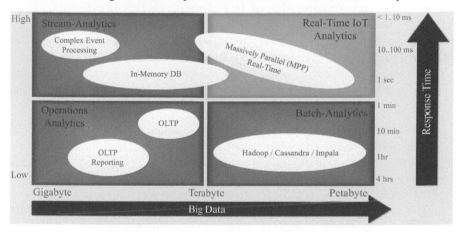

The key capabilities – An IoT data analytics platform in smart synchronization with IoT AEPs and IoT gateways are capable of doing the following. It

- enables interoperable, portable, scalable and reusable application building
- uncovers timely and actionable insights
- works on personal, campus, local, metro, and wide area networks
- enables the realization of smart objects, devices, networks, and environments
- leads to the production of pioneering and people-centric applications and services
- helps to come out with precise predictions and prescriptions
- facilitates process excellence
- embraces IoT protocols such as AMQP, MQTT, XMPP, CoAP, REST, etc.
- guarantees preventive maintenance of infrastructures
- ensures the optimized utilization of distributed assets through monitoring, measurement, and management
- safeguards the safety and security of people and properties
- monitors complex environments to guarantee business performance, productivity, and resilience

There are viable frameworks and management platforms for integrating sensors and devices to remote cloud centers. These enable cloud connectivity to facilitate capabilities such as data capture, rules/policy engine, configuration, and file transfer.

Precisely speaking, with the ready availability of versatile technologies and enabling tools, the long and arduous process of data to information and to knowledge gets accelerated and augmented to fulfill the long-drawn vision of the smarter planet. Actionable insights produced in time go a long way in elevating machines becoming smarter and men the smartest.

10.15   The prime modules of IoT data analytics platforms

Considering the rising complexity of next-generation analytics requirements and hence the enabling platforms, the sophistication of contributing modules for IoT data analytics platforms should be consistently on the climb. In this section, the key modules and their unique features and functionalities are being expounded.

1. Data virtualization, integration and ingestion modules – Millions of connected devices and sensors are pumping out a complicated set of data of their own as well as about their environments and they need to be captured, transformed, and ingested into the underlying IoT database with higher write performance. There are proven ETL and ELT tools in order to speed up data movement

2. Data analytics platforms – There are big, fast, and streaming data analytics platforms in plenty from both open-source software community as well as commercial-grade product vendors. However, IoT data analytics are gaining the mind as well as market shares considering their uniqueness in setting up and sustaining next-generation smarter systems, networks, and environments. Data storage and management systems are very important. There are parallelized, clustered and distributed RDBMS (SQL) systems, NoSQL, and NewSQL systems. For accelerated analytics, there are in-memory databases, in-database analytics, specially made appliances, etc.

3. Data and knowledge visualization platforms – Dashboards, portals, consoles, reports, maps, graphs, charts, etc. are the main components for vividly and vivaciously visualizing the knowledge obtained. The seamless integration with visualization tools for displaying the knowledge obtained in a user-preferred fashion and format is a must for any standard IoT data analytics platform.

4. IoT application enablement platforms (AEPs) – This platform is enabling the aspect of service design, development, deployment, and delivery quickly with a little coding. Typically these platforms come with a variety of libraries, connectors, drivers, adapters, services, etc. and through composing and configuring rather than coding, pioneering applications for all kinds of industry verticals can be accomplished quickly.

On the non-functional aspects, the platforms need to be high-performing, highly scalable, available, and secure, easily configurable, customizable, etc.

10.16   The reference architecture (RA) for IoT data analytics platform

The architecture diagram below illustrates the principal components of the platform in accelerating the IoT data analytics toward squeezing out hidden patterns, beneficial associations, fresh possibilities and opportunities, actionable tips and techniques for enhanced business efficiency and value, lower TCO, higher RoI, and faster time to market, real-time alerts, etc.

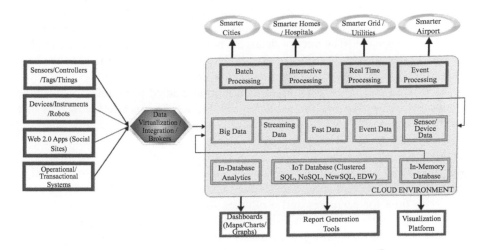

A typical IoT analytics platform has to have the capability to rapidly build and refine extensible models of empowered objects of the physical world and their interrelationships with the artifacts of the cyber world. All kinds of advanced algorithms need to be carefully identified and incorporated to enable deeper and decisive analysis of incoming data, pinpoint possible opportunities and spots of botherations, and deliver insights through visualization tools, dashboards, portals, reports, graphs, maps, charts, etc.

10.17   The renowned use cases for IoT data analytics

As exemplified above, the insights drawn out of IoT data are going to be game-changing for many industry verticals. There are deeper studies and exhortations eulogizing the contributions of IoT data analytics for steadying and steering all kinds of businesses in a safe and smart manner.

Predictive maintenance using sensors-attached assets – Asset tracking and management are gaining attraction across industry verticals. Due to the mission-critical nature of industry machinery, defense equipment, healthcare instruments, robots, connected electronics, cyber-physical systems (CPS) and digitized entities in peoples' lives, identifying their fragile nature and predicting maintenance duration are very vital for ensuring the longevity of assets and the business continuity. Devices are bound to deteriorate over time until they eventually break. By closely monitoring their functioning and contributions, it is possible to spot the pain and problem areas proactively and preemptively. The OA of device data is the way forward for prolonging the device life.

Smarter grids – The voluminous production of smart electricity meters, the arrival of advanced metering infrastructure (AMI) and the real-time analytics of IoT data have led to the realization of smarter grids. Energy conservation and preservation are seeing the light, energy management is getting fully automated, energy utilization is highly optimized, etc. It is all about monitoring and controlling network devices, managing service outages and dispatching crews in time with all the relevant resources. The energy data gets processed in real-time in order to give consumers, distributors and generators all the timely intelligence to plan the best course of actions with all clarity and confidence.

Almost all the industry segments are getting readied to be relevant for their constituents by centralizing the analytics capabilities. The picture below tells that how the IoT data analytics takes the manufacturing domain to greater heights.

Connected cars – This is another celebrated example for IoT analytics. A specialized IoT data analytics platform is capable of bringing the much-needed transformations for the automotive enterprise with a number of new-generation capabilities such as real-time data about vehicles and their parts and pragmatic insights in time for car users and producers through highly advanced diagnostic, predictive, prescriptive and prognostics analytics. Automobile services providers are increasingly collaborating with analytical services providers to bring forth a bevy of insights-driven capabilities to help automotive manufacturers to gain valuable insights by systematically analyzing real-time data being streamed from connected cars. There are big and real-time data analytics platforms for processing sensor data from connected cars for knowledge discovery. The insights include real-time alerts on driver behavior, traffic level, road safety or the need for maintenance and repairs. Any end-to-end platform ensures a single yet comprehensive view of cars' data and the associated insights to inform automotive engineers about the various aspects of the car such as their safety records, predictive maintenance, and performance. Actionable insights are being insisted on realizing smarter parking assistance and traffic management systems, self-driving cars, etc. Precisely not only car drivers, owners, mechanics, and manufacturers, but also all kinds of car occupants gain immense benefits out of the IoT data analytics solutions and services.

In summary, with the amount of IoT data getting generated, collected and subjected to a variety of deeper and decisive investigations is going to be in the range of exabytes, the IT infrastructures and platforms need to be specially and smartly engineered and enhanced to comfortably crunch data heaps to derive actionable intelligence. Therefore, with software-defined clouds emerging as the one-stop IT infrastructure solution, cloud-hosted, end-to-end and converged analytical solutions and services are turning out to be the mandatory ones for the ensuing knowledge era.

The data analytics locations – With IoT data are produced and pumped in big quantities, apart from the well-known infrastructural and platform challenges, there is a fresh set of analytical capabilities and competencies being accentuated these days by IoT luminaries and visionaries to speed up the process of accomplishing IoT data analytics. With the increased complexity, there will be insistence for advanced algorithms. As articulated above, first the analytics can be accomplished at the level and layer of edge /fog devices and second the data can be captured and communicated to a cloud-based analytics platform to carry out historical, batch, ad hoc, and even real-time processing of device and sensor data.

There are a few options being experimented, expounded, and exposed. The edge devices can be clustered together in an ad hoc fashion and enabled to take crucial decisions in time to accordingly feed and activate actuators, controllers, robots, and other devices to embark on the correct journey. That is, forming edge clouds is highly recommended in order to facilitate proximate processing and decision-making as the processing power, storage capacity, and memory range of individual edge devices are typically on the lower side. Through a cloud formation, several devices in the vicinity can be clubbed together to enable the required processing. In other words, the processing and storage capabilities of all the participating devices are being subtly and smartly used to fulfill any analytical needs at the edges itself.

The second option is to leverage IoT and sensor gateways for performing analytical computations out of all the data emanating out of edge devices. Smartphones, Wi-Fi routers, Internet-connected media players, and other reasonably powerful devices in the environment can be tasked to do real-time processing to make right inferences. Further on, a standardized publish–subscribe server software can be deployed on a nearby machine to receive all coming event messages that can be in turn supplied to all the subscribers.

Specific and generic analytical services and applications are being developed, curated and stored in cloud-based service repositories. A standardized OSGi gateway installed at any high-end edge device can download the appropriate services from different cloud registries over the Internet communication infrastructure, install and activate them dynamically to fulfill varying analytical requirements. Device-specific as well as analytics-centric services can be discovered from various remote sources, downloaded, configured, and activated them in runtime in order to empower edge devices as well as to arrive at people and situation-aware services. The OSGi platform brings in the much-needed dynamism and adaptivity. For distributed device analytics, this modularization platform is of immense help. Originally the OSGi framework was developed for embedded devices. However, considering its key differentiators in providing highly modular applications, enterprise-scale applications too overwhelmingly use the OSGi concept to be dynamic and distinct. For edge analytics, the OSGi-sponsored modularity and the Java-induced portability come handy.

Another method is to use a lightweight complex event processing (CEP) engine at the edge side in order to capture and crunch event messages and send all sorts of insights and inferences to respective systems to contemplate countermeasures with all the clarity and confidence. The picture below vividly illustrates how IoT gateway empowered with different software components and capabilities facilitate real-time analytics.

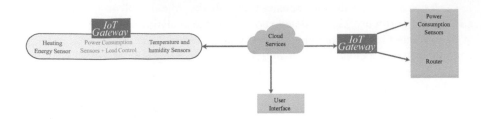

10.18   Why had Cloud-based IoT data analytics?

The following are the major reasons for going ahead with cloud-based data analytics. The cloud landscape is consistently on the growth path. Exceedingly public clouds are leveraged for analytical platforms and applications. The reasons for such a turnaround and transformation are given below. Not only public clouds, the other cloud arrangements such as private, hybrid, and community clouds are also being experimented in order to speed up the analytics process in an efficient and effective fashion. As insisted in this chapter, the idea of edge clouds is flourishing because most of the data are getting generated by edge devices.

That is, besides the astounding journey of conventional clouds, the days of edge clouds are really fascinating. Considering the undiminishing needs of data security and real-time intelligence, performing analytics at edge devices is the right approach and answer.

- Agility and affordability – No capital investment of large-size infrastructures for analytical workloads. Just use and pay. Quickly provisioned and decommissioned once the need goes down.
- Data analytics platforms in clouds – Therefore leveraging cloud-enabled and ready platforms (generic or specific, open or commercial-grade, etc.) are fast and easy
- NoSQL & NewSQL databases and data warehouses in clouds – All kinds of database management systems and data warehouses in cloud speed up the process of next-generation data analytics. Database as a service (DaaS), data warehouse as a service (DWaaS), business process as a service (BPaaS), and other advancements lead to the rapid realization of analytics as a service (AaaS).
- WAN optimization technologies – There are WAN optimization products for quickly transmitting large quantities of data over the Internet infrastructure
- Social and professional networking sites are running in public cloud environments
- Enterprise-class applications in clouds – All kinds of customer-facing applications are cloud-enabled and deployed in highly optimized and organized cloud environments

- Anytime, anywhere, any network and any device information and service access are being activated through cloud-based deployment and delivery.
- Cloud integrators, brokers & orchestrators – There are products and platforms for seamless interoperability among geographically distributed cloud environments. There are collaborative efforts toward federated clouds and the Intercloud.
- Sensor/device-to-cloud integration frameworks are available to transmit ground-level data to cloud storages and processing.

While public clouds are on the verge of reaching out the much-expected maturity in accomplishing well-intended analytic processes, other kinds of clouds are steadily tending toward the mainstream computing resources for ambient analytics.

10.19   The distinct capabilities of IoT data analytics platforms

Several things occur simultaneously. That is the positive news indeed for the total humanity! We all know all sorts of ground-level physical systems are systematically enabled to be smart in their operations and offerings through spontaneous integrations with faraway cyber/virtual systems and services. This fledgling yet fabulous domain of intense study and research is called cyber-physical systems (CPS). On the IoT side, there are conscious efforts to spontaneously integrate digitized/smart/sentient objects. And every kind of everyday devices from specific domains such as manufacturing, retail, utilities, energy, logistics, healthcare, and buildings and cities are linked up with other devices in the vicinity as well as with cloud-based software applications, services, and data sources. Now there are supercharged platforms for collecting and crunching all IoT and CPS data in time to extract value-adding information and insights in time. For getting the intended success and support, the platforms have to be intrinsically blessed with the following functionalities.

- *Scalability* – This is an important factor for large-scale data processing. The envisioned platform has to have this feature (scale-up and out) to enable the underlying database systems as well as the cloud infrastructures.
- *Faster data ingestion* – Typically millions of sensors would transmit their data and hence data loading has to be really quick in order to enable real-time processing and knowledge discovery. The database system has to be designed from the ground up in such a way to load a few millions of rows per second without affecting query performance. There are a number of standards-compliant protocols such as MQTT, CoAP, XMPP, and RESTful for handling massive amounts of messages.
- *Faster query processing* – This is another vital requirement for the IoT era. The database system has to be capable of handling and executing all kinds of queries at high speed to bring forth timely insights.
- *Flexibility and portability* – The platform has to have the innate capability of frictionless running on single as well as cluster servers in on-premise as well as cloud environments.

- *Distributed processing* – The much-maligned distributed architecture is the way forward for efficiently tackling the challenges thrown by big and real-time data. The concept of fog or edge computing insists for initial processing at the end-user devices directly or on some powerful intermediaries locally in order to lessen the data transmission and processing loads on cloud servers. That is, there is a tectonic shift in the processing paradigm. The processing logic increasingly travels to locations wherein data gets generated or resides. The centralized processing steadily paves the way for edge computing. A kind of hybrid processing model based on edge as well as cloud computing models is to emerge and evolve faster in order to enable ground-level devices to partake in the much-complicated processing.
- *Better data compression* – Due to the large size of data, it is paramount to have a good compression mechanism in place so that the data getting persisted and transmitted over any network has to be of lower size.
- *Data analytics* – Batch and real-time processing of big, fast, streaming, and IoT data are essential requirements for spitting out actionable insights. There are several ready-made platforms for capturing different kinds of data at different speeds. The complex event processing (CEP) engine is another indispensable module for making sense out of event messages.
- *Interfaces* – RESTful APIs are being touted as the simple and straightforward way of interfacing with a variety of remote systems. Because of its simplicity, even resource-constrained devices can easily get integrated with enterprise and cloud applications.
- *Deep learning* – The requirement of machine learning capabilities on analytical platforms is being insisted considering the irrefutable fact that machine learning especially deep learning helps to go deeper in order to extract precise and powerful insights.

In summary, any IoT data analytics platform destined for success and stardom has to have the features and facilities for doing path-breaking analytics. The platform has to be modular enough for running on-premise as well as off-premise (cloud) environments. As explained above, edge clouds are the brewing concept for facilitating the much-discoursed edge analytics. As there are powerful devices joining in the network to function as IoT gateways and the age-old decentralized networking aspect is salivatingly resurrecting, analytics at source, intermediaries, and clouds is to see the light. Ultimately it is all about ambient "Analytics as a Service" (AaaS) or analytics everywhere every time toward the world of ambient intelligence (AmI).

10.20   Conclusion

It is a well-known truth that the volume of machine-generated data is much heavier than man-generated data. With the projected trillions of digitized objects, billions of connected devices, and millions of software applications, the data size of poly-structured data is going to grow exponentially. We need to explore and expedite the data analytics processes, platforms, patterns, and practices toward data-driven insights and insights-driven decisions.

The delectable advancements in the spectacular domain of analytics are leading to a variety of innovations for business automation and acceleration. There are platform solutions and services emerging for the batch as well as interactive processing of big data. In this chapter, we have described various analytical capabilities at different levels and layers needed for extracting pragmatic insights out of IoT data. At one end, cloud-based analytics is fast-maturing and stabilizing and at the other end for certain scenarios, IoT data analytics is being recommended by forming edge clouds out of edge devices. Real-time decision-enablement and actuation are made possible through the proximate processing, filtering, and analytics through the lighter versions of various analytical solutions.

Chapter 11

Detection of anomaly over streams using isolation forest

Chellammal Surianarayanan[1] and Saranya Kunasekaran[1]

Abstract

Machine learning algorithms provide useful methods for detecting anomaly over streaming data. There are two major categories of machine learning algorithms, namely supervised and unsupervised algorithms for detecting anomaly. Of these two categories, supervised algorithms need to be trained using huge collection of 'training data', prior to the detection of anomaly in unforeseen data. Here, the training data is required to be labelled data where the label refers to the predefined class. But in reality, labelled data may not always be available to train the machine learning algorithms. In such situations, unsupervised algorithms provide a mechanism of detecting anomaly. In this chapter, the usefulness of unsupervised (clustering) algorithms for anomaly detection over streams is analysed.

11.1 Introduction

Many real-world applications in various domains such as healthcare, business environment, IT parks, governance, stock markets, and monitoring systems tend to generate continuous data with respect to speed. Such continuously flowing data is typically termed as streaming data as the data has neither beginning nor end. Due to the increased usage of the Internet, variety of devices, and smart sensors tend to produce streaming data in huge volume [1]. For example, in one minute 347,222 new tweets on Twitter, about 701,389 logins on Facebook, more than 2.78 million video views on YouTube, and 20.8 million messages on WhatsApp, etc., are getting generated. The Internet of Things (IoT) typically refers to the data streams that are generated by different sensors such as health monitoring sensors, weather monitoring sensors, satellite sensors, mobile phones, smart devices, Tweets from Facebook, and WhatsApp data. Processing of stream data is completely different from that of static data which remains same with respect to time. Very frequently

[1]Department of Computer Science, Government Arts and Science College, Srirangam, Affiliated to Bharathidasan University, India

streaming data needs to be analyzed in real time in order to take timely decisions. Another important characteristic of streaming data is that it may occur with fast speed which results in significant volume of data also. Processing continuous flow of data in real time needs more efficient techniques to handle both volume and velocity of the streams of event [2].

It becomes mandatory for organizations to analyze these streams with minimum latency and make better decision for certain issues such as anomaly detection. Any kind of event that deviates from its normal behavior is termed as anomaly [3]. Anomalies are called using different names according to different domains. For example, in image processing, it may be called as outlier; in healthcare sector, it is named as abnormal; in networking, it is referred as intrusion; in bank transactions, it may be called as fraudulent transaction; and in telecommunication, it is named as malware.

Like any other data, streaming data also contains anomaly. Anomalies present in a dataset needs to be detected as it helps to identify actionable signals within the data and uncovers the outliers primarily gives alert to key events in the data. Unless otherwise these events are detected, it may lead to loss of valuable information (say for example a sudden spike in customer data) to loss of life. The need for processing the data in real time can be understood from the following example. Consider a patient admitted in Intensive Care Unit (ICU). His/her vital parameters, namely, heart rate, respiratory rate, temperature, oxygen saturation, pulse rate, and others are being monitored continuously using bed side monitors. Now what becomes crucial is that analyzing the data instantly at the time of monitoring itself. If the monitored data is found to be abnormal, immediately appropriate decision must be taken to ensure the healthiness of the patient. Here one can realize the significance of processing the data at the time of occurrence.

Equal weightage and importance need to be given for the detection techniques also. Various techniques are in place for the detection of anomaly. Conventionally anomaly detection was manual. With the advent of machine learning techniques, anomalies are being automatically detected. Machine learning algorithms are found to have a significant role in detection of anomalies in various domains [4]. Since a variety of algorithms are being developed for different purposes, again, it becomes crucial to identity appropriate machine learning algorithm for a given domain and for a given problem/situation. For example, one such important criterion needs to be taken into account is with respect to the nature of the data, i.e., whether the available data is labeled data or unlabeled data.

In this chapter, the application of two unsupervised algorithms, namely, one class support vector machine (OCSVM) and isolation forest (IF) have been compared in detecting anomalies over healthcare data set. With this perspective, in this chapter, the performance of two algorithms. The reason behind the selection of this healthcare domain is that detection of critical diseases at their early stage by detecting the presence of anomalies can reduce mortality rate [5]. In addition, the fixing of different operational parameters of the above algorithms has been presented elaborately.

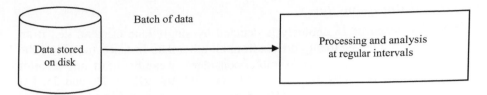

Figure 11.1   Batch processing

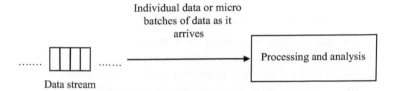

Figure 11.2   Stream processing

11.2   Streaming data

A simple analogy to understand data stream is the way the water flows through a larger river or a tributary. The river has no beginning or end. For example, data generated from traffic light is streaming data which is continuous or discrete and has no start or finish. The streaming data that come from numerous sources are likely to flow into a single, continuous, or combined form. The data format of streams may be structured or unstructured. The real-world examples include streaming data generated in industrial applications, hospitals, networking devices, servers, banking financial domains, sensors, social media, remote sensing, etc. [5]. An important aspect related to streaming data is that since the data arrives with high speed and it is continuous, the storage becomes infeasible and thus the data needs to be processed efficiently during it is arrival.

To provide a better insight for streaming data, its processing may be compared with conventional batch processing. In batch processing, large volume of data will be processed all at once at regular intervals of time whereas streaming data will get processed almost at real time and the output data rate generation is likely to match that of input data. Typical nature of batch processing and stream processing is shown through Figures 11.1 and 11.2, respectively.

11.3   Types of anomalies and need for anomaly detection

Anomalies are of three types, namely, point anomaly, contextual anomaly and collective anomaly [6].

11.3.1 Point anomaly

Here the presence of an anomaly is decided by single data element, i.e., if an individual data element totally differs from all other data instance, then it will be termed as point anomaly. For example, consider a wearable heart rate monitor producing data stream as *66, 74, 67, 71, 85, 102, 94, 91, 77, 79,* and *58*. Let the normal range for heart rate is 60–95 bpm (beats per minute). Any individual element whose value occurs outside the above range is termed as anomaly. Here, *102* and *58* are considered as point anomalies as they deviate from normal range.

11.3.2 Contextual anomaly

If an individual data instance is anomalous within a specific context, then it will represent a contextual anomaly. It may be also called as conditional anomaly. Contextual anomaly involves two attributes such as contextual attributes and behavioral attributes. Contextual attributes are determined based on the context of data instance. For example, in time series data, time is considered as a contextual attribute which determines the position of the instance on the entire sequence. The behavioral attributes define the values of the attributes within a specific context. A data, which is considered as anomaly in a given context, would be normal instance for some other context. For example, in healthcare sector, the range of normal heart rate for adults is 60–95 bpm whereas for athletes, the range of normal heart rate is 40–60 bpm. Here, a heart rate say 60 is abnormal for adults, but normal for athletes.

11.3.3 Collective anomaly

If a collection of data instances is anomalous with respect to the whole data set, then it is represented as collective anomaly [7]. Here an individual data instance itself is not considered as an anomaly, until it appears within a group or a collection. Consider in the same healthcare scenario, a data stream look like *66, 55, 72, 104, 93, 99, 65, 98, 99, 104, 55, 68, 72, 102, 91, 78, etc*. From the above data, *99, 104, 55* is a collective anomaly as it appears as a group of events. But the same data that occur as individual elements in the data set are not considered as collective anomaly, i.e., a collection of related data instances as a group will be anomalous with respect to the whole dataset.

11.3.4 Need for anomaly detection

Anomaly detection is applicable in various domains such as fraud detection in financial domain, intrusion detection in network, and disease detection in healthcare. Thus, any abnormal behavior needs to be detected and analyzed as it contains very important and useful information which is used to take different kinds of control actions depending upon the domain. While detecting anomaly over streaming data is concerned, we need to consider two aspects, namely, (i) some technique to detect the presence of anomaly and (ii) the time at which the anomaly is getting detected. In life critical applications, say for example detecting anomalies in heart beat data of a patient whose vital parameters are continuously being monitored, the detection of anomaly almost in real time is very crucial.

Detecting anomalies is a most challenging task in real-world applications. It may be simpler for data at rest, but it is really harder for data on the fly as the data flow continuous with respect to time. Following are the challenges that occur during anomaly detection over streams in real time.

- The exact perception of anomaly is different for different domains. For example, in medical domain, a small variation from normal behavior is considered as anomaly, while small fluctuation in stock market is considered as normal. Hence, applying techniques to detect anomalies varies from domain to domain.
- The data is likely to have the characteristics of concept drift where the distribution of data changes over time.
- The events in data streams may have undetermined data points which arrives at high rate. The rate of data arrival is not fixed for all the domains. The detection methods should adjust accordingly.
- Anomaly detection technique should be able to handle a wide range of anomalies, types of anomalies and data labels. All these factors are domain dependent.

11.4   Machine learning techniques for anomaly detection

Broadly speaking, two major categories of machine learning algorithms are being used: (i) clustering-based approaches (ii) classification-based approaches.

Clustering approaches can be used when the dataset available has no label associated with it. To facilitate the extraction of knowledge from massive data, clustering technique divides the massive data into clusters of similar objects. That is similar objects are grouped into same cluster. Within a single cluster, the objects are similar whereas the objects belong to different clusters are dissimilar. Similarity is computed using distance measure such as Euclidean distance or density measure such as number of neighbors of an object.

In general, clustering provides first-level knowledge or characterization of data. When clustering needs to perform on streaming data where infinite amount of data arrives as speed, in order to meet the memory and time constraints, clustering in performed in two stages. In the first stage, summary statistics of streaming data are collected using memory efficient data structures such as array and hash functions and, in the second stage, clustering algorithms are employed over the summary data to produce clusters.

In addition, specific clustering algorithms such as STREAM, Balanced Iterative Reducing and Clustering Using Hierarchies (BIRCH), and COBWEB are being used to cluster streaming data. The *STREAM* algorithm [8] applies a divide-and-conquer approach in order to have small space. It divides the stream into many subsets of data and it used K-Means algorithm to each subset to create K clusters. Then it clusters the centers of clusters are assigned with weights according to number of data points. Then the weighted cluster centers are grouped into small number of clusters. BRICH performs clustering of streaming data in an incremental fashion where the algorithm considers a fixed number of data points at a given time. BRICH uses hierarchical data structure, namely feature tree which helps in understanding the features of dataset in a hierarchical pattern. It is more appropriate for vast number of datasets. There is another algorithm called CLUSTREAM [9] which initially clusters the streaming data into K number of micro clusters into which the incoming data points are clustered. In addition, the algorithm stores the summary information about micro clusters. Then based on summary statistics, the micro level clusters are again grouped into macro level clusters.

Classification is a supervised learning task which is used to classify the given data item into the predefined class label. Basically, classification algorithms work in two stages. They are learning stage and classification stage. In the learning stage, the algorithm is trained with huge collection of what is called training data which is supposed to contain all possible combinations of inputs. The output of learning step is classifier or a set of classification rule (which is also called as model). The model has to be validated for its accuracy before it is used for classifying any unknown data. Once the model is found to have sufficient accuracy which is basically decided by concerned application, the model will be put in practice for prediction. As mentioned earlier, streaming data is continuous and rapid in nature, classification algorithms for streaming data have to handle the constraints on memory and processing time. There are two types of classification algorithms. A few examples for classification algorithms that are used for classifying streaming data include Naïve Bayesian, Hoeffding, and Very Fast Decision Tree (VFDT) [10].

11.4.1   Need for selection of algorithm

As mentioned earlier, though there exists a variety of algorithms, we need to select a specific algorithm which is more appropriate for the problem in hand. For example, consider a situation where the available training dataset is unlabeled type. It means that the data items are not associated with predefined class labels. In this case, classification algorithms cannot be used at all as the algorithms can work only with labeled data. Similarly certain algorithms can handle only categorical data. If we have continuous data, it needs to be converted into categorical data before employing prediction algorithm. Thus, suitable preprocessing procedures and algorithms are crucial before going for any processing or analysis. In addition to selection of algorithms, the operating parameters of the algorithms need to be fixed appropriately so that high accuracy of results can be achieved.

In this chapter, two unsupervised, clustering algorithms, namely, OCSVM and IF have been analyzed for their applicability in detecting anomalies. The primary benefit behind the analysis is that, these algorithms are capable of handling unlabeled dataset. In many situations, it is very likely that the datasets are not associated with predefined class labels.

Further, publicly available benchmark dataset that belongs to healthcare data has been taken up for analysis. The dataset is a time stamped one. The remaining portion of the chapter describes, the description of dataset, necessary preprocessing, brief overview about the algorithms used, and experimentation that is carried to fix the suitable values for the operational parameters of the algorithms. Ultimately a better algorithm is suggested for detecting anomaly over streams.

11.4.2   Dataset

As for as streaming data is concerned, there are many data sources such as sensor data, telecommunication data, networking data, geospatial data, satellites, mobile data, healthcare sector, business organizations, social media data and banking [11]. The values of attributes in the datasets may be categorical, numerical, or discrete according to the domain. The datasets are categorized into univariate, bivariate, and multivariate. Univariate represents the dataset which contains only one variable. Bivariate denotes the dataset which contains two attributes. Multivariate refers to the dataset which contains more than two attributes. The detection of anomalies is basically associated with the values of attributes.

The heart rate dataset consisting of 3,19,352 records has been collected from UCI Repository [12]. From the meta data description given in the benchmark data collection, it is understood that, the data has been acquired from individuals using 3 Colibri wireless Inertial Measurement Units (IMUs) sensors which have been placed at different locations on human body, namely wrist, chest, and ankle. The dataset has been collected from a male individual with 27 years old. The individual's height and weight have been measured as 182 cm and 83 kg, respectively. The minimum heart rate has been monitored as 75 beats per minute (bpm) and maximum has been monitored as 193 beats per minute (bpm). The wireless IMU is attached over the wrist of right hand. The detailed description about the data collected from individual is tabulated in Table 11.1.

The individual has to follow a protocol containing 18 different activities like household, sports activities, and other regular activities. These sensors are ready to

Table 11.1   Information about individual and number of records monitored

Individual ID	Gender	Age	Height (cm)	Weight (kg)	Minimum heart rate (bpm)	Maximum heart rate (bpm)	Total records collected
101	Male	27	182	83	75	193	319,352

monitor the heart rate of an individual based on different activities viz., lying, sitting, walking, running, cycling, etc. Each activity is identified with unique ID number. The activities and their unique IDs are given in Table 11.2.

The *activity ID = 0* deals with transient activities that are involved between performing different activities, e.g. going from one location to other or waiting for something to happen. While the individual is undergoing the monitored activities and protocols, the benchmark dataset of above said 319,352 records have been created with four attributes, namely, *Timestamp, Activity ID, Heart rate* along with *target class label*. Here, the class label denotes whether the observed heart rate is anomaly or not. Description about benchmark dataset is presented in Table 11.3.

Table 11.2   Description about activities

Activity ID	Activity description
1	Lying
2	Sitting
3	Standing
4	Walking
5	Running
6	Cycling
7	Nordic walking
9	Watching TV
10	Computer work
11	Car driving
12	Ascending stairs
13	Descending stairs
16	Vacuum cleaning
17	Ironing
18	Folding laundry
19	House cleaning
20	Playing soccer
24	Rope jumping
0	Other (transient activities)

Table 11.3   Description of benchmark dataset

Timestamp (in seconds)	Activity ID	Heart rate (bpm)	Class labels
Starts at 10.03 Ends at 3203.54	9 – Watching TV 11 – Car driving 18 – Folding laundry 19 – House cleaning 0 – Others	Minimum rate – 75 Maximum rate – 193	0 – Normal (9,407) 1– Anomaly (309,945)

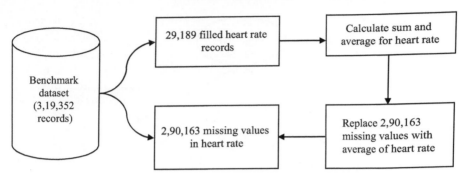

Figure 11.3 Replacing missing value with average

11.4.3 Preprocessing

From the dataset which consists of 319,352 records, it is found that, only 29,189 records are correctly filled with heart rate values and the remaining 290,163 records contain null values. Therefore, it is essential to perform preprocessing in order to get correct outcome. In this work, the null values are replaced with average of heart rate as illustrated in Figure 11.3.

11.4.4 IF

IF [14] is an unsupervised algorithm which is specially designed for anomaly detection. The method starts by constructing a decision tree to classify the data instances. The process of isolation deals with partitioning each data point until it is isolated. *Data points which are more quickly isolated are considered as anomalies* [15]. Detection of anomalies includes two stages, training and testing stage. In the training stage, the algorithm constructs isolation tree using sub-samples of the training set. In the testing phase, test instances are passed through isolation tree and the algorithm assigns anomaly score for each instance according to path length. If the path length is found to be minimum, then the instance will be considered as anomaly. This technique is more efficient in detecting anomalies in streaming data as it has the capacity to scale. This algorithm is being applied in various use cases such as banking, healthcare, and networking. It has the ability of detecting outliers in unlabeled data. The working of IF algorithm is exemplified with following steps:

1. Randomly select an input feature
2. Split the data points by randomly selecting a value between the minimum and maximum of the feature selected

Now, consider two input features, say *age* and *income*. Now, the algorithm constructs tree based on the randomly selected values of the above attributes. One such typical tree is shown in Figure 11.4.

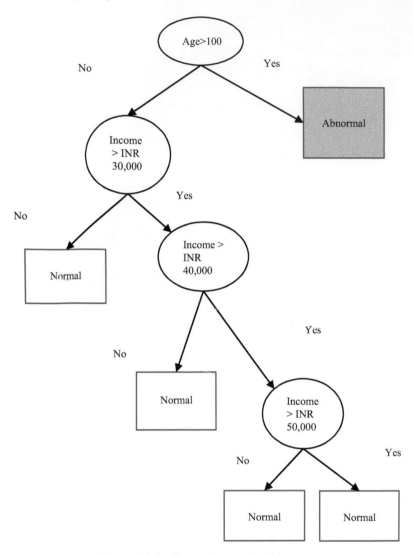

Figure 11.4   Typical tree with four splits

As in the example shown in Figure 11.4, when the age attribute is greater than 100, the data item is declared as anomaly and it is to be noted that the path length of the anomaly is very small when compared with other normal data items where the path length is more. The algorithm calculates the average path length of a data item/instance from the root and assigns an anomaly score, denoted by say s(x, n) where x is the concerned instance and n denotes the number of trees in the forest which will be typically set as an operational parameter. Actually, the above score is computed as the average of anomaly score of the trees in the forest which is normalized over the number of trees in the forest.

The algorithm works with three possible cases:

- Case 1: If the anomaly score is 1, then the path length is very small and the instance is declared as anomaly.
- Case 2: If the anomaly score is below 0.5, the instance is taken as normal.
- Case 3: If the anomaly score is 0.5 for all instances in a dataset, then, it is taken that the dataset does not contain any anomaly.

11.4.5   OCSVM

The OCSVM takes only the positive class which means the data points from the target class [16]. One class SVM handles both linear and non-linear data with the help of kernel functions. Kernel functions are used to take the input data and transform it to the high-dimensional space. There are four kernel functions such as *radial basis function (rbf)*, *linear*, *sigmoid*, and *polynomial*. The other parameters include *nu* parameter both lower bound and upper bound, where the lower bound is the number of samples which are support vectors and upper bound is the number of samples which are wrong side of hyperplane. *Gamma* parameter represents the distance of a training sample reaches. If the value is low means, it denotes far distance. If it is high value means, it denotes close distance. The equations represented for various kernel functions are given in (11.1), (11.2), (11.3), and (11.4).

(i)   **Radial basis function (RBF)**

It depends only on the distance between the input and some fixed point.

$$k(x,y) = \exp\left(-\gamma\|x-y\|^2\right) \tag{11.1}$$

where $k(x,y)$ represents the kernel function on two samples, x and y are feature vectors and $\gamma > 0$ (or) $\gamma = \frac{1}{2\sigma^2}$

(ii)   **Linear**

This function minimizes to a linear equation on the actual attributes to the training data.

$$k(x,y) = x^T y + c \tag{11.2}$$

where $k(x,y)$ denotes the kernel function on two samples, x^T represents the transpose of x sample and c is the constant.

(iii)   **Sigmoid**

It is based on neural networks which use activation function for artificial neurons.

$$k(x,y) = \tanh\left(\alpha x^T y + c\right) \tag{11.3}$$

where the kernel function of sample x and y is denoted as $k(x,y)$, α is the slope, and c is the intercept constant.

(iv)   Polynomial

Polynomial kernels are well suited for problems where all the training data is normalized.

$$k(x, y) = \left(\alpha x^T y + c\right)^d \tag{11.4}$$

where α is the slope, c is the constant, and d represents the degree of polynomial.

11.4.6   Experimentation

11.4.6.1   Fixation of operational parameters for IF

In the proposed work, Scikit-learn, the machine learning library of Python language has been used to implement the automatic anomaly detection. The library provides efficient and robust tools and statistical models for performing different data mining and machine learning tasks such as clustering, classification, regression, association rule mining, and dimensionality reduction with a very convenient and consistent interface.

With the selected data set and machine learning library, a series of experimentation has been carried out to fix the following operational parameters of IF, namely, *n_estimators, max_samples, max_features* and *contamination*.

- n_estimators is the number of isolation trees considered.
- max_samples is the maximum number of samples to consider
- max_features is the maximum number of features that can be considered during the training of the model.
- contamination is the proportion of anomalies in the dataset. In this case, we fix it equal to 0.05.

Datasets consisting of varying record sizes ranging from 100 to 319,352 as: *100, 200, 300, 400, 500, 600, 700, 800, 900, 1000, 40,000, 80,000, 120,000, 160,000, 2,00,000, 2,40,000, 280,000, 3,19,352* have been constructed. The parameters *contamination* and *max_features* have been fixed as 1.0 and 1.0, respectively. Here, +contamination=1.0 instructs the algorithm to identify the first 100 anomaly(i.e. 1*100=100)) in the dataset. Now, *n_estimators* and *max_samples* have to be fixed for various record sizes. At first, keeping n_estimators and record size as constants (say *n_estimators=3* and record size =100), max_samples is varied from 3 to 5 in steps of 1. This step is repeated for other record sizes from 200 to 319,352.

Now, the above procedure has been done for *n_estimators=5* and *n_estimators=10*. Results obtained using IF are given in Tables 11.4.1.a–11.4.3.c. For clarity purpose, the tables are split as follows. The results obtained by using IF, with *n_estimators=3* are given in Tables 11.4.1.a, 11.4.1.b, and 11.4.1.c. Similarly, the results obtained with *n_estimators=5* are given in Tables 11.4.2.a, 11.4.2.b, and 11.4.2.c and the results with *n_estimators=10* are given in Tables 11.4.3.a, 11.4.3.b, and 11.4.3.c.

Table 11.4.1.a   Accuracy obtained for IF with
n_estimators=3 (record size is 100–1,000)

Record size	max_samples	Accuracy of anomaly detection (%)
	3	80.16
100	4	81.26
	5	83.21
	3	80.27
200	4	80.56
	5	81.38
	3	80.27
300	4	81.59
	5	82.11
	3	80.31
400	4	85.25
	5	85.78
	3	81.56
500	4	88.18
	5	89.48
	3	84.98
600	4	90.17
	5	90.16
	3	86.11
700	4	90.21
	5	91.17
800	3	89.49
	4	92.46
	5	92.45
	3	90.19
900	4	93.09
	5	93.26
	3	90.19
1,000	4	93.78
	5	93.19

Table 11.4.1.b   Accuracy obtained for IF with
n_estimators=3 (record size is
40,000–160,000)

Record size	max_samples	Accuracy of anomaly detection (%)
	3	89.01
40,000	4	89.88
	5	90.10
	3	86.67
80,000	4	90.58
	5	92.19
	3	87.20
120,000	4	91.78
	5	92.81
	3	86.23
160,000	4	88.12
	5	90.19

Table 11.4.1.c   Accuracy obtained for IF with n_estimators=3 (record size is 200,000–319,352)

Record size	max_samples	Accuracy of anomaly detection (%)
	3	87.18
200,000	4	87.74
	5	90.16
	3	87.45
240,000	4	88.65
	5	90.11
	3	87.83
280,000	4	89.56
	5	91.12
	3	86.01
319,352	4	86.34
	5	91.15

Table 11.4.2.a   Accuracy obtained for IF with n_estimators=5 (record size is 100 to 1,000)

Record size	max_samples	Accuracy of anomaly detection (%)
	3	73.01
100	4	75.23
	5	77.16
	3	72.18
200	4	72.89
	5	75.67
	3	71.45
300	4	74.89
	5	74.94
	3	72.08
400	4	75.19
	5	77.10
	3	79.33
500	4	79.42
	5	80.17
	3	80.03
600	4	80.46
	5	82.67
	3	81.02
700	4	84.22
	5	86.25
	3	86.35
800	4	88.15
	5	89.17
	3	90.11
900	4	90.89
	5	91.87
	3	90.19
1,000	4	93.45
	5	93.99

Table 11.4.2.b   *Accuracy obtained for IF with n_estimators=5 (record size is 40,000–160,000)*

Record size	max_samples	Accuracy of anomaly detection (%)
40,000	3	88.10
	4	89.88
	5	90.33
80,000	3	86.90
	4	88.89
	5	90.01
120,000	3	87.28
	4	91.74
	5	92.81
160,000	3	86.23
	4	88.12
	5	90.99

Table 11.4.2.c   *Accuracy obtained for IF with n_estimators=5 (record size is 200,000–319,352)*

Record size	max_samples	Accuracy of anomaly detection (%)
200,000	3	87.56
	4	87.64
	5	90.19
240,000	3	87.51
	4	88.65
	5	90.23
280,000	3	87.98
	4	89.56
	5	91.76
319,352	3	86.90
	4	86.54
	5	91.67

From Tables 11.4.1.a to 11.4.3.c, it is found that the IF algorithm gives better performance for n_estimators=10 and max_samples=5. Accuracy obtained with the above setting is given in Table 11.4.4.

11.4.6.2   Fixation of operational parameters for OCSVM

To fix optimal values for the operational parameters of OCSVM, namely, *kernel*, *nu*, and *gamma*, datasets consisting of varying record sizes ranging from 100 to 319,352 as: *100, 200, 300, 400, 500, 600, 700, 800, 900, 1,000, 40,000, 80,000, 120,000, 160,000, 200,000, 240,000, 280,000, 319,352* have been constructed. Nu is the parameter that controls the training errors (and the number of SVs). This

Table 11.4.3.a   Accuracy obtained for IF with n_estimators=10 (record size is 100–1,000)

Record size	max_samples	Accuracy of anomaly detection (%)
	3	84.67
100	4	84.91
	5	84.88
	3	83.27
200	4	84.56
	5	84.88
	3	86.19
300	4	86.71
	5	87.87
	3	85.18
400	4	85.84
	5	87.18
	3	85.17
500	4	86.38
	5	80.17
	3	80.19
600	4	80.48
	5	82.87
	3	85.02
700	4	85.22
	5	86.25
	3	86.87
800	4	88.15
	5	89.17
	3	90.28
900	4	91.54
	5	91.87
	3	90.06
1,000	4	92.19
	5	93.26

Table 11.4.3.b   Accuracy obtained for IF with n_estimators=10 (record size is 40,000–160,000)

Record size	max_samples	Accuracy of anomaly detection (%)
	3	85.37
40,000	4	89.78
	5	90.31
	3	85.39
80,000	4	83.89
	5	87.41
	3	87.28
120,000	4	90.74
	5	92.81
	3	86.23
160,000	4	88.12
	5	90.18

Table 11.4.3.c Accuracy obtained for IF with n_estimators=10 (record size is 200,000–319,352)

Record size	max_samples	Accuracy of anomaly detection (%)
	3	87.35
200,000	4	87.64
	5	90.19
	3	87.45
240,000	4	89.65
	5	90.46
	3	87.78
280,000	4	89.15
	5	91.88
	3	86.65
319,352	4	86.89
	5	91.77

Table 11.4.4 Operating parameters for IF

n_estimators	max_samples	Contamination	max_features	Accuracy (%)
10	5	1.0	1.0	88.52 (average)

Table 11.5.1.a Performance measures obtained for OCSVM (size is 100–1,000)

		Performance measures			
Record size	Kernel	Accuracy of anomaly detection (%)	Precision (%)	Recall (%)	F-score (%)
	Rbf	5	2	1	1
	Linear	4	2	2	2
100	Sigmoid	100	100	100	100
	Poly	4	1	1	2
	Rbf	5	2	3	2
	Linear	4	1	2	2
200	Sigmoid	100	100	100	100
	Poly	4	1	1	3
	Rbf	5	2	2	1
	Linear	5	1	1	3
300	Sigmoid	100	100	100	100
	Poly	5	2	3	3
	Rbf	5	2	3	2
	Linear	5	3	2	4
400	Sigmoid	100	100	100	100

(Continues)

Table 11.5.1.a   *(Continued)*

Record size	Kernel	Performance measures			
		Accuracy of anomaly detection (%)	Precision (%)	Recall (%)	F-score (%)
	Poly	5	3	4	4
	Rbf	5	4	3	4
	Linear	5	2	4	1
500	Sigmoid	100	100	100	100
	Poly	5	3	4	2
	Rbf	5	2	1	1
	Linear	5	3	4	2
600	Sigmoid	100	100	100	100
	Poly	5	2	4	4
	Rbf	5	2	2	1
	Linear	5	2	4	3
700	Sigmoid	100	100	100	100
	Poly	5	1	2	1
	Rbf	5	2	4	3
	Linear	5	1	2	4
800	Sigmoid	100	100	100	100
	Poly	5	1	4	3
	Rbf	5	1	3	1
	Linear	5	3	2	4
900	Sigmoid	100	100	100	100
	Poly	5	4	2	1
	Rbf	5	4	3	2
	Linear	5	2	1	4
1,000	Sigmoid	100	100	100	100
	Poly	5	4	2	3

parameter is always within the range (0,1]. Gamma parameter determines the influence of radius on the kernel. The parameters nu and gamma have been fixed as 0.05 and 0.05, respectively.

Now, kernel has to be fixed for various record sizes. At first, keeping record size as constant (say record size =100), kernel is varied as rbf, linear, sigmoid, and polynomial in steps of 1. This step is repeated for other record sizes from 200 to 319,352. Results obtained using OCSVM are given in Tables 11.5.1.a–11.5.1.c. For clarity purpose, the tables are split as follows. The results obtained by using OCSVM, with record sizes 100 to 1,000 are given in Table 11.5.2.a.

Similarly, the results obtained with record sizes 40,000–160,000 are given in Table 11.5.2.b and the results obtained with record sizes 200,000–319,352 are given in Table 11.5.2.c.

From Tables 11.5.1.a, 11.5.1.b, and 11.5.1.c, it is found that the OCSVM algorithm gives better performance for sigmoid kernel function. Accuracy obtained with the above setting is given in Table 11.5.3.

Table 11.5.2.b   Performance measures obtained for OCSVM (size is 40,000–160,000)

| Record size | Kernel | Performance measures | | | |
		Accuracy of anomaly detection (%)	Precision (%)	Recall (%)	F-score (%)
	Rbf	24	18	13	23
	Linear	5	2	3	7
40,000	Sigmoid	90	65	64	66
	Poly	5	2	3	6
	Rbf	24	11	16	15
	Linear	6	3	2	5
80,000	Sigmoid	90	77	63	68
	Poly	5	3	1	3
	Rbf	24	21	19	20
	Linear	6	2	4	3
120,000	Sigmoid	80	73	66	65
	Poly	6	5	3	6
	Rbf	25	20	16	18
	Linear	8	5	6	8
160,000	Sigmoid	80	71	69	66
	Poly	8	5	4	7

Table 11.5.2.c   Performance measures obtained for OCSVM (record size is 200,000–319,352)

| Record size | Kernel | Performance measures | | | |
		Accuracy of anomaly detection (%)	Precision (%)	Recall (%)	F-score (%)
	Rbf	29	25	19	22
	Linear	9	8	8	4
200,000	Sigmoid	90	77	65	54
	Poly	9	7	8	9
	Rbf	29	27	23	25
	Linear	9	8	7	7
240,000	Sigmoid	80	69	59	71
	Poly	9	6	8	6
	Rbf	31	28	25	21
	Linear	8	8	7	6
280,000	Sigmoid	80	69	61	65
	Poly	8	6	7	4
	Rbf	31	29	27	26
	Linear	7	7	4	6
319,352	Sigmoid	80	76	68	71
	Poly	7	4	4	5

Table 11.5.3   Operating parameters for OCSVM

Kernel	Nu	Gamma	Accuracy (%)	Precision (%)	Recall (%)	*F*-score (%)
Sigmoid	0.05	0.05	92.77 (average)	87.61 (average)	84.16 (average)	84.77 (average)

Table 11.6   Comparative analysis of anomaly detection techniques based on accuracy

	Anomaly detection accuracy (%)	
Record size	IF	OCSVM
100	84.88	100
200	84.88	100
300	87.87	100
400	87.18	100
500	80.17	100
600	82.87	100
700	86.25	100
800	89.17	100
900	91.87	100
1,000	93.26	100
40,000	90.31	90
80,000	87.41	90
120,000	92.81	80
160,000	90.18	80
200,000	90.19	90
240,000	90.46	80
280,000	91.88	80
319,352	91.77	80

11.4.6.3   Comparative analysis

The accuracy for various record sizes obtained using IF and OCSVM with optimal setting are given in Table 11.6.

In addition, the accuracy of different algorithms is given in graphical format in Figure 11.5.

From Table 11.6 and Figure 11.5, random forest is found to give 100% accuracy for the entire record sizes. Also, the average accuracy of IF is found to be 88.52%. Similarly, the average accuracy of OCSVM is found to be 92.77%.

11.4.7   Real-time anomaly detection using discretized streams

After fixing the operational parameters of algorithms, the next step is to perform analysis on the accuracy of anomaly detection for stream. To find this aspect, different discretized streams have been created by varying the time between two

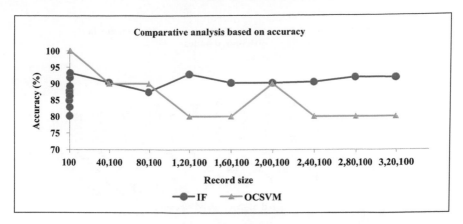

Figure 11.5   Comparative analysis based on accuracy

Table 11.7   Accuracy of anomaly detection for different discretized streams

Discretized streams	Speed of discretized stream	Anomaly detection accuracy (%)	
		IF	OCSVM
Stream-1	10 dps/sec	68.00	61
Stream-2	20 dps/sec	69.50	61
Stream-3	25 dps/sec	72.00	65
Stream-4	50 dps/sec	74.40	61
Stream-5	100 dps/sec	78.50	60
Stream-6	200 dps/sec	76.40	60
Stream-7	250 dps/sec	76.96	63
Stream-8	500 dps/sec	73.16	61
Stream-9	1,000 dps/sec	66.90	60
Stream-10	10,000 dps/sec	67.92	62
Stream-11	40,000 dps/sec	70.34	60
Stream-12	50,000 dps/sec	69.88	60
Stream-13	100,000 dps/sec	67.26	61
Stream-14	200,000 dps/sec	64.88	58

data items. The generation of different stream have been created using Apache Kafka asynchronous messenger (note, an elaborate discussion about Apache Kafka messenger has been presented in the succeeding chapter). For example, there are 10 data points in 1 sec, then its speed is 10 data points per sec (dps/sec). Different streams, namely, stream-1, stream-2, stream-3, stream-4, stream-5, stream-6, stream-7, stream-8, stream-9, stream-10, stream-11, stream-12, stream-13, and stream-14. The speeds of the above streams are given in Table 11.7. Further, the accuracy of anomaly detection for various streams has been given in graphical format in Figure 11.6.

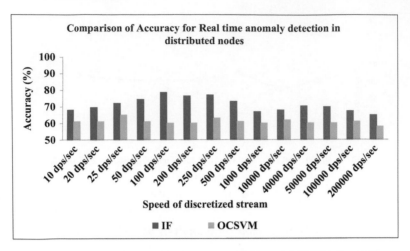

Figure 11.6   Accuracy of anomaly detection of IF and OCSVM for different discretized streams

From Table 11.7, it is found that the accuracy of OCSVM is comparatively less than that of IF, but it seems that the accuracy of detection almost remains stable. When we look into the accuracy of IF, the accuracy of detection is higher than that of OCSVM. Also, when we go to streams of higher speeds, it is found that the accuracy seems be alright and it is higher than that of OCSVM.

Thus, as mentioned in the introduction of the chapter, with the details analysis of performance of two algorithms, it is recommended to employ IF, when the dataset in hand is not associated with labels. Further, when we have labeled data, we need to carry out performance analysis of classification or supervised algorithms. This aspect is presented in the succeeding chapter.

11.5   Conclusion

While detecting anomalies over streams, the nature of streaming datasets plays a crucial role in choosing the machine learning algorithm for anomaly detection. In this chapter, a primary aspect i.e., whether the dataset is associated with predefined class labels or not has been considered. The performance of anomaly detection of IF and OCSVM have been analyzed. By experimentation with benchmark dataset, IF is found to have outperformed OCSVM.

References

[1]   Ounacer Soumaya, Talhaoui Mohamed Amine, Ardchir Soufiane, Daif Abderrahmane and Aouuazi Mohamed, "Real time data stream processing challenges and perspectives", International Journal of Computer Issues

(IJCSI), vol. 14, no. 5, pp. 6–12, September 2017, p-ISSN: 1694-0814, e-ISSN: 1694-0784.

[2]   Fatih Gurcan and Muhammet Berigel, "Real-time processing of Big Data streams: lifecycle, tools, tasks and challenges", in: *Proceedings of the 2nd International Symposium on Multidisciplinary Studies and Innovative Technologies* (*ISMSIT*), 19–21 October 2018, pp. 1-6, e-ISBN: 978-1-5386-4184-2.

[3]   Varun Chandola, "Anomaly detection: a survey", ACM Computing Surveys, vol. 41, pp. 1–72, 2009.

[4]   Edin Sabic, David Keeley, Bailey Henderson and Sara Nannemann, "Healthcare and anomaly detection: using machine learning to predict anomalies in heart rate data", AI & Society, vol. 36, pp. 149–158, 2020.

[5]   Bharadwaj Veeravalli, Chacko John Deepu and DuyHoa Ngo, "Real-time, personalized anomaly detection in streaming data for wearable healthcare devices", in: Handbook of Large-Scale Distributed Computing in Smart Healthcare, Scalable Computing and Communications, Springer, New York, NY, pp. 403–426, 2017.

[6]   Leornado Querzoni and Nicolo Rivetti, "Tutorial: data streaming and its application to stream processing", in: *Proceedings of the 11th ACM International Conference on Distributed and Event-based Systems*, June 2017, pp 15–18.

[7]   Michael A. Hayes and Miriam A. M. Capretz, "Contextual anomaly detection framework for big sensor data", Journal of Big Data, vol. 2, no. 1, pp. 1–22, 2015.

[8]   Mounir Hafsa and Farah Jemili, "Comparative study between Big Data analysis techniques in intrusion detection", Big Data and Cognitive Computing, vol. 3, no. 1, pp. 1–13, 2018.

[9]   Dmitry Namiot, "On Big Data stream processing", International Journal of Open Information Technologies, vol. 3, pp. 48–51, January 2015, ISSN: 2307-8162.

[10]   Rutuja Jadhav and Neha Sharma, "Classification methods for data stream mining", Open Access International Journal of Science and Engineering, vol. 3, special issue 1, pp. 94–97, March 2018, e-ISSN: 2456-3293.

[11]   D. P. Acharjya and P. Kauser Ahmed, "A survey on Big Data analytics: challenges, open research issues and tools", International Journal of Advanced Computer Science and Applications *(IJACSA)*, vol. 7, no. 2, pp. 511–518, 2016.

[12]   Reto Wettstein, *"Real-time body temperature and heart rate monitoring system for classification of physiological response patterns using wearable sensors and machine learning technology"*, Master Thesis, Universitat Helderberg Hochschule Heilbronn, pp. 1–97, 17 December 2018.

[13]   https://archive.ics.uci.edu/ml/datasets/PAMAP2+Physical+Activity +Monitoring

[14]   Sahand Hariri, Matias Carrasco Kind and Robert J. Brunner, "Extended isolation forest", IEEE Transactions on Knowledge and Data Engineering, vol. 32, no. 8, pp. 1–12, 8 July 2020.

[15]   Hongyu Sun, Qiang He, Kewen Liao, et al., "Fast anomaly detection in multiple multi-dimensional data streams", in: *Proceedings of the 2019 IEEE International Conference on Big Data (Big Data)*, IEEE, Los Angeles, CA, 24 February 2020, pp. 1218–1223, p-ISBN: 978-1-7281-0859-9, e-ISBN: 978-1-7281-0858-2.

[16]   Bouchra Lamrini, Augustin Gjini, Simon Daudin, Francois Armando, Pascal Pratmarty and Louise Trave-Massuyes, "Anomaly detection using similarity-based one-class SVM for network traffic characterization", in: *Proceedings of the 29th International Workshop on Principles of Diagnosis*, August 2018, pp. 1–8.

Chapter 12

Detection of anomaly over streams using big data technologies

Chellammal Surianarayanan[1] and Saranya Kunasekaran[1]

Abstract

Anomaly detection serves as a method for identifying and recognizing abnormal events that may occur over data in various application domains. Anomaly detection is very useful as it provides valuable and actionable information such as detection of fraud in financial domain, detection of intrusion in networking etc. Detecting anomaly over streaming data requires efficient tools and techniques as streaming data is continuously flowing one with no start or end. As streaming data is associated with speed, big data-based platforms provide the fundamental base over which machine learning algorithms can be employed so that the detection of anomaly over streaming data can be performed efficiently. This chapter describes Apache Kafka-based architecture in which detection of anomaly over streams is being done using machine learning algorithm.

12.1 Introduction

As discussed in the previous chapter, streaming data is one which does not have any start or end and it is continuously flowing. Like any other data, it also contains abnormal events called anomaly. The detection of anomaly is mandatory in many application domains as the anomalies are representatives of very crucial events such as intrusion in networks, fraudulent event in financial domains, and critical patient in healthcare. As far as anomaly detection over streams are concerned, two aspects gain importance, (i) appropriate techniques for detection of anomaly and (ii) appropriate technique for handling streams of large size/volume with real-time features. There are two different tracks of techniques to meet the above aspects, machine learning techniques and big data techniques as shown in Figure 12.1.

As seen in the previous chapter, anomaly detection is one of the key issues in several domains particularly in healthcare application as detecting anomalies in

[1]Department of Computer Science, Government Arts and Science College, Srirangam, Affiliated to Bharathidasan University, India

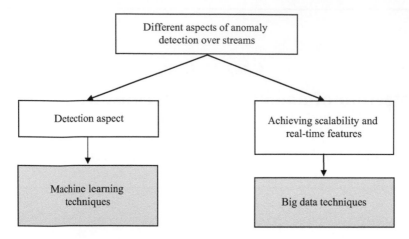

*Figure 12.1   Different aspects of anomaly detection with corresponding
techniques*

right times enables physicians to take appropriate decisions [1]. In the previous
chapter, the usefulness of unsupervised clustering-based algorithms was discussed
with heart beat dataset. The labels in the dataset were ignored. Here, specific focus
has been given to two aspects, namely labeled dataset and detection of anomaly in
real time. It is mandatory to have effective techniques for anomaly detection in real
time. In this chapter, a scalable approach has been presented to detect the anomaly
over heart beat data using Random Forest algorithm and big data-based high-
throughput architecture that is established using Apache Kafka distributed, asynchronous messenger. The remaining portion of the chapter at first presents a brief
overview about machine learning algorithms with specific focus on Random Forest
& Apache Kafka and then detailed discussion about the elaborate experimentation
on selection of operational parameters of the above algorithm and how the anomaly
can be detected in a scalable manner using Apache Kafka in real time.

12.2   Brief overview about machine learning algorithms

The most predominant technique is considered as machine learning as it is capable
of dealing with most of the research issues. There are various machine leaning
techniques such as *Support Vector Machine (SVM), Bayesian Networks (BN), K-
Nearest Neighbors (K-NN), Local Outlier Factor (LOF), Random Forest (RF),
Isolation Forest (IF)*, and *One Class Support Vector Machine (OCSVM)*. As far as
anomaly detection is concerned, we can broadly *SVM* is basically binary classifier
which classifies data points as normal and anomaly by constructing a hyperplane
which separates the classes. The algorithm tries to reduce classification error by
maximizing the margin between the classes using support vector. It has kernel

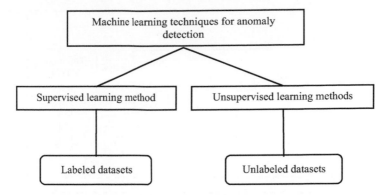

Figure 12.2   Selection of machine learning techniques for the proposed research

functions for transforming non-linear relationship between data and target labels into a linear problem in a higher dimension. *Bayesian Networks* is a probabilistic model used for anomaly detection in multi scenarios [2].

K-NN [3] assigns anomaly score method and detects a data instance as anomaly by comparing it with a threshold. The *LOF* [4] is an unsupervised detection technique which is derived from DBSCAN. The objective of this approach is that the density around an outlier data point is totally different from the density around its neighbors. *IF* is an unsupervised algorithm which is specially designed for anomaly detection. The methods start with constructing a decision tree to classify the data instances. The process of isolation deals with partitioning each data point until it is isolated. Data points which are more quickly isolated are considered as anomalies [5].

The *OCSVM* is an unsupervised learning algorithm which is trained only on normal data points [6]. The model learns the boundaries of normal points and treats the points which are outside the boundaries as anomalies.

RF is an ensemble method that uses a collection of decision trees to process the data and provides a consolidated result obtained from the results of individual trees with a voting mechanism.

As in Figure 12.2, RF comes under supervised category. IF and OCSVM comes under unsupervised category. RF has been widely used in heart rate domain, credit card fraudulent [7], intrusions in networking [8], industrial IoT data [9], and the importance of RF in detecting anomalies has been described in [10]. RF can perform fast classification over large dataset. In addition, it can do both regression and classification. It can work with multi-classes. It is an ensemble algorithm.

12.2.1   RF

RF is an ensemble-based supervised machine learning method that trains several decision trees in parallel as in Figure 12.3 with bootstrapping approach where the individual decision trees are trained in parallel on various subsets of dataset with differently available features. In this approach, each decision tree is able to produce different output and the final decision is taken based on the majority of votes. The

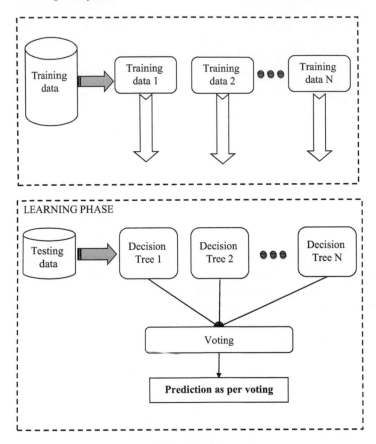

Figure 12.3   Workflow of RF

main feature of this method is that it performs efficiently on larger datasets with more features and handles imbalanced data [11]. In RF, training data is chosen randomly. Each trained tree gives its own classification result in order to analyze the missing value and calculates the error. The advantage of random forest is that it can be used for both classification and regression problems. This work deals with random forest classifier as it aims to classify the input data into anomaly and the normal one. This technique is widely used in many applications like banking, stock market, medicine, business organizations, etc. in order to detect abnormal behavior in an efficient way. Since the training is done in parallel, it is very fast. As it is an ensemble of algorithms, error is minimized.

The algorithm has the following operational parameters such as, *n_estimators* denotes the number of trees to construct the model, *random_state* looks for best split at each node *max_depth* represents the largest path between the root node and the leaf, *criterion* has been fixed as *gini index* which represents the function to measure of inequality of a tree split. The degree of *gini index* varies between 0 and

1, where 0 represents that all elements belong to same class, 1 denotes that the elements are distributed randomly across several classes and 0.5 specifies that the elements are equally distributed into some classes.

The formula used to calculate *gini index* is given in (12.1):

$$\text{Gini} = 1 - \sum_{i=1}^{n} (p_i)^2 \tag{12.1}$$

where p_i is the probability of ith object that belongs to one of classes and n denotes the number of classes. Gini impurity measures the degree or probability of a particular variable being wrongly classified when it is randomly chosen. While building the decision tree, we would prefer choosing the attribute/feature with the least Gini index as the root node. The degree of Gini index varies between 0 and 1, where,

- 0 denotes that all elements belong to a certain class or if there exists only one class.
- 1 denotes that the elements are randomly distributed across various classes.
- 0.5 denotes that the objects equally distributed elements into some classes.

  Along with the above operational parameters, to validate the model, K-fold cross validation method with k=10 is used, i.e. the entire dataset is split into ten groups;

  For each group, the following steps are followed to evaluate the model:
  o Consider the group as test data and the remaining other groups as training data.
  o Fit a model on the training set and evaluate it on the test set
  o Retain the evaluation score and discard the model.

Ultimately the model is evaluated using the average of the all-evaluation scores. This method of evaluating the model is less biased one as the models gets evaluated with all samples.

Now, toward analyzing the potential of the algorithms for anomaly detection in real time, an architecture consisting of Apache Kafka has been proposed. Apache Kafka is a distributed messenger having high throughput of *two million writes/sec*. It is a scalable architecture. This chapter describes a series of experiments that has been carried out for real time analysis, using RF in environment of Kafka. The chapter also details the proposed architecture along with a brief overview about Apache Kafka.

12.3   High level Apache Kafka architecture

Apache Kafka is especially designed for distributed messaging system for gaining high throughput. The features supported by Kafka are built in partitions, replication, fault tolerance, and scalability [12]. Its throughput is two million writes/second. The high-level architecture of Kafka messenger is shown in Figure 12.4.

Components of Apache Kafka are *Kafka producer*, *Kafka broker*, *Kafka topic*, *Kafka consumer*, and *Zookeeper*. Kafka Producer will produce or publish the

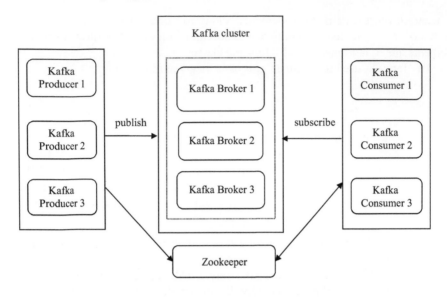

Figure 12.4   High-level Kafka architecture

messages on one or more topics, which are delivered to consumer through the broker. Kafka cluster consists of one or more servers called Kafka broker which has the great responsibility for maintaining the published data. Kafka topic is located within the Kafka broker. Topic is the area where the messages are store and published. For each topic, Kafka maintains minimum of one partition. Topics may have many partitions also. Each partitioned message has a unique sequence id called offset. Kafka consumer consumes messages from brokers by subscribing the required topic. Kafka provides various APIs, namely, *Producer API*, *Consumer API*, *Streaming API*, and *Connector API* which enable the communications between various components. The producer API allows an application to publish a stream of records to one or more Kafka topics. The consumer API allows an application to subscribe to one or more topics and process the stream of records produced to them. The streaming API allows an application to act as a stream processor. The connector API allows building and running reusable producers or consumers that connect Kafka topics to existing applications. Zookeeper serves as the coordination interface between the Kafka brokers and Kafka consumers. Kafka allows zookeeper to store information about topics, brokers, consumers and so on.

12.4   Fixation of operational parameters of RF

For any machine learning algorithm, fixing its operational parameters to its optimal values plays a major role in deciding the accuracy of the algorithm. Also, each algorithm has its own operational parameters. These parameters are needed to be fixed, while the algorithms are trained with training data, by experiments. So, a series of experiments have been conducted as discussed in the next chapter. Here, in Table 12.1, the hyper parameters of different algorithms are given for reference.

Parameters of RF have been fixed by performing a series of experimentation with a runtime environment consisting of CPU having Ubuntu 16.10 as operating

Table 12.1   Operational parameters of RF algorithm

S. no.	Machine learning techniques used	Parameter selection			
1	RF	n_estimators	criterion	random_state	max_depth

Table 12.2.1.a   Performance measures obtained for RF with n_estimators=3 (record size is 100–1,000)

Record size	max_depth	Performance measures			
		Accuracy of anomaly detection (%)	Precision (%)	Recall (%)	F-score (%)
100	2	100	100	100	100
	3	100	100	100	100
	5	100	100	100	100
200	2	100	100	100	100
	3	100	100	100	100
	5	100	100	100	100
300	2	100	100	100	100
	3	100	100	100	100
	5	100	100	100	100
400	2	100	100	100	100
	3	100	100	100	100
	5	100	100	100	100
500	2	100	100	100	100
	3	100	100	100	100
	5	100	100	100	100
600	2	100	100	100	100
	3	100	100	100	100
	5	100	100	100	100
700	2	100	100	100	100
	3	100	100	100	100
	5	100	100	100	100
800	2	100	100	100	100
	3	100	100	100	100
	5	100	100	100	100
900	2	100	100	100	100
	3	100	100	100	100
	5	100	100	100	100
1,000	2	100	100	100	100
	3	100	100	100	100
	5	100	100	100	100

system, processor with Intel Core i3-4005U CPU @ 1.70GHz x 4, 64-bit OS type and 8 GB RAM. The necessary code has been developed in Python. Python is one of the most popular programming languages for this task and it has replaced many languages in the industry, one of the reasons is its vast collection of libraries. Python libraries that used in Machine Learning include, Numpy, Scipy, Scikit-learn, Theano, TensorFlow, Keras, PyTorch, Pandas, and Matplotlib.

Table 12.2.1.b   Performance measures obtained for RF with n_estimators=3 (record size is 40,000–160,000)

Record size	max_depth	Performance measures			
		Accuracy of anomaly detection (%)	Precision (%)	Recall (%)	F-score (%)
	2	100	100	100	100
40,000	3	100	100	100	100
	5	100	100	100	100
	2	98.66	96.45	94.52	95.26
80,000	3	98.57	96.23	94.12	94.67
	5	97.15	96.35	94.78	94.66
	2	97.45	95.36	95.27	94.49
120,000	3	97.84	96.17	95.10	94.46
	5	98.26	97.27	95.37	94.16
	2	98.16	97.69	95.19	95.39
160,000	3	98.32	97.11	95.68	95.11
	5	98.35	97.10	95.30	96.98

Table 12.2.1.c   Performance measures obtained for RF with n_estimators=3 (record size is 200,000–319,352)

Record size	max_depth	Performance measures			
		Accuracy of anomaly detection (%)	Precision (%)	Recall (%)	F-score (%)
	2	98.45	94.16	95.67	94.81
200,000	3	98.67	94.87	95.55	94.56
	5	98.58	94.78	96.47	97.72
	2	98.12	95.36	96.98	93.15
240,000	3	99.46	95.03	95.12	95.43
	5	99.78	96.67	93.19	94.38
	2	98.16	98.11	96.77	91.10
280,000	3	99.29	94.64	93.54	93.89
	5	99.78	97.19	95.47	92.08
	2	98.54	95.47	96.17	96.45
319,352	3	99.10	97.46	96.53	95.39
	5	99.89	97.65	96.22	97.87

To fix optimal values for the operational parameters of RF, namely, *n_esti-mators, criterion, random_state* and *max_depth*, datasets consisting of varying record sizes ranging from 100 to 319,352 as: *100, 200, 300, 400, 500, 600, 700, 800, 900, 1,000, 40,000, 80,000, 120,000, 160,000, 200,000, 240,000, 280,000, 319,352* have been constructed. Criterion has been fixed as gini index and random_state has been fixed as 1.

Now, n_estimators and max_depth have to be fixed for various record sizes. At first, keeping n_estimators and record size as constants (say n_estimators=3 and record size =100), max_depth is varied from 2 to 5 in steps of 1. This step is repeated for other record sizes from 200 to 319,352.

Table 12.3.1.a   Performance measures obtained for RF with n_estimators=5 (record size is 100–1,000)

Record size	max_depth	Performance measures			
		Accuracy of anomaly detection (%)	Precision (%)	Recall (%)	F-score (%)
	2	100	100	100	100
100	3	100	100	100	100
	5	100	100	100	100
	2	100	100	100	100
200	3	100	100	100	100
	5	100	100	100	100
	2	100	100	100	100
300	3	100	100	100	100
	5	100	100	100	100
	2	100	100	100	100
400	3	100	100	100	100
	5	100	100	100	100
	2	100	100	100	100
500	3	100	100	100	100
	5	100	100	100	100
	2	100	100	100	100
600	3	100	100	100	100
	5	100	100	100	100
	2	100	100	100	100
700	3	100	100	100	100
	5	100	100	100	100
	2	100	100	100	100
800	3	100	100	100	100
	5	100	100	100	100
	2	100	100	100	100
900	3	100	100	100	100
	5	100	100	100	100
	2	100	100	100	100
1,000	3	100	100	100	100
	5	100	100	100	100

Table 12.3.1.b   Performance measures obtained for RF with n_estimators=5 (record size is 40,000–160,000)

Record size	max_depth	Performance measures			
		Accuracy of anomaly detection (%)	Precision (%)	Recall (%)	F-score (%)
	2	100	100	100	100
40,000	3	100	100	100	100
	5	100	100	100	100
	2	98.61	94.78	94.66	95.67
80,000	3	98.69	95.36	94.49	95.55
	5	98.82	95.03	94.46	96.47
	2	98.12	96.67	94.16	96.98
120,000	3	98.46	94.78	95.39	95.12
	5	98.23	95.36	95.11	93.19
	2	99.03	93.54	96.98	98.69
160,000	3	99.45	95.47	94.66	98.82
	5	99.64	96.17	94.49	98.12

Table 12.3.1.c   Performance measures obtained for RF with n_estimators=5 (record size is 200,000–319,352)

Record size	max_depth	Performance measures			
		Accuracy of anomaly detection (%)	Precision (%)	Recall (%)	F-score (%)
	2	98.26	96.09	93.15	94.66
200,000	3	99.18	98.82	95.43	94.49
	5	99.53	98.12	94.38	94.46
	2	98.12	93.54	91.10	94.16
240,000	3	99.68	95.47	93.89	95.39
	5	99.85	96.17	92.08	95.11
	2	99.28	94.66	93.15	96.98
280,000	3	99.46	94.49	95.43	94.66
	5	99.55	94.46	94.38	94.78
	2	99.37	94.16	98.69	95.36
319,352	3	99.50	95.39	98.82	95.03
	5	99.89	95.11	98.12	94.16

The above procedure has been done for n_estimators=5 and n_estimators=10. Results obtained using RF are given in Tables 12.2.1.a to 12.2.1.c. For clarity purpose, the tables are split as follows.

Table 12.4.1.a   *Performance measures obtained for RF with n_estimators=10 (record size is 100–1,000)*

Record size	max_depth	Performance measures			
		Accuracy of anomaly detection (%)	Precision (%)	Recall (%)	F-score (%)
	2	100	100	100	100
100	3	100	100	100	100
	5	100	100	100	100
	2	100	100	100	100
200	3	100	100	100	100
	5	100	100	100	100
	2	100	100	100	100
300	3	100	100	100	100
	5	100	100	100	100
	2	100	100	100	100
400	3	100	100	100	100
	5	100	100	100	100
	2	100	100	100	100
500	3	100	100	100	100
	5	100	100	100	100
	2	100	100	100	100
600	3	100	100	100	100
	5	100	100	100	100
	2	100	100	100	100
700	3	100	100	100	100
	5	100	100	100	100
	2	100	100	100	100
800	3	100	100	100	100
	5	100	100	100	100
	2	100	100	100	100
900	3	100	100	100	100
	5	100	100	100	100
	2	100	100	100	100
1,000	3	100	100	100	100
	5	100	100	100	100

The results obtained by using RF, with n_estimators=3 are given in Table 12.2.1.a, 12.2.1.b, and 12.2.1.c. Similarly, the results obtained with n_estimators=5 are given in Table 12.3.1.a, 12.3.1.b, and 12.3.1.c and the results with n_estimators=10 are given in Table 12.4.1.a, 12.4.1.b, and 12.4.1.c.

From Tables 12.4.1.a to 12.4.1.c, it is found that the RF algorithm gives better performance for n_estimators=10 and max_depth=5. Performance measures obtained with the above setting are given in Table 4.4.

*Table 12.4.1.b   Performance measures obtained for RF with n_estimators=10
(record size is 40,000–160,000)*

Record size	max_depth	Performance measures			
		Accuracy of anomaly detection (%)	Precision (%)	Recall (%)	F-score (%)
	2	100	100	100	100
40,000	3	100	100	100	100
	5	100	100	100	100
	2	98.34	94.28	95.39	95.03
80,000	3	98.37	94.91	95.11	94.16
	5	100	100	100	100
	2	98.29	93.66	94.38	91.12
120,000	3	98.67	93.68	94.69	94.68
	5	100	100	100	100
	2	98.91	94.50	95.12	94.12
160,000	3	99.12	92.89	93.18	91.68
	5	100	100	100	100

*Table 12.4.1.c   Performance measures obtained for RF with n_estimators=10
(record size is 200,000–319,352)*

Record size	max_depth	Performance measures			
		Accuracy of anomaly detection (%)	Precision (%)	Recall (%)	F-score (%)
	2	97.72	94.38	93.72	93.08
200,000	3	98.85	91.21	92.10	94.24
	5	100	100	100	100
	2	99.08	93.01	93.45	94.38
240,000	3	99.24	92.87	93.24	91.10
	5	100	100	100	100
	2	98.46	94.38	94.56	93.67
280,000	3	99.17	90.89	92.76	91.99
	5	100	100	100	100
	2	99.71	96.08	95.38	96.03
319,352	3	99.79	95.24	91.81	93.43
	5	100	100	100	100

12.5   Proposed architecture

An architecture using Kafka and machine learning algorithms has been for real-time anomaly detection. It consists of three entities, (i) stream data generator, (ii) Kafka broker, and (iii) anomaly detector. Basically, the proposed architecture is

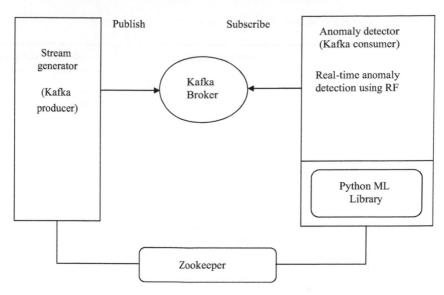

Figure 12.5   Proposed architecture

Table 12.5   Operating parameters for RF

n_estimators	criterion	random_ state	max_ depth	Accuracy (%)	Precision (%)	Recall (%)	F-score (%)
10	Gini	1	5	100	100	100	100

capable of yielding the required scalability for large-scale applications. The establishment of the proposed architecture is shown in Figure 12.5.

The key functions of the entities are as follows:

- Kafka message producer is the one which generates the streams. One can generate streams of desired speeds.
- Kafka broker is the one which communicates the messages generated by producer to consumer.
- Anomaly detector – in the proposed architectures, anomaly detector is implemented in Kafka consumer.

Machine learning algorithm is implemented using Python machine library. Python becomes very popular due its extensive support for different libraries. Scikit-learn (Sklearn), the most powerful machine learning library of Python, provides a selection of efficient tools for machine learning and statistical modeling including classification, regression, clustering, and dimensionality reduction via a consistence interface.

The main entities involved are configured in a single node as shown in Figure 12.5.

Table 12.6   Accuracy obtained for different discretized streams

Discretized streams	Speed of discretized stream	Anomaly detection accuracy (%) RF
Discretized Streams-1	10 dps/sec	86
Discretized Streams-2	20 dps/sec	90
Discretized Streams-3	25 dps/sec	83
Discretized Streams-4	50 dps/sec	88
Discretized Streams-5	100 dps/sec	92
Discretized Streams-6	200 dps/sec	97
Discretized Streams-7	250 dps/sec	96
Discretized Streams-8	500 dps/sec	97
Discretized Streams-9	1,000 dps/sec	96
Discretized Streams-10	10,000 dps/sec	97
Discretized Streams-11	40,000 dps/sec	98
Discretized Streams-12	50,000 dps/sec	97
Discretized Streams-13	100,000 dps/sec	98
Discretized Streams-14	200,000 dps/sec	99

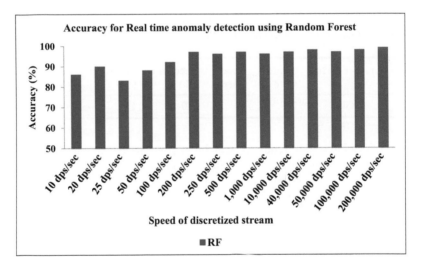

Figure 12.6   Anomaly detection using Random Forest for streams having different speeds

12.6   Experimentation

In this experimentation, the speeds of discretized streams have been changed and the anomaly detection accuracy of RF algorithm has been measured. The values are given in Table 12.6.

From Table 12.6, the accuracy of RF algorithm is found to vary from 86% to 99% for the discretized streams having speed from 100 data points/millisecond to 100,000 data points/microsecond. The key point is that the accuracy is increasing with respect to record size.

Further, the results are shown as a graph in Figure 12.6.

12.7   Conclusion

This chapter presents an architecture consisting of Kafka messenger and RF algorithm for detection of anomaly in streams. The present architecture needs to extend to accommodate scalability. More experimentation needs to carried out with different datasets to draw more meaningful inferences.

References

[1]   Salima Omar, Asri Ngadi and Hamid H. Jebur, "Machine learning techniques for anomaly detection: an overview", *International Journal of Computer Applications*, vol. 79, no. 2, pp. 33–41, 2013.

[2]   Riyaz Ahamed Ariyaluran Habeeb, Fariza Nasaruddin, Abdullah Gani, Ibrahim Abaker Targio Hashem, Ejaz Ahmed and Muhammad Imran, "Real-time big data processing for anomaly detection: a survey", *International Journal of Information Management*, vol. 45, pp. 289–307, April 2019.

[3]   Edin Sabic, David Keeley, Bailey Henderson and Sara Nannemann, "Healthcare and anomaly detection: using machine learning to predict anomalies in heart rate data", *AI & Society*, vol. 36, pp. 149–158, 2020.

[4]   Nerijus Paulauskas and Azuolas Faustas Bagdonas, "Local outlier factor use for the network flow anomaly detection", *Security and Communication Network*, vol. 2015, no. 8, pp. 4203–4212, 2015.

[5]   Fei Tony Liu, Kai Ming Ting and Zhi-Hua Zhou, "Isolation forest", in: *Proceedings of the Eighth IEEE International Conference on Data Mining*, New York, NY: IEEE, pp. 413–422, December 2008, p-ISBN: 978-0-7695-3502-9, p-ISSN: 1550-4786, e-ISSN: 2374-8486.

[6]   Aleksandra Solarz, Maciej Bilicki, Mariusz Gromadzki, Agnieszka Pollo, Anna Durkalec and Michał Wypych, "Automated novelty detection in the wise survey with one-class support vector machines", *Astronomy and Astrophysics (A&A)*, vol. 606, no. 39, pp. 1–13, 21 July 2017.

[7]   Dejan Varmedja, Mirjana Karanovic, Srdjan Sladojevic, Marko Arsenovic, and Andras Anderla, "Credit card fraud detection – machine learning methods", in: *Proceedings of the 18th International Symposium Infotech – Jahorina*, New York, NY: IEEE, pp. 1–5, March 2019, e-ISBN: 978-1-5386-7073-6, p-ISBN: 978-1-5386-7074-3.

[8]   Rifkie Primartha and Bayu Adhi Tama, "Anomaly detection using random forest: a performance revisited", in: *Proceedings of the 2017 International Conference on Data and Software Engineering (IcoDSE)*, New York, NY:

IEEE, pp. 1–6, 12 February 2018, e-ISBN: 978-1-5386-1449-5, p-ISBN: 978-1-5386-1450-1.

[9]   Simon D. Duque Anton, Sapna Sinha and Hans Dieter Schotten, "Anomaly-based intrusion detection in industrial data with SVM and random forests", in: *Proceedings of 27th International Conference on Software, Telecommunications and Computer Networks (SoftCOM)*, vol. 1, 2019, pp. 1–6.

[10]   Zhiruo Zhao, Kishan G. Mehrotra, and Chilukuri K. Mohan, "Online anomaly detection using random forest", in: *Proceedings of the 31st International Conference on Industrial Engineering and Other Applications of Applied Intelligent Systems, Recent Trends and Future Technology in Applied Intelligence*, Montreal, Canada: Springer Verlag, vol. 10868 LNAI, pp. 135–147, 1 January 2018, p-ISSN: 0302-9743, e-ISSN: 1611-3349.

[11]   Phyu Thi Htun and Kyaw Thet Khaing, "Anomaly intrusion detection system using random forests and k-nearest neighbor", *International Journal of P2P Network Trends and Technology (IJPTT)*, vol. 3, no. 1, pp. 39–43, 2013, ISSN: 2249-2615.

[12]   Jay Kreps, Neha Narkhede and Jun Rao, "Kafka: a distributed messaging system for log processing", in: *Proceedings of the 6th International Workshop on Networking Meets DataBases (NetDB'11)*, Athens, Greece, 2011.

Chapter 13

Scalable and real-time prediction on streaming data – the role of Kafka and streaming frameworks

Pethuru Raj[1] and Steve Jefferson[2]

Abstract

Increasingly data gets generated and streamed from different and distributed data sources. In order to make sense out of any streaming data, the market is flooded with a variety of features-rich streaming data analytics platforms and frameworks. Lately, the role and responsibility of Kafka, an open source streaming data platform, are growing steadily. In this chapter, we have written about the noteworthy contributions of Kafka in producing timely, trendsetting and predictive insights out of streaming data.

A new breed of "Fast Data" architectures has evolved to be stream-oriented, where data is processed as it arrives, providing businesses with a competitive advantage. The demand for stream processing is increasing every day in the digital era. The main reason behind it is that processing only volumes of data is not sufficient but processing data at faster rates and making insights out of it in real time is very essential so that organization can react to changing business conditions/sentiments in real time. And hence, there is a need to understand the concept "stream processing "and technology behind it. This collateral is prepared with the noble intention of articulating the need for scalable and real-time prediction on streaming data. There are competent technologies, tools, and techniques for real-time prediction out of streaming data in a highly elastic manner. All these details are covered in this document in order to enlighten our readers. The major topics illustrated here include

1. Streaming concepts
2. Apache Kafka
3. Apache Kafka streams
4. Apache Spark
5. A sample machine learning (ML) application for real-time prediction out of streaming data in a scalable fashion

[1]Edge AI Division, Reliance Jio Platforms Ltd., Bangalore, India
[2]Department of Engineering Mathematics, University of Bristol, UK

13.1   Streaming concepts

It is undeniably true that most of the business activities can be modeled as a stream of events. There is a lot of hype around "machine-generated data" and "Internet of things." These buzzwords may have a different meaning for different people, but a considerable part of these areas is about the collection and processing of big data streams. Like any other domain, stream processing has its own set of challenges and concepts.

Detaching Fallacies – The popularity and increasing demand for stream processing is a natural progression of big data evolution. Most of the stream processing platforms are built by taking capabilities from the big-data batch processing world and making them available for a low-latency domain. This approach created some misconception around the notion of stream processing.

Stream processing vs. analytics – People often take stream processing synonymous with real-time analytics. Real-time analytics is one important use case of stream processing. However, it does not always mean analytics. There are many more applications of real-time stream processing. More often, your stream processing application would implement core functions in the business rather than computing analytics about the business. Analytics may be an individual service along with many other services on your streaming platform. Stream processing is a backbone infrastructure and a set of services that coordinate with analytics function. It is more like the glue that binds your platform to deliver the business processes that may also include analytics.

Stream processing vs. ETL – Some people take the stream processing as an ETL pipeline that works in real-time. That might be a good starting point on stream processing. However, stream processing applications require addressing needs that are very different from the ETL domain of conventional big-data processing. Stream processing application is more like microservices rather than a scheduled job. Like a typical microservice, stream processing applications might not be processing requests over HTTP, but they operate on asynchronous event streams over a pull mechanism. You can take the stream processing applications as an application programming model for asynchronous services rather than an ETL framework.

Stream processing vs. cluster computing – Cluster computing or the distributed computing is all about sharing the workload over a pool of resources in the cluster of computers. This is often implemented using a framework that is responsible for providing the fault tolerance, scalability, and many other orchestration capabilities. These cluster management frameworks manage the resources in the form of containers which is nothing but a logical bundle of cluster resources such as memory, CPU, networking, and in many cases operating system image as well. This area is going under a separate evolution, and we can see a further decoupling of responsibilities for greater flexibility. Docker containers have decoupled the container configuration and packaging from the cluster management. The Kubernetes is trying to solve the problem of resource allocation and placement of containers in a fault-tolerant and scalable cluster.

On the other side, a stream processing application has a different domain of problems and challenges while dealing with the stream of events in the real-time. They have nothing to do with the cluster management and resource allocation, and in fact, you would want to have the flexibility to take advantage of the separate developments that are happening in the cluster computing space.

Many of the big-data processing frameworks such as Apache Spark assumes the responsibility of packaging the dependencies, serialize your code, and send it to the workers over the network. This process has an inherent delay to start the execution, and it also imposes a restriction on packaging and deployment flexibility that in turn takes away a bunch of advantages of CI/CD and few other things.

To summarize this discussion, when you are designing a stream processing solution, you may not want to get trapped into the cluster management requirements. You stream processing application should not have a dependency on the cluster management frameworks. In fact, the cluster management platform should be entirely optional for your streaming application as well as you should have the flexibility to take advantage of any of such mature platforms.

Stream processing vs. batch processing – The first and most obvious thing that you would notice about the stream processing is that you are going to deal with an unbounded, ever growing, and infinite dataset that is continuously flowing to your system. In contrast, the batch processing is dealing with a bounded, fixed, and finite data set that has already landed at your system in the past. If you carefully think about the bounded dataset, it is nothing but a small subset of the unbounded dataset that is chopped into a smaller set from the stream.

The approach taken up by a micro-batch processing system is a bottom-up approach where they first solved a subset of the problem by processing smaller batches and tried to enhance and extend the batch method to solve a much bigger problem of dealing with infinite streams. However, the systems that are initially designed for the stream processing in mind, they would have the flexibility to take a radical approach to solve a bigger problem, and then use the same method to deal with the smaller batches of bounded data, that are in fact a subset of the problem that the stream processing system already solved. The point is straight. A well designed, efficient stream processing system will eventually eliminate the need for the batch processing systems.

Like any other technical domain, stream processing also poses a unique set of challenges. Before we start working with streams, it is critical to have some good sense of the difficulties that you are going to handle while dealing with the event streams.

Time domain – One of the capabilities of the stream processing system is the power to extract value out of the time-sensitive events before the value vanishes. For example, healthcare systems want to send an alert to nurses as soon as possible. With time, the value of such alarm disappears. This time sensitivity is not only associated with the life-critical systems. Time makes sense in many other use cases. For example, your application is processing a stream of ticket booking events.

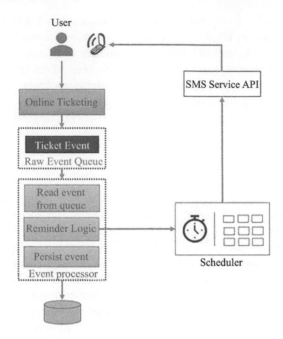

As the event is received to your application, you want to schedule a reminder that should be sent a couple of hours before the show. However, such a reminder does not make sense If the ticket is booked fifteen minutes before the show, and hence you want to filter out those tickets from flowing to the scheduler. The point is straight. The time stamping of the event is critical for many stream processing use cases, and hence you may have to attach a timestamp with your events.

Event-time vs. processing-time – For a stream processing system, we often care about two types of timestamps.

1. Event time
2. Processing time

Event time is the time that an event happened in the real world. For example, the time when a ticket was booked by an online ticket booking platform. Another example would be the time when the search button is clicked by the user to search some product on your eCommerce website.

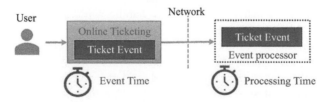

Processing time is the time that the event is observed by the machine that is processing it. For example, the time when the ticket booking event is received at your stream processing system that takes a decision to schedule an alert. Both notions of time are useful depending on the application. For example, a ticket is booked at 10.30 AM for the show that starts at 11.00 AM. For some strange reasons, the ticket booking event reaches your stream processing application at 11.05 AM. You may not want to send the reminder notification now. The show should have already started. In this case, the processing time makes more sense over the event time.

On the other hand, if you are computing a search pattern over time to learn what products are being searched on your eCommerce website in the morning, vs. afternoon, vs. evening. For such computations, the event time makes more sense. In an ideal world, the event time and the processing time should be same assuming it takes no time to reach the machine that processes the event. However, in a real world, the processing time would be later than the event time due to the network latency, resource sharing and a variety of other reasons. These differences in event time and processing time may be as small as few milliseconds to many hours or even days. For example, you are collecting usage patterns for some mobile application that works online as well as offline. This data can be transmitted to your servers only when the mobile device has connectivity. If the user goes to an area where he loses the connectivity for a few hours, you may get those events after hours. If the user switches off the mobile data for a couple of days, this delay may be as significant as a few days.

Time window – Many of the standard data processing operation appears to be time-agnostic such as filter, join, and grouping. Let us assume that you are processing web traffic log entries. You want to group the records by the country of origin and count them. For this simple requirement, you may not have to consider event time or the processing time. However, the number of users by country may not be a useful metric because it keeps increasing forever. Breaking the ever-growing count in temporal boundaries should make more sense. For example, the number of users per hour or per minute for a given country would be more meaningful. The point is straightforward. Some of the requirements would need you to slice the time domain in precise time windows. You would want to collect the events generated or received within the window and perform some analysis on the whole set. Your time window may be of two types: tumbling (fixed) or sliding.

Tumbling window – This window is fixed and non-overlapping time window. To visualize the notion of tumbling window, let us consider an input stream as shown below.

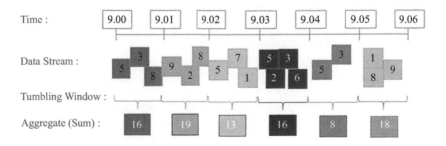

The first row represents the time. Each number in the second row represents a data point. The next line groups the data by a tumbling window of one minute. Finally, we take a sum of the data points for each tumbling window.

Sliding window – These windows are fixed length, but they slide over the period. Let's consider the same input stream that we used in the tumbling window and see how a sliding window gives you a different perspective of the time.

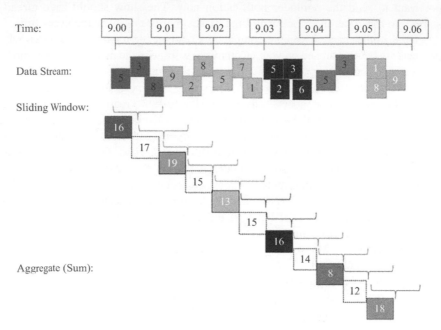

The first row represents the time. Each number in the second row represents a data point. The next line groups the data by a window of one minute that slides every thirty seconds. Finally, we take a sum of the data points for each sliding window. Now let us talk about how these two windows are different. While using a tumbling window, you would buffer the data for a minute and then take a sum of all the data points. In this case, every computation has a delay of one minute. However, the sliding window updates the sum every thirty seconds for the most recent one minute. You would eventually get the same result as the fixed window, but you also get an early sense by an intermediate result after every 30 sec.

Watermarks and triggers – We learned that you may want to slice up your event stream into time-based windows and aggregate your results over time such as per second or per minute. However, the windowing introduces a new problem of latecomers. The stragglers can jeopardize the correctness of your results.

Let us assume that you are you are monitoring traffic by computing the number of vehicles pass by every minute. You started at 9.00.00 AM and wanted to sum up the number of cars that passed by between 9.00.00 and 9.01.00. However, the event takes five seconds to reach your application. So, the event that generated at 9.00.00 will arrive at your system at 9.00.05, and similarly, the event created at 9.00.59 will reach to your system by 9.01.04.

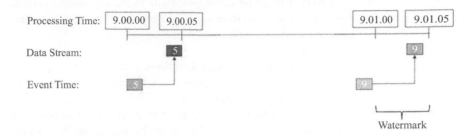

So, to compute the correct results, you should wait until 9.01.05 to ensure that all events that are generated between 9.00 and 9.01 successfully reached your application. If you calculate your sum before that time, your output is incorrect. The notion of waiting for the stragglers is known as watermarks or the triggers. Different stream processing system handles it differently. However, the idea is termed as the watermark. Watermarks are a feature of streaming systems that allow you to specify how late they expect to see data in event time. The triggers in this respect are the mechanism to end the waiting of the new events and trigger the computation. Watermarks and triggers are essentially an approach to handle stragglers.

Handling late record is one of the most complex problems of the stream processing system for the fact that you cannot accurately predict the delay in most of the cases. It is tough to guarantee that your application has received all the data that are generated before specific event time, and you do not have anything hanging somewhere due to some unknown reasons. This uncertainty of stragglers is the greatest streaming challenge.

Other window approaches – Time is one of the most common approaches to implement the notion of a window. One of the main reasons to use the time for windowing is that the time always goes on, and the time window will eventually close for sure. Another approach is to implement a window on the count of events. In this approach, we wait for some x number of records to trigger the computation. For example, you may want to wait for 100 records to arrive and then trigger the calculations. Such notions should be implemented with extra care because in certain conditions, you may be waiting forever as you never got 100 records.

Another common approach is to base your window on the notion of session. In general sense, a session is a period of activity that is preceded and followed by a period of inactivity. For example, a series of interactions of a user on a website, followed by no further response for a certain period may be termed as an end of the session. Sessions are often implemented using timeouts because they typically do not have a set duration or a set number of interactions. The timeout basically specifies how long we want to wait until we believe that a session has ended.

Stateful streams – A state is nothing but a persistent and durable store where the application can buffer or store some data for later reference. Many of the stream processing use cases are stateless, and they do not need to maintain any state. For example, when you are processing one event at a time, and all you need to do is to transform the event and pass it to some other processor to take necessary action. Simple transformations and filers on individual events are the most common examples that may not need to maintain a state.

However, most of the stream processing applications need to keep some state, and hence they should be categorized as stateful applications. Your application is stateful whenever it needs to aggregate, implement a window, perform a join operation, or ensure that they can be stopped and resumed. One of the common reasons for streaming applications to maintain a state is to avoid reprocessing of huge volumes in case of failures. You may need the ability to resume from wherever you were paused or stopped. Since a streaming application works on a continuous stream of data, and if they need to go back in time and reprocess all the data once again for some reason, they may not be able to catch up with the new data in due time and hence defy the whole purpose of stream processing.

Stream table duality – Stream table duality is one of the most talked topics in the stream processing domain. The idea is quite simple. However, it can take you a long way to conceptualize your stream processing solutions. The notion of stream table duality talks about the relationship between data streams and database tables, and how you can create one from the other. When implementing stream processing solutions in practice, you need streams as well as the database tables. For example, when you are processing an eCommerce transaction as an event stream, your stream processing application may want to join the transaction with the customer information from a database table. Streams are everywhere. However, the database tables are also everywhere. The point is straight. Tables are the reality, and you cannot avoid them. Tables make perfect sense in a stream processing solution as well. So, you may want to combine the ideas from both worlds and design a practical solution.

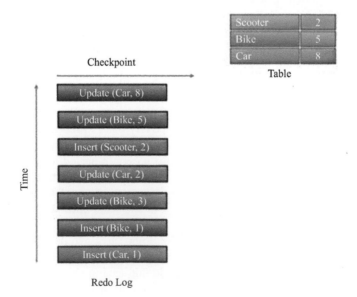

The relationship between stream and tables can be understood more clearly by realizing the fact that a table is nothing but an aggregated view of a stream at a given point in time. This idea is applied by the databases to create tables. In most of the databases, transactions are recorded in a log file in chronological order. The log file is a representation of a stream as it records immutable and continuous events. The databases read this log and apply them in a sequence to materialize the table. The table represents the latest state of each unique record however the log represents a sequence of transactions as they arrive. In fact, the database is converting a stream into a table. On the other side, a table can also be converted into a stream. The idea is implemented by most of the change data capture (CDC) tools such as Oracle golden gate and HVR. These tools monitor all the changes to the table at one end of the pipeline and stream the changes to the other end of the pipe.

In summary, event stream processing (ESP) works with an infinite stream of data with continuous computation, as it flows, with no need to collect or store the data to act on it. It is used to query continuous data stream and detect conditions, quickly, within a small time period from the time of receiving the data. Some insights are more valuable shortly after it has happened with the value diminishes very fast with time. Stream processing enables such scenarios, providing insights faster, often within milliseconds to seconds from the trigger.

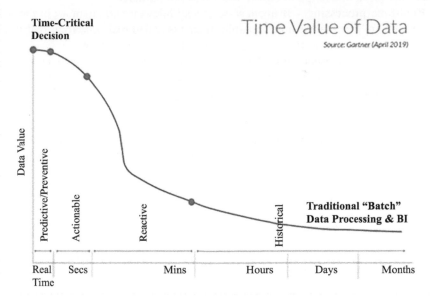

Batch using streaming – It is possible to obtain batch features directly using modern stream processors

Bounded data is a finite stream of data whereas unbounded data represents an infinite stream of data

Near real-time vs. real-time – There is a delay introduced between the occurrence of an event and the processing of the data. The events are processed as soon as possible by the stream processor.

Data analytics and ML – ML advancements such as neural networks and deep learning algorithms can discover hidden patterns in unstructured data sets and uncover new information, vital for companies. Actually, when ML and streaming data meet, amazing things can happen.

Amazon Web Services (AWS) defines "Streaming Data" is data that is generated continuously by thousands of data sources, which typically send in the data records simultaneously, and in small sizes (order of Kilobytes). This data needs to be processed sequentially and incrementally on a record-by-record basis or over sliding time windows and used for a wide variety of analytics including correlations, aggregations, filtering, and sampling. In stream processing method, continuous computation happens as the data flows through the system. Stream processing is highly beneficial if the events you wish to track are happening frequently and close together in time. It is also best to utilize if the event needs to be detected right away and responded to quickly.

There is a subtle difference between stream processing, real-time processing (near real-time) and complex event processing (CEP). Let us quickly look at the examples to understand the difference.

Stream processing – Stream processing is useful for tasks like fraud detection and cybersecurity. If transaction data is stream-processed, fraudulent transactions can be identified and stopped before they are even complete.

Real-time processing – If event time is very relevant and latencies in the second's range are completely unacceptable, then it is called real-time (rear real-time) processing. For example, flight control system for space programs.

Complex event processing (CEP) – CEP utilizes event-by-event processing and aggregation (e.g., on potentially out-of-order events from a variety of sources, often with large numbers of rules or business logic).

Radicalbit data management platform offers a set of tools specifically designed around data scientist's needs, a simple yet powerful way to reduce the time to market in deploying ML enhanced analytics applications.

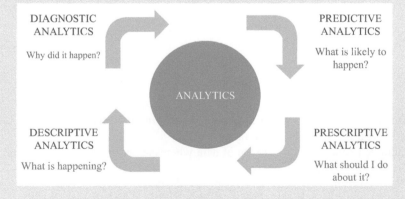

DIAGNOSTIC ANALYTICS

Why did it happen?

PREDICTIVE ANALYTICS

What is likely to happen?

ANALYTICS

DESCRIPTIVE ANALYTICS

What is happening?

PRESCRIPTIVE ANALYTICS

What should I do about it?

From Lambda to Kappa architecture – The solutions developed by Radicalbit are based on the Kappa Architecture, a powerful and agile approach able to manage natively streaming data sources together with batch.

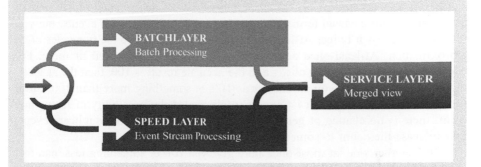

This is a popular big data architecture for data processing. It is typically batch based, and treats streaming sources in a separate flow that needs to be merged at a later stage. This is a streaming-oriented and event-based architecture for data processing. It matches streaming and batch requirements in a unique flow.

Apache Flink – Stream processing framework for distributed, high-performing, always-available, and accurate data streaming applications.

Apache Kafka – Event broker/distributed streaming platform.

Apache Spark – Distributed Cluster computing framework.

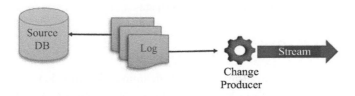

The point is straightforward. The data exists in two related forms: streams and tables. Both are essential constituents of a practical solution.

Exactly once processing – The correctness of your results is of prime importance in most of the cases. However, some use cases are based on approximation, and a nearly accurate result is well accepted. The argument of accuracy and approximation are intensely discussed in the stream processing domain with three notions.

1. At least once processing
2. At most one processing
3. Exactly once processing

At-least-once processing talks about ensuring that we do not lose any event and each record is processed at least once. However, at the same time, at-least-once will leave a possibility for duplicate events. It accepts that an event is computed more than once but guarantees that none of the events are lost. On the other hand, at-most-once processing focuses on avoiding duplicates. It guarantees that an event should not be processed more than once. However, it is acceptable to lose some of the events. In more casual terms, it means that you can miss some events, but you will never process it twice. At-least-once and at-most-once are the two sides of an approximation. At-least-once approximates the value to the actual or more. For example, if you are counting clicks and the accurate result is 100, then the at-least-one approach will give you an answer as 100, or something more than 100. Since you chose to implement at-least-once and eliminated the possibility of losing any event, there is no chance of getting less than 100. However, the duplicate events may increase the count to something more than 100.

On the other side, at-most-once may give you 100 or something less than that as you accepted losing some events but ensured that you do not count any event twice. At-least-once and at-most-once are about accepting tread-off depending on what makes more sense in your use case.

Exactly-once processing is ensuring that every event is processed exactly once without losing any event, and without duplicating anything as well. Exactly-once appears to be the best and the most desirable choice. However, implementing exactly-once is hard in a practical sense. One of the main problems is the delay in arriving records at the processor. You cannot keep waiting for the event forever, and it is almost impossible to ensure that the event reaches at your processor within an acceptable timeline or before the practically feasible watermark.

Some systems allow you to achieve exactly-once processing. However, that involves implementing database like transactional features to ensure that the transaction is successfully committed exactly-once. Implementing such transactions comes at the cost of additional complexity and that is why we often resolve to at-least-once, or at-most-once schematics whenever approximation is an acceptable thing.

13.2   Apache Kafka

Apache Kafka is a community-distributed streaming platform that has three key capabilities: publish and subscribe to streams of records, store streams of records in a fault-tolerant durable way, and process streams as they occur. Apache Kafka has several success cases in the Java world, including website activity tracking, metrics collection and monitoring, log aggregation, and real-time analytics.

Apache Kafka core concepts – Kafka is run as a cluster on one or more servers that can span multiple data centers. A Kafka cluster stores a stream of records in categories called topics, and each record consists of a key, a value, and a timestamp. As seen in the official documentation, Kafka has four core APIs:

- The producer API – Allows an application to publish a stream of records to one or more Kafka topics.

- The consumer API – Allows an application to subscribe to one or more topics and to process the stream of records published to those topics.
- The streams API – Allows an application to act as a stream processor, consuming an input stream from one or more input topics, and producing an output stream to one or more output topics to effectively transform the input streams to output streams.
- The connector API – Allows building and running reusable producers or consumers that connect Kafka topics to existing applications or data systems.

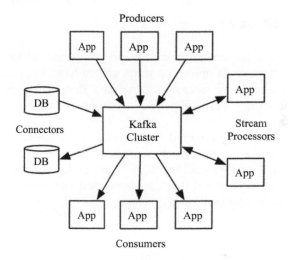

A few of the critical attributes that make Kafka such an alluring alternative are vividly illustrated below.

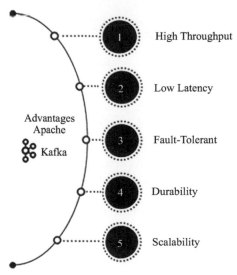

Apache Kafka is a distributed streaming platform. At its core, it allows systems that generate data (called producers) to persist their data in real-time in an Apache Kafka Topic. Any topic can then be read by any number of systems who need that data in real-time (called consumers). Therefore, at its core, Kafka is a Pub/Sub system. Behind the scenes, Kafka is distributed, scales well, replicates data across brokers (servers), can survive broker downtime, and much more.

13.3   Kafka Streams

Kafka Streams is a customer library for preparing and investigating data put away in Kafka. It expands upon important stream handling ideas, for example, appropriately recognizing occasion time and developing time, windowing backing, and necessary yet useful administration and constant questioning of utilization states.

Kafka Streams gives purported state stores, which can be utilized by stream preparing applications to store and inquire information. A vital ability while actualizing chained and cascading tasks. Each undertaking in Kafka Streams installs at least one state stores that can be reached employing APIs to store and question information required for preparing.

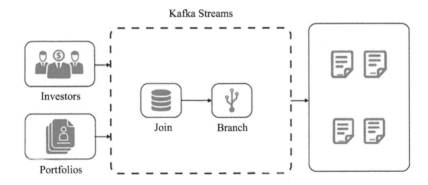

These state stores can either be a persevering key-esteem store, an in-memory hash-map, or another advantageous information structure. Kafka Streams offers adaptation to internal failure and programmed recuperation for neighborhood state stores. Kafka Streams permits coordinated read-only inquiries of the state stores by strategies, strings, procedures or applications outside to the stream preparing application that made the state stores. It will be given through a component called Interactive Queries. All stores are named, and Interactive Queries uncovered just the read activities of the fundamental usage.

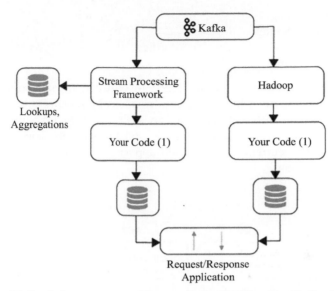

Apache Kafka bolsters an extensive variety of utilization Kafka Streams use cases as a broadly useful data management framework for situations where high throughput, dependable conveyance, and level versatility are imperative. Apache Storm and Apache HBase both work exceptionally well in tandem with Kafka. Typical functions and cases that can be conducted include:

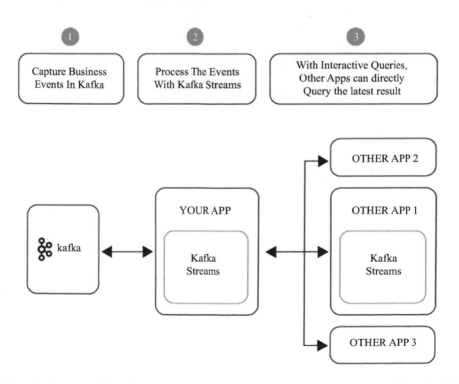

- Stream processing
- Site activity tracking
- Measurements collection and monitoring
- Log aggregation

Kafka Streams have a low hindrance to obstructions and errors. You can rapidly compose and run a little scale confirmations by running extra occasions of your application on different machines to scale up to high-volume generation remaining tasks at hand. Kafka Streams straightforwardly handles the heap, adjusting various occurrences of a similar application by utilizing Kafka's unique multitasking functions.

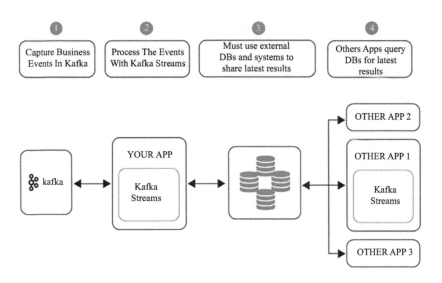

Outlined as an essential and lightweight customer library, Kafka Streams can be effectively inserted in any Kafka streams Java application and incorporated with any current bundling. It can be added to any arrangement and operational devices that clients have for their data-centric applications.

- Puts no external conditions on frameworks other than Apache Kafka itself as the inward informing layer.
- It utilizes Kafka's parceling model on a level plane scale handling while at the same time keeping up steady requesting streams.
- Streams can seamlessly deal with any Kafka Streams join operations that are done on the data, which empowers quick and proficient tasks like windowed joins and conglomerations.
- It backs precisely once to prepare semantics to ensure that each record will be handled once and just once notwithstanding when there is an error on

either Stream for customers or Kafka intermediaries highly involved with handling.

- Utilizes one-record at any given moment preparing to accomplish millisecond handling inactivity and backs occasionally based on time-based windowing activities with late entry of records.
- Offers essential stream handling natives, alongside an abnormal state streams DSL and a low-level processor API.

	Apache Spark	Apache Flink	Apache Storm	Apache Samza	Apache Kafka streams
Process Model	Micro-batching Batch	Event Micro-batch Batch	Event	Event	Event
Cluster Management	Mesos, Yarn, Standalone	Yarn, Tez, Standalone	Mesos, Yarn	Yarn	Mesos, many others
Delivery Guarantee	Exactly Once	Exactly once	-At least Once -Exactly Once (with Trident)	-At least once	-At least once
Reference Data	-In Memory Cache	-In Memory Cache DBMS inside Cluster	Remote DBMS	-In memory Cache -Per client DBMS -Remote DBMS	-Remote DBMS
Programming Model	Declarative	Declarative	Compositional	Compositional	Compositional
Programming Language	Java/Scala Python	Java/Scala	JVM Languages	Java	Java
Latency	Medium	Low	Very Low	Low	Low
Maturity	High	Low	High	Medium	Low
Community Adaption	Wide Adaption	Growing Adaption	Selective Adaption	Selective Adaption	Not in production yet

13.4   Kafka Streams topology

- A stream is an essential function given by Kafka Streams. It speaks to an unbounded, ceaselessly refreshing informational collection.
- A stream is an arranged, re-playable, and blames a tolerant succession of changeless information records, where an information record is characterized as a key-esteem match.
- A stream preparing application is any program that makes utilization of the Kafka Streams library. It portrays its computational rationale through at least one processor topologies, where a processor Kafka Streams topology is a diagram of stream processors (hubs) that are associated by streams (edges). These can exist as a virtual machine on Kafka streams java JVM as well.
- A stream processor is a hub in the processor topology. It speaks to a handling venture to change information in streams by accepting one information record at once from its upstream processors in the topology, applying its activity to it, and may along these lines deliver at least one yield records to its downstream processors.

You can run one or more instances of your app. They run independently
but will automatically discover each other and collaborate.

Your
App

| App Instance 1 | App Instance 2 | App Instance 3 |
| Kafka Streams API | Kafka Streams API | Kafka Streams API |

You can easily add and
remove app instances during
live operations. If one instances
dies, then the other instances
will take over its work.

Kafka
Cluster

A source processor is an uncommon kind of stream processor that does not
have any upstream processors. It delivers an information stream to its topology
from one or various Kafka subjects by expending records from these points and
sending them to its down-stream processors. A sink processor is a different sort of
stream processor that does not have down-stream processors. It sends any got
records from its up-stream processors to a predetermined Kafka theme.

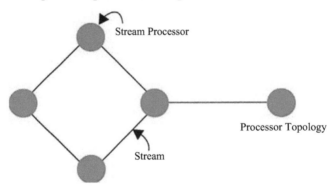

Stream Processor

Processor Topology

Stream

Note that in ordinary processor hubs, other remote frameworks can likewise be
reached while handling the present record. Consequently, the handled outcomes can
either be spilled once again into Kafka or kept in touch with an outer framework.

Kafka Streams offers two different ways to characterize the stream preparing
topology that often jumbles the arrangement and handling of data at larger scales.
Kafka Streams DSL gives the most widely recognized information change activities, for example, delineate, Kafka stream join and totals out of the container. The
lower-level processor API permits designers to characterize and associate custom
processors and in addition to collaborating with state stores. Similar APIs can be
created using a Kafka Streams Scala bundle. Kafka Streams Scala bundles are often
packaged as separate products by providers.

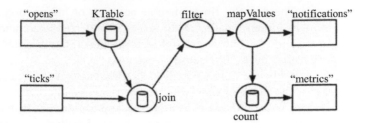

A processor topology merely is a coherent reflection for any stream preparing code. At runtime, the intelligent topology is instantiated and recreated inside the application for parallel computation.

Kafka Streams supports a tightly built framework that eliminates a number of the pesky issues that beguile industries and companies that play around with massive data. It has become a favorite for tech companies mainly due to many factors.

- Versatility – Conveyed framework are scaled effortlessly with no downtime.
- Solidness and memory – Holds on messages on a plate, and gives intra-bunch replication.
- Unwavering quality – Repeats information underpins different supporters and naturally adjusts purchasers if there should be an occurrence of errors.
- Execution – High throughput for both distributing and buying in.
- Time – A fundamental viewpoint in stream handling is the thought of the time, and how it is displayed and coordinated. For instance, a few tasks, for example, Kafka Streams windowing are characterized because of time limits.

13.5   Talking about the time

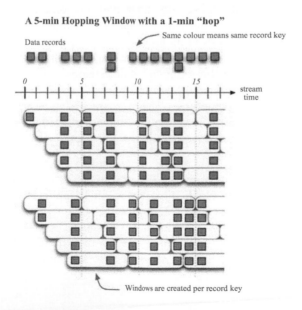

- Occasion time – The point in time when an occasion or information record happened, i.e., was initially made "at the source" is referred to commonly as the occasion time and is a central idea to Kafka Streams. If the source is a geo-area change revealed by a GPS sensor in an auto, at that point the related occasion time would be the time when the GPS sensor caught the area change.
- Handling time – The point in time when the occasion or information record happens to be prepared by the stream preparing application, i.e., at the point when the record is expanded, is the handling time. The handling time might be milliseconds, hours, or days and so forth later than the first occasion time. Imagine an investigation application that peruses and procedures the geo-area information announced from auto sensors to display it to an administration dashboard. Here, preparing time in the examination application may be milli-seconds or seconds (e.g., for continuous pipelines in light of Apache Kafka and Kafka Streams) or hours (e.g., for clump pipelines in light of Apache Hadoop or Apache Kafka streams Spark) after occasion time.
- Ingestion time – The point in time when an occasion or information record is put away in a subject parcel by a Kafka agent is the ingestion time. The distinction to occasion time is that this ingestion timestamp is produced when the record is attached to the actual subject by the Kafka intermediary, not when the record is made "at the source." The distinction to handling time is that pre-paring time is the point at which the stream preparing application forms the record. For instance, if a document is not prepared, there is no idea of handling time for it, however despite everything it has an ingestion time.

The decision between occasion time and holding-time is made through the design of Kafka (not Kafka Streams): From Kafka 0.10.x onwards, timestamps are consequently inserted into Kafka messages. Contingent upon Kafka's design, these timestamps speak to occasion time or ingestion-time.

- The particular Kafka design setting can be indicated on the intermediary level or per point. The default timestamp extractor in Kafka Streams will recover these implanted timestamps in its present condition.
- Thus, the powerful time semantics of your application relies upon the successful Kafka design for these implanted timestamps.
- Kafka Streams relegates a timestamp to each datum record through the Timestamp Extractor interface. These per-record timestamps depict the advancement of a stream concerning time and are utilized by time-subordinate tasks, for example, Kafka streams window activities.

Accordingly, this time will propel when another record lands at the processor. We call this information-driven time the stream time of the application to separate with the divider clock time when this application is executing. Substantial usage of the Timestamp Extractor interface will then give different semantics to the stream time definition. For instance, recovering or figuring timestamps because of the actual substance of information records, for example, an installed timestamp field to give occasion time semantics, and restoring the present divider clock time subsequently yield handling time semantics to stream time. Designers would thus be able to implement diverse ideas of time contingent upon their business needs.

At last, at whatever point a Kafka Streams application composes records to Kafka, at that point, it will likewise dole out timestamps to these new records. The way the timestamps are allowed relies upon the specific situation:

- At the time when new yield records are produced through handling some information record, for instance, context. Forward () activated all the while() work call, yield record timestamps are acquired from input record timestamps straightforwardly.
- At the point when new yield records are produced using occasional capacities, for example, Punctuator#punctuate(), the yield record timestamp is characterized as the current inner time (acquired through context.timestamp()) of the stream assignment.
- For accumulations, the timestamp of a subsequent total refresh record will be that of the most recent arrived input record that set off the refresh.

Handling user cases and states – Some stream handling applications do not require state, which implies the preparing of a message is autonomous from the handling of every other message.

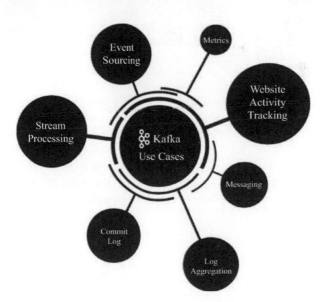

Notwithstanding, having the capacity to keep upstate opens up numerous conceivable outcomes for complex stream preparing applications. You can join input streams, or gathering and total information records. The Kafka Streams DSL gives various administrators.

In-stream handling, a standout question is "does stream preparing framework ensure that each record is prepared once and just once, regardless of whether a few errors are experienced while trying to?" Failing to ensure precisely once stream process will delineate the entire process against which the framework has multiple layers of protection. These layers ensure that processing occurs smoothly even in the case when things turn bizarre which is rarely common in such an advanced system.

13.6   What the Kafka Streams API is made of?

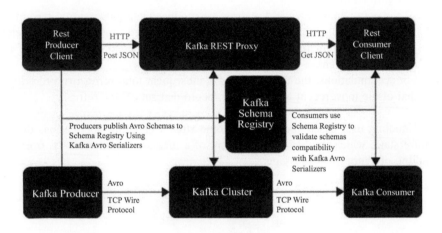

The Kafka Streams API enables you to make ongoing applications that power your central business. It is the simplest to utilize the most ground-breaking innovation yet to process information put away in Kafka. It gives business the use of standard classes of Kafka. A distinctive element of the Kafka Streams API is that the applications you work with it are typical applications. These applications can be bundled, sent, and observed like some other application, with no compelling reason to introduce external groups or unnecessary third-party add-ons.

- Abnormal state DSL
  - o Abnormal state DSL contains officially actualized strategies prepared to utilize classes and cases. It is made out of two fundamental components: KStream and Kafka Streams KTable or Global KTable.

- KStream
  - o A KStream is a reflection of record stream where every datum is a vital key esteem combine in the unbounded dataset. It gives numerous useful approaches to control stream information like an outline, mapValue,

Kafka Streams flatMap, Kafka Streams flatMapValues, and Kafka Streams Ktable.

o It additionally gives joining strategies for joining different streams and collection techniques on stream information.

- KTable or GlobalKTable
  o A KTable is a deliberation of a changelog stream.
  o In this changelog, each datum record is viewed as an Insert or Update (Upsert) contingent on the presence of the key as any current column with a similar key will be overwritten.

- Processor API
  o The low-level Processor API gives a customer to get to stream information and to play out business rationale on the approaching information stream and send the outcome as the downstream information.
  o It is done through broadening the unique class AbstractProcessor and superseding the procedure strategy which contains the class strategies.
  o This procedure strategy is called once for each key-esteem combine.
  o Where the abnormal state Kafka streams DSL furnishes prepared to utilize techniques with useful style, the low-level processor API gives the adaptability to actualize handling rationale as indicated by the company's needs.
  o The trade-off is only the lines of code to be composed for particular situations thus making Kafka Streams DSL important to the final functional capabilities.
  o Commands for python can be entered through the Kafka Streams terminal which makes it more user-friendly without complex coding required for execution.

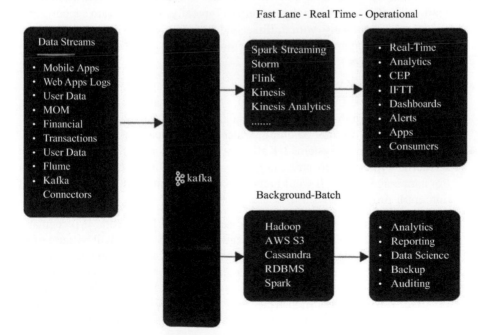

Kafka Streams is built upon important stream processing concepts such as properly distinguishing between event time and processing time, windowing support, and simple (yet efficient) management of application state. It is based on many concepts already contained in Kafka, such as scaling by partitioning. Also, for this reason, it comes as a lightweight library that can be integrated into an application. The application can then be operated as desired, as mentioned below.

1. Standalone, in an application server
2. As a Docker container, or
3. Directly, via a resource manager such as Mesos.

13.7   Why Apache Kafka Streams?

- Elastic, highly scalable, and fault-tolerant
- Deploy to containers, VMs, and bare metal (BM) servers
- Equally viable for small, medium, & large use cases
- Fully integrated with Kafka security
- Write standard Java and Scala applications
- Exactly-once processing semantics
- No separate processing cluster required
- Develop on Mac, Linux, and Windows

On concluding, Kafka is actually a message broker with a really good performance so that all your data can flow through it before being redistributed to applications. Kafka works as a data pipeline. Typically, Kafka Stream supports per-second stream processing with millisecond latency. Kafka Streams is a client library for processing and analyzing data stored in Kafka. Kafka streams can process data in two ways.

- Kafka -> Kafka: When Kafka Streams performs aggregations, filtering etc. and writes back the data to Kafka, it achieves amazing scalability, high availability, high throughput, etc. if configured correctly.
  It also does not do mini batching, which is "real streaming."
- Kafka -> External Systems ('Kafka -> Database' or 'Kafka -> Data science model'): Typically, any streaming library (Spark, Flink, NiFi, etc.) uses Kafka for a message broker. It would read the messages from Kafka and then break it into mini time windows to process it further.

Kafka Streams is a quick, adaptable, and error-free framework. It is regularly utilized instead of conventional message agents like JMS and AMQP because of its higher throughput, consistent quality, and replication. Kafka can message geospatial information from an armada of whole deal trucks or sensor information from warming and cooling hardware in places of business. Whatever the business or project case, Kafka dealers monstrous message streams for low-dormancy examination in enterprise Apache Hadoop.

13.8   Apache Spark Streaming

Spark Streaming receives live input data streams, it collects data for some time, builds RDD, divides the data into micro-batches, which are then processed by the Spark engine to generate the final stream of results in micro-batches. Following data flow diagram explains the working of Spark streaming.

Spark Streaming provides a high-level abstraction called discretized stream or DStream, which represents a continuous stream of data. DStreams can be created either from input data streams from sources such as Kafka, Flume, and Kinesis, or by applying high-level operations on other DStreams. Internally, a DStream is represented as a sequence of RDDs. Think about RDD as the underlying concept for distributing data over a cluster of computers.

It makes it very easy for developers to *use* a single framework to satisfy all the processing needs. They can *use* MLib (*Spark's* ML library) to train models offline and directly *use* them online for scoring live data in Spark *Streaming*. In fact, some models perform continuous, online learning, and scoring. Not all real-life use-cases need data to be processed at real real-time, few seconds delay is tolerated over having a unified framework like Spark Streaming and volumes of data processing. It provides a range of capabilities by integrating with other spark tools to do a variety of data processing.

13.9   Spark Streaming vs. Kafka Stream

Now that we have understood high level what these tools mean, it is obvious to have curiosity around differences between both the tools. Following table briefly explain you, key differences between the two.

Spark streaming	Kafka Streams
Data received form live input data streams is divided into micro-batches for processing	Processes per data stream (real-time)
Separated processing cluster is required	No separated processing cluster is required
Needs re-configuration for scaling	Scales easily by just adding java processes, no reconfiguration required
At least one semantics	Exactly one semantics
Spark streaming is better at processing group of rows (groups, by, ml, window functions, etc.)	Kafka streams provide true a-record-at-a-time processing capabilities. It is better for functions like rows parsing, data cleansing, etc.
Spark streaming is standalone framework	Kafka stream can be used as part of microservice, as it is just a library

Broadly, Spark Streaming is suitable for requirements with batch processing for massive datasets, for bulk processing and has use-cases more than just data streaming. Kafka Streams is still best used in a 'Kafka -> Kafka' context, while Spark Streaming could be used for a 'Kafka -> Database' or 'Kafka -> Data science model' type of context. Although, when these two technologies are connected, they bring complete data collection and processing capabilities together and are widely used in commercialized use cases and occupy significant market share.

13.10   A sample ML application

Text mining and analysis of social media, e-mails, support tickets, chats, product reviews, and recommendations have become a valuable resource used in almost all industry verticals to study data patterns in order to help businesses to gain insights, understand customers, predict and enhance the customer experience, tailor marketing campaigns, and aid in decision-making. Sentiment analysis uses ML algorithms to determine how positive or negative text content is. Example use cases of sentiment analysis include

- Quickly understanding the tone from customer reviews
  - To gain insights about what customers like or dislike about a product or service
  - To gain insights about what might influence buying decisions of new customers
  - To give businesses market awareness
  - To address issues early

- Understanding stock market sentiment to gain insights for financial signal predictions
- Determining what people think about customer support
- Social media monitoring
- Brand/product/company popularity/reputation/perception monitoring
- Discontented customer detection monitoring and alerts
- Marketing campaign monitoring/analysis
- Customer service opinion monitoring/analysis
- Brand sentiment attitude analysis
- Customer feedback analytics
- Competition sentiment analytics
- Brand influencers monitoring

Manually analyzing the abundance of text produced by customers or potential customers is time-consuming; ML is more efficient and with streaming analysis, insights can be provided in real time. This section discusses the architecture of a data pipeline that combines streaming data with ML and fast storage. In this first part, we will explore sentiment analysis using Spark ML data pipelines. We will work with a dataset of Amazon product reviews and build a ML model to classify reviews as positive or negative. In the second part of this, we will use this ML model with streaming data to classify documents in real time. The second part will discuss using the saved model with streaming data to do real-time analysis of product sentiment, storing the results in MapR Database, and making them rapidly available for Spark and Drill SQL.

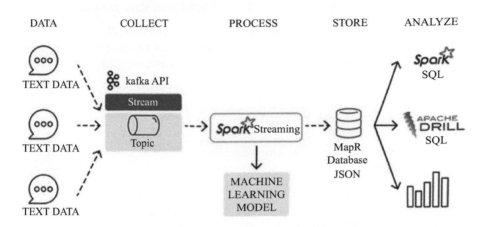

Classification – This is a family of supervised ML algorithms that identify which category an item belongs to (such as whether an e-mail is spam or not), based on labeled data (such as the e-mail subject and message text). Some common use cases for classification include credit card fraud detection, e-mail spam detection, and sentiment analysis. Classification takes a set of data with known labels and predetermined features and learns how to label new records, based on that information. Features are the properties that you can use to make predictions. To build a classifier model, you explore and extract the features that most contribute to the classification.

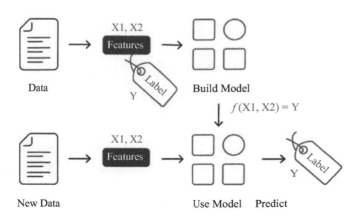

Let us go through an example for sentiment analysis for text classification of positive or negative.

- What are we trying to predict?
  - In this example, the customer review ratings are used to label reviews as positive or not. A review with 4 to 5 stars is considered a positive review, and a review with 1 to 2 stars is considered a negative review.

- What are the properties that you can use to make predictions?
  - The review text words are used as the features to discover positive or negative similarities in order to categorize customer text sentiment as positive or negative.

13.11   A standard ML workflow

Using ML is an iterative process, which involves

1. Data discovery and model creation
    - Analysis of historical data
    - Identifying new data sources, which traditional analytics or databases are not using, due to the format, size, or structure
    - Collecting, correlating, and analyzing data across multiple data sources
    - Knowing and applying the right kind of ML algorithms to get value out of the data
    - Training, testing, and evaluating the results of ML algorithms to build a model

2. Using the model in production to make predictions
3. Data discovery and updating the model with new data

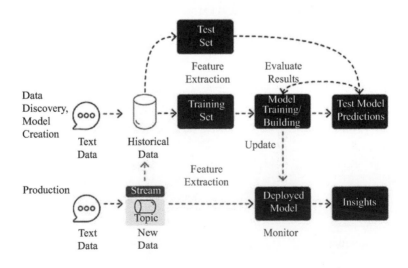

Feature extraction – Features are the interesting properties in the data that you can use to make predictions. Feature engineering is the process of transforming raw data into inputs for a ML algorithm. In order to be used in Spark ML algorithms, features have to be put into feature vectors, which are vectors of numbers representing the value for each feature. To build a classifier model, you extract and test to find the features of interest that most contribute to the classification.

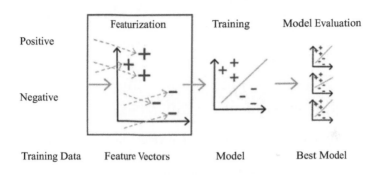

(Image reference O' Reilly Learning Spark)

13.12   Apache Spark for text feature extraction

The Term Frequency–Inverse Document Frequency (TF-IDF) feature extractors in SparkMLlib can be used to convert text words into feature vectors. TF-IDF calculates the most important words in a single document compared to a collection of documents. For each word in a collection of documents, it computes:

- Term frequency (TF), which is the number of times a word occurs in a specific document
- Document frequency (DF), which is the number of times a word occurs in a collection of documents
- TF-IDF, which measures the significance of a word in a document (the word occurs a lot in that document, but is rare in the collection of documents)

For example, if you had a collection of reviews about bike accessories, then the word "returned" in a review would be more significant for that document than the word "bike." In the simple example below, there is one positive text document and one negative text document, with the word tokens "love," "bike," and "returned" (after filtering to remove insignificant words like "this" and "I"). The TF, DF, and TF-IDF calculations are shown. The word "bike" has a TF of 1 in 2 documents (word count in each document), a document frequency of 2 (word count in set of documents), and a TF-IDF of ½ (TF divided by DF).

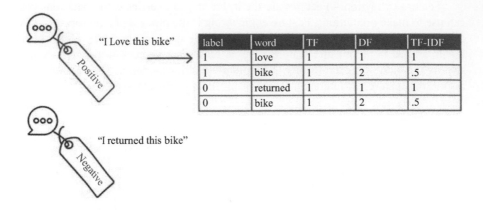

13.13   Logistic regression

Logistic regression is a popular method to predict a binary response. It is a special case of generalized linear models that predicts the probability of the outcome. Logistic regression measures the relationship between the Y "Label" and the X "Features" by estimating probabilities using a logistic function. The model predicts a probability, which is used to predict the label class.

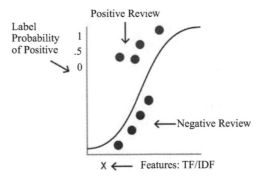

In our text classification case, logistic regression tries to predict the probability of a review text being positive or negative, given the label and feature vector of TF-IDF values. Logistic regression finds the best fit weight for each word in the collection of text by multiplying each TF-IDF feature by a weight and passing the sum through a sigmoid function, which transforms the input x into the output y, a number between 0 and 1. In other words, logistic regression can be understood as finding the parameters that best fit:

$$\log\left(\frac{p}{1-p}\right) = \hat{\alpha} + \hat{\beta}_1 X_1 + \hat{\beta}_2 X_2 + \cdots + \hat{\beta}_p X_p.$$

Where:
- p is the probability that Y is 1

- $\hat{\beta}_1, \hat{\beta}_2, \ldots, \hat{\beta}_p$ are the coefficient weights

- $X_1, X_2 \ldots$ are the features

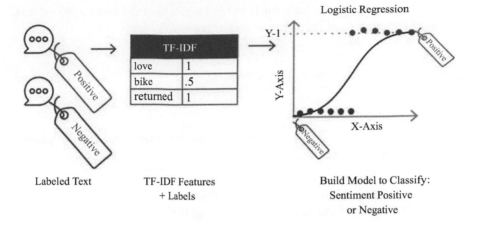

| Labeled Text | TF-IDF Features + Labels | Build Model to Classify: Sentiment Positive or Negative |

Logistic regression has the following advantages:

- Can handle sparse data
- Fast to train
- Weights can be interpreted
  - Positive weights will correspond to the words that are positive
  - Negative weights will correspond to the words that are negative

13.14   Data exploration and feature extraction

We will be using a dataset of Amazon sports and outdoor products review data. The dataset has the following schema; we will use the fields highlighted in red for sentiment analysis

reviewerID – ID of the reviewer, e.g., A2SUAM1J3GNN3B
asin – ID of the product, e.g., 0000013714
reviewerName – name of the reviewer
helpful – helpfulness rating of the review, e.g., 2/3
reviewText – text of the review
overall – rating of the product
summary – summary of the review
unixReviewTime – time of the review (Unix time)
reviewTime – time of the review (raw)
The dataset has the following JSON format:
{
    "reviewerID": "A1PUWI9RTQV19S",
    "asin": "B003Y5C132",
    "reviewerName": "kris",
    "helpful": [0, 1],

"reviewText": "A little small in hind sight, but I did order a .30 cal box. Good condition, and keeps my ammo organized.",
"overall": 5.0,
"summary": "Nice ammo can",
"unixReviewTime": 1384905600,
"reviewTime": "11 20, 2013"
}

In this scenario, we will use logistic regression to predict the label of positive or not, based on the following:

Label :

- overall – rating of the product 4–5 = 1 Positive
- overall – rating of the product 1–2 = 0 Negative

Features

- reviewText + summary of the review → TF-IDF features

13.15   Using the Spark Ml package

Spark ML provides a uniform set of high-level APIs, built on top of DataFrames with the goal of making ML scalable and easy. Having ML APIs built on top of DataFrames provides the scalability of partitioned data processing with the ease of SQL for data manipulation.

Spark ML Workflow

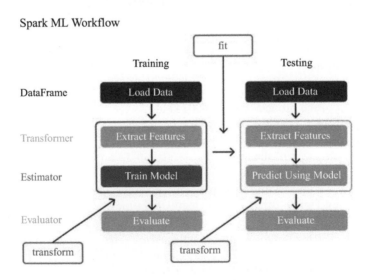

We will use an ML Pipeline to pass the data through transformers in order to extract the features and an estimator to produce the model.

13.16   Train the model

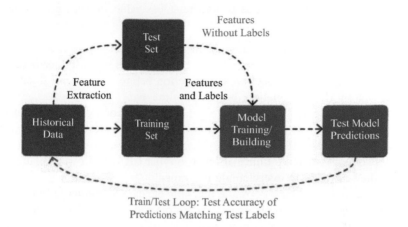

Train/Test Loop: Test Accuracy of
Predictions Matching Test Labels

There are a plenty of great tools to build classification models. Apache Spark provides an excellent framework for building solutions to business problems that can extract value from massive, distributed datasets. ML algorithms cannot answer all questions perfectly. But they do provide evidence for humans to consider when interpreting results, assuming the right question is asked in the first place.

13.17   Scalable ML in production with Apache Kafka

Intelligent real-time applications are a game changer in any industry. ML and its sub-topic, deep learning, are gaining momentum because ML allows computers to find hidden insights without being explicitly programmed where to look. This capability is needed for analyzing unstructured data, image recognition, speech recognition, and intelligent decision making.

While the concepts behind ML are not new, the availability of big data sets and processing power allow every enterprise to build powerful analytic models. A plenty of use cases exist in any industry to increase revenue, reduce cost or improve customer experience by applying analytic models in enterprise applications and microservices. This discusses potential use cases for ML in mission-critical real-time applications leveraging Apache Kafka as central, scalable, mission-critical nervous system plus Apache Kafka's Streams API to build intelligent streaming applications.

Scalable, mission-critical real-time applications – The emergence of the Internet, smartphones, and always-on thinking has changed how people behave today. This includes people's expectations about how devices, products, and services interact with them: people expect information in real time now. The challenge for enterprises is to act on critical business moments before it is too late. Batch processing is not sufficient anymore. You need to act immediately, or even better: proactively.

Traditional enterprises can implement very powerful real-time processing for their daily business. Often, domain knowledge is needed to understand the scenario and build new streaming analytics to add business value. Stream processing use cases exist in every industry, for example

- Fraud detection – correlate payment information with other historical data or known patterns to detect fraud before it happens. This typically needs very fast processing as you must decline a transaction before settling the stock movement, sharing the information, or shipping the item.
- Cross-selling – correlate customer big data to make context-specific, personal, customized offers or discounts before the customer leaves the store. You leverage real-time information (like location-based data, payment data), but also historical data (like information from your CRM or Loyalty platform) to make the best offer to every single customer.
- Predictive maintenance – correlate machine big data to predict failure before it happens. This allows replacing parts before they break. Depending on the industry and use case, this can save a lot of money (e.g., manufacturing), increase revenue (e.g., vending machines) or increase customer experience (e.g., telco network failure prediction).

The key in all these use cases is that you process big data while it is in motion. You need to handle the event before it is too late to act. Be proactive, not reactive! Your system should make decisions before a fraudulent transaction happens, before the customer leaves the store, before a machine breaks.

This does not always mean that you need millisecond response time, though. Even batch processing of events is fine in several use cases. For example, in most manufacturing or Internet of Things (IoT) use cases for predictive maintenance, you monitor time windows of several hours or even days to detect issues in infrastructure or devices. Replacement of defective parts is sufficient within a day or week. This is a huge business case and saves a lot of money, because you can detect issues and fix them before they happen or even also destroy other parts in the environment.

Intelligent real-time applications leveraging ML – mission-critical real-time applications like the above have been built for years – without ML. If you read about ML and its sub-topic, deep learning, you often see examples like these

- Image recognition – upload a picture to your Facebook timeline, and objects like your friends, the background, or the beer in your hand are analyzed.
- Speech translation – this enables chat bots that communicate with humans via generated text or speech.
- Human-like behavior – IBM Watson has beaten the best Jeopardy players; Google's AlphaGo has beaten professional Go players.

These examples become more and more relevant for enterprises looking to build innovative new applications and differentiate from competitors. In the same way, you can apply ML to more "traditional scenarios" like fraud detection, cross selling, or predictive maintenance to enhance your existing business processes and make better data-driven decisions. The existing business process can stay as it is. You merely replace the simpler custom coded business logic and rules by analytic models to improve the automated decision. The following sections show how to build, operate, and monitor analytic models in a scalable, mission-critical way by leveraging Apache Kafka as a streaming platform.

13.18   ML – the development lifecycle to deploy analytic models

Let us first think about the development lifecycle of analytic models:

1. Build – use ML algorithms like generalized linear model (GLM), Naive Bayes, Random Forest, Gradient Boosting, Neural Networks or others to analyses historical data to find insights. This step includes tasks like collection, preparation or transformation of data.
2. Validate – use techniques such as cross validation to double-check that the built analytic model works on new input data.
3. Operate – deploy the built analytic model to a production environment to apply it on new incoming events in real time.
4. Monitor – watch the outcomes of the applied model. This contains two parts: send alerts if a threshold is reached (business monitoring). Assure that the accuracy and other metrics are good enough (analytic model monitoring).
5. Continuous loop – improve the analytic model by going through all above steps continuously. This can be done in manual batch mode (say, once a week) or online, where the model is updated for every incoming event.

The whole project team must work together from the beginning to discuss questions like

*   How does it need to perform in production?
*   What technology does the production system use or support?
*   How will we monitor the model inference and performance?
*   Do we build a complete ML infrastructure covering the whole lifecycle or using existing frameworks to separate model training from model inference?

For example, a data scientist can build a Python program, which creates a model that scores very well with high accuracy. But this does not help as you cannot deploy it to production because it does not scale or perform as needed. You can already imagine why Apache Kafka® is a perfect fit for productionizing analytic models. The following section will explain the usage of Apache Kafka® as a streaming platform in conjunction with ML/deep learning frameworks (think Apache Spark) to build, operate, and monitor analytic models.

Reference architecture for ML with Apache Kafka – Let us look at a reference architecture for building, operating, and monitoring analytic models with Kafka.

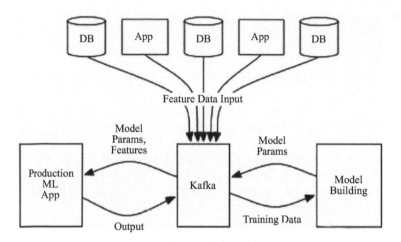

The essence of this architecture is that it uses Kafka as an intermediary between the various data sources from which feature data is collected, the model building environment where the model is fit, and the production application that serves predictions.

Feature data is pulled into Kafka from the various applications and databases that host it. This data is used to build models. The environment for this will vary based on the skills and preferred toolset of the team. The model building could be a data warehouse, a big data environment like Apache Spark or Hadoop, or a simple server running python scripts. The model can be published where the production application that gets the same model parameters can apply it to incoming examples (perhaps using Kafka Streams to help index the feature data for easy usage on demand). The production app can either receive data from Kafka as a pipeline or even be a Kafka Streams application itself.

Kafka becomes the central nervous system in the ML architecture to feed, build, apply, and monitor analytic models. This establishes huge benefits

- Data pipelines are simplified
- Building analytic modules is decoupled from servicing them
- Usage of real time or batch as needed
- Analytic models can be deployed in a performant, scalable, and mission-critical environment

In addition to leveraging Kafka as a scalable, distributed messaging broker, you can also add optional components of the Kafka ecosystem like Kafka Connect, Kafka Streams, Confluent REST Proxy, Confluent Schema Registry, or KSQL instead of relying on the Kafka Producer and Consumer APIs.

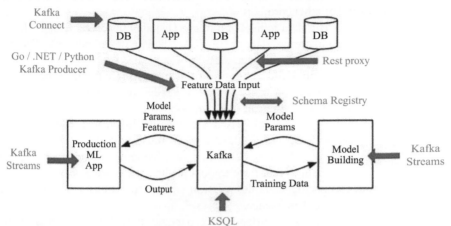

KSQL

The next section explains how to leverage Kafka's Streams API to easily deploy analytic models to production.

Example for ML development lifecycle – Let us now dive into a more specific example of an ML architecture designed around Kafka.

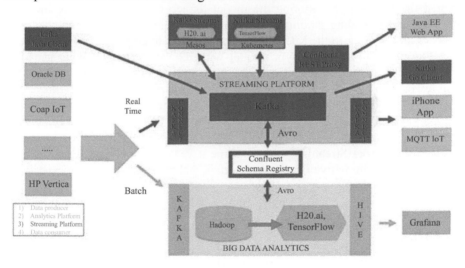

In green, you see the components to build and validate an analytic model. In orange, you see the streaming platform where the analytic model is deployed, infers to new events, and monitoring. Data producers send messages continuously. The analytics platform receives this data either in batch or real time. It uses ML algorithms to build analytic models. The analytic models are deployed to the streaming platform. The streaming platform applies the analytic models to new events to infer a result (i.e., do a prediction). The outcome is sent to a data consumer. In this example, we separate model training from model inference, which is the typical setup in most of today's ML projects

Model training – Big data is ingested into a Hadoop cluster via Kafka. H2O.ai is used to analyses the historical data in Hadoop to build a neural network. The data scientist can use its preferred interface – R, Python, Scala, Web UI Notebook, etc. for this. The model building and validation runs on the Hadoop cluster processing the data at rest. The result is a trained analytic model generated as Java code by H2O.ai. This is ready for production deployment.

Model inference – The neural network is then deployed to a Kafka Streams application. The Kafka Streams application can run anywhere, whether it is a standalone Java process, a Docker container, or a Kubernetes cluster. Here, it is applied to every new event in real time to do a prediction. Kafka Streams leverages the Kafka cluster to provide scalable, mission critical operations of analytic models, and performant model inference.

Online model training – Instead of separating model training and model inference, we can also build a complete infrastructure for online model training. This alternative has several trade-offs. Most traditional companies use the first approach, which is appropriate for most use cases today.

Model monitoring and alerting – Deployment of an analytic model to production is just the first step. Monitoring the model for accuracy, scores, SLAs, and other metrics, and providing automated alerting in real time, is just as important. The metrics are fed back to the ML tool through Kafka to improve or replace the model.

Development of an analytic model with H2O.ai – The following shows an example of building an analytic model with H_2O, which is an open source ML framework which leverages other frameworks like Apache Spark or TensorFlow under the hood. The data scientist can use his or her favorite programming language like R, Python, or Scala. The great benefit is the output of the H_2O engine: Java code. The generated code typically performs very well and can be scaled easily using Kafka Streams. Here are some screenshots of H2O.ai Flow (web UI/notebook) and alternative R code to build an analytic model.

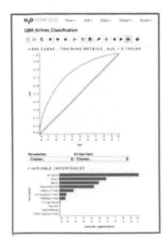

13.19   Building an analytic model with H_2O flow web UI

```
library(h2o)
h2o.init()
airlines.hex <- h2o.uploadFile(path = h2o::::.h2o.locate("/tmp/allyears2k_headers.zip")

r <- h2o.runif(airlines.hex)
air_train.hex <- airlines.hex[r < 0.6,]
air_valid.hex <- airlines.hex[(r >= 0.6) & (r < 0.9),]
air_test.hex  <- airlines.hex[r >= 0.9,]
myX <- c("Origin","Dest","DayofMonth", "DayOfWeek")

air.model <- h2o.gbm(
  y = "IsDepDelayed", x = myX,  distribution="bernoulli",
  training_frame = air_train.hex,
  validation_frame = air_valid.hex,
  ntrees=100, max_depth=4, learn_rate=0.1,
  sample_rate=0.6, col_sample_rate=0.7,
  nfolds=5)
```

The output is an analytic model, generated as Java code. This can be used without re-development in mission-critical production environments. Therefore, you do not have to think about how to "migrate" a Python or R model to a production system based on the Java platform. While this example uses H_2O's capabilities to generate Java code, you can do similar things with other frameworks like TensorFlow, Apache MXNet, or DeepLearning4J.

Deployment of an analytic model with Apache Kafka's Streams API – Deployment of the analytic model is easy with Kafka Streams. Simply add the model to your stream processing application – which is just a Java application – to apply it on new incoming events.

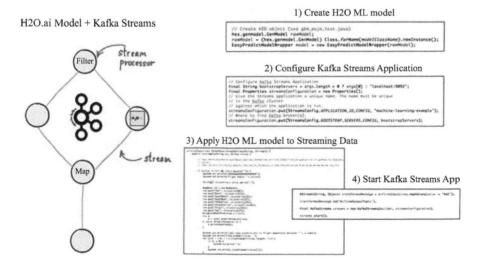

Apache Kafka's Streams API to embed H_2O.ai model into Kafka Streams – Since the Kafka Streams application leverages all Kafka features under the hood, this new application is ready for scale and mission-critical usage. There is no additional need to tweak the model because of production considerations. Simply clone the project, run the Maven build, and see how the H_2O model is used in the Kafka Streams application. This example will continue to evolve, with more sophisticated examples and use cases leveraging H_2O and other ML frameworks like TensorFlow or DeepLearning4J.

Such an implementation of applying ML to stream processing can easily be integrated into any automated continuous integration workflow using your favorite tool stack for CI/CD environments, such as Maven, Gradle, Chef, Puppet, or Jenkins.

Sharing of an analytic model between training and inference using open standards – As discussed earlier already, you need to use an appropriate technology for building your analytic model. Otherwise you will not be able to deploy it into production in a mission-critical, performant, and scalable way. Some alternatives to share and update models between data scientists to develop and improve the model and DevOps teams to embed and productize the model.

- Native model – Directly deploy a model to the stream processing engine, like deploying a Python model via JNI in a Java application
- Generated code – Independent of the language used to build the model, a generated binary or source code can be deployed to the stream processing engine, which is optimized for performance. For example, the model is generated Java bytecode, even though the data scientist used R or Python to train it.
- External server – Call to an external analytics server via request-response using analytics tools like SAS, MATLAB®, KNIME, or H_2O. This is typically done via a REST interface.
- Portable format for analytics (PFA) – A modern standard, including pre-processing in addition to the model. PFA leverages JSON and Apache Avro, and supports Hadrian.

There are various trade-offs between these alternatives. For instance, using a standard like PFA creates additional efforts and restrictions but adds independence and portability. From Kafka perspective, where you typically have mission-critical deployments with high volume, the preferred option today is often generated Java code, which is performant, scales well, and can easily embedded into a Kafka Streams application. It also avoids communication with an external REST server for model inference.

Using a streaming platform to deploy analytic models into mission-critical deployments – ML can create value in any industry. Also, Apache Kafka® is rapidly becoming the central nervous system in many enterprises. ML is a fantastic use case for it! You can leverage Kafka for

- Inference of the analytic model in real time
- Monitoring and alerting

- Online training of models
- Ingestion into the batch layer/analytics cluster to train analytic models there

You have seen some code examples in this section how to leverage Apache Kafka and its Streams API to build a scalable, performant, mission-critical infrastructure for applying and monitoring analytic models.

13.20   The reviews processing batch pipeline

Before jumping straight in, it is very important to map out the current process and see how we can improve each component. Below are a few assumptions

- When a user writes a review, it gets POSTed to a Web Service (REST Endpoint), which will store that review into some kind of database table.
- Every 24 h, a batch job (could be Spark) would take all the new reviews and apply a spam filter to filter fraudulent reviews from legitimate ones.
- New valid reviews are published to another database table (which contains all the historic valid reviews).
- Another batch job or a SQL query computes new stats for courses. Stats include all-time average rating, all-time count of reviews, 90 days average rating, and 90 days count of reviews.
- The website displays these metrics through a REST API when the user navigates a website.

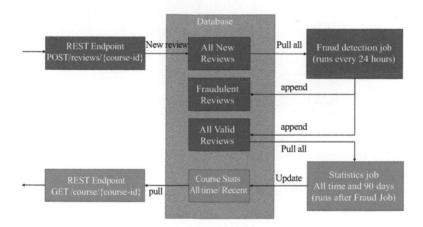

13.21   Transforming batch pipeline into a scalable, real-time and distributed pipeline with Apache Kafka

The target architecture – When building a real-time pipeline, you need to think microservices. Microservices are small components designed to do one task very well. They interact with one another, but not directly. Instead, they interact indirectly by using an intermediary, in our case a Kafka topic. Therefore, the contract between two microservices is the data itself. That contract is enforced by leveraging schemas. To summarize, our only job is to model the data, because data is king. Note all of the microservices used here are just normal Java applications, lightweight, portable, and you can easily put them in Docker containers.

1. Review Kafka producer – When a user posts a review to a REST Endpoint, it should end up in Kafka right away.
2. Fraud detector Kafka Streams – We are going to get a stream of reviews. We need to be able to score these reviews for fraud using some real-time ML, and either validate them or flag them as a fraud.
3. Reviews aggregator Kafka Streams – Now that we have a stream of valid reviews, we should aggregate them either since a course launch, or only taking into account the last 90 days of reviews.
4. Review Kafka Connect sink – We now have a stream of updates for our course statistics. We need to sink them in a PostgreSQL database so that other web services can pick them up and show them to the users and instructors.

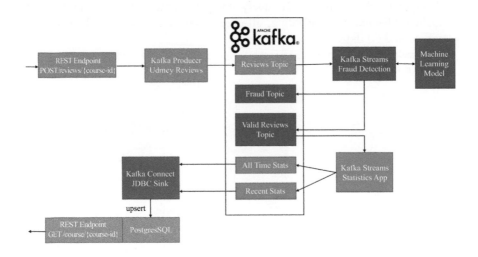

This is the target architecture for our real-time pipeline. Every color is a micro service:

1. Reviews Kafka producer – To get the reviews data, let us use the external REST API Udemy which provides to fetch a list of existing and published reviews for a course. The producer API helps you produce data to Apache Kafka. It will take an object combined with a Serializer (a class that allows you to transform your objects in raw bytes) and send it across. So here, we have two steps to implement:

1. Create a way to fetch reviews for any course using the Udemy REST API.
2. Model these reviews into a nice Avro Object and send that across to Kafka.

Fetching Udemy reviews – Getting reviews is actually easy. We are just going to figure out how many reviews a course has in total, and then repeatedly call the REST API from the last page to the first. We add the reviews to a java queue. The queue has a fixed size of 100 so it is blocking until not full

Sending the reviews to Kafka – Sending the reviews to Kafka is just as easy as creating and configuring a Kafka Producer

2. Fraud detector Kafka Streams –At this stage, we have simulated a stream of reviews in Kafka. Now we can plug in another service that will read that stream of reviews and apply a filter against a dummy ML model to figure out if a review is or is not spam.

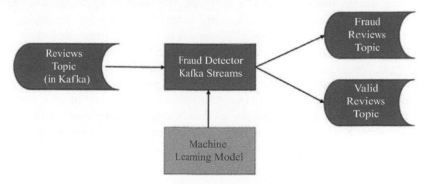

For this, we will use Kafka Streams. The Kafka Streams API is made for real-time applications and micro-services that get data from Kafka and end up in Kafka. It has recently gained exactly-once capability when running against a cluster that is version ≥ 0.11.

Fraud detection algorithm – Currently, my algorithm deterministically classifies a review as a fraud based on a hash value and assigns 5% of the reviews as Spam. Behind this oversimplified process, one can definitely apply any ML library to test the review against a pre-computed model. That model can come from Spark, Flink, H_2O, and anything.

3. Reviews aggregator Kafka Streams – Our third application is also a Kafka Streams application. It is a stateful one so the state will be transparently stored in Kafka. From an external eye, it looks like the following.

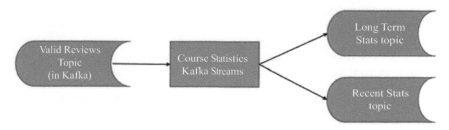

13.22   Architecture for the stateful Kafka Streams application

KStream and KTables – In the previous section, we learned about the early concepts of Kafka Streams, to take a stream and split it in two based on a spam evaluation function. Now, we need to perform some stateful computations such as aggregations, windowing in order to compute statistics on our stream of reviews.

Thankfully we can use some pre-defined operators in the high-level DSL that will transform a KStream into a KTable. A KTable is basically a table, that gets new events every time a new element arrives in the upstream KStream. The KTable then has some level of logic to update itself. Any KTable updates can then be forwarded downstream.

Aggregation key – In Kafka Streams, aggregations are always-key based, and our current stream messages have a null key. We want to aggregate over each course therefore we first have to re-key our stream (by course-id). Re-keying our stream in Kafka Stream is very easy. When you re-key a KStream, and chain that with some stateful aggregations (and we will), the Kafka Streams library will write the re-keyed stream back to Kafka and then read it again. That network round trip has to do with data distribution, parallelism, state storage, recovery, and it could be an expensive operation. So be efficient when you change the key of your stream!

We have the guarantee that all the reviews belonging to one course will always go to the same Kafka Streams application instance. As our topic holds all the reviews since inception, we just need to create a KTable out of our stream and sink that somewhere.

Let us note the aggregation computation is exactly the same. The only thing that changes over time is the data set we apply that aggregation onto. We want it to be recent (from the past 90 days), over a time window, and making sure that window advances every day. In Kafka Streams, it is called a Hopping Window. You define how big the window is, and the size of the hop. Finally, to handle late arriving data, you define how long you are willing to keep a window for:

Defining a hopping window of 90 days – Note that this will generate about 90 different windows at any time. We will only be interested in the first one. We filter only for recent reviews (really helps speed up catching up with the stream), and we compute the course statistics over *each time window*: The aggregation is similar as before, but we now have an additional parameter. That operation can become a bit costly as we keep 90 time windows for each course, and only care about one specific window (the last one). Unfortunately, we cannot perform aggregations on sliding windows (yet), but hopefully, that feature will appear soon! It is still good enough for our needs. In the meantime, we need to filter to only get the window we are interested in: it is the window which ends after today and ends before tomorrow:

Although the Kafka Streams syntax looks quite simple and natural to understand, a lot happened behind the scenes. Here are a few things to note

- Exactly once – As we want that aggregation to be perfectly accurate, we need to enable exactly-once processing semantics (EOS). This feature appeared in

0.11, and the name stirred up a lot of debate. So, to make it short and clear, it means "effectively once" and is exactly what we need (pun intended). That means no reviews will somehow be counted twice in case of broker, network, or application failure. Neat!

- Incoming data format – As mentioned before, it'll be awesome if the data had a "new" and an "old" field. This would allow to handle updates in reviews and compute the correct average in case of updates to a review.
- Windowed aggregations – There is a massive performance hit to computing 90 windows only to discard them all and keep the last one. I have evaluated it and found it to be 25 times less efficient than using the (way more advanced) lower level API.
- Lower level API – Using this API, you can create your own transformers and compute exactly what you need. In the source code, you can find how to do the recent statistics computations using that API, although I would not discuss it in this post as it goes way beyond the already immense quantity of information I just threw at you.
- Performance – These apps can be parallelized to the number of partitions in the incoming topic. It has horizontal scaling natively which is quite awesome. Kafka Streams in that regards makes it really easy to scale without maintaining some sort of back-end cluster.

4. Kafka Connect Sink – exposing that data back to the users – Eventually, all we care about is people browsing the Udemy website and visualizing the course statistics. As with most web services, serving information is often backed by some sort of database. For my example, here a relational database (PostgreSQL) is chosen, but one could choose a NoSQL one like MongoDB, or a search index such as ElasticSearch. Possibilities are endless, and there exists Kafka Connect Sinks for pretty much any technology out there.

Kafka Connect – Kafka Connect is a framework upon which developers can create connectors. These connectors can be of two kinds: Source and Sink. Source are producers and Sink are consumers. The beautiful thing behind Kafka Connect is that it provides you infrastructure to run any connector. For an end user, running a connector is as easy as pushing configuration. Re-using other people's work sounds like a dream, right? Well, that is what Kafka Connect is about.

13.23   Conclusion

Machine and deep learning algorithms are flourishing and signaling the realization of prediction and prescription insights. With the availability of big data, the prediction accuracy is going up. Now there are several business domains generating a lot of data continuously. Thus, capturing and making sense out of streaming data have become a huge challenge for business houses. That is, predicting things based on streaming data in real time acquires special significance for postulating and producing next-generation applications. Real-time prediction is an important capability for enterprises in order to be right and relevant to their constituents. For bringing forth people-centric solutions and services, customer delight, pinpointing fresh avenues for increased revenues, heightening productivity, etc., the aspects such as prediction with greater accuracy and in time are being given prime importance. There are competent technologies, artificial intelligence (AI) algorithms, integrated data analytics platforms, knowledge visualization tools, etc. in order to simplify and speed up real-time prediction.

Now with the surging popularity of cloud infrastructures and the general availability of software infrastructure such as Apache Kafka and Kafka streams, the ML applications can be easily scaled out in order to tackle big data and to crunch them in real-time. This document clearly described the various aspects of accomplishing real-time and scalable prediction out of streaming data.

Chapter 14

Object detection techniques for real-time applications

C. Jyothsna[1] and B. Narendra Kumar Rao[2]

Abstract

Object detection is a method of identifying and locating items in a continuous image or video stream using computer vision. Background subtraction, optical flow, and frame difference are object detecting approaches. In this study, we will explore Object Detection Algorithms, such as Convolutional Neural Network algorithm families (CNN, R-CNN, Fast R-CNN, Faster R-CNN) and YOLO as well as associated applications and frameworks. Object Detection Algorithms will be used by real-time applications and will get their goals.

This book chapter discusses the Introduction about computer vision, object detection, object detection architectures, object detection methods, object detection techniques, applications of object detection, and implementation sources for object detection.

14.1 Introduction

14.1.1 Introduction to computer vision

Artificial Intelligence has a subfield called computer vision in which algorithms are used to identify objects represented in digital images and videos provided by cameras thus enable computers to see. The computer must evaluate what it sees and then do suitable analysis or act on that information. Computer vision techniques can be used in various real-life applications such as computer vision in healthcare, agriculture, transportation, retail and manufacturing, picture classification, object detection, object tracking, and content-based image retrieval are some of the computer vision tasks.

14.1.2 Introduction to object detection

Object detection is a computer vision technology that allows you to find and locate objects in an images or videos, such as individuals, buildings, or

[1]Department of CSE, JNTUA, India
[2]Department of CSE, Sri Vidyanikethan Engineering College, India

automobiles. Objects can be detected in two different ways: one is constant object detection and second is moving object detection. Object detection seeks to recognize a specified set of thing classes such as animals, people, and automobiles and to characterize the position of each detected object in an image using bounding boxes.

14.2   Architectures

14.2.1   *Object detection architectures*

Object detection architectures can be two different types: single-stage architectures and two-stage architectures.

14.2.1.1   Single-stage architectures

A single-stage object detector requires only a single pass through the neural network and predict all boundary boxes in one step. Example for single-stage architecture algorithms is YOLO (2016), SSD (2016), Squeeze Det, Detect Net, Retina Net (2017), YOLOV3 (2018), YOLOV4 (2020), and YOLOR (2021). Object detectors with only one stage is faster than those with two-stage object detectors. The following diagram describes as a one-stage object detection architecture (Figure 14.1).

14.2.1.2   Two-stage architecture

Two stage networks also called as multi-stage architecture. In this first stage, extract regions of objects and in the second stage to classify and localization of objects. This method is slow compare to one-stage detectors. Examples for two-stage architecture algorithms are CNN, region-based CNN (R-CNN), Fast R-CNN, Faster R-CNN, Mask R-CNN, and granulated RCNN (G-RCNN). The following diagram describes as two-stage object detection architecture (Figure 14.2).

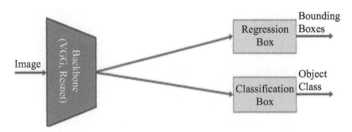

Figure 14.1   One-stage object detection architecture

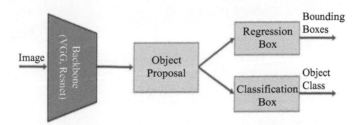

Figure 14.2   Two-stage object detection architecture

14.3   Methods

14.3.1   Object detection methods

Object detection methods include frame difference, background removal, and optical flow.

14.3.1.1   **Frame differencing**

Frame differencing method is used to identify an object in motion [1]. This method is mainly used to analyze the difference between adjacent frames in image sequence. Frame detection method mainly used surveillance cameras. The frame detection method comprises the temporal information required to distinguish between the foreground (moving objects) and the background.

Example for frame differencing. Here we consider as two different situations, first there is a movement in the frames and second there is no movement in the frames.

Case 1: There is no movement in the frames as shown in Figure 14.3.

When there is no movement in the frames or picture sequences, the difference between the two images reveals a black binary output image, indicating that there is no difference in a single pixel [1].

Case 2: There is movement in the frames, as shown in Figure 14.4.

When there is motion in the picture When there is movement in the scenes, the binary picture of the difference between the two frames indicates motion with white color and no change with black color [1].

14.3.1.2   **Background subtraction**

Background subtraction is a method for calculating foreground items that involve subtracting the current frame from a background model comprising the static portion of the scene, as seen in Figure 14.5.

14.3.1.2.1   Flow-chart for background subtraction

As shown in Figure 14.6, take input as video frames and this video frame is passed to preprocessing step, by using this step to reduce noise in the stream. In preprocessing step using temporal or special smoothing is used to reduce noise levels.

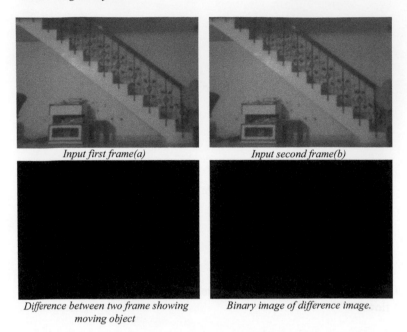

Input first frame(a)   *Input second frame(b)*

Difference between two frame showing   *Binary image of difference image.*
moving object

Figure 14.3   Two-image sequences where there is no movement

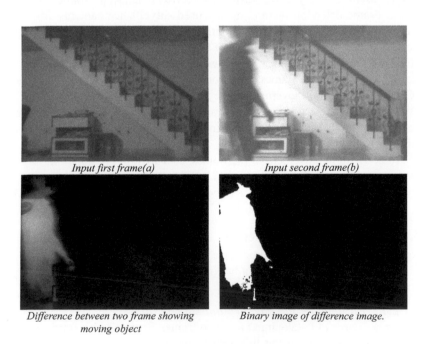

Input first frame(a)   *Input second frame(b)*

Difference between two frame showing   *Binary image of difference image.*
moving object

Figure 14.4   Two-image sequences where there is movement

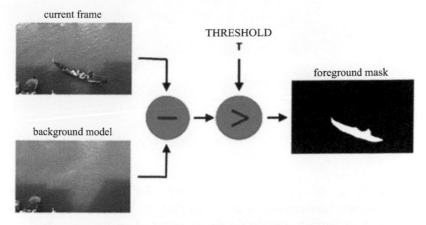

Figure 14.5 Foreground subtraction from background model

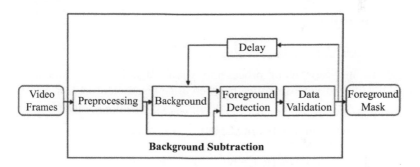

Figure 14.6 Background subtraction flow chart

In preprocessing, the data format used by the background subtraction. Most of the algorithms handles luminance intensity, which is one scalar value for each pixel. Color images are more popular in background subtraction.

14.3.1.3 Optical flow

Optical flow is the movement of objects between consecutive frames of a series caused by the relative movement of the item and camera. The optical flow problem can be stated as follows:

When we may represent the picture intensity (I) as a function of location (x,y) and time between subsequent frames (t). We get the new picture $I(x+dx,y+dy,t+dt)$ by moving the pixels in the original image $I(x,y,t)$ by (dx,dy) over t time. Optical flow may be employed in a variety of applications where object motion information is critical. Optical flow is often used in video editors for compression, stabilization, and slow-motion effects, among other things. Optical flow is also used in action recognition activities and real-time tracking systems. Optical flow is the task of estimating per-pixel motion between two consecutive frames in a video. The

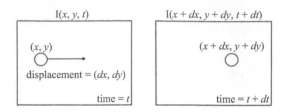

Figure 14.7   Displacement of pixel

optical flow job entails calculating the shift vector for a pixel as a difference in object displacement between two neighboring pictures. The basic principle behind optical flow is to estimate the displacement vector of an item generated by its motion or camera motions, as shown in Figure 14.7.

14.4   Algorithms

14.4.1   Object detection techniques

Deep learning are capable of processing visual data. Detecting and localizing objects in photos and videos may be handled using neural networks. The following are some of the most important deep learning object identification techniques [2]:

1. Convolutional neural network (CNN)
2. Region-based CNN (R-CNN)
3. Fast region-based CNN (R-CNN)
4. Faster region-based CNN (R-CNN)
5. Mask R-CNN (2017)
6. G-RCNN (2021)
7. Histogram of oriented gradients (HOG)
8. Single shot detector (SSD)
9. Spatial pyramid pooling (SPP-Net) (2014)
10. YOLO (YOLO V3 (2018), YOLO V4 (2020), YOLO (2021))
11. Retina net

In image classifications, we will be able to classify whether given image is dog or cat from given first image as shown in Figure 14.8(a). In second image, Figure 14.8(b) unable to detect images individually. In real life, problems always have multiple objects condensed into a single image. This is the importance of object detection comes [2].

One of the most essential jobs in computer vision is image categorization. As indicated in the illustration, image categorization, as shown in Figure 14.9, is the class of assigning one or more labels to a given image. Object detection is another frequent computer vision topic that involves detecting and finding objects of specific kinds in a picture. Item localization can be interpreted in a variety of ways,

(a)   (b)

Figure 14.8   (a) Dog image in photograph. (b) Dog and cat images in photograph

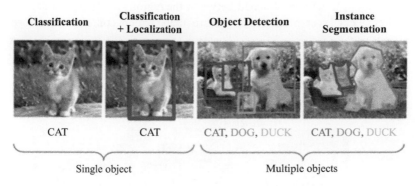

Figure 14.9   Image classification and object localization

such as by drawing a bounding box around the object or by identifying every pixel in the picture that includes the object (a process known as segmentation), as seen in Figure 14.9.

14.4.2   General algorithm for object detection

The basic steps in object detection algorithm are

- Step 1: First take input, here input is an image.
- Step 2: The image is then dividend into various regions in the second step.
- Step 3: The step is to treat each region as if it were a separate image.
- Step 4: The fourth step is to submit all of these regions to a specific algorithm, which will classify into distinct categories.
- Step 5: After splitting each region into its proper class, the original image with recognized objects is combined from all of these regions.

14.4.3   CNN

The CNN is a multi-layered artificial neural network architecture. To recognize patterns in a visual image, a convolutional neural network is used. Three fundamental layers make up the convolutional neural network design [2] as shown in Figure 14.10. They are

1. Convolutional layer
2. Pooling layer
3. Fully connected layer

14.4.3.1 Convolution layer

The feature from the given input picture or video is extracted using the convolution layer. A kernel or filter is used to detect important features in a given input image. Convolutional layer is a mathematical action that takes place between an input image and a filter of a specific size such as M×M size. By moving over the original image, the dot product is performed between the regions of the input image and the taken filter. This layer produces a feature map, which contains the information about the image.

As in Figure 14.11 extracting the features from the image of nine.

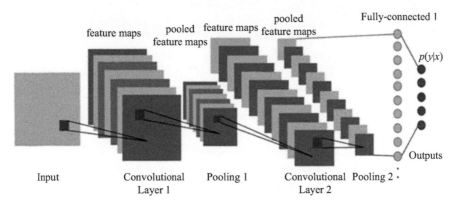

Figure 14.10   Basic CNN architecture

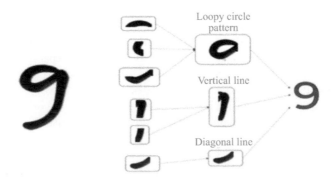

Figure 14.11   Features of image 9

14.4.3.2   Pooling layer

It convolutional neural network's second layer. The pooling layer comes after the convolutional layer. The layer's primary goal is to minimize the size of the convolved feature. Pooling operations can be divided into two categories.

(i) Max pooling
(ii) Average pooling

(i) Max pooling
The maximum element from the region of the feature map covered by the filter is selected in a max pooling technique. The filter size of a feature is 2 by 2, the maximum element in first region is 9, then it will be displayed as output value as shown in Figure 14.12.

(ii) Average pooling
The average of items present in the region of the feature map covered by the filter is computed in an average pooling technique. The filter size of a feature is 2 by 2, the average element in first region is 4.25, then it will be displayed as output value as shown in Figure 14.13.

The pooling layer bridge between the convolutional layer and fully connected layer.

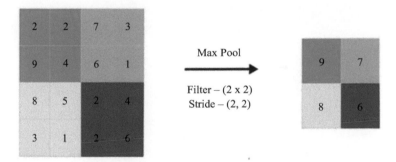

Figure 14.12   Max pooling operation with filter size 2×2

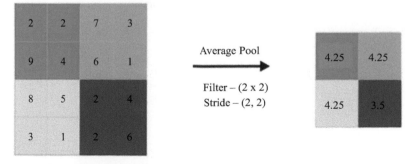

Figure 14.13   Average pooling operation with filter size 2×2

14.4.3.3 Fully connected layer

This fully connected network is a feed forward network. This layer consists of the biases and weights along with neurons. The neuron connects between two different layers. In which each pixel is considered as a separate neuron. As in fully connected network number of different classes to be predicted. As shown in Figure 14.14.

Other operations in CNN architecture:

14.4.3.4 ReLU

ReLU is a rectified linear unit, this is not separate component of convolutional process. The purpose of applying the rectifier function is to maximize the non-linearity in our image. Naturally image is nonlinear. This is an activation function. The activation function determines which information from the model should be sent forward.

ReLU has a derivative of either 0 or 1 depending whether its input is negative or not as shown in Figure 14.15. ReLU function is applied after convolution operation.

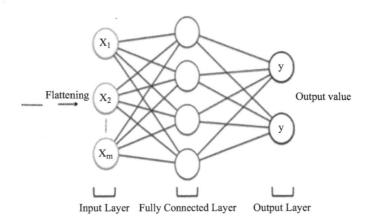

Figure 14.14   Fully connected neural network

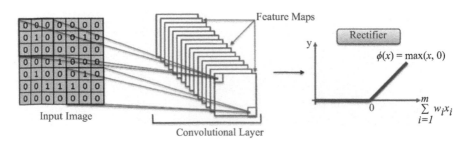

Figure 14.15   Rectifier linear unit

14.4.3.5 Dropout

Another operation is the dropout layer. Dropout referrers to ignoring units during the training phase to overcome the over fitting. Over fitting is nothing but only model works for given training data set, if new data comes to your model, it gets negative that means cannot predict the results. Dropout operation is as shown in Figure 14.16.

14.4.3.6 Flattening

Flattening operation is converting the data set into one-dimensional data for input to the next layer which is the fully connected layer as shown in Figure 14.17.

14.4.4 Region-based CNN

A form of machine learning model is a region-based CNN. It is used to do computer vision tasks, particularly object detection. For object classification, the CNN method is employed, and for object detection, the R-CNN algorithm is used. The R-CNN method suggests a set of bounding boxes in the provided picture and determines whether or not the boxes include an item [3].

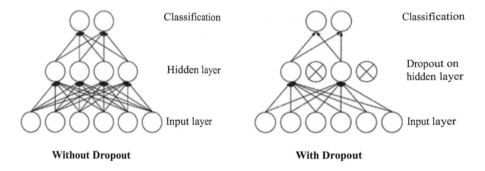

Figure 14.16   Dropout operation in CNN

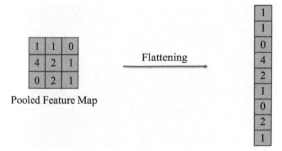

Figure 14.17   Flattening operation in CNN

Selective search algorithm is used by R-CNN algorithm to generate approximately 2,000 region proposals as shown in Figure 14.18. The CNN architecture, which computes CNN features, receives the 2,000 region recommendations. These features are loaded into support vector machine (SVM) model, which is used to classify the item in the region proposals. Region proposals are parts of the picture that may contain the items in the input image.

14.4.4.1   Selective search algorithm

The selective search algorithm is used to identify areas in a picture. An item is made up of four areas. There are variety of sizes, colors, textures, and encloses to chosen from. Selective search detects these patterns in the image and recommends different places based on them. This algorithm accepts an image as input and outputs region recommendations based on it.

14.4.4.2   Steps in selective search algorithm

Step 1: First take image as an input, as shown in Figure 14.19.
Step 2: By using proposal methods to get region of interest (RoI), as shown in Figure 14.20.
Step 3: All these regions are reshaped as per the input image of the CNN, and each region is passed to the ConvNet, as shown in Figure 14.21.
Step 4: Finally, a bounding box regression (Bbox) is used to predict the bounding box for each identified region, as shown in Figure 14.22.

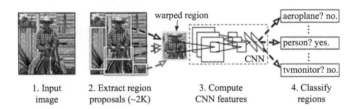

Figure 14.18   *Region-based convolutional network architecture*

Figure 14.19   *Input image*

Figure 14.20 RoI of input image

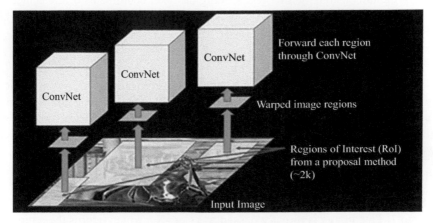

Figure 14.21 Each region of input image is passed to ConNet

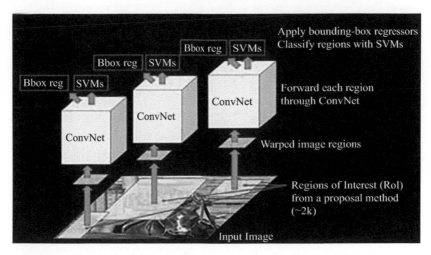

Figure 14.22 Bounding boxes for identified region

14.4.4.3 SVM

The CNN-generated feature vector is consumed by the binary SVM, which is trained individually on each class. The SVM model provides a confidence score indicating the presence of an item in that area based on the feature vector generated by the prior CNN architecture.

14.4.4.4 Bounding box regressor

For determining the bounding box probabilities in the image, we use a scale in variant linear regression model called bounding box regressor. To train this model, we use predicted and ground truth pairing of four dimensions of localization (x, y, w, h) are the dimensions, with x and y being the pixel coordinates of the center of the enclosing box. The width and the height of bounding boxes are represented by w and h.

14.4.5 Fast region-based CNN

The method is similar to the R-CNN algorithm. Rather than supplying region recommendations to the CNN, we get it the input image to create a convolutional feature map. So that it can be fed into a layer that is fully connected as illustrated in Figure 14.23. We employ a soft matrix layer to predict the class of proposed region as well as the bounding box offset values on the RoI feature vector.

14.4.5.1 Steps in fast R-CNN

Step 1: Take an image as input, as shown in Figure 14.24.

Step 2: This image is directly passed to a ConvNet which returns the region of interests accordingly, as shown in Figure 14.25.

Step 3: Then, as shown in Figure 14.26, we apply the RoI pooling layer to the extracted regions of interest to ensure that they are of the same size 26.

Step 4: Finally, these areas are sent to a fully connected network, which classifies them and produces the bounding boxes using softmax and linear regression layers at the same time, as seen in Figure 14.27.

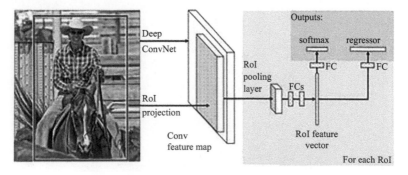

Figure 14.23   Fast region CNN architecture

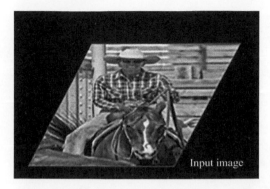

Figure 14.24   Input image

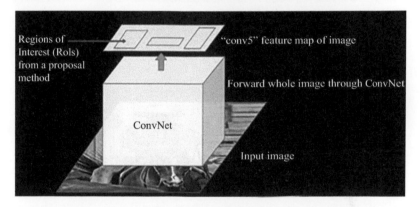

Figure 14.25   Whole input image is passed to ConvNet

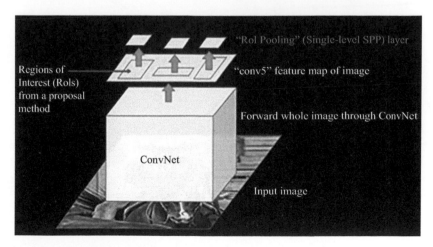

Figure 14.26   Extracted region of equal size

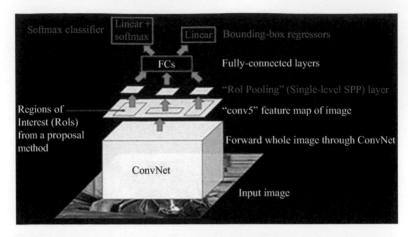

Figure 14.27   Regions are passed on to a fully connected network

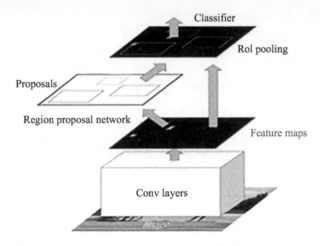

Figure 14.28   Faster region-based CNN architecture

14.4.6   Faster region-based CNN

Faster R-CNN is a truncated version of Fast R-CNN. The main distinction is that fast R-CNN generates regions of interest by selective search, whereas faster R-CNN generates regions of interest using "Region Proposal Network," aka RPN. Figure 14.28 shows how RPN takes picture feature maps as an input and creates a series of object suggestions, each with an objectness score as output [4].

14.4.6.1   Steps in faster R-CNN approach

1. Feed the input image to the ConvNet, which will output a feature map for that input image.

2. To obtain areas of an image, this feature map employs a region proposal network. This method returns an object's score as well as object suggestion.
3. By using the RoI pooling method an proposals, all proposals will be the same size.
4. To categorize and output them bounding boxes, the recommendations are given to a fully connected layer with a soft matrix layer in a linear regression layer on top.

14.4.7 Mask region-based CNN

Mask R-CNN can automatically segment and build pixel-wise masks for every item in an image. We will use mask R-CNNs on both photos and video clips to construct a mask for each object in our image, allowing us to separate the foreground from the background dreaming. Figure 14.29 depicts a mask R-CNN.

For each item in the image, image segmentation generates a pixel-by-pixel mask. Mask R-CNN is essentially a faster R-CNN extension. R-CNN is extensively utilized for object detection jobs since it is faster. It returns the class label and bounding box coordinates for each item in a supplied picture.

14.4.8 YOLO algorithm

YOLO stands for You Only Look Once. The YOLO algorithm is a method for detecting objects. When compared to typical object detection methods, it is far faster and more accurate. The YOLO Algorithm is a neural network design with a single step. It is a detection technique for many objects. It is based on a regression model, and rather than picking a portion of an image, it predicts classes and bounding boxes for the whole picture in a single algorithm run. Four parameters

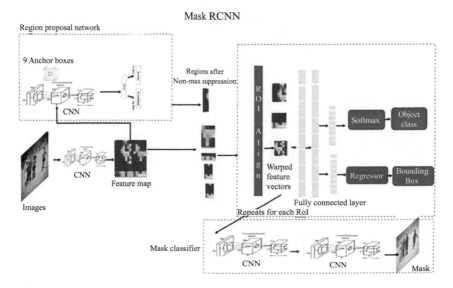

Figure 14.29 Mask R-CNN architecture

100

100

Figure 14.30   Input image

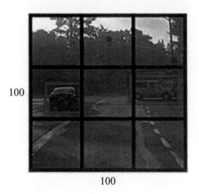

100

100

Figure 14.31   Take input image into grids

can be used to characterize each bounding box. Those are center of the bounding box $(b_x b_y)$, width (b_w), height (b_h), class of object (c). The probability that there is an object in the bounding box (p_c). $y = (p_c, b_x, b_y, b_h, b_w, c)$.

14.4.8.1   Steps in YOLO Algorithm

Step 1: First takes input as image, as shown in Figure 14.30.

Step 2: YOLO algorithm separates the input image into grids, as shown in Figure 14.31.

Step 3: For each grid, image classification and localization were applied.

Step 4: Finally, for a multi-class classification, YOLO predicts the bounding boxes and accompanying class probabilities for detected objects, typically using soft max.

14.5   Applications

Now a days various real-time applications are using these object detection techniques to reach their real-life problem-solving goals. The following are applications of object detection.

1. Face recognition
2. Anomaly detection
3. Crowd counting (person counting)
4. Retail
5. Healthcare (X-ray image analysis, cancer detection)
6. Industrial quality check
7. Image captioning
8. Video surveillance
9. Vehicle number plate recognition
10. Self-driving cars (autonomous vehicles)

14.5.1 Object detection algorithms and its applications

S. no.	Object detection algorithms	Applications
1	CNN	Facial recognition, hand written recognition
2	Region-based CNN	Gaming, pedestrian detection, automatic license plate detection
3	Fast region-based CNN	Retail, healthcare, image captioning
4	Faster region-based CNN	Image analysis in medicine, X-ray image analysis, cancer detection
5	Mask region-based CNN	Sports field, autonomous vehicles, tumor detection, detecting features related to corona virus
6	YOLO	Detecting traffic signals, people count, self-driving cars

14.6 Result and discussion

14.6.1 Hand written detection using CNN

The ability of computer to receive and interpret handwritten input from sources such as photograph, paper documents, and transformed into a digital form is shown in Figure 14.32.

Various uses in handwritten character recognition are postal address interpretation, handwriting biometrics, and signature verification.

14.6.2 Face detection using CNN

Face detection is a computer vision task that involves finding faces in photos. Face detection is important in biometric authentication in security and surveillance, verification for identity in banking field and electronic commerce. Example face detection model is shown in Figure 14.33.

14.6.3 Autonomous driving cars for multi object detection by using YOLO algorithm

The YOLO algorithm can be used in self-driving automobiles to recognize various items such as vehicles, pedestrians, and parking signals. Object

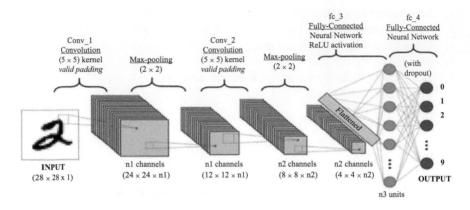

Figure 14.32   *Handwritten character 2 recognized by machines by using convolutional neural network*

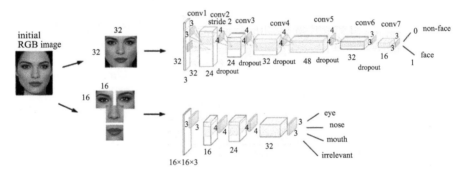

Figure 14.33   *Face detection by using CNN*

detection is used in self-driving automobiles to avoid collisions. To collect data from roadways, automobiles have cameras installed in the front that snap pictures of the road ahead every few seconds while driving. Gather all these images into a folder and labeled those images and drawing bounding boxes around every image you found by using YOLO algorithm draw bounding box on every image as shown in Figure 14.34.

14.6.4   Real-time applications in computer vision

14.6.4.1   Computer vision in manufacturing

14.6.4.1.1   Quality management

Smart camera applications allow smart factories to automate visual inspection and quality control of production processes and assembly lines. Deep learning, as seen

Figure 14.34 Self-driving car with object detection by using YOLO algorithm

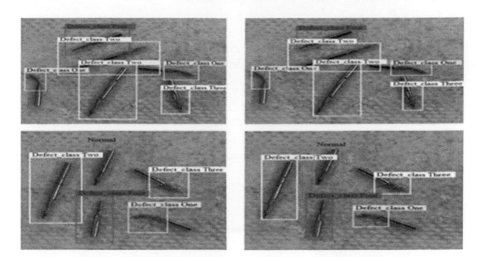

Figure 14.35 Finding defect product from normal product

in the image, uses real-time object identification to outperform rigorous manual inspection in terms of detection accuracy, speed, objectivity, and reliability as shown in Figure 14.35 [5].

14.6.4.2 Computer vision in healthcare

14.6.4.2.1 Cancer detection

Machine learning is being used in the medical industry to diagnose breast and skin cancer. Image recognition, for example, enables scientists to recognize subtle distinctions between malignant and non-cancerous pictures and to analyze data from magnetic resonance imaging (MRI) scans.

14.6.4.2.2   COVID-19 diagnosis

Coronavirus control can be accomplished with the use of computer vision. There are several deep learning computer vision models available for X-ray-based COVID-19 diagnosis. COVID-Net is the most widely used for identifying COVID-19 instances using digital chest X-ray radiography (CXR) pictures.

14.6.4.3   Computer vision in agriculture

14.6.4.3.1   Animal monitoring

A significant method of smart farming is animal monitoring using computer vision. Machine learning monitors the health of individual animals such as pigs, cattle, or poultry using video feeds. As illustrated in figure, smart vision systems strive to analyze animal behavior in order to boost productivity, health, and wellbeing of the animals, and hence affect yields and economic advantages in the industry as shown in Figure 14.36.

14.6.4.4   Computer vision in transportation

14.6.4.4.1   Parking occupancy detection

Visual parking spot monitoring is used to identify parking lot occupancy. Computer vision applications, particularly in smart cities, enable decentralized and efficient systems for visual parking lot occupancy detection based on a deep CNN, as seen in Figure 14.37.

14.6.4.4.2   Automated license plate recognition (ALPR)

Many of today's transportation and public safety systems rely on license plate identification and extraction from images or videos. ALPR has changed the public safety and transportation industries in numerous ways. These number plate recognition systems allow modern tolled highway solutions, resulting in considerable

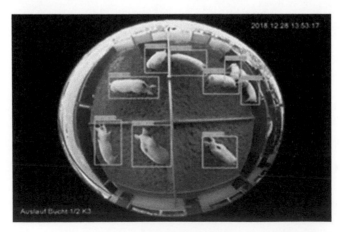

Figure 14.36   Health monitoring of animals

Figure 14.37 Parking occupancy detection

operational cost savings through automation and the introduction of whole new market capabilities.

14.6.4.4.3 Pedestrian detection

Pedestrian is nothing but moving a particular object such as a person or vehicle. Pedestrian detection is a significant task in intelligent video surveillance system. Pedestrian detection is demand for intelligent transportation systems (ITS). Autonomous driving, infrastructure surveillance, traffic management, transit safety, and efficiency. In pedestrian detection, standard CCTV and integrated RGB cameras are all used. Person detectors, also known as infrared signatures, may be created by combining infrared signatures, form characteristics, gradient data, machine learning, and motion features. Deep CNN-based pedestrian identification has made great improvement, especially in the detection of strongly obstructed pedestrians.

14.6.5 Computer vision framework

Computer vision is a rapidly expanding scientific discipline that deals with extracting information from digital photos and videos in order to get a high-level knowledge of the surroundings. The use of computer vision tools and software in healthcare, agriculture, smart cities, security, automotive, and other industries have skyrocketed in the IT sector. In recent years, this has been complemented by the creation of various toolkits, frameworks, and software libraries relating to this topic.

14.6.5.1 List of the most popular computer vision tools

1. OpenCV
2. TensorFlow
3. CUDA
4. Viso Suite
5. MATLAB®
6. Keras
7. SimpleCV

8. BoofCV
9. CAFFE
10. OpenVINO
11. DeepFace
12. YOLO

14.7   Conclusion

Object detection techniques are a challenging problem in computer vision, computer vision is subarea of Artificial Intelligence. These object detection mechanisms are used in many real-time applications to achieve their goals. Some the main real-life applications are face recognition for biometry and self-driving cars to reduce collisions on roads. Deep learning and machine learning object detection techniques are used to implementing those important real-life applications

References

[1] N. Singla, "Motion detection based on frame difference method", *International Journal of Information & Computation Technology*, 4(15), 2014, pp. 1559–1565, ISSN 0974-2239.

[2] C. Bhagya and A. Shyna, "An overview of deep learning based object detection techniques", in: *2019 1st International Conference on Innovations in Information and Communication Technology (ICIICT)*, 2019, pp. 1–6.

[3] A. Vahab and M.S. Naik, "Applications of object detection system", *International Research Journal of Engineering and Technology*, 6, 2019, pp. 4186–4192 e-ISSN: 2395-0056.

[4] J. Deng and X. Xuan, "A review of research on object detection based on deep learning", *Journal of Physics: Conference Series*, 1684, 2020, 012028.

[5] M. Apoorva Raghu Nandan, "Object detection algorithm for video surveillance applications", in: *International Conference on Communication and Signal Processing*, April 3–5, 2018, India.

[6] K.U. Sharma and N.V. Thankur, "A review and an approach for object detection in image", *International Journal of Computer Vision and Robotics, Research Gate*, 7, 2017, 196.

[7] L.R. Galvez, A.A. Bandala and E.P. Dadios, "Object detection using convolutional neural networks", in: *Proceedings of TENCON 2018 – 2018 IEEE Region 10 Conference*, Jeju, Korea, 28–31 October 2018.

[8] Z.-Q. Zhao, P. Zheng, S.-T. Xu, and X. Wu, "Object detection with deep learning: a review", *IEEE Transactions on Neural Networks and Learning Systems*, 30, 2019, 3212–3232.

[9] K.L. Masita, A.N. Hasan and T. Shongwe, "Deep learning in object detection: a review", in: *2020 International Conference on Artificial Intelligence, Big Data, Computing and Data Communication Systems (icABCD)*, 2020.

[10]   W. Wei, "Small object detection based on deep learning", in: *2020 IEEE International Conference on Power, Intelligent Computing and Systems (ICPICS)*.

[11]   J. Wang, T. Zhang and Y. Cheng, "Deep learning for object detection: a survey", *Computer Systems Science & Engineering*, 38, 2021, 165–182, doi:10.32604/csse.2021.017016.

[12]   G. Sunil, "Study of object detection methods and applications on digital images", *International Journal of Scientific Development and Research*, 4, 2019, pp. 491–497, IJSDR1905088.

[13]   S.R. Balaji and S. Karthikeyan, "A survey on moving object tracking using image processing", in: *International Conference on Intelligence and Control*, 2017, 978-1-5090-2717-0/17.

Chapter 15

EdgeIoTics: leveraging edge cloud computing and IoT for intelligent monitoring of logistics container volumes

S. Durga[1], Esther Daniel[2], S. Seetha[3] and N. Susila[1]

Abstract

In logistics enterprises, a significant amount of space available in vehicles goes unused. Currently, there is no method to measure and estimate the dimension and volume of shipments in real-time and use this data to prepare an efficient load procedure. This in turn leads logistical services to employ inefficient methods that drastically increase their resource needs and workload. To facilitate this, this chapter offers an intelligent monitoring service that uses Internet of Things (IoT), Edge Cloud, and web services to record and capture data about shipments. It uses this information to efficiently create a load procedure for parcels based on the company's available assets. The proposed system continuously monitors capacity and position throughout container shipping and analyses the data on a remote cloud server to warn partners when a certain condition or violation occurs. In a real-life setting, we tested the system and discovered that it correctly notifies partners when certain undesirable environmental conditions or events that occur.

15.1   Introduction

In the logistics industry, a large amount of space in containers goes underutilized. This is because no system manages the loading that can quickly and efficiently do the task of allotting the packages based on real-time data [1]. This will enhance capacity and profits for the Logistical Service enterprises. The primary goal is to provide a service using modern technologies such as IoT devices and web services to create a system that actively gathers information and data via networked IoT devices and process the captured data through a robust software suite that uses technologies and services such as Amazon Web Services, IoT (Raspberry Pi), and

[1]Department of IT, Sri Krishna College of Engineering and Technology, India
[2]Karunya Institute of Technology and Sciences, India
[3]CMR Institute of Technology, India

Django REST FrameWork to create a highly efficient and cost-effective loading system/service for the logistical service that will enhance its workflow considerably. It is mathematically impossible to implement a well-organized supply chain that maximizes the use of space and equipment. However, through the smart use of new technologies such as IoT, web services, and online databases, we aim to provide a system/service that is responsible for recording, managing, and analyzing data obtained by intelligent interconnected IoT devices through robust and secure software suite.

The IoT is providing the insight that the trucking and logistics industry requires to boost quality and safety [2]. Sensors in an IoT deployment can generate reams of data, which must be stored and evaluated. These data need to be sent to a cloud server or a centralized data center, but they must be transmitted [3]. There are several sectors in the transportation business where data transmission through cellular or satellite becomes too expensive or suffers from sporadic connectivity. In an edge computing paradigm, data is collected, processed, and analyzed at the point closest to its source, then sent to the cloud for viewing, reporting, and sharing. Even if a network connection is not accessible, edge computing technology keeps running. This chapter proposes a novel approach EdgeIoTics that incorporates IoT and Edge cloud-based data analysis for determining the remaining space available in storage containers.

15.1.1   Background

The IoT continuously generates, manages, and transmits data. The current data streaming solutions assist in the administration of various ongoing data sources. This data trend will grow as sensors and devices become more widely used. It is changing a lot of industries: logistics can now track vehicles in real-time and even provide on-demand services, as well as understand the details of transportation lines and predict issues before they happen; the automotive industry is using sensors not only for self-driving cars but also to provide deeper, real-time insights, equipping engineers to fix the issues in advance. Radio-frequency identification (RFID) tags are used in IoT-based logistics to track items as they arrive at their destination. Equipment like onboard sensors, or even a tablet or cell phone, can be used to monitor and optimize vehicle operation and driver behavior in real time. Drivers can prevent delays by using real-time traffic and weather monitoring. Data streamed from various IoT devices is more time-sensitive, has a larger volume, and may or may not have long-term value after processing. The main challenge in IoT streaming data integration is synchronizing data from several sources that arrive at different times and dealing with data redundancy.

15.1.2   IoT and data analytics

Data analytics is critical in the IoT because it is used to make sense of the massive amounts of data generated by IoT devices. It mixes data streams from various IoT devices to produce consistent and trustworthy results.

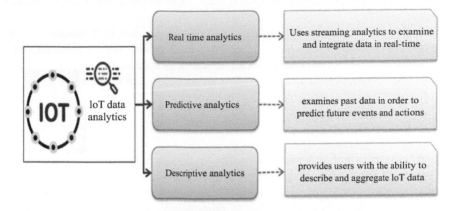

Figure 15.1 IoT data analytics types

In an IoT context, there are three types of analytics: real-time analytics that alerts for abnormalities on the fly; predictive analytics that yields a prediction and a confidence level as a post-process; and descriptive analytics that reports on past, present, or future data with visualizations that frequently offer the most insightful results [4]. Figure 15.1 shows the three types of IoT data analytics. Machine learning is used in predictive analytics to analyze historical data and generate a probability for how the device will behave in the future. Organizations can anticipate faults or service requirements before the equipment fails.

Hundreds of sensors record massive amounts of unstructured data ranging from data streams to camera feeds, in an IoT infrastructure. The need for a trustworthy storage facility to do analytics on IoT data is a big challenge. Furthermore, rather than simply dumping data into storage without first formatting it, preprocessing is required. Upsolver, Apache Spark, and Amazon Kinesis Streams are data stream processing frameworks that can save IoT data to a data reservoir in a format that facilitates SQL-based analysis by standard analytics tools [4,5]. Stream processing analyses uninterrupted data flow in memory, only sending state changes to a storage device. It saves time by allowing a machine to recognize relevant data while discarding less useful stuff. Stream Analytics from Microsoft Azure [6] integrates with open source cloud platforms to enable real-time analytics on data from IoT applications and devices. The IoT analytics offered by Amazon Web Services (AWS) contains ready-to-use models for popular Application areas such as predictive maintenance and smart hearth care [6].

Container volume-centered analytics has resulted from the growth of logistic apps, connected vehicles, and IoT devices. When a space scarcity is noticed, the applications or devices are configured to automatically send out alerts and prompt a response from officials. For example, sensors installed in the truck provide real-time monitoring of available spaces as well as monitoring devices for cargo loading management. This chapter employs AWS stream processing and real-time data analytics for the proposed edge cloud-based monitoring of logistics container volumes.

The rest of the section is organized as follows: Section 15.2 summarizes the related work. Section 15.3 explains the proposed approach with a block diagram. The implementation details and outcomes are discussed under Section 15.4 and Section 15.5 concludes the chapter with the conclusion and future work.

15.2   Related work

The gathered information assists a company to develop and become more effective in a range of areas, including optimizing pick-and-place operations, enhance and expediting commodities handling at the storage unit, minimizing picking mistakes, choosing the right technology for the storage facility, significantly increasing storage area utilization, improve freight bill accuracy, and streamline transportation and packing [7]. The main concerns in IoT-based logistics applications are cost and management issues [8]. The Smart Logistics review identifies outstanding issues such as how to effectively handle the challenges of rapidly changing customer expectations, leverage on new technological opportunities, and facilitate new business models [9]. An IoT-based logistic architecture based on RFID tracking and management systems has been developed for the manufacturing industry. It emphasizes the important factors for the systematic development of current logistics [10]. A smart logistics solution was presented that includes logistics tracking, auxiliary sorting, speedy loading and unloading, and cargo positioning and inventory. The authors used RFID as the core while combining NB-IoT and deep learning technologies. This technology has the potential to boost the level of automation across the logistics industry [11]. For agri-food supply chains, a reference design for IoT-based logistic information systems was presented [12]. It emphasizes a hybrid solution that incorporates IoT and cloud computing. By utilizing technology enablers, the architecture facilitates the supply of economical custom-tailored solutions. Although recent research into the possibilities of IoT in logistics applications has yielded some useful insights, there is still a lack of comprehensive and objective solutions for container volume management [13–15].

15.3   IoT and edge cloud-based intelligent monitoring of logistics container volumes

For container volume management, an edge cloud and IoT-based approach employ edge node servers, which have significantly better computational capability. Any Indian transportation and logistics firm, in general, has to know the exact size and weight of its goods [16]. This ensures that their storage capacity is fully utilized and trucks are not overburdened. Figure 15.2 depicts a block diagram of the proposed EdgeIoTics method, which includes an IoT module, an Edge Module, and a Public cloud Module.

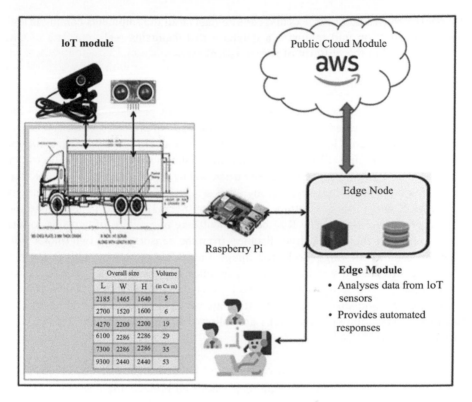

Figure 15.2   Block diagram of EdgeIoTics approach

15.3.1   IoT module

Through comprehensive transparency and faster detection of faults, IoT in collaboration with developing technologies such as Edge cloud provides an effective
supply chain platform for the logistics business. The most crucial aspects of a
linked logistics system are inventory management and warehousing. Companies
may simply obtain information about the remaining space available within container trucks using IoT-enabled sensors. The proposed approach uses a USB camera
and ultrasonic sensors to record speedy and accurate measurements of the parcel's
exterior edges to automatically record the volume and weight of their shipments.
This new system/service would gather data from IoT devices and sensors about the
various attributes of the shipment such as dimensions, volume, and weight, and
load the data to a web service to be analyzed and stored in a database. This data is
then manipulated and accessed by a software solution through an API that enables
the user to control his/her shipments and their movement on any device or platform
through the use of API calls. Raspberry Pi 4 has been used to collect and transfer
the data to the edge cloud. The system is designed to be installed in the entrances of

transport vehicles and/or trucks and capture data on all the shipments coming in and out of the location and maintain a database that maintains real-time data of any shipments within the custody of the logistical service.

15.3.2   Edge Cloud module

Streaming analytics have been used in places where processing and storage are convenient, such as edge devices, the cloud, and on-premises servers. Data is examined and filtered locally by edge servers before being sent to the back-end for additional processing. With edge computing, supervisors will be unnecessary because the remaining space within the truck will be discovered and communicated with each other with ultra-low latency edge servers stationed at strategic locations will collect and process continuous data from the IoT module to determine the container volume status. The Raspberry pi will take two photos of two sides of the box along with their respective distance from the sensor. These two photos will then be sent to an Edge node for image processing, where it will generate a bounding box based on the images submitted by the IoT device. The three dimensions of the Box were computed using these two pieces of data (object bounding box and distance). These files are saved on a public cloud server for future use. The following two steps are followed to process the data from the IoT module.

15.3.2.1   Step 1. Dimension calculation from image

With the use of a lens, the resulting camera image projects the three-dimensional scene onto a two-dimensional sensor [17,18]. Figure 15.3 depicts the height projection. H_{object} stands for the height of the object of interest in pixels of the image. P_{sensor} represents the sensor resolution depending on image size. Distance and focal

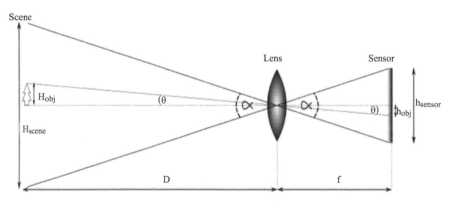

*Figure 15.3   Generic camera measurements [17]. Source: https://stackoverflow.
com/questions/42035721/how-to-measure-object-size-in-real-world-
in-terms-of-measurement-like-inches-cen/42355269*

represent the distance from the camera and the focal length of the camera. Equation (15.1) shows the correlation used by expressing angles in radians:

$$focal \cdot \theta = H_{object} \tag{15.1}$$

The camera's vertical field of view $Vertical_{FoV}$ is a crucial component for camera and lens calculations. The Field of View entity will be computed directly using the following equation with the focal length of the lens and the size of the sensor known:

$$Direct_{FoV} = Distance \cdot \frac{H_{object}}{P_{sensor}} \cdot Vertical_{FoV} \tag{15.2}$$

15.3.2.2   Step 2. Data analysis, send alert to stakeholder and store at public cloud

PackageID is unique, and VehicleID corresponds to the company that owns the package. The initial piece of data in PackageDetails is directly inserted from the IoT Device when it finishes evaluating its images. PackageLength, PackageWidth, and PackageHeight are the object's estimated dimensions, whereas Package Volume represents its volume. Figure 15.4 shows the entity-relationship model diagram of the data used. The edge node will determine whether the newly arrived package will fit into the container after determining the remaining space available within the container and the expected space required to insert the newly arrived parcel into the container.

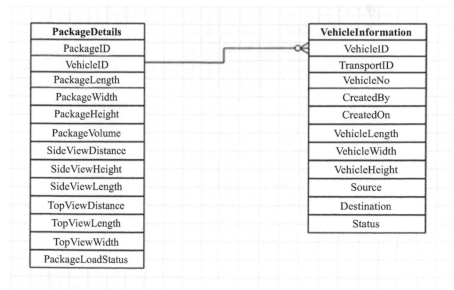

PackageDetails	VehicleInformation
PackageID	VehicleID
VehicleID	TransportID
PackageLength	VehicleNo
PackageWidth	CreatedBy
PackageHeight	CreatedOn
PackageVolume	VehicleLength
SideViewDistance	VehicleWidth
SideViewHeight	VehicleHeight
SideViewLength	Source
TopViewDistance	Destination
TopViewLength	Status
TopViewWidth	
PackageLoadStatus	

Figure 15.4   Entity-relationship model diagram of the data used

15.3.3   Public Cloud module

Pushing the processing of data to the edge reduces the time taken to transfer data to the cloud for centralized processing. However, due to deployment and maintenance costs, positioning the edge servers in all of the locations throughout the transport is quite difficult. The IoT module can transfer data directly to the public cloud for processing in places where the edge node is not identifiable. The goal of the Public Cloud is to create a set of open application programming interfaces (APIs) and orchestration capabilities that will enable cross connectivity between the Edge and the Public Cloud. Image data was stored in the Amazon S3 storage cloud for future use and prediction. By capturing and altering data in the RDS database, the data can then be manipulated by an API on AWS EC2 services [19]. REST API requests made using URLs are also used to build a load order passing the data through a bin packing algorithm that allows the data according to the user's requirements.

Figure 15.5 shows the Cloud-only data processing sequences of the proposed approach. AWS ReKognition, a well-known pre-trained, and customized computer visioning platform were used to extract and process the image data.

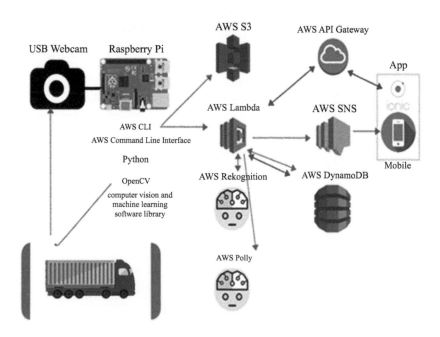

Figure 15.5   Cloud-only data processing sequence of the proposed approach.
Source: https://docs.aws.amazon.com/iot/latest/developerguide/
connecting-to-existing-device.html

15.4   Implementation and outcomes

The implementation of the proposed approach has two sections, namely, (1) implementation at the Edge – Laptop with Core i5, 8GB hard disk was used as the edge node. Apache tomcat server has been used for processing the sensor data at the edge and inference at the edge. And (2) Deployment of the proposed approach at the Public Cloud – it uses public cloud platforms to host the training process and model database. The proposed approach is implemented using Python 3. The following steps are used to describe the outcome of data processing.

Step 1: Find the current top of PackageId.

Step 2: Get image and distance data and upload the image to AWS S3.

Step 3: Let images be processed by AWS ReKognition via S3 which gives a JSON string as output.

Step 4: Use the data from step 3 and the distance reading from the sensor to get three dimensions of the object and consequently upload all data to the PackageDetails AWS database.

Step 5: This data can then be used by API calls to do various actions. Data of set of packages and truck details are input into an API and that gives the output as shown in Figure 15.6.

The API calls are developed and Packagedetails gets the details of the specified package with the web address URL: http://127.0.0.1:8000/api/pckdetails/ <packageid>.

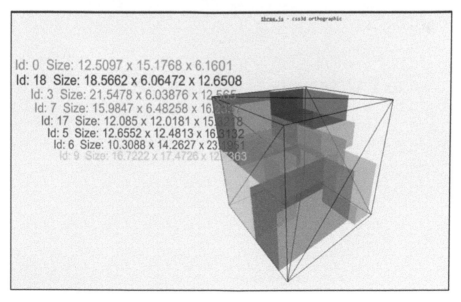

Figure 15.6   Visual representation after PackIt4Me sorting of boxes

Output string of Packagedetails API call, output string of vehdim API call, output string of vehallot API call are shown in Figures 15.7, 15.8, and 15.9, respectively. Vehdim gets the dimensions of a specific vehicle. url: http://127.0.0.1:8000/api/vehdimdetails/<vehicleidid>.

Packagedetails

```
GET /api/pckdetails/7

HTTP 200 OK
Allow: GET, POST, DELETE, HEAD, OPTIONS
Content-Type: application/json
Vary: Accept

{
    "status_code": "S200",
    "message": "success",
    "pckDetails": {
        "packageid": 7,
        "vehicleid": 8,
        "packagelength": 15.9847,
        "packagewidth": 16.2337,
        "packageheight": 6.48258,
        "packagevolume": 1682.17,
        "sideviewdistance": 36.53,
        "sideviewheight": 6.4469,
        "sideviewlength": 15.9847,
        "topviewdistance": 36.62,
        "topviewlength": 6.51826,
        "topviewwidth": 16.2337
    }
}
```

Figure 15.7   Output string of Packagedetails API call

Vehdim Details

```
GET /api/vehdimdetails/7

HTTP 200 OK
Allow: OPTIONS, GET
Content-Type: application/json
Vary: Accept

{
    "status_code": "S200",
    "message": "success",
    "vclDetails": {
        "vehiclelength": 20.0,
        "vehiclewidth": 20.0,
        "vehicleheight": 20.0
    }
}
```

Figure 15.8   Output string of vehdim API call

Figure 15.9   Output string of vehallot API call

Vehallot details gets the details of packages allotted to a specified vehicleid runs it through the Packit4ME algorithm and if the set of packages do not fit into the specified vehicleid it automatically allots the package to a different vehicle with the same source and destination and the appropriate status else it displays the packages.

url: http://127.0.0.1:8000/api/pckdetails/<packageid>

15.5   Conclusion and future work

To find and express the greatest data insights that can be leveraged to drive timely decisions, data visualization is necessary. As bid data continues to grow at an extremely high rate, data storage, and management are critical. Managing and storing such a large amount of data on a centralized server are a massive task. Edge computing is used to reduce network traffic and latency while also addressing the issue of data loss at centralized servers.

For intelligent monitoring of logistics container quantities, an IoT and Edge-Cloud computing-based approach was presented. Rather than transmitting data over a cellular network, IoT sensors deliver all data to an edge device. This compute device gathers data from various endpoints, analyses it, and conducts intelligent container volume discovery in a much faster, practically real-time manner. The main scope covered with cloud support is real-time data gathering, storing shipments and packages for the logistical industry, and providing recommendations. Our findings will aid in the monitoring of logistics container volumes and provide practitioners with a better understanding of the present state of container space. Enabling continuous video feed processing and detection, as well as camera calibration and volume estimation using AI-based learning to rectify acquired data [20], will be investigated in the future. Federated analytics is a future research direction that allows data to be reviewed and aggregated wherever it is kept, including at the edge, in the distributed core, and the cloud.

References

[1]   von Stietencron, M., Hribernik, K., Lepenioti, K., *et al.* (2021). Towards logistics 4.0: an edge-cloud software framework for big data analytics in logistics processes. *International Journal of Production Research*, 1–19, DOI: 10.1080/00207543.2021.1977408.

[2]   Golpîra, H., Khan, S.A.R. and Safaeipour, S. (2021). A review of logistics internet-of-things: current trends and scope for future research. *Journal of Industrial Information Integration*, 22, 100194.

[3]   Durga, S., Daniel, E., and Leelipushpam, P.G.J. (2022). A novel request state aware resource provisioning and intelligent resource capacity prediction in hybrid mobile cloud. *Journal of Ambient Intelligence and Humanized Computing*, 13, 2637–2650.

[4]   Adi, E., Anwar, A., Baig, Z. and Zeadally, S. (2020). Machine learning and data analytics for the IoT. *Neural Computing and Applications*, 32(20), 16205–16233.

[5]   Marculescu, R., Marculescu, D. and Ogras, U. (2020). Edge AI: systems design and ML for IoT data analytics. In *Proceedings of the 26th ACM SIGKDD International Conference on Knowledge Discovery & Data Mining* (pp. 3565–3566).

[6]   Mohammadi, M., Al-Fuqaha, A., Sorour, S., and Guizani, M. (2018). Deep learning for IoT big data and streaming analytics: A survey. *IEEE Communications Surveys & Tutorials*, 20(4), 2923–2960.

[7]   Qu, T., Lei, S.P., Wang, Z.Z., Nie, D.X., Chen, X. and Huang, G.Q. (2016). IoT-based real-time production logistics synchronization system under smart cloud manufacturing. *The International Journal of Advanced Manufacturing Technology*, 84(1–4), 147–164.

[8]   Ngo, T.T., Abdukhakimov, A. and Kim, D.S. (2019). Long-range wireless tethering selfie camera system using wireless sensor networks. *IEEE Access*, 7, 108742–108749.

[9]   Ding, Y., Jin, M., Li, S. and Feng, D. (2021). Smart logistics based on the internet of things technology: an overview. *International Journal of Logistics Research and Applications*, 24(4), 323–345.

[10]   Jianli, S. (2012). Design and implementation of IOT-based logistics management system. In *2012 IEEE Symposium on Electrical & Electronics Engineering (EEESYM)* (pp. 603–606). New York, NY: IEEE.

[11] Pang, J., Shen, L., Zhang, Q., Xu, H. and Li, P. (2019). Design of modern logistics management system based on rfid and nb-iot. In *Workshops of the International Conference on Advanced Information Networking and Applications* (pp. 561–569). Cham: Springer.

[12] Verdouw, C.N., Robbemond, R.M., Verwaart, T., Wolfert, J., and Beulens, A.J. (2018). A reference architecture for IoT-based logistic information systems in agri-food supply chains. *Enterprise Information Systems*, 12(7), 755–779.

[13] Ghosh, A.M. and Grolinger, K. (2019). Deep learning: Edge-cloud data analytics for iot. In *2019 IEEE Canadian Conference of Electrical and Computer Engineering (CCECE)* (pp. 1–7). New York, NY: IEEE.

[14] Pahl, C. and Lee, B. (2015). Containers and clusters for edge cloud architectures – a technology review. In *2015 3rd International Conference on Future Internet of Things and Cloud* (pp. 379–386). New York, NY: IEEE.

[15] Hassan, N., Gillani, S., Ahmed, E., Yaqoob, I. and Imran, M. (2018). The role of edge computing in internet of things. *IEEE Communications Magazine*, 56(11), 110–115.

[16] Zhu, D. (2018). IOT and big data based cooperative logistical delivery scheduling method and cloud robot system. *Future Generation Computer Systems*, 86, 709–715.

[17] White, P.J., Podaima, B.W. and Friesen, M.R. (2014). Algorithms for smartphone and tablet image analysis for healthcare applications. *IEEE Access*, 2, 831–840.

[18] Katti, H., Peelen, M.V. and Arun, S.P. (2017). How do targets, nontargets, and scene context influence real-world object detection? *Attention, Perception, & Psychophysics*, 79(7), 2021–2036.

[19] Mishra, A. (2019). *Machine Learning in the AWS Cloud: Add Intelligence to Applications with Amazon SageMaker and Amazon Rekognition*. New York, NY: John Wiley & Sons.

[20] Sood, S.K. (2021). Smart vehicular traffic management: an edge cloud centric IoT based framework. *Internet of Things*, 14, 100140.

Chapter 16

A hybrid streaming analytic model for detection and classification of malware using Artificial Intelligence techniques

Esther Daniel[1], S. Durga[2], N. Susila[2], S. Seetha[3] and T. Sujatha[2]

Abstract

In this era of technology and network, the battleship between security experts and malware developers is a never-ending fight as every day a new signatures malware comes into the battle to fight. To compete in this technological battle, AI-based technique would effectively combat and triumph. Various machine learning and deep learning techniques involved in the process of malware detection and classification with good accuracy are analyzed. ML-based techniques perform very well and were able to detect and classify even zero-day malware. A new hybrid methodology for the efficient detection and classification of malware is proposed. The accuracy of malware detection is improved by the proposed ensemble method.

16.1 Introduction

Malicious software is increasing at an alarming rate, according to recent studies, viruses can hide in the system utilizing various obfuscation tactics. The malware must be recognized before it impacts a large number of systems. To safeguard computer systems and the Internet from malware various malware detection methods are increasing. However, malware identification, on the other hand, continues to be a challenge. Almost every member of society has used the Internet in their daily lives in recent years. This is because doing anything without the Internet is nearly impossible, including social connections, online banking,

[1]Department of Computer Science and Engineering, Karunya Institute of Technology and Sciences, India
[2]Department of AI&DS, Sri Krishna College of Engineering and Technology, India
[3]Department of Information Science & Engineering, CMR Institute of Technology, India

health-related transactions, and marketing. Criminals have begun to commit crimes on the Internet rather than in the actual world as the Internet has grown in popularity. To initiate cyber-attacks on target devices, criminals typically use malicious software. Malware is defined as software that executes malicious payloads on victim machines (computers, smartphones, computer networks, and so on). Malware comes in many forms, including viruses, worms, Trojan horses, rootkits, and ransomware. Each malware type and family are designed to affect the original victim machine in different ways such as causing harm to the targeted system, allowing remote code execution, stealing confidential information, and so forth [1]. Cloud-based malware detection with blockchain is an emerging trend in the detection of zero-day malwares [2]. Malware is designed to gain unauthorized access or disturb normal operation and adversely affect computers and mobile devices [3,4].

A data stream is a real-time continuous, ordered sequence of data packets based on the arrival time or timestamp. Data streams are usually a massive amount of data that arrives at a high speed [5]. The stream of data is a sequence of log tuples that consist of attributes that are related to the interactions between the entities. The transactional data streams deal with interactions between the clients and servers. The data gathered can vary from sensor data, image data, and network web data traffic. The websites receive streams of various types of data for every click and numerous queries.

The characteristics of data streams are

• Voluminous continuous data
• Effectively captures required data used for processing
• Swift and updated real-time response
• Require multi-dimensional and multi-level processing
• Stores the summarized results of the huge collection of data

Streaming data is where data is continuously generated by various data sources such as sensors, data centers, and Internet traffic. Streaming data includes a wide variety of log files that are generated by web-based applications, social networks, financial, and stock services. The data are processed sequentially and incrementally using data analytics methods ranging from correlations, aggregation, filtering, and sampling. The data analytic result enables to consolidate the activity, usage, and to evolve with a decision for better productivity and visibility. Processing of the data stream has various challenges to be met as the data is of multiple, continuous, and ordered streams. The scalability, fault tolerance, and durability of the data stored and processed have to be considered for efficient data processing. The processing of streaming data requires a storage and processing layer. The storage layer deals with ordering a large stream of data for swift read/write access. The processing layer handles the computation of the data from the storage layer.

Malware classification is becoming more difficult these days, as some malware cases exhibit traits from numerous classifications at the same time. The malware was created for simple goals, in the beginning, making it easy to detect.

Traditional conventional malware is an example of this type of malware. New generation malware, on the other hand, is malware that may function in kernel mode and is more destructive and difficult to detect than traditional malware. This malware can easily get around security software that runs in kernel modes, such as firewalls and antivirus software. Traditional malware typically consists of a single process and does not employ complex tactics to conceal itself. New generation malware, on the other hand, runs numerous existing or new processes at the same time and employs obfuscated techniques to conceal itself and remain persistent in the system. New generation malware can carry out more devastating operations, such as targeted and persistent attacks, that have never been seen before, and the attacks can involve more than one type of malware. The traditional method of identifying malware depends on signature-based malware detection. But nowadays, the malware attacks that occur are mostly zero-day malware which increases the difficulty in detecting and classifying malware. Zero-day malware is a specific kind of malware or malicious software that has only recently been discovered where we would not be able to classify or detect these malware [6].

Artificial Intelligence (AI) revolutionizes malware detection techniques and enables to detection and classify these types of malware. Various machine learning and deep learning algorithms are used to detect these types of malware and hopefully gives a better result. Machine learning (ML) models are broadly classified as supervised learning, unsupervised and semi-supervised learning. ML models in the detection of malware are becoming quite common in recent days due to the rising number of malwares that propagates into different devices with different techniques. So, the malware reverse engineers came up with different approaches which use different techniques or algorithms such as label propagation, support vector machines (SVM), KNN, CNN, Naïve Bayes, and DT. In all these learning model's malware are identified with different accuracy rates and different false positive rates (FPS). In supervised learning first, the model is trained with enough data sets of malwares, and the predictions or output is obtained. In an unsupervised model, the training phase is not present instead the model is programmed to classify the malware or programs based on particular features or signatures on its own. In semi-supervised learning, the model is trained and later the classification or prediction part comes this is considered as the best approach even though the above two approaches are used for different cases. Machine learning models treat data in batches and streams. The batch learning model has limited learning capacity as the training data are required to be available at once, thus fitting a model for a specified dataset and not considering any updates is not a suitable learning model. Every update that is taken into account for training the model is up to date when the data is processed as streams i.e., bit by bit or byte by byte instead of huge blocks of data. This model evolves to deal with any concept datasets and is easier for better learning and predictions. Even though we use machine learning certain mistakes take place which can cause serious troubles. The false-positive rates give us unwanted false alarms about something good. The true-negative rates do not give us alarms when something is bad assuming that it is good. It is critical to develop a hybrid methodology for the detection and classification of malware.

16.2   Related works

The possibility of detecting malware is remaining problematic because theoretically, it is a hard problem, and practically malware creators use complicated techniques such as obfuscation to make the detecting process very challenging. The known malware signature- and heuristic-based detection approaches perform well. Machine learning-based malware analysis to detect malware is growing enormously. Windows is one of the most vulnerable OS to malware as connected to the internet various machine learning techniques can be implemented to detect through various techniques involved using static, dynamic, or hybrid features mostly. Ihab Shahadat, Bara' Bataineh, Amena Hayajneh, Ziad A. Al-Sharif [7] utilize ML-based predictions that include binary and multi-classification methods for data splitting and cross-validation for feature selection. First, convert the binary malware file into a gray-scale picture and utilized visual-AT ML visualization to classify malware [8]. This model deals with adversarial examples and gives a high precision rate. Visual-AT produces an accuracy of 97.73%. Conventional security methods to detect malicious code use signatures that are developed by reverse engineering malware. The traditional signature-based detection became ineffective against the recent malware [9]. The main tasks in a malware process are malware detection and classification. Malware detection analysis is of two types they are dynamic analysis and static analysis. Malware identification continues to be a challenge. Although signature-based and heuristic-based detection systems are both quick and effective in detecting known malware, neither has been successful in detecting novel malware. For unknown and difficult malware, on the other hand, behaviour-based, model-checking-based, and cloud-based approaches work well; deep learning-based, mobile device-based, and IoT-based approaches also emerge to detect some fraction of known and unknown malware. A thorough examination of malware detection approaches as well as recent detection methods that employ these approaches is examined. A broad understanding of malware detection approaches as well as the benefits and drawbacks of each detection strategy and the methods employed in these techniques are elaborated. For crucial embedded and cyber-physical systems (CPS) [10], a unique malware detection technique to detect malicious activities, the system uses electromagnetic (EM) side-channel signals from the device. The technology uses a neural network to represent EM emanations from an uncompromised device during training. Many computer systems, from embedded systems and mobile devices to desktop workstations and cloud servers, have been vulnerable to micro-architectural side-channel assaults [11]. Side-channel vulnerabilities arising from fundamental micro-architectural performance aspects, such as the most prevalent caches, out-of-order execution, and speculative execution, are exploited in such attacks. Prior work has concentrated on detecting and assessing these security flaws, as well as devising and deploying a countermeasure new method for identifying microarchitectural side-channel attacks that has a broad range of possible applications, as demonstrated by a case study utilizing the Prime + Probe attack family [12]. Rather than focusing on the side effects of side-channel assaults on micro-architectural elements like hardware performance counters, the focus is on high-level semantics and invariant issues. Cyber security continues to be a difficult issue for society especially as the number of networked systems grows [13]. Side-channel information leaked from hardware has been shown to reveal secret information in systems such as encryption keys, side-channel information can be utilized to detect malware on a computer platform without requiring access to the code. The network traffic is analyzed for efficient malware detection.

A hybrid model with the combination of random forest (RF) and multi-layer perceptron (MLP) using 12 hidden layers has very high true positive (TP) and low false positive (FP). The accuracy obtained is very low so different combinations have to be analyzed [14]. MalDy a portable framework for feature extraction and various machine learning models to classify is developed. It is dependent on the execution environment report system that possibly tries to reduce the dependency on the exec env report system [15]. PCA a feature-hybrid malware variant model is used to reduce dimension and an ensemble model is used for prediction. Less static features are analyzed [16]. MalFCS produces the data structures using entropy graphs rather than gray-scale images and an SVM classifier is used for classification. Adversarial network (AN) implementation when incorporated gives better efficiency [17]. Visual-AT ML visualization to classify the malware handles adversarial examples. This model build [18] first converts the binary malware file into a gray-scale picture and utilized visual-AT ML visualization to classify malware. This model deals with adversarial examples and gives a superior precision rate. Adversarial examples are taken care of in this model that gives an exactness of about 97.73%. In this model [19], the malware dataset is gathered and imported into the cuckoo sandbox. They arranged API call sequences utilizing a bidirectional long short-term memory (LSTM) model. Programming interface call affiliation and recurrence is examined utilizing the AMHARA algorithm. At that point, RF and LSTM are joined and anticipated which gives a superior outcome. ML and deep learning (DL) are both consolidated in this model. A small dataset is utilized that gives an exactness of 96.7%. These researchers have fabricated a multi-modular profound learning system known as HYDRA which comprises four fundamental segments, for example, API-based parts, Mnemonics-based segments, Byte-based segments, and the element combination and characterization component. The impediments of end-end learning have been limited in utilizing this method. The double substance can likewise be included with the current model which may give a superior result of 99.75% is the precision identified while actualizing multi-modal deep neural network [20]. From the literature, it is evident that malware analysis is important and the use of an ensemble model for classification and prediction of malware is essential. The visualization technique to convert a malware file into an image file and train the system for malware detection is crucial.

16.3   Ensemble-based malware detection model

To detect malware in a real-world environment as well as prevent any mishap due to malware is the primary objective. To meet the objective of an ensemble-based model for detecting and classifying malware using AI-based techniques is used. An efficient ensemble model will be able to classify and predict malware with a good accuracy rate, high true positive rate, and low false positive rate. An ensemble model which comprises three models is discussed. The first one is a machine learning model where the model is trained with malicious network activity along with usual network traffic such that any malicious activity in the network will be detected. Behind every malware attack, there will be always a communication to the host i.e. the attacker, this is why the first model monitors the network traffic. As discussed above, nowadays zero-day malware attack is rapidly increasing and to detect such type of malware attacks, the malware file is converted into an image and it is noted that there is a lot of similarity between the malware. Hence, in the second model, we will be converting malware files into a gray-scale image and train a machine learning model by extracting the features from those images, and on constructing this model, the zero-day malware attack can be prevented. And when it comes to image-based detection, there is a wide possibility that the model can be attacked by adding some epsilon values to the images, the third model is constructed in such a way that the image generated before will be converted into adversarial examples just by adding some epsilon values to the images. These adversarial examples are then trained with a deep learning model. On constructing this hybrid model, the malware attack can be prevented based on network and files which will be more sufficient to detect malware. The first model gives an accuracy of about 99%, and the accuracy of 93% is obtained from the second model, and, at last, the third model gives an accuracy rate of 86%. In the further section, we will be discussing a complete methodology involved in constructing these models.

The proposed ensemble model, image and network-based malware classification (IANBMC) is described in detail. IANBMC can be divided into three different models where each model takes different features as an input then is trained with various machine learning and deep learning algorithms to find the best model among that and gives us the accuracy on combining the best of those models. At the start, the overview of IANBMC is provided in this section. Second, how each model is built is described in a detailed manner in Section 16.3.2. Finally, we elaborate on how the detection model could be enhanced when combined.

16.3.1   Overview

The architecture of the image and network-based malware detection methodology consists of three different models as shown in Figure 16.1. By using ensemble learning, the accuracy is obtained by combining all three models. The first model is built using machine learning algorithms like SVM, random forest,

K-nearest neighbor, and a few more, and the best model for this dataset is noted and kept as a base classifier. The dataset of the first model consists of network traffic HTTP and TCP connections and has features like source and destination IP address, source and destination port number, and a few more. Second, the malware binary files dataset BIG 2015 is downloaded from a well-known website like Kaggle. The downloaded binary files are then converted into a greyscale image using python which will be considered as the input features and then various ML algorithms are treated with this dataset and the best is noted down. Third, the same malware files are converted into the greyscale image but now we will be adding some noise to the images which can be noted as adversarial training and CNN is trained with the noised image dataset and the accuracy is noted down. Once all the accuracy is noted down, an average of the second model and the third model accuracy is calculated and with the average accuracy combined with first model accuracy, voting is done which gives us the final output.

16.3.2 IANBMC

The first model is built in such a way that it only detects any suspicious activity on the network traffic. The dataset for the first model is downloaded from the

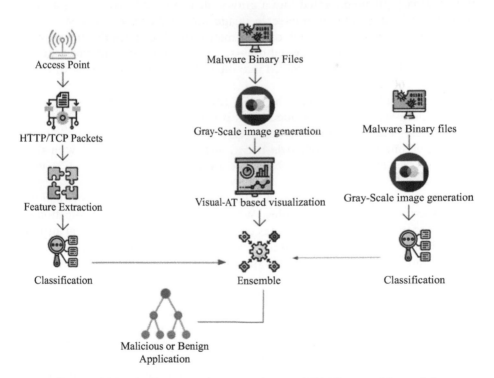

Figure 16.1 Architecture diagram of the IANBMC ensemble model

well-known website Kaggle which has around 25192 rows and 42 columns which contain TCP, User Datagram Protocol (UDP), and Internet Control Message Protocol (ICMP) protocol types. The downloaded dataset is loaded into a data frame and is filtered into TCP protocol type. Label encoding is performed on the constructed data frame and then it is categorized as a training and testing dataset such that 75% of the dataset is categorized as training whereas 25% of the remaining dataset is categorized into the testing dataset. Machine learning algorithms like SVM, random forest, KNN, Ada-boost, and Bagging are used for the classification and on which random forest stands at the top with 99.7% of accuracy.

The next phase of the ensemble model is constructed such that the model will be able to classify using the malware based on the binary files. Microsoft BIG 2015 dataset is downloaded from Kaggle and extracted into the project folder which consists of 10,868 binary files of type .asm belonging to nine different malware families with trainLables.csv file. The downloaded CSV file contains the ID and class of the malware which is loaded into the data frame. The file list is obtained by running through the dataset folder and is made to run in a loop to generate gray-scale images only for the malware is present in the data frame. On the gray-scale image generation process, the binary files are the first-byte list of hexadecimal decimal values, and then with those byte lists a byte matrix according to the size of the image (Figure 16.2). Using the PIL library the byte matrix is then converted into a gray-scale image and saved under a folder named jpg. The generated gray-scale image will not be in the same size as the size of the file denotes the size of byte matrix which denotes the size of gray-scale images and so the generated gray-scale images are then rescaled into the same size where images are resized into the width of 800 and the length of 1600 (i.e.) 800*1600.

After rescaling the images, the GIST features are extracted from the images using a gray-scale co-occurrence matrix using Mahotas Haralick functionality. Once these features are extracted, various machine learning models like SVM, random forest, KNN, Ada-boost, and Bagging are trained with those features. The high accuracy noted by constructing this model is 91% using Ada-boost.

The third model is built in such a way that it will be able to classify malware images using adversarial examples. When it comes to image classification the model constructed to classify images can be fooled by adding a random attribute in the images that need to be classified such a method of fooling can be resolved by generating adversarial examples and building the model with those examples. The same rescaled images are given as the input for generating adversarial examples. Vgg16, Resnet34, Resnet50 and Resnet152 are the models used to train those images. On the total of the rescaled image, 80% of the images are used for training, and 20% is used for testing, the image is also validated by the module ImageDataGenerator and once validated, the model is trained and tested which is gives a decent accuracy. Then the adversarial examples are generated with the help of the constructed model and the epsilon value (random attribute) is calculated using NumPy and the permutation is calculated using Fast Gradient

Malware Files	Byte List	Byte Matrix	Grayscale Images	Rescaled Images

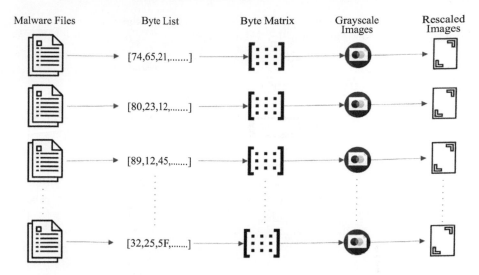

Figure 16.2 Binary files to gray-scale image generation process

Sign Method, where signed_grad of gradient descent is the permutation value (Figure 16.3). The calculated epsilon value and the permutation are passed as an i/p to the rescaled image which gives a new image that can be called an adversarial image. Once the adversarial examples are generated, these images are trained with the same architecture but a new deep learning model. Resnet152 tops the other entire algorithm and gives the accuracy of 86% on running 10 epochs.

The ensemble method will provide better accuracy results for classification and prediction.

Algorithm 1

Input: The dataset file with data that need to be trained
Output: Accuracy of the model
Load the dataset from the ".csv" file into a panda data frame
Perform label encoding on the loaded data frame
Split the whole data frame
X,Y=get75PercentageofData(data),get25PercentageofData(data)
bestAlgorithm=findTheBestAlgorithm(X, Y)
return getAccuracy(bestAlgorithm)

The first algorithm will extract the data of HTTP and TCP packets from the access points. The packets features are extracted and are classified as malicious or non-malicious.

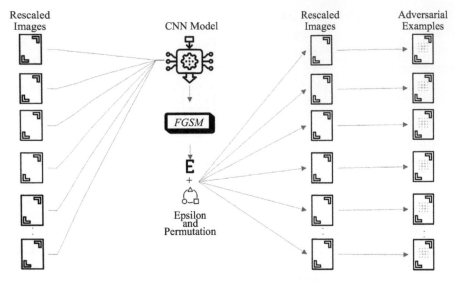

Figure 16.3   Adversarial example generation process

Algorithm 2

Input: The downloaded Microsoft BIG 2015 malware binary dataset
Output: Accuracy of the model while(input directory contains ".asm" file)
file list.add(filename) while(file in file list)
convert ".asm" file to hexadecimal values convert hexadecimal value to bytes convert bytes to byte matrix
generate a greyscale image using byte matrix
rescale the generated greyscale image
bestAlgorithm=findTheBestAlgorith(rescaledImages) return
get accuracy(bestAlgorithm)

Algorithm 2 downloads malware binary files and the binary files are converted to gray-scale images. The visual adversarial examples techniques will avoid the Epsilon value attacks. Algorithm 3 will train and test the model by using various machine learning models for providing better accuracy.

Algorithm 3

Input: The rescaled images generated from algorithm 2
Output: Accuracy of the model
Two new folder train and test is created with subfolders as class name
The total dataset is split into test and train and with respective, to the class, the images are placed

Using ImageDataBunch the dataset is loaded
Using the cnn_learner Restnet34 model is downloaded and trained with the dataset
giving us the accuracy.

The proposed model performs label encoding to remove the string values thus boosting the ML model's accuracy. The random forest provides high accuracy when compared with other ML algorithms. This method used ensemble learning which gives a better result when compared to a normal machine learning approach. Malware mostly attacks systems using a network and tries to download some malicious code, so the base starts with analyzing the network traffic. We have taken that into account analyzing the binary files which gives us a better result compared to models analyzing only the malware files. As CNN_AT model is used for gray-scale image classification which prevents adversarial example attacks.

16.4   Implementation results

In this section, the malware detection and classification model with the libraries and the algorithms used are discussed. The experimental programs are implemented in Python with the operating system Linux release. The libraries used are Pandas for loading the data and feature engineering, and Scikitlearn is used for classifiers, model evaluation, metrics, cross-validation, and label encoding. Matplotlib for Data visualization and PIL for image processing. Mahotas generates co-occurrence matrix. SVM, KNN, random forest, AdaBoost, Bagging, and CNN are the algorithms used for the evaluation.

16.4.1   Accuracy

On implementation of model 1, the accuracy is obtained by various models on detecting malicious activity in the network and it is observed that the entire model gives the best accuracy and in which random forest gives the accuracy of about 99.7%. The rest of the accuracy can be noted in Figure 16.4. Figure 16.5 shows the accuracy obtained by various models on detecting malware families based on binary files and it is observed that the entire model gives good accuracy and in which Ada-Boost gives the accuracy of about 93.3%. On constructing the third model as it is a deep learning model, the accuracy obtained in every ten epochs is figured in Figure 16.6 and shows that the accuracy obtained by various models on detecting malware families based on binary files and conclusion all the model gives the best accuracy and in which resnet152 gives the better accuracy of about 87%.

16.4.2   Performance metrics

The performance metrics of the first two models are calculated using a confusion matrix and are portrayed in Figure 16.7 for the model I and at Figure 16.8 for model

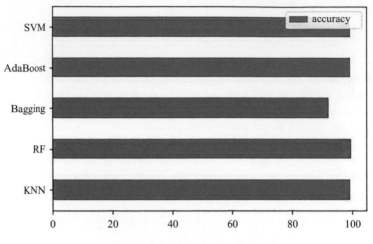

Figure 16.4   Accuracy of model

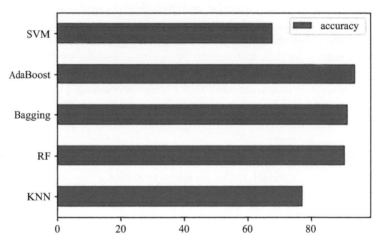

Figure 16.5   Accuracy of model II

II, the confusion matrix is calculated only for the algorithm that stands top among five of them. And for the deep learning model, the performance metrics are figured using the training and validation loss of the respective model and are converted into a graph and pictured in Figure 16.9 as training loss and Figure 16.10 as validation loss.

The adversarial images are generated using Fast Gradient Sign Attack (FGSM) technique and are trained with the CNN model. The re-scaled images are trained with the CNN model. Using FGSM, epsilon and permutation values are obtained

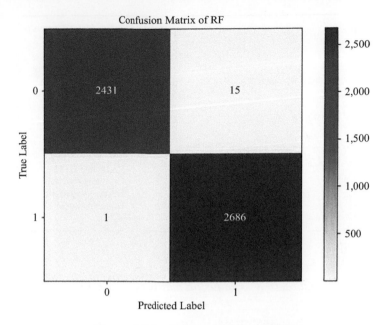

Figure 16.6   Accuracy of model III

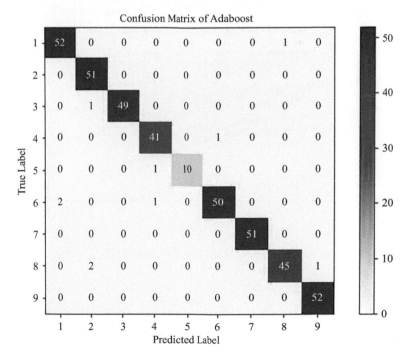

Figure 16.7   Confusion matrix of random forest

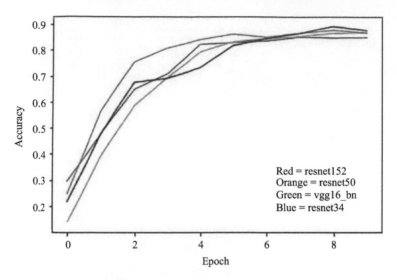

Figure 16.8   Confusion matrix of Ada-Boost

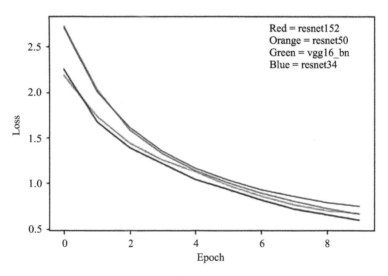

Figure 16.9   Train loss of model III

and are applied to the re-scaled image to generate the adversarial examples. These adversarial examples are used for training the CNN model to prevent any AE attacks. The ensemble model for detection of malware with better accuracy is achieved by ResNet 152 CNN model.

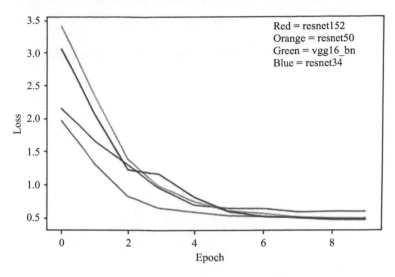

Figure 16.10   Valid loss of model III

16.5   Conclusion

The need for malware detection and classification has increased now in this technology era of the Internet. The initial phase for malware detection starts with static
and dynamic analysis. Other than this signature-based malware detection gives a
better result. But nowadays, zero-day malware is drastically increasing which paves
the way to machine learning and deep learning technologies. In this chapter, we
have discussed various machine learning and deep learning techniques involved in
the detection and classification of various malware. The IANBMC model comprising of three phases provides better accuracy.

References

[1]   Daniel, E., Susila, N. and Durga, S. (2021). "A panoramic view of cyber
      attack detection and prevention using machine learning and deep learning
      approaches". In *Applied Learning Algorithms for Intelligent IoT* (pp. 77–98).
      Boca Raton, FL: Auerbach Publications.
[2]   Aslan, Ö., Ozkan-Okay, M. and Gupta, D. (2021). "A review of cloud-based
      malware detection system: opportunities, advances and challenges".
      European Journal of Engineering and Technology Research, 6(3), 1–8.
[3]   Gandotra, E., Bansal, D. and Sofat, S. (2014). "Malware analysis and classifi-
      cation: a survey". *International Journal of Information Security*, 5(2), 56.
[4]   Makandar, A. and Patrot, A. (2017). "Malware class recognition using image
      processing techniques". In *Proceedings of the International Conference on*

Data Management on Analytics and Innovation (ICDMAI), 2017 (pp. 76–80). New York, NY: IEEE.

[5]   Golab, L. and Ozsu, M.T. (2003). "Issues in data stream management". *ACM SIGMOD Record*, 32, 5–14.

[6]   https://www.techopedia.com/definition/29741/zero-day-malware

[7]   Shhadat, I., Bataineh, B., Hayajneh, A. and Al-Sharif, Z.A. (2020). "The use of machine learning techniques to advance the detection and classification of unknown malware". *Procedia Computer Science*, 170, 917–922.

[8]   Liu, X., Lin, Y., Li, H. and Zhang, J. (2020). "A novel method for malware detection on ML-based visualization technique". *Computers & Security*, 89, 101682.

[9]   Aslan, Ö.A. and Samet, R. (2020). "A comprehensive review on malware detection approaches". *IEEE Access*, 8, 6249–6271.

[10] Khan, H.A., Sehatbakhsh, N., Nguyen, L.N., Prvulovic, M. and Zajic, A. (2019). "Malware detection in embedded systems using neural network model for electromagnetic side-channel signals". *Journal of Hardware and Systems Security,* 3(4), 305–318, https://doi.org/10.1007/s41635- 019-00074-w.

[11] Sukno, F.M., Waddington, J.L. and Whelan, P.F. (2015). "3-D facial landmark localization with asymmetry patterns and shape regression from incomplete local features", *IEEE Transactions on Cybernetics*, 45(9), 1717.

[12] Sabbagh, M., Fei, Y. and Wahl, T. (2018). "SCADET: a side-channel attack detection tool for tracking prime+probe". In *IEEE/ACM International Conference on Computer-Aided Design* (*ICCAD '18*), November 5–8, 2018, San Diego, CA. New York, NY: ACM, 8 pages, https://doi.org/10.1145/3240765.3240844.

[13] Dunlapa, S., Butts, J., Lopezc, J., Rice, M. and Mullins, B. (2016) "Using timing-based side channels for anomaly detection in industrial control systems", *International Journal of Critical Infrastructure Protection*, 15, 12–26.

[14] Yoo, S., Kim, S., Kim, S. and Kang, B.B. (2021). "AI-HydRa: advanced hybrid approach using random forest and deep learning for malware classification". *Information Sciences*, 546, 420–435.

[15] Karbab, E.B. and Debbabi, M. (2019). "MalDy: portable, data-driven malware detection using natural language processing and machine learning techniques on behavioral analysis reports". *Digital Investigation*, 28(Suppl), S77–S87.

[16] Zhang, J., Qin, Z., Yin, H., Ou, L. and Zhang, K. (2019). "A feature-hybrid malware variants detection using CNN based opcode embedding and BPNN based API embedding". *Computers & Security*, 84, 376–392.

[17] Xiao, G., Li, J., Chen, Y. and Li, K. (2020). "MalFCS: an effective malware classification framework with automated feature extraction based on deep convolutional neural networks". *Journal of Parallel and Distributed Computing*, 141, 49–58.

[18] Liu, X., Lin, Y., Li, H. and Zhang, J. (2020). "A novel method for malware detection on ML-based visualization technique". *Computers & Security*, 89, 101682.

[19] Xiaofeng, L., Fangshuo, J., Xiao, Z., Shengwei, Y., Jing, S. and Lio, P. (2019). "ASSCA: API sequence and statistics features combined architecture for malware detection". *Computer Networks*, 157, 99–111.

[20] Gibert, D., Mateu, C. and Planes, J. (2020). "HYDRA: a multimodal deep learning framework for malware classification". *Computers & Security*, 95, 101873.

[21] Tatbul, N. (2010). "Streaming data integration: challenges and opportunities". In *2010 IEEE 26th International Conference on Data Engineering Workshops (ICDEW 2010)* (pp. 155–158). New York, NY: IEEE.

Chapter 17

Performing streaming analytics on tweets (text and images) data

Anmol Choubey[1], Shivika Manglick[1] and R. Maheswari[1]

Abstract

In today's world, Twitter is one of the most popular and powerful social networking platforms. People interact, voice out their opinions, express their thoughts, start conversations about various issues through "tweets" and the market has started analyzing these tweets to get a better understanding of how the general public feels about their products, schemes, or new policies. This helps them to get their perspective directly and work towards making them more people-friendly. Different organizations and consumers are using various mechanisms to perform the sentiment analysis. In this work, two different methods are proposed to perform Twitter sentiment analysis. One of them is using Node-RED and IBM services where real-time data is harvested i.e. tweets from Twitter using Twitter's API from its developer tool. Data is then stored into the IBM cloudant and then the tweets are classified into positive, negative or neutral based on their sentiment score which lies between −5 and +5. Using IBM Watson's text to speech service, the tweets are converted to the audio format so that the user could listen to them one by one and the IBM Watson image analyzer is used to analyze what the image represents and it also shows the confidence and different features of the image. Using the visual recognition service, the tone of the tweet is analyzed among emotions like joy, anger, disgust, etc. and the Node-RED dashboard can be created to see the sentiment scores of various tweets. The other proposed method is using Python in machine learning where the sentiment analysis of the tweets is performed with the sentiment score using different classifiers and those classifiers are compared based on their precision, recall, f1 score, and accuracy to conclude which one of them is the most appropriate one for this work. Real-time data is harvested from Twitter, converted into a CSV file and analyzed into positive, negative, or neutral according to their sentiment scores using the classifiers.

[1]School of Computer Science and Engineering, Vellore Institute of Technology, India

17.1   Introduction

Internet of Things (IoT) has become a major part of our daily life. Almost every organization, system, company, and even our home have integrated the Internet of Things and find it difficult to function without it anymore. It has significantly reduced our labor cost, increased efficiency, and decreased the time people used to invest. Small tasks can be done in less time by sitting on our chairs. For example, in an office, if someone has to check if a conference room is empty or not, instead of going up to check they can use sensors to alert them when the rooms will be empty and can also book those for them. These methods have positively impacted companies to save time and allocate these costs to better and more efficient use [1]. IoT devices have also conquered our homes using smart home automation where lights and fans can be adjusted according to the outside conditions, the air conditioning can be set adjusted according to the room temperature automatically, security can be improved, intrusion can be detected, and prevented in lesser time, and much more.

As can be seen from the above examples, the IoT is the present and the future as it is the evolution of things that can be connected to other things like cars, homes, offices, electrical appliances, shelves, and much more. It can also transfer and receive huge amounts of data, store it in the cloud, and also harvest real-time data. IoT is solving a lot of our daily life problems and has helped every industry to make their work more efficient [2]. For example, IoT helps the agriculture industry by automatically detecting the weather conditions like temperature, humidity, rainfall, and the necessary steps to be taken to prevent any loss using sensors. It also helps big companies and organizations with data transfer and analytics.

Therefore, it can be said that IoT is about data transfer, its analysis and processing. Data can be retrieved in different formats from sensor readings, through some input commands or instructions and other information [3].

This can be used for research in various fields. One of them is sentiment analysis. Sentiment analysis refers to computerized methods that are used to analyze whether someone's opinion is negative, positive, or neutral. As social media platforms keep on growing at a fast pace, sentiment analysis has become one of the most important areas of research for product marketing, businesses, political campaigns, and people's opinions about ongoing issues and their appraisals.

General research modules in sentiment analysis include (i) extracting features and identifying the data elements which can be used to interpret the opinions [4]; (ii) classification and prediction of users' emotions whether they are positive, negative, or neutral [5]; (iii) aggregation and visualization of the condensed version of predicted opinions' set; and (iv) analysis of opinions associated with a topic in the posts. These developed methods can also be used to harvest and classify real-time data from social media networks [6].

Therefore, this project proposes a method to analyze the sentiments of the users on Twitter using IoT. Every day we see different hashtags trending on Twitter about various issues and people spend hours going through thousands of tweets to get a gist of its concept and what the backstory is to understand the public's reactions. Whereas this process can be done in a few seconds using IoT and data mining where the system can harvest real-time tweets from Twitter for each issue using the hashtags, download them, save them in the cloud for future work, analyze the data, give out sentiment score, predict the sentiment and the tone of the user, prepare a summary of the data, visualize it with the help of different graphs, and present it in a much more organized manner [7]. Thus, in this work, two methods are proposed to analyze the sentiments of the tweets. One is using Node-Red and the other is using Python in machine learning.

The rest of the work is organized as follows. Section 17.2 presents an overview of the literature survey done for this work by following different papers. Sections 17.3 and 17.4 present an overview of the existing system for this method and our proposed system. The next sections present the system design of the proposed work, working modules along with the description of each of the modules. The last section gives the concluding remarks and the prospects for future work.

17.2   Literature survey

There are various ways to analyze the sentiments of the tweets. In their work, the authors have proposed a sentiment analysis of tweets with the use of machine learning algorithms and attempted to classify whether the tweets are negative or positive by taking the dataset from Kaggle [8]. The models that are used for classification work on different methodologies. The authors aim to classify tweets into negative or positive by using models based on probabilities in their work and taking the dataset from Kaggle and Sentiment140 [9]. Abdullah Alsaeedi and Mohammad Zubair Khan [10] have provided theoretical comparisons of the existing approaches. They have classified the sentiments according to the polarity of the text documents. Along with the analysis, it is important to visualize the results in a user-friendly manner. Aliza Sarlan, Chayanit Nadam, and Shuib Basri [11] have represented their results in a pie chart and HTML page which helps the user to conclude their work more efficiently. In another work, out-performing the state-of-the-art baseline, the authors have introduced a POS-specific prior polarity feature along with the use of a tree kernel [12].

Understanding the need for analysis is one of the most important steps in any procedure. The analyst has to get a gist of the applications of the results for them to get the desired result. The authors have conducted systematic literature reviews in their work to provide the applications of the analysis [13]. One of the applications of the analysis of the text is to decipher if the text has some vulgar content or not and to remove them before any community gets hurt. The authors in their work have designed a system to analyze the pragmatic aspects of the vulgarity of the tweets. They have incorporated the demographic traits of the users in the analysis to get the percentage of vulgar tweets out of total tweets sent by any particular user [14]. Some more applications of sentiment analysis include using it for trend analysis [15], for business intelligence [16], and it can also help the researchers to identify quality research papers using a constructed annotated corpus [17].

Segregation of the data into a training set is an essential step in machine learning. In their work, the authors have also used the training set to show that when the size of the training set is sufficiently large their model performance approaches the inter-annotator agreement [18]. Another method for sentiment analysis is using R for the acquisition, pre-processing, and analyzing the tweets. Ankita Sharma and Udayan Ghose [19] have used R in their work to perform sentiment analysis and gain an insight into the opinion polarity of the public concerning the elections held in India by collecting the tweets from a specific period. Onam Bharti and Monika Malhotra [20] have proposed a different method in their work which uses a modified K means algorithm with Naive Bayes classification and KNN to perform sentiment analysis. Deep learning architectures are another method to perform sentiment analysis which Pinkesh Badjatiya, Shashank Gupta, Manish Gupta, and Vasudev Verma [21] have used in their work to classify a tweet as racist, sexist, or neither by performing extensive experiments. Emotion recognition has also gained popularity in recent times and the authors in this work [22] have developed a conversational AI that depends on the use of both contextual and multimodal information to detect emotions in conversations. Another method is the ontology learning techniques which Victor Sosa [23] has used in his work using linguistic patterns.

Considering a large number of methods available to perform sentiment analysis, it is essential to decide which one fulfills our requirements. This survey by M. Indhraom Prabha and G. Umarani Srikanth [24] provides a comparison between various flavors of deep learning methods along with their performance parameters.

17.3   Existing work

The already existing work [25] provides a method to analyze the tweets using the machine learning algorithm with Python where it takes the data from already existing datasets, for example from Kaggle. They use the CSV file, perform sentiment analysis, get the sentiment score and using them, classify the tweets into positive or negative. They used the Naïve Bayes classifier to classify the tweets, Tweepy to get the Twitter API, and TextBlob which is a python library to process the textual data.

17.4   Proposed work

17.4.1   Node-RED

In this method, the Node-RED platform is used to harvest real-time tweets from Twitter by getting the Twitter API using the Twitter developer tool. The flow is implemented to get the sentiment scores of the tweets by putting in particular hashtags which lie in the range of −5 to +5 using which the tweets were classified into negative (sentiment score<0), positive (sentiment score>0) and neutral (sentiment score=0). IBM Watson services are used to include various features in this work. The tone of the tweets (joy, disgust, sad, etc.) is analyzed using Watson Tone Analyzer, tweets were converted to audio using Watson Text to Speech service, images attached to tweets were analyzed using Watson Visual Recognition Service. A dashboard is built for the sentiment scores of the tweets and they were stored in the Cloudant database for historical analysis.

17.4.2 Machine learning using Python

Real-time data is harvested from Twitter and converted into a CSV file for the data to be processed. The data is cleaned by filtering out the null values, the emoticons and the special characters which would not be considered while analyzing the tweet. A training set is made for the dataset and sentiment analysis is performed to get the sentiment score which lies in the range −5 to +5 and the tweets are classified into positive and negative according to their sentiment scores. Different classifiers (SVM, Naïve Bayes, Logistic Regression, Random Forest Boost, Decision Tree) are used to perform the sentiment analysis and extract their F1-score, recall score, precision value, and accuracy to conclude which among these classifiers is best suited for this work so that an accurate value of our analysis is obtained.

17.4.3 System design of proposed work

Figure 17.1 is the proposed architecture diagram which shows the flow of the work. First, the tweets are collected and segregated into positive tweets and negative tweets using different nodes in Node-red. Then feature extraction is carried out using the

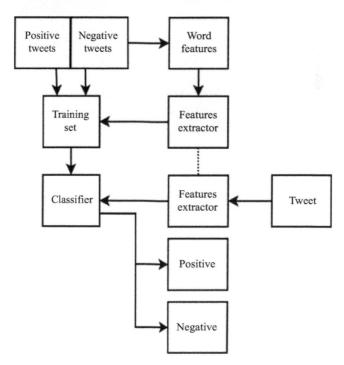

Figure 17.1   Block diagram of sentiment analysis

training data which is used to train the classifiers and then predict the sentiment score which hence will provide the sentiment type i.e. positive or negative.

17.5   Modules

17.5.1   *Node-RED*

17.5.1.1   Harvesting real-time tweets from Twitter and classifying them into positive and negative

In this Node-RED flow (Figure 17.2), real-time tweets are harvested from Twitter using the Twitter API from Twitter Developer Portal (Figure 17.3)

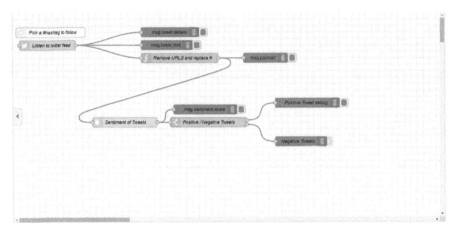

Figure 17.2   Node-RED flow for classification

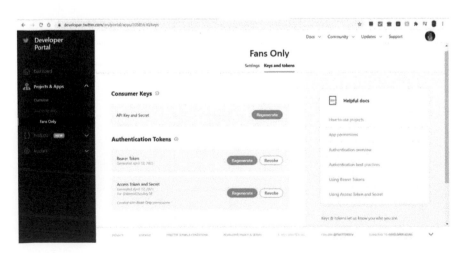

Figure 17.3   Twitter developer portal

(https://developer.twitter.com/en/apps). With the help of Sentiment of Tweets Node, the sentiment score of each tweet is obtained which lies in the range −5 to +5 and then accordingly classifies it into positive and negative.

17.5.1.1.1 Configuration of nodes

Here, the configuration of nodes for the above function is depicted using the screenshots of the configuration of nodes.

Figure 17.4 is the configuration of a "Twitter in" node where one has to provide a Twitter ID, search type like all public tweets, and a hashtag for collecting or harvesting the tweets on a particular topic.

In the Twitter ID field (Figure 17.5), one has to provide a few more details like API key, Access token which are generated while making API in Twitter Developer Portal (Figure 17.3).

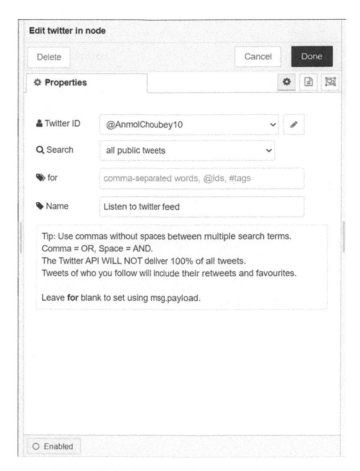

Figure 17.4   "Twitter in" node configuration

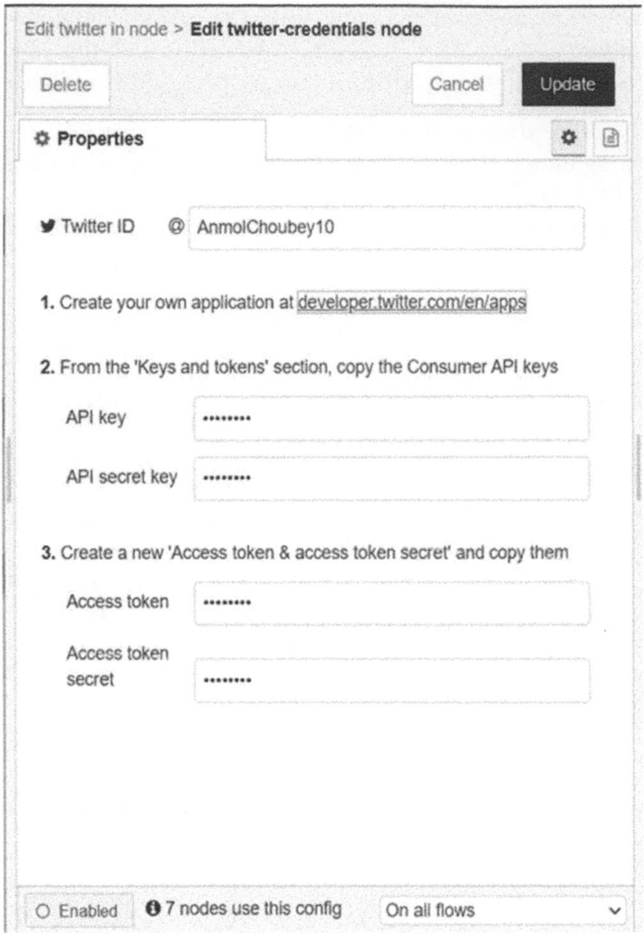

Figure 17.5   Twitter credentials

Figure 17.6 is the function node that is used to remove the URLs and replace them with #. Figures 17.7 and 17.8 show the configurations of the switch node and sentiment node.

17.5.1.2   Tweet reader

Using the Text to Speech Watson IBM service, the tweets are converted to audio so that the users can listen to them rather than reading them. The node red flow for this is shown in Figure 17.9.

17.5.1.2.1   Configuration of nodes

The screenshots in Figures 17.10 and 17.11 depict all the configurations of different nodes used for the Tweet Reader flow.

Figure 17.6   Function node to remove URL

Figure 17.7   Sentiment node configuration

Figure 17.8   Switch node configuration

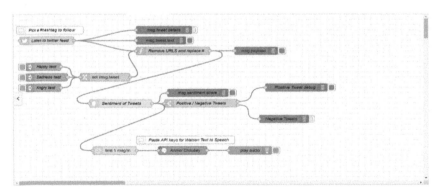

Figure 17.9   Flow for tweet reader

17.5.1.2.2   IBM Watson Text To Speech service

The Text to Speech service converts textual data to audio by synthesizing the audio back for a natural voice with minimum delay. This service can be used for various applications which are voice automated. The portal is shown in Figure 17.12.

Figure 17.10   Configuration of speech node

Figure 17.11   Configuration of delay node

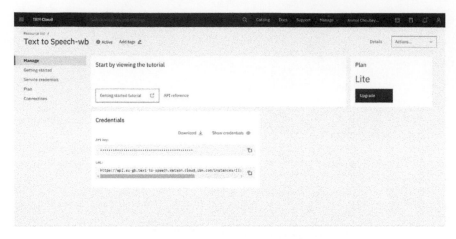

Figure 17.12   IBM Watson Text to Speech-wb configuration and credentials

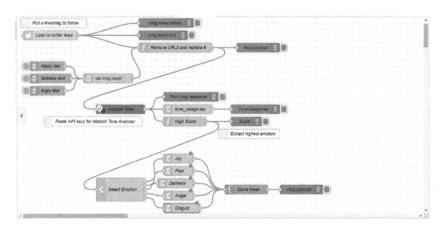

Figure 17.13   Flow for tweet tone

17.5.1.3   Tweet tone

In this flow which is shown in Figure 17.13, the tone of the tweet is analyzed i.e. the emotions that the user is trying to present (among joy, fear, sadness, anger, disgust) in their tweet by using some keywords and high score node.

17.5.1.3.1   Configuration of nodes

Figures 17.14–17.18 depict all the configuration of different nodes used for the Tweet Tone flow.

17.5.1.3.2   IBM tone analyzer

On social media, people show various emotions/tones such as fear, anger, joy, disgust, sadness which have an adverse effect on the conversations. Tone analyzer

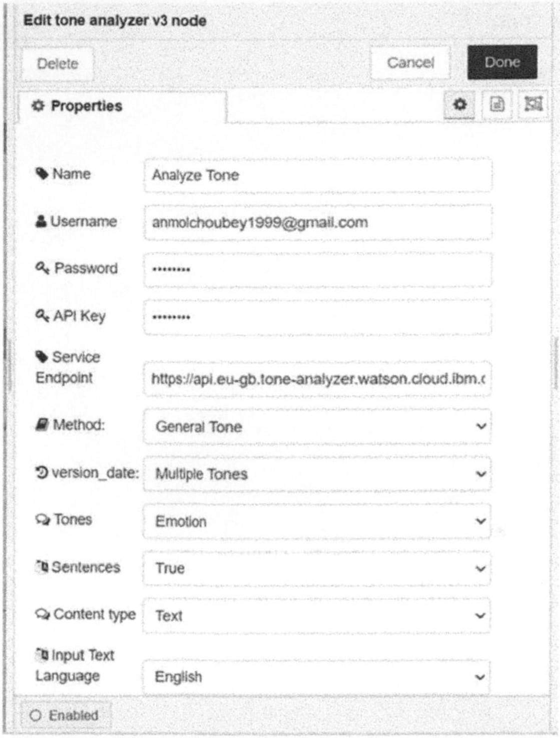

Figure 17.14   Tone analyzer node configuration

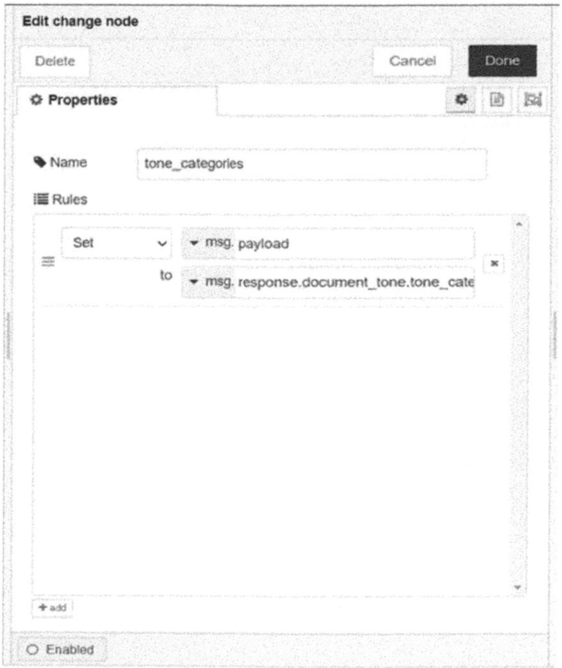

Figure 17.15   Change node configuration

Edit function node

Delete   Cancel   Done

⚙ Properties

🏷 Name   High Score

| Setup | **Function** | Close |

```
1   var emotions = [];
2   emotions = msg.response.document_tone.tone_categories
3                   .filter(function(c){
4                       if (c.category_id == "emotion_tone")
5                       {return c; }
6                   })[0].tones;
7
8   var myscore = 0;
9   for (var i=0; i<emotions.length; i++) {
10      if(emotions[i].score > myscore) {
11          msg.payload = emotions[i].score;
12          msg.topic = emotions[i].tone_name;
13          myscore = emotions[i].score;
14      }
15  }
16
17  return msg;
```

⤬ Outputs   1

○ Enabled

Figure 17.16   High tone function node

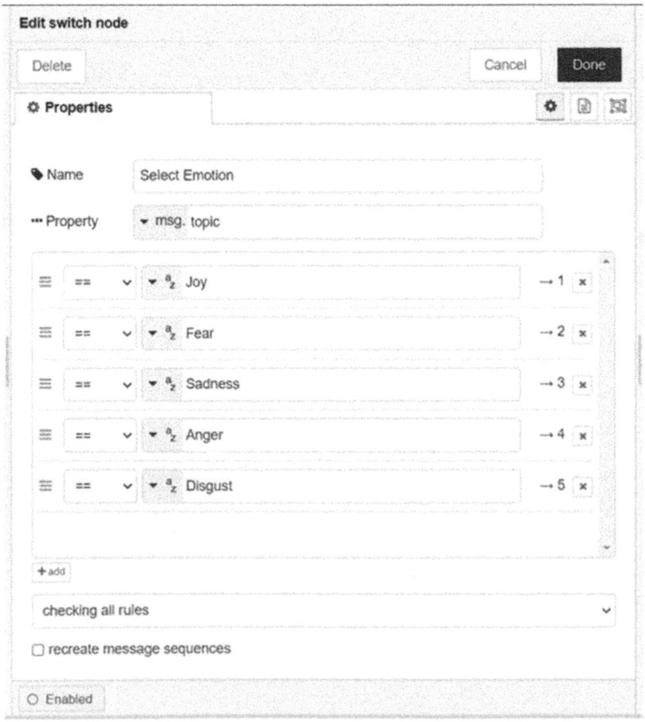

Edit switch node

Delete   Cancel   Done

⚙ Properties

🏷 Name   Select Emotion

••• Property   ▾ msg. topic

≡	== ∨	▾ ª_z Joy	→ 1 ✕
≡	== ∨	▾ ª_z Fear	→ 2 ✕
≡	== ∨	▾ ª_z Sadness	→ 3 ✕
≡	== ∨	▾ ª_z Anger	→ 4 ✕
≡	== ∨	▾ ª_z Disgust	→ 5 ✕

+add

checking all rules   ∨

☐ recreate message sequences

○ Enabled

Figure 17.17   Switch node configuration

Figure 17.18   Template node config

identifies these tones which can help in improving communication. Figure 17.19 shows the portal.

17.5.1.4   Dashboard

The dashboard presents the particular tweet along with the gauge showing the sentiment score and sentiment score graph. The Node-Red flow created for this is shown in Figure 17.20.

17.5.1.4.1   Configuration of nodes

Figures 17.21–17.23 depict all the configurations for the Dashboard flow.

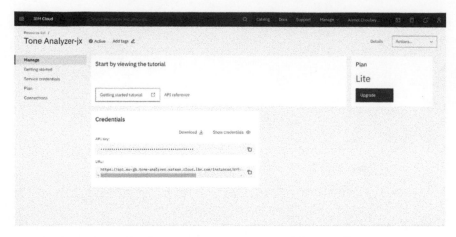

Figure 17.19   *IBM Watson Tone analyzer configuration and credentials*

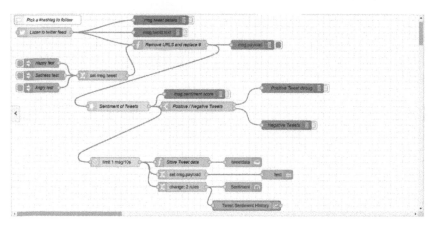

Figure 17.20   *Flow chart for the dashboard*

17.5.1.5   Image analysis

In the Node-RED flow shown in Figure 17.24, the images attached along with the tweets are analyzed and show what it represents with the confidence score using IBM Watson Visual Recognition Service.

17.5.1.5.1   Configuration of nodes

Figures 17.25–17.28 are the configurations of the nodes used in the image analysis Node-Red flow.

Using the function node, we will write the script to extract the tweet image URL.

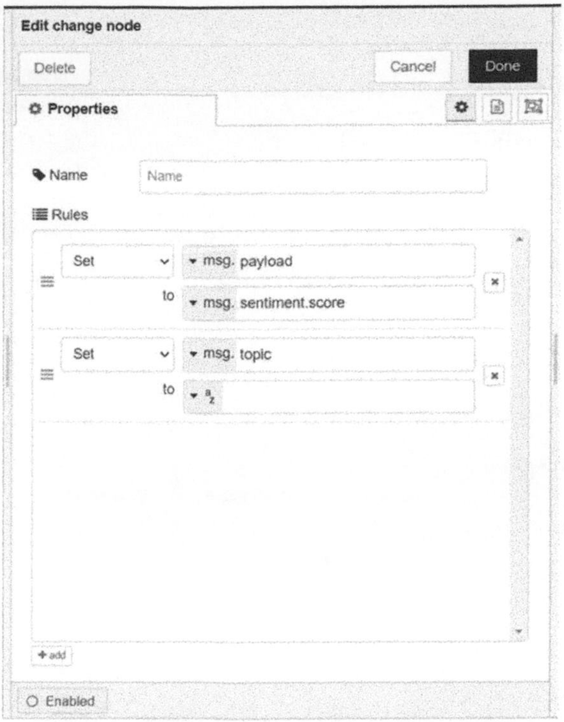

Figure 17.21   Change node configuration

Figure 17.22   Gauge node configuration

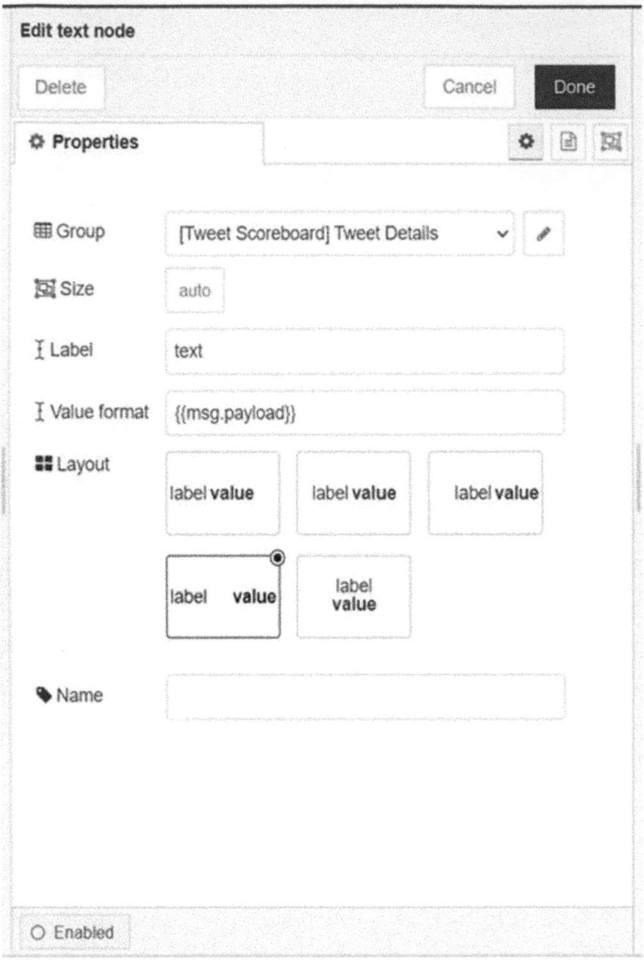

Edit text node

Delete   Cancel   **Done**

⚙ **Properties**   ⚙ ▤ ◱

▦ Group   [Tweet Scoreboard] Tweet Details   ∨   ✎

◲ Size   auto

Ⲓ Label   text

Ⲓ Value format   {{msg.payload}}

▦ Layout

| label **value** | label **value** | label **value** |

| label   value | label
                    value |

🏷 Name

○ Enabled

Figure 17.23   Text node for displaying tweet details on the dashboard

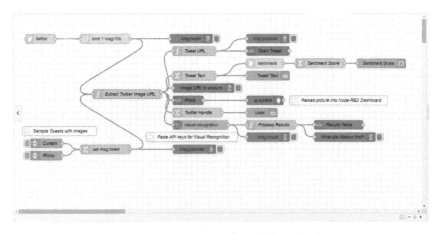

Figure 17.24   Flow for image analysis

Figure 17.25   Delay node config

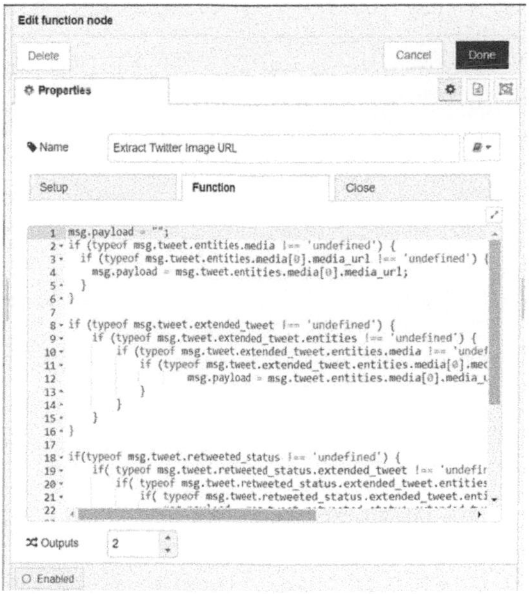

Figure 17.26   Extract Twitter image function

Figure 17.27   Tweet URL node configuration

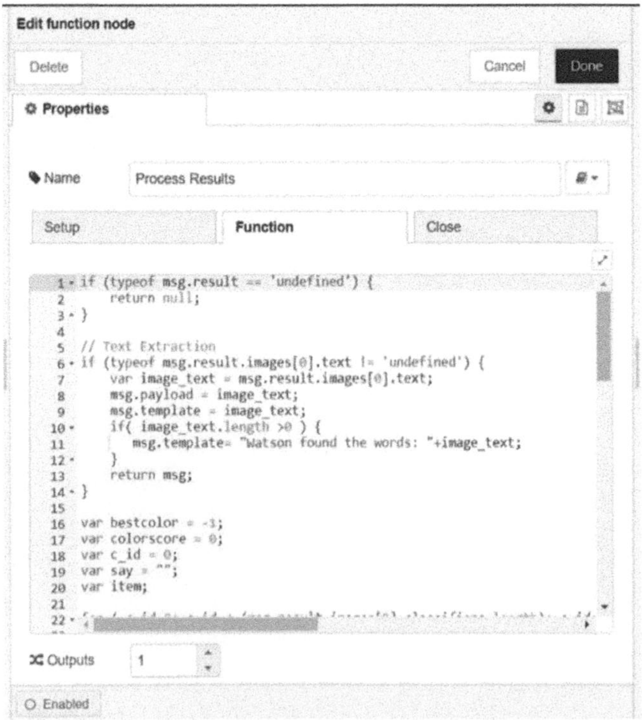

Figure 17.28   Process results function node

17.5.1.5.2 Dashboard nodes

Figures 17.29–17.31 show the configurations of the flow to set up the dashboard of image analysis.

17.5.1.5.3 IBM Watson Recognition Service – Hx

The Visual Recognition Service (Figure 17.32) analyzes the images attached for objects or different types of content. It also gives out a confidence score to understand what is happening in the image.

17.5.1.6 Storing tweets in cloudant

In the Node-RED flow shown in Figure 17.33, the tweets are stored in the IBM cloudant database which can also be read at any time.

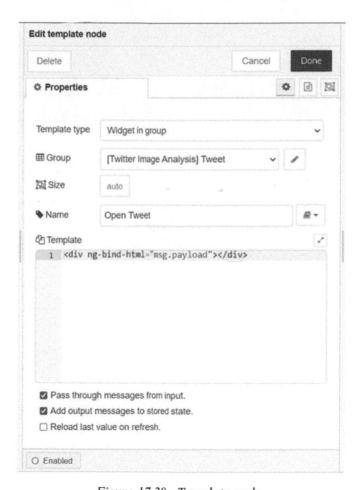

Figure 17.29   Template node

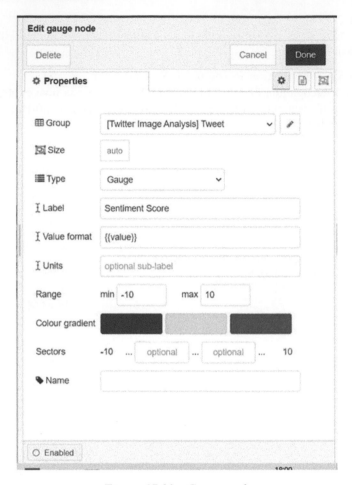

Figure 17.30   Gauge node

17.5.1.6.1   Configuration

Figures 17.34 and 17.35 depict the configuration of nodes available in the cloudant Node-RED flow.

17.5.1.6.2   IBM Cloudant service

IBM Cloudant is a cloud-based service that provides data management and analytics engine. Databases can be created and stored in the cloud using this service where users can read and write data. The Cloudant portal is shown in Figures 17.36 and 17.37.

Figure 17.31   Text node

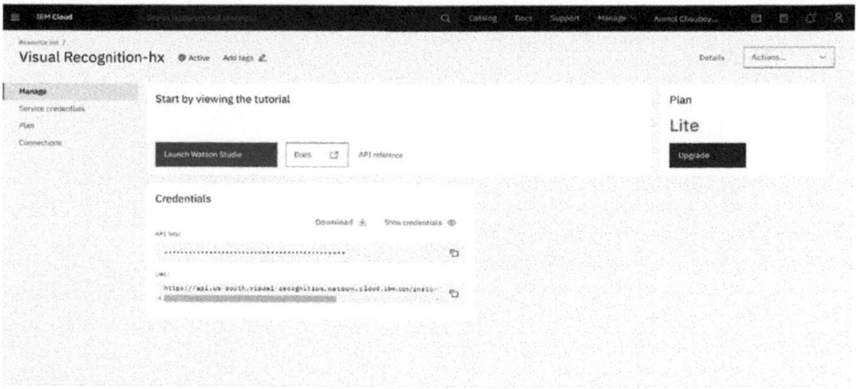

Figure 17.32   IBM Watson visual recognition configuration and credentials

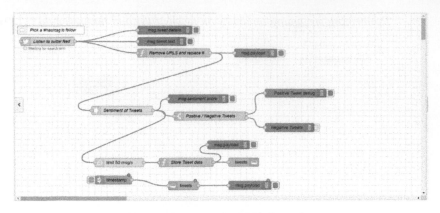

Figure 17.33   Node-RED flow chart

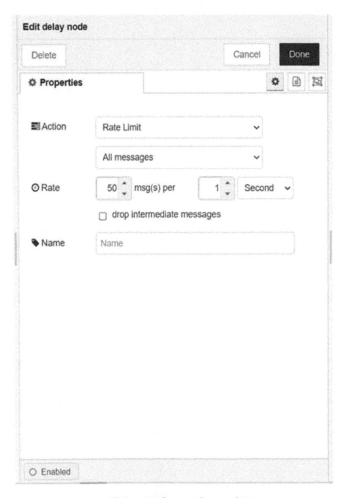

Figure 17.34   Delay node configuration

Figure 17.35   Cloudant out node configuration

17.5.2   Machine learning using Python
17.5.2.1   Reading tweet details from IBM Cloudant and writing it into CSV File along with sentiment score

The program is connected to the Cloudant database which was created above in the Node-Red flow. The tweets are stored in the database with the help of which users can write the tweets into a CSV file and read the data from there to perform sentiment analysis. The sentiment scores of each tweet are also stored along with the

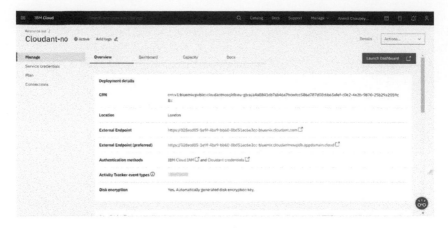

Figure 17.36   IBM Cloudant configuration and credentials

Figure 17.37   Databases dashboard

tweets in the CSV file to be used for analysis. The CSV file is saved in the local directories of our system and can be accessed locally.

17.5.2.2   Sentiment analysis

The CSV file created above is accessed. The null values from our dataset are removed. By using the sentiment scores, the number of neutral (sentiment score=0), positive (sentiment score>0) and negative (sentiment score<0) tweets are visualized along with the frequency of the maximum sentiment scores and the lengths of each tweet. The dataset is then cleaned by removing the punctuation marks, emoticons, and the stopwords of English (like I, my, are, is, etc.) which are not useful in analyzing the sentiment of the text. Count Vectorizer is used which converts the given text into vectors which are done on the basis of the frequency of each word that is occurring in the entire text. Then the dataset is divided into a test dataset and training dataset to analyze the tweets. Five different classifiers which are Naïve Bayes Multinomial DB, Logistics Regression, Decision tree, SVM, and Boosted Forest Random classifier are used to predict the sentiment score. Then these classifiers are compared on the basis of F1 score, Recall score, Precision, and Accuracy to conclude which of these is best suited for this work to analyze the tweets in an accurate and efficient way. It is implemented on Jupyter Notebook.

17.6 Outputs

17.6.1 Node-RED

17.6.1.1 Tweet sentiments

The sentiment of each tweet is calculated and printed in the debug window (Figure 17.38) of Node-RED.

17.6.1.2 Tweet reader

Tweets are collected and are read out loud with the help of IBM text to speed as shown in Figure 17.39.

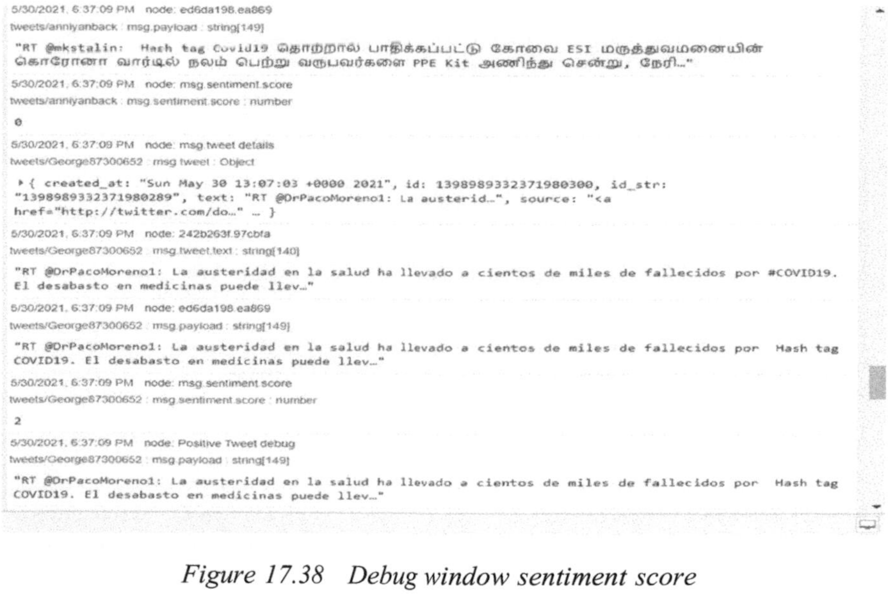

Figure 17.38 Debug window sentiment score

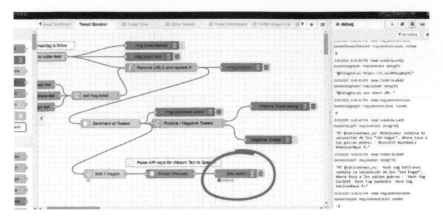

Figure 17.39   *Node-RED flow to convert text to audio*

Figure 17.40   *Tweet expression type (sadness, joy, etc.)*

17.6.1.3   Tweet tone

Tweets are analyzed using the tone analyzer and displayed what type of expression the tweet expresses as shown in Figure 17.40.

17.6.1.4 Tweets dashboard

The dashboard (Figure 17.41) displays the tweet details and sentiment score using a gauge and a chart that displays sentiment score over a period of time.

17.6.1.5 Image analysis

The tweet details with the tweeted image are displayed and are analyzed using IBM visual recognition. It recognizes and displays what the image contains as shown in Figures 17.42 and 17.43.

The image is recognized as a gray color rhinoceros and all other features too with the confidence level of the recognition.

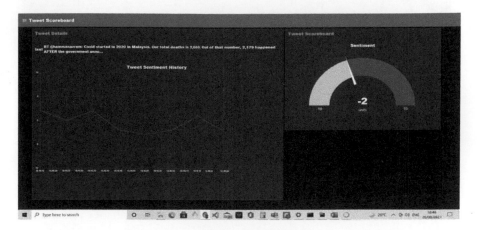

Figure 17.41   Dashboard

Figure 17.42   Tweet details and image (Rhino)

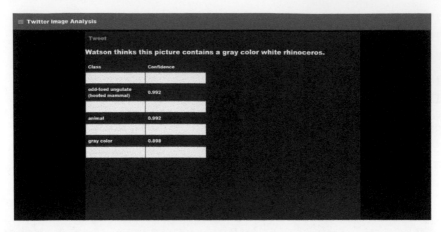

Figure 17.43   *Image is recognized*

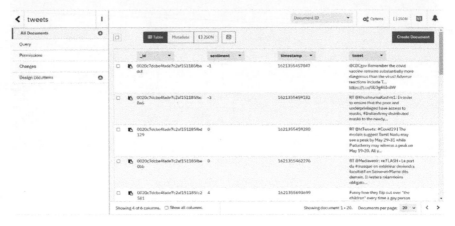

Figure 17.44   *"Tweet" database cloudant*

17.6.1.6   Store tweets to cloudant

The harvested tweets are collected and stored in the cloudant where a database "Tweet" is created (Figure 17.44). It contains tweet id, sentiment score, timestamp, and the tweet.

17.6.2   *Machine learning*

17.6.2.1   Generated CSV file stored in cloudant

The tweet details which were stored in cloudant were converted into a CSV file (Figure 17.45) and saved in the local directory using the python code.

17.6.2.2   Sentiment analysis

17.6.2.2.1   *Dataset head*

The generated CSV file is used as a dataset (Figure 17.46) for analysis.

	A	B	C	D	E	F	G	H	I
1	ID	TWEETS	SENTIMEN	SENTIMENT					
2	1.39E+18	@CDCgov	-1	negative					
3	1.39E+18	RT @Khusl	-3	negative					
4	1.39E+18	RT	0	nuetral					
5	1.39E+18	RT @Medi	0	nuetral					
6	1.39E+18	Funny how	4	positive					
7	1.39E+18	RT	0	nuetral					
8	1.39E+18	RT	-1	negative					
9	1.39E+18	RT @Khusl	-3	negative					
10	1.39E+18	BugÃ¼n de	0	nuetral					
11	1.39E+18	RT	0	nuetral					
12	1.39E+18	RT @buyd	0	nuetral					
13	1.39E+18	RT @SGIRI	0	nuetral					
14	1.39E+18	RT	0	nuetral					
15	1.39E+18	RT @BRAV	-3	negative					
16	1.39E+18	Bile orang	0	nuetral					
17	1.39E+18	RT @stpiin	2	positive					
18	1.39E+18	RT @Kancl	-2	negative					
19	1.39E+18	RT @Mack	1	positive					

Figure 17.45   Generated CSV file

	ID	TWEETS	SENTIMENT_SCORE	SENTIMENT
0	1394691992727302100	@CDCgov Remember the covid vaccine remains sub...	-1	negative
1	1394691998326481000	RT @KhushnumaKashm1: In order to ensure that t...	-3	negative
2	1394691998737604600	RT @htTweets: #Covid19	The models suggest Ta...	0	nuetral
3	1394692011303788500	RT @Mediavenir: FR FLASH - Le port du #masque ...	0	nuetral
4	1394692981962145800	Funny how they flip out over "the children" ev...	4	positive

Figure 17.46   Dataset for analysis

```
<class 'pandas.core.frame.DataFrame'>
RangeIndex: 2063 entries, 0 to 2062
Data columns (total 4 columns):
 #   Column           Non-Null Count   Dtype
---  ------           --------------   -----
 0   ID               2063 non-null    int64
 1   TWEETS           2063 non-null    object
 2   SENTIMENT_SCORE  2063 non-null    int64
 3   SENTIMENT        2063 non-null    object
dtypes: int64(2), object(2)
memory usage: 64.6+ KB
```

Figure 17.47   Non-Null count with data type

17.6.2.2.2   Dataset information

Dataset is checked whether it contains null values and data type of the column (Figure 17.47).

17.6.2.2.3   Tweets
All the tweets are displayed ignoring all other columns as shown in Figure 17.48.

17.6.2.2.4   Sentiment score plot
The frequency of sentiment score of tweets is plotted in Figure 17.49.

17.6.2.2.5   Sentiment plot
The frequency of sentiment type (negative, neutral, positive) of all tweets is shown in Figure 17.50.

17.6.2.2.6   Dataset with tweet length
The tweets lengths are calculated and added as a column in the dataset (Figure 17.51).

```
0        @CDCgov Remember the covid vaccine remains sub...
1        RT @KhushnumaKashm1: In order to ensure that t...
2        RT @htTweets: #Covid19 | The models suggest Ta...
3        RT @Mediavenir: FR FLASH - Le port du #masque ...
4        Funny how they flip out over "the children" ev...
                            ...
2058                                    #Indianeedfmg
2059     RT @AIGHospitals: We are delighted and extreme...
2060     RT @RadioChinar: #COVID19 Awareness Drive in D...
2061     RT @HNM_MemeChanger: This is a Personal attack...
2062     Portugal today recorded two deaths attributed ...
Name: TWEETS, Length: 2063, dtype: object
```

Figure 17.48   Tweets

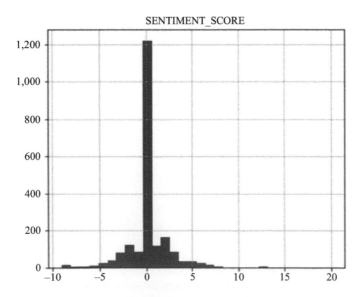

Figure 17.49   Sentiment score of all tweets

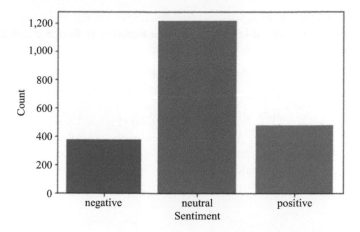

Figure 17.50   Sentiment type of all tweets

	ID	TWEETS	SENTIMENT_SCORE	SENTIMENT	lengths
0	1394691992727302100	@CDCgov Remember the covid vaccine remains sub...	-1	negative	140
1	1394691998326481000	RT @KhushnumaKashm1: In order to ensure that t...	-3	negative	139
2	1394691998737604600	RT @htTweets: #Covid19	The models suggest Ta...	0	nuetral	140
3	1394692011303788500	RT @Mediavenir: ꜰʀ FLASH - Le port du #masque ...	0	nuetral	140
4	1394692981962145800	Funny how they flip out over "the children" ev...	4	positive	140

Figure 17.51   Tweet details

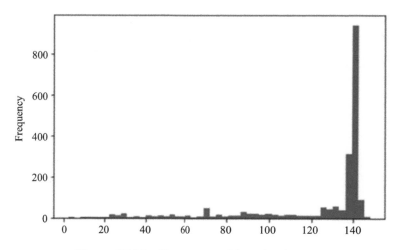

Figure 17.52   Frequency of length of tweets

17.6.2.2.7   Frequency of length of tweets plot

The frequency of length of all tweets is plotted as in Figure 17.52. It is observed that mostly tweets are of length = 140.

The details of the dataset after adding the length are shown in Figure 17.53.

All tweets which have a length of 140 are displayed in Figure 17.54 since it is the most counted tweet length.

17.6.2.2.8   Comparison of various models

The various model classifiers were used which are Logistic Regression classifier, Decision Tree classifier, Boosted Random Forest classifier, SVM classifier, and Gaussian NB classifier. The following comparison (Figure 17.55) of the classifiers was obtained using F1 score, Accuracy, Precision, and Recall.

	ID	**SENTIMENT_SCORE**	**lengths**
count	2.063000e+03	2063.000000	2063.000000
mean	1.394946e+18	0.120213	122.865730
std	5.993214e+13	2.150292	31.643732
min	1.394692e+18	-9.000000	2.000000
25%	1.394967e+18	0.000000	125.000000
50%	1.394970e+18	0.000000	140.000000
75%	1.394973e+18	0.000000	140.000000
max	1.394975e+18	20.000000	148.000000

Figure 17.53   Dataset details

	ID	TWEETS	SENTIMENT_SCORE	SENTIMENT	lengths
0	1394691992727302100	@CDCgov Remember the covid vaccine remains sub...	-1	negative	140
2	1394691998737604600	RT @htTweets: #Covid19	The models suggest Ta...	0	nuetral	140
3	1394692011303788500	RT @Mediavenir: ↳ FLASH - Le port du #masque ...	0	nuetral	140
4	1394692981962145800	Funny how they flip out over "the children" ev...	4	positive	140
5	1394692982708883500	RT @cavoust5: 💬 - C'est la photo d'un visage q...	0	nuetral	140
...	...	...	...	...	...
2055	1394974653463019500	RT @LawrenceSellin: What was the role of the W...	0	nuetral	140
2057	1394691984665759700	Che poi uno si chiede se il #COVID19 non abbi...	0	nuetral	140
2059	1394691998536257500	RT @AIGHospitals: We are delighted and extreme...	7	positive	140
2061	1394692012264198100	RT @HNM_MemeChanger: This is a Personal attack...	-1	negative	140
2062	1394692982754918400	Portugal today recorded two deaths attributed ...	-4	negative	140

Figure 17.54   Tweets with length = 140

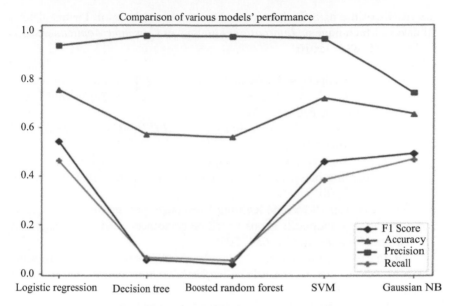

Figure 17.55   Comparison of various models

17.7   Conclusion

In this work, a method to analyze the sentiments of Twitter with the help of integrated IoT using Node-RED and machine learning is proposed. It was discovered that the logistic regression classifier yields the most accurate results and should be used for the analysis of tweets. This algorithm can be used to analyze the tweets of any given event and would prove to be an asset for brand marketing and even political campaigns.

17.8   Future work

Future work includes improving the mechanism to present the most important and dominant tweets for any particular event and include more sentiment tones. This mechanism can be used in homes and companies.

References

[1]   S.M. Alzahrani, "Development of IoT mining machine for Twitter sentiment analysis: mining in the cloud and results on the mirror", in: *2018 15th Learning and Technology Conference (L&T)*, 2018, pp. 86–95, doi: 10.1109/ LT.2018.8368490

[2]   V.A. Kharde and S.S. Sonawane, "Sentiment analysis of Twitter data: a survey of techniques", *International Journal of Computer Applications*, 139 (11), 0975–8887, 2016.

[3]   N. Yadav, O. Kudale, A. Rao, S. Gupta and A. Shitole, "Twitter sentiment analysis using supervised machine learning", in: Hemanth J., Bestak R., Chen J.I.Z. (eds.) *Intelligent Data Communication Technologies and Internet of Things*, February 2021.

[4]   G. Gunjan, *"Twitter Sentiment Analysis – A NLP Use-Case for Beginners"*, Data Science Blogathon, 2021.

[5]   J. Singh, G. Singh and R. Singh, "Optimization of sentiment analysis using machine learning classifiers", *Human-Centric Computing and Information Sciences*, 7, 32, 2017.

[6]   S. Yi and X. Liu, "Machine learning based customer sentiment analysis for recommending shoppers, shops based on customers' review", *Complex & Intelligent Systems*, 6, 621–634, 2020.

[7]   A. Ligthart, C. Catal and B. Tekinerdogan, "Systematic reviews in sentiment analysis: a tertiary study", *Artificial Intelligence Review*, 54, 1–57, 2021.

[8]   N. Mahendran and T. Mekala, "A survey: sentiment analysis using machine learning techniques for social media analytics", *International Journal of Pure and Applied Mathematics*, 118(8), 419–423, 2018.

[9]   M. Kabir, M.Md. Jahangir Kabir, S. Xu and B. Badhon, "An empirical research on sentiment analysis using machine learning approaches", *International Journal of Computers and Applications*, 43, 1011–1019, 2019.

[10] A. Alsaeedi and M.Z. Khan, "A study on sentiment analysis techniques of Twitter data", *International Journal of Advanced Computer Science and Applications*, 10(2), 361, 2019.

[11] A. Sarlan, C. Nadam and S. Basri, "Twitter sentiment analysis," in: *Proceedings of the 6th International Conference on Information Technology and Multimedia*, 2014, pp. 212–216.

[12] A. Agarwal, B. Xie, I. Vovsha, O. Rambow and R. Passonneau, "Sentiment analysis of Twitter data", in: *Proceedings of the Workshop on Language in Social Media* (*LSM 2011*) Columbia University, 2011.

[13] Z. Drus and H. Khalid, "Sentiment analysis in social media and its application: systematic literature review", in: *The Fifth Information Systems International Conference*, 2019.

[14] I. Cachola, E. Holgate, D. Preotiuc-Pietro and J.J. Li, "The socio-dynamics of vulgarity and its effects on sentiment analysis in social media", in: *Proceedings of the International Conference on Computational Linguistics* (*COLING*), 2018, pp. 2927–2938.

[15] J.-d. Wang, "A novel approach to compute pattern history for trend analysis", in: *2011 Eighth International Conference on Fuzzy Systems and Knowledge Discovery (FSKD)*, 2011.

[16] S. Chaturvedi, V. Mishra and N. Mishra, "Sentiment analysis using machine learning for business intelligence," in: *2017 IEEE International Conference*

on Power, Control, Signals and Instrumentation Engineering (ICPCSI), 2017, pp. 2162–2166, doi: 10.1109/ICPCSI.2017.8392100

[17]   D.M. El-Din, "Analyzing Scientific Papers Based on Sentiment Analysis", 2016, doi: 10.13140/RG.2.1.2222.6328.

[18]   I. Mozetič, M. Grčar and J. Smajlovic, "Multilingual Twitter sentiment classification: the role of human annotators", *PLoS ONE*, 11, e0155036, 2015.

[19]   A. Sharma and U. Ghose, "Sentimental analysis of Twitter data with respect to general elections in India", *Procedia Computer Science*, 173, 325–334, 2020.

[20]   O. Bharti and M. Malhotra, "Sentiment analysis on Twitter data", *International Journal of Computer Science and Mobile Computing*, 5(6), 601–609, 2016.

[21]   P. Badjatiya, S. Gupta, M. Gupta and V. Varma, "Deep learning for hate speech detection in Tweets", in: *2017 International World Wide Web Conference Committee (IW3C2)*, published under Creative Commons CC BY 4.0 License, 2017.

[22]   S. Poria, D. Hazarika, N. Majumder, G. Naik, E. Cambria and R. Mihalcea, *Information Systems Technology and Design*, Singapore: SUTD, 2019.

[23]   V. Sosa, "Discovering hypernyms using linguistic patterns on web search", in: *2011 7th International Conference on Next Generation Web Services Practices*, 2011.

[24]   M.I. Prabha and G. Umarani Srikanth, "Survey of sentiment analysis using deep learning techniques," in: *2019 1st International Conference on Innovations in Information and Communication Technology (ICIICT)*, 2019.

[25]   B. Gupta, M. Negi, K. Vishwakarma, G. Rawat and P. Badhani, "Study of Twitter sentiment analysis using machine learning algorithms on Python", *International Journal of Computer Applications*, 165(9), 29–34, 2017.

Chapter 18

Machine learning (ML) on the Internet of Things (IoT) streaming data toward real-time insights

Pethuru Raj[1] and R.S. Saundharya Thejaswini[1]

Abstract

The world generates an unfathomable amount of data every day. The speed with which the data gets generated, transmitted, ingested, and crunched is nothing but spectacular in the recent past. Expert thinkers and pundits across the globe are of the opinion that data is the transformation agent. Data is positioned as a strategic asset for any institution, innovator, and individual to grow and glow and is being reasoned as the new fuel for bringing in real and sustainable business transformation. It is a universally accepted fact that data can be methodically processed, mined, and analyzed to produce actionable insights. There are batch and real-time data processing methods to make sense of data heaps. Further on, there are integrated data analytics platforms in plenty, to extract hidden patterns, associations, and other useful insights out of data volumes. The data analytics ecosystem grows continuously considering the importance of data-driven insights and insights-driven decisions for businesses as well as people to be agile, adaptive and adroit in their dealings and deeds.

Off late real-time data capture, storage, analytics, decision-making, and action are being insisted upon vehemently considering the evolving business dynamics. Any data or message has to be carefully captured, cleansed, and crunched immediately in order to be really beneficial for businesses and commoners. It is indisputable that the data value goes down sharply with time. Another facet is that agile and autonomous business systems are extremely event-driven. That is, any business event may trigger a suite of events across. Thus, all kinds of event data/messages have to be received and processed in real time in order to activate and automate one or more business operations. In short, for envisaging and realizing real-time services, applications and enterprises, real-time data analytics capability is very much indispensable. Enterprises are therefore keenly strategizing and setting up analytics infrastructure modules with all the clarity and alacrity to make sense out of both internal and external data in time. Such a futuristic and flexible capability helps business houses to be sagaciously steered in the right direction.

[1]IBM, Bangalore, India

18.1   Introduction

Without an iota of doubt, this is the IoT era. All kinds of physical, mechanical, electrical, electronics and IT systems are accordingly modernized with digitization and edge technologies. Such empowered devices are subsequently hooked to the Internet. These networked and embedded devices are termed the Internet of Things (IoT) devices.

These IoT devices in conjunction with a stream of digital technologies (software-defined clouds, data analytics platforms, Artificial Intelligence (AI) models, blockchain databases, microservices and event-driven architectures, cybersecurity, digital twins, etc.) are capable of bringing in the much-needed digital transformation across industry verticals. Such a seamless and spontaneous connectivity with cloud-hosted software services and data enables everyday devices to be distinct and deft in their actions and reactions. In a nutshell, the integration with cloud applications through the Internet, which is being recognized as the world's largest communication infrastructure, has set a stimulating foundation for visualizing and realizing next-generation software solutions.

The point to be noted here is that all sorts of devices in and around us are being digitized and connected. Such IoT devices generate a variety of voluminous data in different velocities. Sophisticated use cases are being devised and developed when IoT data gets meticulously collected, cleansed and crunched. Smart homes, hotels, hospitals, etc. are being envisaged and implemented through the power of IoT devices. Data-driven insights and insights-driven decisions/deals/deeds come in handy in propelling the concept of smart cities across the continents and countries.

In brief, path-breaking IoT use cases can be built and released by applying big, real, and streaming analytics methods on IoT data in order to extract actionable insights. Data analytics play a very vital role in translating raw IoT data into useful and usable knowledge. There are integrated data analytics platforms in plenty from commercial-grade product vendors. The open-source community is responding to the growing need for data analytics. However, it is neither straightforward nor easy to embark on a data analytics journey.

In the recent past, there are a number of powerful improvements in the AI space. Several machine and deep learning (ML/DL) algorithms and their significant variants came up to automate several manual and error-prone data analytics processes [1].

18.2   The explosion of streaming data from IoT devices and sensors

Sensors are penetrative, pervasive, and persuasive too. There are single and multi-purpose sensors widely used in manufacturing machinery, humanoid robots, connected drones, vehicles, defense equipment, consumer electronics, smartphones, medical electronics, avionics, etc. In the past, sensor data gets captured and stocked in operational databases such as the operational historian.

> **Operational Historian** is a kind of operational database solution. Generally, the operational historian is collocated at the plant with other control system components including instrumentation and SCADA. These databases facilitate data capture, compression, validation, and aggregation. Historian software is built-in or used together with control systems like DCS and PLCs.

This database software stores historical and time-based data that flows from a myriad of sensors and are optimized for time-dependent analysis. Historian technology captures event data from hundreds of sensor types and other real-time devices. These dedicated data historians can survive harsh conditions, such as a production floor and oil wells so they continue capturing and storing data even if the main data store is unavailable. Historian software often includes complementary tools for reporting and monitoring historic data, and can detect trends or correlations. When an issue is flagged, the system can alert an operator about the potential problem. However, with the fast proliferation of multifaceted IoT devices and sensors, there is a need for streaming systems, streaming analytics platforms, storage appliances, data lakes, cloud infrastructures, etc.

There are a number of improvisations in the IoT space. Connected sensors have become miniaturized, low-cost, low-power, long-range, and multifaceted. The advancement in the fields of microelectronics and nanoelectronics has clearly impacted the design of disappearing sensors and actuators. These can form ad hoc, dynamic, and purpose-specific meshes in order to perform large-scale data processing to accomplish greater things.

With the widespread deployment of 5G communication infrastructures across the world, sensors can communicate with cloud-based IoT-enablement and analytics systems directly or indirectly. With such connectivity, we can easily aspire to visualize greater things. There are devices and sensor-centric wireless and wired communication protocols. Wi-Fi connectivity is becoming important for local communication. To take full advantage of IoT data streams, business houses have to have the capability to filter out, mashup, correlate, corroborate, contrast, interpolate, and extrapolate the IoT data volumes.

Streaming data is the continuous flow of real-time data generated by different and distributed sources. By using stream processing technology, data streams can be received, processed, stored, analyzed, and acted upon in real-time. Precisely speaking, the term "streaming data" is used to describe continuous and neverending data streams with no beginning or end. Streaming data can be formally utilized/acted upon without needing it to be downloaded first.

Data volume, velocity, variety, viscosity, and virtuosity are enigmatically varying indeed. IoT devices and sensors, IT infrastructure modules (compute, storage and networking), security appliances, business applications, personal and professional gadgets and gizmos, are the prominent data-generating sources. Click streams, transactional, operational, analytical, and location data can all be aggregated to be subjected to a variety of deeper and decisive investigations to emit useful and usable information in real time.

It is almost impossible to regulate data structure, data integrity, or control the volume or velocity of the IoT data getting generated. Traditional analytical solutions are built to ingest, process, and structure data before it can be acted upon. But streaming solutions have the ability to consume, persist to storage, enrich, and analyze data in motion. Thus, any streaming application has to be supported by two vital software infrastructure solutions: storage and processing. The storage system must be able to record large streams of data in a way that is sequential and consistent. The streaming data processing systems must be able to interact with storage solutions, consume, and analyze the data immediately in order to emit actionable insights.

Thus, capturing streaming data is the first step for any data-driven organization to strive ahead with full confidence and clarity. By ingesting and analysing streaming data through automated tools, real-time insights can be derived. Thereby innovators can envisage people-centric, business-critical, process-aware, service-oriented, event-driven, knowledge-filled, cloud-native, real-world and real-time services and applications, which lead to real-time and Intelligent enterprises. It is projected by leading market watchers and researchers that there will be billions of IoT devices and trillions of IoT sensors in the years to unfold across the globe. These devices and sensors can generate a massive amount of multi-structured data and stream it to cloud storage. Cloud-hosted data analytics platforms then fetch and crunch the data to extract actionable insights in time. Thus, streaming solutions in association with streaming data analytics platforms enable the discovery of useful information and insights in time. IoT systems make use of the derived insights to exhibit adaptive behaviour. Intelligent IoT environments such as smart homes, hotels, and hospitals can be gleefully realized to empower service providers and consumers alike with sincerity and sagacity.

18.3   The potentials of streaming data

As indicated above, streaming data is a flow of data collected from many sources in various formats and quantities. It can be collected from software applications, connected sensors and actuators, bank transactions, website activities, server log files, etc. By collecting, cleansing and crunching streaming data, getting meaningful information is made possible. Stream processing is taking an action on a series of data points. With more data emanating from a rapidly growing number of data sources, data analytics becomes mandatory for companies to march ahead in their purposes and pursuits. With the pervasive deployment of IoT sensors and devices, there is a massive amount of IoT data getting generated. Companies place high importance on capturing and castigating IoT data to streamline and smoothen the journey. The following recommendations were made by pundits and pioneers to be benefited from all the recent advancements in real-time streaming analytics.

1. Corporates have to deploy sophisticated streaming solutions along with data storage and analytics platforms in enterprise or cloud servers to readily make sense of IoT streaming data. All kinds of business events have to be minutely monitored and mined to emit useful information for business executives and stakeholders to plan ahead and execute the plan with extreme clarity, confidence, and alacrity.
2. Such a setup can facilitate the timely unraveling of hidden patterns in data heaps, which originate from different and distributed data sources.
3. Through predictive analytics, it is easy and fast to appropriately respond to a variety of business events.
4. The system response can be swift and automated. Further on, such a capability through automated tools helps to take intelligent actions instantly with less intervention, interpretation and involvement of humans.

The figure below vividly illustrates how streaming data analytics gets accomplished.

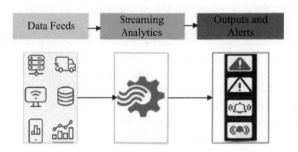

18.4   The needs for real-time data analytics

Real-time insights are needed for implementing a variety of people-centric and business-critical use cases. Patient monitoring, autonomous vehicles, predictive maintenance of mission-critical assets, etc. are some of the renowned use cases yearning for real-time data capture, storage, processing, decisions, and actions. For example, for patient monitoring, all body parameters of patients have to be minutely monitored, measured, and analyzed to extract actionable intelligence in time. The knowledge discovered helps caregivers and specialists gain all the right and relevant remediation details in time. Otherwise, there might be a possibility for patients to suffer severely.

There are multifaceted IoT sensors being manufactured in larger quantities to capture various body conditions with greater accuracy. Smartphones can act as the IoT gateway to aggregate and transfer to cloud-based message broker/queue and to the data analytics platform. Increasingly for producing real-time insights, edge device clusters/clouds are being increasingly leveraged. That is, instead of sending to faraway cloud-based streaming platforms, local or proximate processing is being preferred considering the time delay that can be potentially caused by network slowdown. That is, streaming data analytics platforms and toolkits are being deployed as edge devices to neatly fulfill real-time needs.

Realistically streaming analytics platforms can handle massive amounts of data at scale. Businesses are keenly strategizing and planning to have streaming analytics capability in order to simplify the realization and sustenance of real-time services and applications. Streaming analytics platforms have turned out to be an excellent investment for worldwide corporates to succulently envisage sophisticated and premium offerings to their partners, consumers, and employees. These platforms enable the ingestion of tremendous quantities of data.

With the steady arrival of feature-rich software and hardware solutions, the long-pending goal of real-time analytics of big data is seeing the light. Timeliness and trustworthiness of insights derived from data heaps go a long way in envisaging and elegantly realizing sophisticated software solutions for the ensuing digital era.

18.5   The emergence of real-time analytics systems

There are several instances and incidents wherein streaming data originates and pours in continuously. Feature-rich IoT devices and sensors are prominent and pertinent in producing and transmitting data, which gets streamed across for different purposes. Making sense out of data quickly is a primary purpose. Mission-critical and life-saving machinery, instruments, equipment, appliances, etc. emit out and stream valuable data ceaselessly. Industry assets always generate and stream data to be captured, cleansed, and crunched immediately toward knowledge discovery and dissemination. The real-time analytics of streaming data goes a long way in technologically protecting and prolonging their lives. If there is a small lapse in managing and maintaining them, then the result may be irreparable and catastrophic. That is, preventive and predictive maintenance of important machinery is vital to ensure business continuity. If there is a discontinuity or slow down, then the brand value of that organization is bound to go down sharply. Thus, streaming data and its real-time processing through a host of competent technologies and tools open up fresh possibilities and opportunities.

Real-time analytics platforms – Having understood the growing need for real-time data analytics, there came a number of open-source and commercial-grade platforms for facilitating real-time data analytics. Let us focus on some of the open-source systems. Apache Samza, a distributed stream processing framework, which allows you to build stateful applications that process data in real time from multiple sources including Apache Kafka, is discussed below. There are also numerous other powerful products including Apache Flink [2]. The diagram below vividly illustrates the various software infrastructure components needed to build and run real-time systems.

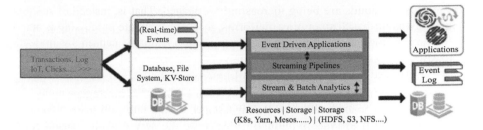

Apache Storm is another popular open source distributed real-time computation system which makes it easy to reliably process unbounded streams of data. Storm is famous for doing real-time processing whereas Apache Hadoop is for batch processing. Apache Storm [3] has many use cases: real-time analytics, online machine learning (ML), continuous computation, distributed RPC, ETL, and so on. Apache Storm is fast, scalable, and fault-tolerant and it integrates with the queuing and database technologies. Apache Storm topology consumes streams of data and processes those streams in arbitrarily complex ways. Collectively these technologies are used to build a real-time data pipeline that moves data across the systems and applications. There are also several powerful supporting systems needed for empowering real-time data analytics.

Streaming systems – These solutions are insisted to consistently and cognitively support real-time businesses. For example, Apache Kafka is a market-leading streaming solution. Apache Kafka is an open-source distributed event streaming platform and it plays a very influential role in high-performance data pipelines, streaming analytics, data integration, and mission-critical applications. However, to be useful, Kafka has to be seamlessly and spontaneously integrated with other allied software infrastructure products such as in-memory databases and grids, container-enablement and management platforms, and real-time data analytics systems with machine-learning capabilities. Let us discuss each of them in detail.

While Apache Kafka may be the most popular solution for data streaming needs, Apache Pulsar is coming up fast as one of the most powerful streaming software for the future. Apache Pulsar is a cloud-native, distributed messaging, and streaming platform. Pulsar is a multi-tenant, high-performance solution for server-to-server messaging. It is to address the shortcomings of Kafka by enabling easier scalability and adding missing features like geo-replication [4].

In terms of architecture, each Pulsar instance can consist of multiple clusters. These clusters, in turn, consist of multiple brokers as well as ZooKeeper and BookKeeper clusters. Herein, brokers are getting decoupled from the storage layer. Pulsar introduces more configuration parameters than

Kafka. On the other hand, Kafka uses ZooKeeper, which is being replaced by the new quorum controller, and hence all the metadata responsibilities will be handled by the Kafka cluster itself.

Message consumption – When it comes to Kafka, consumers pull messages from the server. Long-polling ensures that new messages are consumed almost instantaneously. Pulsar is based on the pub–sub pattern (publish–subscribe). Producers publish messages to the server while consumers need to subscribe in order to receive them.

Storage – While Kafka uses logs that are distributed among brokers, Pulsar uses Apache BookKeeper for storage. BookKeeper also offers tiered storage, which means that older and less used data can be stored on cost-saving solutions.

Brokers – A Kafka client communicates with Kafka brokers to write or read events. Once received, the brokers will store the events in a durable and fault-tolerant manner for as long as needed. However, Apache Pulsar uses stateless brokers. These brokers can be started quickly and in large numbers to accommodate higher demand.

In Kafka, each broker uses a complete log for its partitions. These brokers need to synchronize data with all the other brokers for the same partition as well as their replicas. Pulsar, on the other hand, stores the state outside of the brokers which separates them completely from the data storage layer.

Stream processing – Pulsar stream processing relies on the Pulsar Functions interface which is only suited for simple callbacks. On the other hand, Kafka Streams and ksqlDB are more complete solutions. You could use them to build streaming applications with stateful information, sliding windows, etc. In short, Kafka aims for high throughput while Pulsar is invested in low latency.

In-memory computing – This computing model gains surging popularity these days as real-time computing requirements grow drastically. The size of random access memory (RAM) of recent computing machines is rapidly growing. With the enhanced memory availability, IoT data gets gleaned and stocked in RAM in order to aid in faster computation. Also, there are several breakthrough solutions to facilitate this futuristic computing paradigm.

In-memory databases are purpose-built databases that rely primarily on memory for data storage. This is in contrast to databases that store data on disk or SSDs. In-memory data stores are designed to enable quick data access. In-memory databases are ideal for applications that require microsecond response times or have large spikes in traffic such as real-time data analytics.

In Memory Data Grid (IMDG) – This is a set of networked/clustered computers that pool together their RAM to let applications share their data with other applications running in the cluster. IMDGs are built for faster and larger data processing. They enable the building and running of large-scale applications and guarantee the highest application performance by using RAM along with the processing power of multiple computers that run tasks in parallel.

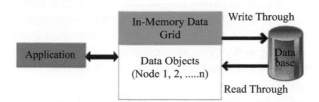

An IMDG works by running specialized software on every computer in a cluster to coordinate access to data for applications. The software keeps track of all data on each individual node so that the data can be shared with any other node or any application. This orchestration hides the complexity of retrieving and updating data across the network.

Data in an IMDG is often stored in the form of objects, such as maps, lists, and queues. Each of these objects and data types is represented as variables in an application, and the application logic references these variables as if they resided in the same computer that is running the application. This makes the programming paradigm easier. IMDGs are ideal when data is continually accessed and modified as a part of complex computations.

One prominent use case for IMDGs [5] is payment processing. During a payment transaction, several important calculations have to be performed quickly. Typically, payment authentication and payment network selection are two of the key actions, but fraud detection is arguably the most computationally heavy operation. Fraud detection requires a comparison of the transaction in question against a long list of previous transactions to measure the probability of fraud. Fraud detection is one of the prime objectives of payment processors. Also, it is important to reduce the number of false positives. Fortunately, there are pioneering ML algorithms to reduce the number of false positives. In short, we need faster and better fraud detection capability. The performance advantage of IMDGs lets payment processors run these multiple algorithms while maintaining the millisecond-level responsiveness that they need to maintain a positive customer experience.

Apache Ignite [6] is a distributed in-memory computing platform that can be deployed on a cluster of commodity servers. It is an open source IMDG getting inserted between an existing application and a disk-based database. Ignite also can serve as a standalone in-memory database for new applications. Ignite pools the available CPUs and RAM of the cluster and distributes data and compute to the individual nodes. The Ignite home page says that it is a distributed database for creating high-performance applications that inherently support in-memory speed. Ignite can ingest massive amounts of data in real time. With all data remaining in memory, the Ignite software uses MapReduce to execute Massively Parallel Processing (MPP) across the distributed cluster. Leveraging both in-memory data caching and MPP, the Ignite solution provides up to a $1,000\times$ increase in application performance at scale versus applications that use a disk-based database.

Ignite users can also leverage the native Kafka integration to make it easy to ingest streaming data from IoT devices into the in-memory computing cluster. Further on, Apache Ignite can be used to build a digital integration hub (DIH) for aggregating and processing data from multiple on-premise datastores, cloud-based data sources, and streaming data feeds. As a digital hub, Apache Ignite contributes as a high-performance data access layer that makes the aggregated data available to multiple business applications in real time.

With in-memory data grids and streaming solutions in place, there is a need for real-time data analytics platforms. Fortunately, there are many powerful and integrated analytics solutions. Apache Spark [7] is a distributed computing engine used for processing and analyzing large amounts of data. Spark handles both batch and streaming data. Spark performs exploratory data analysis (EDA) on petabyte-scale data. In short, Spark simplifies scalable computing.

Spark can take advantage of the Apache Ignite in-memory computing platform to rapidly analyze the huge amounts of data being ingested via the streaming pipeline. Spark can also use Ignite as an online datastore. This enables Spark users to append data to their existing DataFrames or RDDs and rerun Spark jobs. Spark supports SQL analytics: execute fast, distributed ANSI SQL queries for dash-boarding and ad hoc reporting.

For ML use cases, Apache Ignite includes integrated, fully distributed ML and deep learning libraries that have been optimized for massively parallel processing. Spark in connivance with Ignite enables businesses to create continuous learning applications where ML or deep learning algorithms run locally against the data residing in-memory on each node of the cluster. Spark aids ML. You can train ML algorithms on a laptop and then use the same ML model to scale to fault-tolerant clusters of thousands of machines.

Building and leveraging real-time analytics systems gather momentum with the combination of in-memory databases and data grids, streaming solutions, and MPP systems. By integrating with 360-degree dashboards, knowledge discovery, and dissemination get streamlined and speeded up significantly. Thus, with the faster maturity and stability of in-memory databases and data grids, the in-memory computing phenomenon gains speed and sagacity. Real-time services and applications can be realized with such pioneering infrastructure transformation.

18.6 Cluster management

For running large-scale, enterprise-grade and high-performing software applications, clusters of computers are being increasingly leveraged. However, managing clusters is not a straightforward task. Therefore, there came a number of cluster management software for efficient and effective monitoring, management, and maintenance of computing clusters. The prime purpose of cluster management software is to maximize the output that a cluster of computers can perform and provide. A cluster manager typically balances workload to reduce bottlenecks, monitors the health of each of the cluster's members, and manages failover when a compute machine fails.

In the recent past, we hear and read a lot about the Kubernetes platform, which is gaining surging popularity due to the overwhelming utilization of containers. Containers speed up application composition and act as the most optimal runtime for a variety of software packages including business software, backend databases, middleware solutions (message brokers and queues, etc.), and platforms (development, deployment, integration, orchestration, governance, security, etc.). Kubernetes automates the deployment and management of containerized applications. Containers are turning out to be an excellent runtime environment for microservices, which are being presented as the most optimal building block for enterprise-class applications. Now there are multiple container instances being used for hosting and running one microservice. Such a setup establishes and ensures a highly available and adaptive IT environment for successfully and succulently running mission-critical applications.

Kubernetes is the market-leading container lifecycle management software. It intelligently manages containers across compute clusters in IT environments (private, public and edge clouds). A Kubernetes cluster is a set of physical or virtual machines for running containerized applications and is the base and promise for scheduling and running containers across a group of homogeneous or heterogeneous machines. This cluster has a desired state that defines which applications should be running, which images they have to use for those applications, which compute resources should be made available for them to deliver their assigned functionalities, and other such configuration details. Kubernetes will automatically manage any cluster to match the desired state. For the containerized world and the world of virtual machines, Kubernetes play a very vital role. In the recent past, it has emerged as the platform for managing not only containers but also virtual machines. Hence, both containerized and virtualized workloads can be automatically tackled through the power of Kubernetes.

The role of Kubernetes in managing and running containers, in specific, is extremely important. It has the wherewithal to manage multiple clusters of nodes spread across private and public clouds. Each node, in turn, can accommodate several containers. There are containerization-enablement platform solutions readily available to simplify the process of containerizing software infrastructures such as Apache Ignite and streaming platform solutions. Well-written APIs enable Kubernetes to manage these high-end containerized software solutions.

IoT applications and data get increasingly distributed across clusters and clouds. With in-memory computing capability, making sense of IoT data and empowering IoT applications to make intelligent decisions in time are seeing the light at the end of the tunnel. Kubernetes play a very sagacious role in edifying the IoT era [8].

18.7   Demystifying the IoT architecture

The device ecosystem grows rapidly. We have a plenty of purpose-specific and agnostic devices and sensors deployed in our living, relaxing and working environments. For example, machinery on manufacturing floors, medical instruments at hospitals, equipment at national borders for ensuring homeland security, IT infrastructures (compute, storage, network, etc.) at cloud centers, kitchen utensils and wares, consumer electronics, smartphones, personal gadgets and gizmos, robots and drones, point of sales (PoS) at retail stores, etc. are being produced in large numbers and are methodically digitized through the application of digitization and edge technologies. There are powerful edge technologies such as barcodes, nano-scale chips, RFID tags, stickers, beacons, disappearing microcontrollers, LED lights, and single board computers (SBCs) to transition all kinds of physical, mechanical, and electrical systems to be digitized. With multiple connectivity options and network infrastructures, digitized elements are being connected with one another in the vicinity. Also digitized entities are being hooked into the Internet in order to access and leverage web, cloud embedded and mobile applications, services and data. That is, digitized systems become connected. This is being termed the Internet of Devices (IoD) and Things (IoT).

There is also a field of cyber physical systems (CPS). That is, physical systems at the ground are being hooked into cyber systems and services to be succulently empowered. Another related concept is digital twins. For any physical system, there is a corresponding digital version in order to collect operational, log, performance, security, transaction, and health condition data and crunch them quickly to extract useful information and insights, which, are then, fed into the right devices in time.

Real-time data analytics platforms and AI algorithms contribute immensely to empowering connected systems to be cognitive in their actions and reactions. We call IoT devices edge devices. They are fully digitized and connected. They can form ad hoc, purpose-specific, and dynamic clusters out of homogeneous and heterogeneous edge devices. Such device clusters/clouds come in handy in facilitating proximate data processing and in producing real-time insights.

IoT use cases are becoming sophisticated when integrated with digital technologies such as AI, streaming analytics, 5G communication, blockchain, digital twins, and containerization. IoT data grows in scope, speed, and structure. IoT data exponentially grows in size. IoT systems are accelerating, augmenting, and automating business operations intelligently. IoT architecture has to accommodate the trends and transitions. Typically there are four layers in the IoT architecture:

- **Hardware/sensing layer** – This layer is the device layer. There are a variety of IoT edge sensors and actuators in any important environment these days to monitor and manage things there. To enable IoT device data transmission across, one or more IoT gateways built on Raspberry Pi modules or Arduino microcontrollers are being fixed in that environment. Sensors and actuators form mesh networks to cognitively address bigger challenges and concerns. There are both wired/wireless and wireless communication capabilities.
- **Network/gateway layer** – This layer acts as the bridge between the first layer (hardware/sensing layer) and IoT analytics systems running in nearby or faraway cloud environments. This layer receives the digital data emanating from multiple IoT edge devices and does some mediation activities. There are communication options such as wired and wireless communications between IoT devices and gateways. Further on, there are special protocols: Message Queue Telemetry Transport (MQTT), Advanced Message Queuing Protocol (AMQP), Constrained Application Protocol (CoAP), and HTTP.
- **Platform layer** – There are IoT-enablement and analytics platform solutions getting hosted in cloud environments (local, remote, and edge). IoT data gets subjected to a variety of deeper investigations to squeeze out actionable insights.
- **Application layer** – The knowledge discovered gets disseminated to IoT applications and services.

18.8   Real-time stream processing for IoT

Multi-faceted IoT devices generate multi-structured data in large quantities. IoT device data gets streamed to be captured and crunched to produce useful insights in real time. IoT data has to be transformed in order to simplify and streamline data processing and analytics. Data has to be extracted and prepared to be right and relevant for the target environment. Data enrichment is another critical requirement to derive insights with higher accuracy. Context details have to be attached to IoT data in order to smoothen the path toward knowledge discovery. Finally, IoT data gets ingested into data storage systems. There are data ingestion products such as Apache Ni-Fi, Scoop, Flume and a host of ELT and ETL tools.

With the proliferation of IoT devices and sensors in our everyday environments such as homes, offices, retail stores, hospitals, hotels, factories, vehicles, warehouses, etc. Devices talk to other devices. Or devices have to connect and communicate with cloud-based analytics platforms, data storage appliances, 360-degree dashboards, etc. They may need to provide streaming data to all of these platforms.

IoT devices generally have fewer computational and network resources. Further on, these devices write data in short intervals and hence the number of data messages is huge (that is, the throughput is very high). One of the challenges is having a protocol that is compact and robust enough to meet the distinct requirements of IoT devices and machines. The pervasive HTTP protocol is found to be unsuitable for IoT device communication and data transmission as it consumes more resources.

One viable and venerable solution is Message Queuing Telemetry Transport (MQTT) protocol. MQTT is a lightweight communication protocol and is based on the publishing and subscribe model. If an IoT device (publisher/client) wants to send information out, it will publish the data to a topic of an MQTT broker. The broker then sends the information to all other clients that have subscribed to receive publications on the topic.

Using MQTT with streaming data – IoT devices emit out data in the fire-and-forget form to minimize bandwidth and power consumption. For example, a Raspberry Pi deployed in a paddy or cornfield can act as a monitoring station. The Pi module provides data such as air and soil temperatures, humidity, hydration, and pH levels. All this information is made visible in the farmer's dashboard, which can run on his smartphone, tablet/laptop, in-vehicle infotainment screen, etc. Logistics firms extensively use MQTT to track fleets and shipments. An MQTT broker acts as an intermediary for sensors attached to planes, trains, trucks, and cars by transferring the sensor-captured data with a company's database/data lake and analytical systems at the backend.

MQTT is proving to be an indispensable technology for the IoT era. IoT applications are being built and deployed in cloud environments. IoT devices and gateways at the other end are the prominent data generators and transmitters. The MQTT protocol plays a decisive role in shaping up the next-generation IoT use cases.

Storing IoT data in a time-series database makes data analytics simpler and faster. InfluxDB is a popular time-series database and is designed for fast and high-availability storage and retrieval of time-series data. This is especially suitable for handling application metrics, IoT sensor data, and real-time analytics. Data in InfluxDB is organized by time-series. A time-series can contain zero or many points. A point represents a single data record that has four components – measurement, tag-set, field-set, and timestamp.

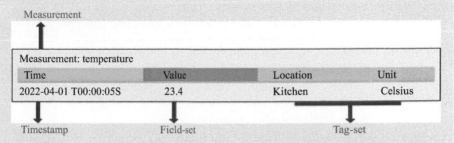

First, the timestamp shows the UTC date and time associated with a particular point. Field-set is comprised of one or more field-key and field-value pairs. They capture the actual data with labels for a point. Similarly, the tag-set is comprised of tag-key and tag-value pairs, but they are optional. They basically act as metadata for a point and can be indexed for faster query responses.

Finally, a database acts as a logical container for users, retention policies, continuous queries, and time-series data. InfluxDB is part of the InfluxData platform that offers several other products to efficiently handle time-series data.

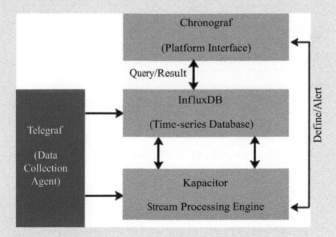

Apart from InfluxDB, the platform includes Chronograf, which offers a complete interface for the InfluxData platform. Further, it includes Telegraf, an agent for collecting and reporting metrics and events. Finally, there is Kapacitor, a real-time streaming data processing engine.

All kinds of IoT data are written to a topic in the MQTT message broker. The next task involves a streaming platform. As discussed at the beginning of this chapter, there are several streaming data platforms. Apache Kafka is currently one of the most prevalently used data streaming platforms.

Amazon Kinesis [9] is a real-time data analytics platform hosted in AWS cloud. Kinesis makes it easy to collect, process, and analyze streaming data in real time to get timely insights. Through Amazon Kinesis, it is possible to ingest real-time data such as video, audio, application logs, website click-streams, and IoT telemetry data.

Once the data is written to the MQTT broker, a Kinesis producer sub-scribes to it and pulls the data and writes it to the Kinesis stream. Then, from the Kinesis stream, the data gets pulled by Kinesis consumers. Then, the pulled data gets processed and written into an InfluxDB, which is a time-series database.

Finally, Grafana, which is a well-known tool for analytics and monitoring, is used to do data analytics and visualization.

Martin Štufi and Boris Bačić have published a research paper titled, "Designing a Real-Time IoT Data Streaming Testbed for Horizontally Scalable Analytical Platforms: Czech Post Case Study" [10].

As indicated above, enterprise-grade IoT systems need real-time and hor-izontally scalable data processing capability to quickly discover and disseminate actionable insights. Real-time data processing platforms receive and act upon data streams, which flow from sensors attached to self-driving cars, security solutions for homes and businesses, etc. The macro-level architecture says all explicitly.

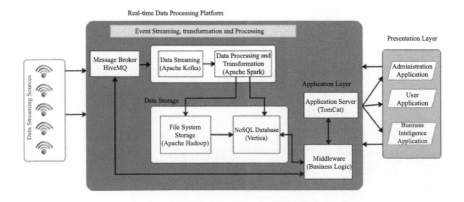

18.9   Macro-level real-time stream processing system architectures

The high-level real-time IoT data analytics architecture diagram is taken from [11]. The diagram vividly illustrates the various stages and the software products used to achieve the desired process flow. As explained above, a typical IoT architecture usually structures itself into four different layers. Let us understand how the data actually originates and flows through these layers.

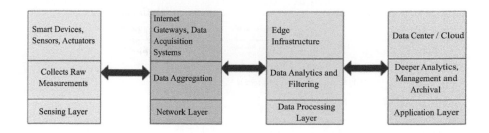

First, the sensing layer comprises of a dazzling array of heterogeneous sensors that are designed and destined to gather different measurements. Typically, all kinds of environmental data and the various operational parameters of assets deployed in that environment are being collected by the sensors. Then, the network layer helps in aggregating the raw data and sending it over the Internet for processing. Further, the data processing layer filters the raw data and generates early analytics. Finally, the application layer employs powerful data processing capabilities to perform deeper analysis and management of data.

There are a few data collection and ingestion methods. One prominent approach is **MiNiFi**, a subproject of Apache NiFi, which is a complementary data collection approach that supplements the core tenets of NiFi in dataflow management. This is focusing on the collection of data at the source of its creation. Apache MiNiFi agents can be deployed in Raspberry Pi devices. This lightweight agent can collect data from the sensor and route it to the Apache NiFi. From here, it is possible to route the data to multiple destinations. MiNiFi design goals are clear: small size and low resource consumption, central management of agents, and edge intelligence. MiNiFi can be easily integrated with NiFi through site-to-site protocol (S2S) to build an end-to-end flow management solution that is scalable and secure.

The other option is to do direct ingestion from an MQTT broker/server instance and route it to several backend systems. At the edge level, sensors collect information on the digital world and send them to a gateway through a variety of wired and wireless protocols (Serial, RS-485, MODBUS, CAN bus, OPC UA, BLE, WiFi, etc.). The gateway is a Raspberry Pi running a Mosquitto Broker and a MiNiFi agent.

There are many MQTT brokers available to be used for testing and for real applications. Mosquitto [12] is an open-source message broker that implements the MQTT protocol. It is lightweight and is suitable for use on all devices from low-power SBCs to full servers. The MQTT protocol provides a lightweight method of carrying out messaging using a publish/subscribe model. This is therefore suitable for IoT devices and sensors. The Mosquitto project also provides a C library for implementing MQTT clients. Websockets allow you to receive MQTT data directly into a web browser. This is important as the web browser may become the DE-facto interface for displaying MQTT data.

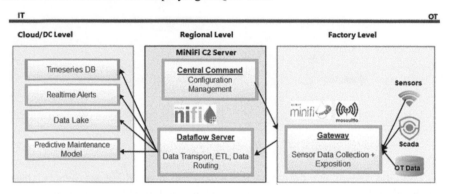

The second option is to use StreamSets [13]. With the advent of huge numbers of digitized entities (IoT devices) and connected sensors, manufacturing companies and enterprises have to devise a new approach to collecting digital data. The number of IoT devices and sensors on the edge is big in number. The majority of IoT devices are resource-constrained and hence data storage and running large-scale software on them turn out to be a difficult proposition. Furthermore, they often go through a dysconnectivity period. StreamSets Data Collector (SDC) Edge brings the edge within reach, delivering an ultralight yet powerful data ingestion solution for resource-constrained systems. Developers can build robust ingestion pipelines that are deployed in a small footprint and low resource utilization package. A drag-and-drop GUI makes it easy to prototype and deploys edge pipelines to huge populations of systems.

As discussed, there are data storage and processing systems to take care of the rest. The format in which Google Cloud accomplishes real-time IoT data processing is illustrated through the following diagram [14].

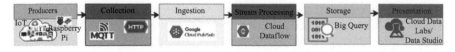

The Cloud Pub/Sub is used to listen to the data from the MQTT broker. Cloud Pub/Sub is a messaging system that can handle a real-time data stream. It also natively connects to other Cloud Platform services, gluing together data import, data pipelines, and storage systems. After ingesting the data from the IoT device, Cloud Pub/Sub further sends the data to the Cloud Dataflow for data processing. Cloud Dataflow is used to create the data pipeline to perform some data transformations which sends the processed data to BigQuery. BigQuery provides a fully managed data warehouse with a familiar, SQL-like interface. And further Cloud DataLab is used for the data representation.

The diagram vividly depicts how the same gets implemented using the AWS cloud.

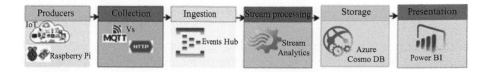

Here Kinesis Stream is used for the data ingestion process. For this, there is a necessity to define the Kinesis action, which will collect data from MQTT and send it to Kinesis Analytics for further processing. After stream-processing, the processed data is sent to Amazon Redshift and Amazon S3. In this, we can use Amazon QuickSight for the data representation using which we can build our visualization dashboards perform ad hoc analysis, and quickly get business insights from data.

The same can be elegantly implemented through Microsoft Azure Cloud. The pipeline for which, is given below.

Microsoft Azure Events Hub connects to MQTT via Cloud Gateway and consumes the data published by Raspberry Pi on the MQTT broker. Azure provides Stream Analytics for data processing. Above all, we can use the data stream from Events Hub and process the real-time data stream. After processing, the data is sent to Azure CosmoDB and can be further visualized on Power BI by using the CosmoDB connector.

18.10   The end-to-end enterprise integration architecture

IoT integration architectures need to integrate the edge (devices, machines, cars, etc.) with the cloud environments (public, private, and edge) to be able to process IoT data.

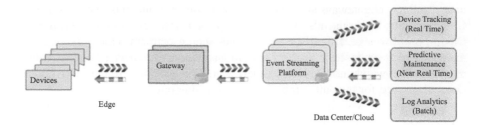

18.11   A lightweight ML architecture for IoT stream

Håkon Hapnes Strand has come out with a lightweight ML architecture for IoT streams [15]. Running ML models is getting a lot of attention these days. For building and releasing real-time services and systems, applying ML/DL algorithms to streaming data has captured the interest of researchers and practitioners. For example, by analyzing the movements of buses on public roads deeply, it is possible to predict their arrival and departure times at bus stops in an accurate fashion. By installing one or two IoT gateways in each of the buses plying on the roads, it is quite easy and elegant to capture their movement data precisely. By taking the captured data to a nearby cloud environment and by crunching it, it is possible to predict when a bus would come to a particular stop and when it will depart from it. Such details can be displayed at bus stops. Travelers can benefit immensely from such systems. The distinct capability of performing real-time data analytics and the derived insights obtained from it, in time, go a long way in envisaging and providing a bevy of people-centric services. Real-time analytics play a very stellar role in shaping up setting up and sustaining real-time enterprises.

With big data comes big responsibility – A single sensor may capture and share many messages in a day. Based on the size of the messages being shared, the total message size may come up to approximately 5 MB of data. But a typical IoT solution may involve thousands of sensors and on summing up the messages readied and rendered by all the participating sensors, due to which the amount of data getting generated, captured, stocked, and used becomes massive. Not only sensors, but there are also a variety of networked embedded devices including one or more IoT middleware products, which are to polish off data collection, aggregation, and enrichment requirements.

Leading market watchers and researchers have forecast that there will be billions of IoT devices across the world in the years to come. They are capable of producing a huge amount of poly-structured data. That is, big data demands big computation to generate big insights. However, with more data, the prediction accuracy is bound to go up significantly. The quick maturity and stability of ML algorithms have simplified and streamlined the process of knowledge discovery from big data.

The typical IoT system architecture involves a large number of IoT devices in any mission-critical environment. For transmitting IoT data to faraway cloud environments, IoT gateways are being put up in those environments to collect, filter out superfluous data, and transmit IoT data to a nearby or distant cloud-based message broker/queue. IP-enabled IoT devices such as cameras can send the captured data to cloud-based middleware solutions directly. Otherwise, the aspect of transmitting telemetry is nicely and neatly accomplished through the leverage of IP-capable IoT gateways, illustrated by the below diagram.

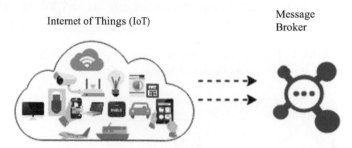

There are powerful communication protocols such as MQTT and AMQP. There are cloud-based message brokers such as Azure IoT Hub, AWS Kinesis, etc. Further on, there are open-source frameworks (Apache Kafka, Flink, etc.). These technologies and tools can ingest messages from millions of IoT devices. That is, the ready availability of event streaming platforms in cloud environments enables the ingestion of a large amount of event data and messages.

The subsequent steps are the key to the intended success. Just having data is serving no purpose at all. The captured and cleansed data has to be subjected to a variety of deeper and more decisive investigations to emit actionable insights out of the data volumes. That demands the usage of additional software infrastructure modules to transition data into information and into knowledge. The enhanced architecture to facilitate knowledge discovery and dissemination is given below.

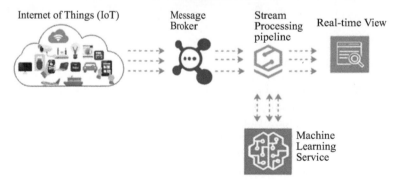

A stream processor is added to the architecture. The main purpose of a stream processor is to subscribe to messages from the message broker and to reactively process them on the fly. Then it immediately feeds that to a live view of the enriched data. Within a few hundred milliseconds of the time, the original IoT device message gets recorded and the results are made available in live view. There are multifaceted dashboards giving 360-degree views. Further, there are report-generation toolkits in plenty to deliver and display the insights drawn out of IoT data heaps.

Then a ML microservice is hooked to the stream processor in order to perform predictive analytics. The extracted predictive insights also form a part of the live output. Thus, message broker, stream processing engine, and ML model micro-service team up together to create a powerful and real-time IoT data analytics system.

A lightweight IoT data analytics solution – Stream processing uses the technique of time windowing as depicted below.

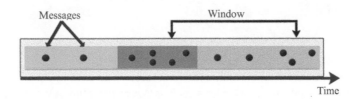

This simple function is called a tumbling window and this feature is being natively supported by all the stream processing engines in the market. By looking at fixed-size time windows, it is possible to aggregate the data in some way. It is also possible to process only the latest message in the batch of messages. That allows for a slightly different architecture.

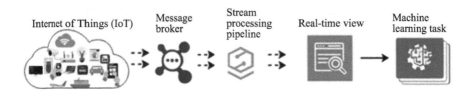

In this setup, a scheduled task, such as a cron job, wakes up at preferred time intervals, looks at the latest output from the streaming pipeline, and generates predictions before going back to sleep. Previously the predictions are kept alive as we wait for the task to trigger again. For soft real-time requirements, the predictions are valuable for some finite amount of time. Such a lightweight approach sharply reduces the system costs. As the data analytics system runs on the cloud, there is no need to pay for the processing units all the time. That is, when the processing systems are sitting idle, then there is no charge.

As described in the chapter [15], the prediction and training functionality is detached from the streaming layer. That functionality is put into separate Docker containers in order to spin up the container instances whenever needed.

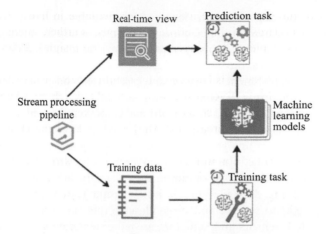

This results in a self-contained infrastructure that keeps training models on fresh data and generating live predictions as long as the streaming pipeline receives IoT data and messages.

Here the infrastructure and operational costs are very minimal. This lightweight system is currently processing a couple of million messages a day and is costing around $60 monthly. That includes everything including the cloud infrastructure cost [15]. This is achieved by exploiting the offerings such as containers-as-a-service (CaaS) and function-as-a-service (FaaS). As we all know, containers support application portability, real-time scalability, immutability, etc. There are container lifecycle management platforms. Kubernetes is the market-leading container orchestration platform. Through a host of automated tools, running containerized software applications, middleware solutions, platform solutions, databases, etc. in cloud environments is being termed as the way forward. Through containerization, the much-demanded resource-utilization efficiency goes up drastically. Now, the emergence of serverless computing has deepened the automation thereby there is less work for cloud administrators. The infrastructure setup and sustenance tasks are being automated through serverless platform solutions. On-demand scalability of serverless applications through elastic infrastructure modules goes a long way in sharply reducing operational costs.

The chapter [15] highlights and trumpets the fact that the lightweight system is running on a minimal infrastructure at a surprisingly low cost while satisfying the performance requirements. This system is currently running on Microsoft Azure cloud. This system teaches a lot to data scientists while designing complex systems for running ML models for quickly analysing IoT streaming data for squeezing out actionable insights. Data loses its value as time goes by. Thus, timeliness and trustworthiness guaranteed by machine and deep learning models are important in order to achieve the intended success.

18.12 Streaming data analytics: the benefits & use cases

Batch processing is found to be insufficient for enterprises to be right and relevant to their partners, employees and consumers. Fulfilling the goal of customer satisfaction can be done through deriving real-time insights and by delivering premium services. Therefore, real-time stream processing is needed. Real-time processing is insisted across industry verticals. For example, fraud detection has to be done immediately to avoid financial losses. For retail service providers, dynamic inventory and replenishment management capabilities and a seamless shopping experience across multiple devices are being realized through real-time processing. Business applications have to be designed and empowered to integrate data from multiple applications and data sources. They need to have the embodied intelligence to process, filter, analyze, and react accordingly and astutely to any event data or message in time. Enterprises gain immensely with streaming data and through the intrinsic capability of capturing and analyzing continuously flowing data. Thus, streaming data analytics is an important feature for forward-looking business behemoths to survive and surge ahead in this cut-throat competition.

Typically, IoT sensors and actuators are prominent data generators. IoT data, which is streaming in nature, has to be gathered and directed to streaming solutions such as Kafka, which serves data to be analyzed by sophisticated analytics platforms such as Apache Spark, Storm, Flink, and Samza. These platforms are capable of doing parallel data processing to emit insights in time. By leveraging IoT data, business applications are supplied with context-sensitive data. That is, context-aware applications and services can be realized through the real-time processing of IoT data. In this section, we are to discuss a few prominent use cases of streaming data analytics.

Log analytics – Log files gleaned from a variety of business workloads, IT services and IoT devices are being analyzed through pioneering real-time log analytics solutions to get the trustworthy intelligence to deeply understand the root cause of any problem and to cognitively troubleshoot IT infrastructure modules, edge devices, business applications, etc. This facilitates quick recovery and business continuity. The log data, which is streamed and subjected to deeper analytics, plays a very vital role to nip any problematic security attack in the budding stage.

Security information and event management (SIEM) – This real-time security analytics solution could acquire and analyze event data to empower proactive and pre-emptive threat detection. As told above, security event data gets streamed and captured to do a thorough investigation to extract the details about any impending cyberattack.

Retail industry– Real-time insights derived from IoT devices and connected sensors can definitely help in bringing in a bevy of intelligent automation and can revolutionize operations. The ready availability of real-time stream processing systems has laid down a stimulating foundation for all these noteworthy advancements.

Typically, an IoT device generates a continuous flow of real-time data (one or more log data per second). If there are 50 sensors in a retail store, then we can easily anticipate 100 multiplied by 60 data values per second. That is, 2,160,000 values will be generated from a retail store per day. If there are hundreds of stores, then it becomes big data and without automated tools, keeping track of log data to tune up the stock management turns out to be a challenge. Thus, real-time data analytics is essential for next-generation retail services.

The retail industry is gaining a lot through real-time streaming data analytics. A variety of retail and its allied data can be sourced from myriads of sources including point of sales (POS) systems, e-commerce transactional data, in-store sensor data, supply chain systems, and social media. There are other data sources such as inventory, replenishment, and in-store robots. Stream analytics platforms enable analyzing of real-time data and also are helping to match with other retail-related data such as purchase history, festival and holiday seasons, and promotion campaigns. By such empowerment, proper and profit-looking product recommendations can be given to appropriate people at right time. This helps retail giants in precisely exploring and exploiting fresh avenues to increase revenues.

Through real-time streaming analytics, the flourishing retail industry can visualize sophisticated features/functionalities/facilities to attract shoppers and online buyers to sell more with less. E-commerce giants are solidly leveraging the distinct advancements happening in the stream analytics space. Cloud environments (private and public) are being blessed with open source and commercial-grade streaming data analytics platforms to speed up the unraveling of personalized, predictive, and prescriptive insights. In the recent past, streaming platforms are being deployed in resource-intensive IoT edge devices and gateways to accomplish real-time computing and analytics.

Real-time integration between mobile applications, customer activity, and back-end services like CRMs, loyalty systems, geolocation, and weather information create a context-specific customer view and allow for better cross-selling, promotions, and other customer-facing services.

- **Retail inventory management system** – This is for monitoring the number of products currently available in every store and warehouse. With such a data processing system in place, retailers can get a real-time update on out-of-stock situations. Streaming data architecture lowers the required workforce, simplifies processes, and provides monitoring that can manage inventory at a global scale.
- **Data streaming in video analytics** – Retail stores and warehouses use CCTV cameras to monitor user traffic. CCTV cameras are also being used to regulate shoppers, understand customer behaviour, and predict in-store wait time as well. Stream processing of videos throws a lot of light on the various aspects of retail store management.
- **Inventory optimization** – Increasingly powerful IoT sensors are used to minutely monitor retailers' inventory. This is to ensure that some important items are kept at optimum levels. Customers always prefer fresh food items. Hence established grocery retailers are using IoT solutions for preventing temperature spikes and for keeping food from spoiling. The installation of temperature sensors in fridges and freezers keeps their products fresh by continuously monitoring their condition and streaming data about current temperature levels. Managers and facility engineers can be immediately alerted when appliances do not adhere to set conditions. Therefore, inventory losses are greatly reduced and customers are extremely happy with the product.

Industry 4.0 applications – Factories, manufacturing floors, and assembly lines are being stuffed and sandwiched with a dazzling array of Industrial Internet of Things (IIoT) assets in order to sumptuously reap several noteworthy IT-enabled benefits including automated operations. Cloud environments are increasingly famous for realizing optimized and organized IT infrastructures. Further on, there are a few strategically sound digital technologies such as AI, digital twins, edge computing, 5G communications, and blockchain. With the blending of digital technologies, the long-standing goal of ambient intelligence (AmI) is to see the light. Realistically speaking, all kinds of industrial systems are being succulently digitized through digitization and edge technologies. Subsequently, they are connected to scores of business applications, transactional and analytical platforms, digital twins, storage systems, data lakes, etc. running in cloud environments. The connectivity empowers industrial equipment and toolkits to be distinct and deft. But at the same time, cyberattacks on connected entities are on the rise.

The matured and stabilized real-time streaming data analytics comes in handy in pinpointing security vulnerabilities of the connected systems and in nullifying them before making any damage. Threat detection is one of the prime advantages of real-time processing. Predictive maintenance of mission-critical and expensive industry assets is another popular use case of real-time data analytics. It is prudent to know the performance level and health condition in order to plan a repair or rest for critical assets. Such advancement helps administrators and operators to spot problems before they create an issue. This helps to understand whether there is any spot of botheration beforehand. Thus, for substantially increasing the asset-utilization efficiency, preventive, predictive and prescriptive insights are needed. The contributions of streaming analytics are definitely immense for worldwide enterprises to be smarter and steady in fulfilling customer delight.

Autonomous vehicles – Self-driven vehicles are getting a lot of minds and market shares these days. There are path-breaking sensors such as cameras, GPS, light detection and ranging (LIDAR), and other in-vehicle and on-board sensors. These sensors are being attached to each vehicle to minutely monitor and collect a lot of decision-enabling, value-adding, and accuracy-guaranteeing data from various components of the vehicle. Data captured by these sensors is being methodically analyzed to derive actionable insights, which, in turn, provide greater safety and security for vehicles and their occupants. Sensors also monitor vehicle performance and health condition of each critical component of the vehicle. By intelligently processing the data captured, the driving and travel experience is to be remarkably enhanced. Any kind of impending dangers, road conditions, traffic snarls, etc. can be understood beforehand to plan and proceed with full confidence, care, and cognition.

Healthcare analytics – We have a variety of purpose-specific medical instruments, sophisticated scanners and sensors to precisely capture various body parameters. The field of medical electronics is flourishing fast. Medical devices are connected and these IoT edge devices are contributing immensely to enhancing patients' healthcare experience. Patient monitoring and management can be automated through real-time analytics of IoT streaming data. The advancements in the edge computing space are being seen as a positive indication to achieve more for visualizing intelligent healthcare services and applications. The IoT devices are allowing doctors to track their patients whether their health condition is improving owing to the treatment or not.

Smart cities – Any smart city initiative across the world has to involve many verticals such as energy, transportation, and parking. Further on, smart homes, hospitals, hotels, and factories are a prominent part of smart city projects. IoT devices and sensors are being touted as the major contributor to setting up and sustaining smart cities. With the ready availability of cloud-hosted real-time data analytics platforms, implementing smart city services and applications becomes easier and more elegant. Thus, any lively and lovely places can be transitioned into active and people-centric environments through a host of IoT sensors and actuators. And the capability of real-time data processing is very much required. With the faster maturity and stability of 5G communication, cloud-native and edge computing models, a lot of improvisations are being worked out. Disappearing yet powerful IoT devices, which can be artistically clustered to accomplish bigger and better tasks, are being manufactured and deployed in large quantities across important junctions, entertainment plazas, eating joints, stadiums, railway stations, airports, malls, conference halls, classrooms, tunnels, expressways, etc. In short, real-time processing of IoT streaming data has laid down a series of stimulating and sparkling use cases for empowering people in their decisions, deals and deeds.

18.13 Conclusion

AI is being positioned as the next-generation paradigm for producing intelligent systems across industry verticals. All kinds of internal and external data from various sources get methodically collected, cleaned, and transformed into actionable insights through a host of automated toolkits. The knowledge discovered gets disseminated into our devices, networks, business workloads, and IT services in time. Such technological empowerment is capable of transitioning ordinary items into extraordinary artifacts and dumb objects into animated ones. Everything becomes smart, every device becomes smarter and every human being becomes the smartest. In short, AI is being primed for the best technology for society as a whole.

There are a few implementation technologies in the AI space. ML and DL algorithms play a very vital role in pinpointing and procuring distinct patterns in datasets. The extracted insights are then meticulously used for making systems to be cognitive in their actions and reactions. In this chapter, we have explained how IoT streaming data gets converted into useful information and insights in time through the leverage of ML algorithms. ML models are appropriate and awesome for working with big data. The accuracy levels of predictions being made by ML models are being constantly increased through a host of pioneering technologies. Also, ML models are inherently capable of learning from data continuously to bring forth fresh insights with clarity and alacrity.

References

[1] Cui, L., Yang, S., Chen, F., Ming, Z., Lu, N. and Qin, J. (2018). A survey on application of machine learning for Internet of Things. *International Journal of Machine Learning and Cybernetics*, 9, 1399–1417. doi: 10.1007/s13042-018-0834-5.

[2] Apache Flink. https://flink.apache.org/

[3] Apache Storm. https://storm.apache.org/

[4] Pulse vs Kafka. https://memgraph.com/blog/pulsar-vs-kafka

[5] IMDGs. https://hazelcast.com/glossary/in-memory-data-grid/

[6] Apache Ignite. https://ignite.apache.org/

[7] Apache Spark. https://spark.apache.org/

[8] Vayghan, L., Saied, M., Toeroe, M. and Khendek, F. (2019). Kubernetes as an Availability Manager for Microservice Applications. https://doi.org/10.48550/arXiv.1901.04946

[9] Amazon Kinesis. https://aws.amazon.com/kinesis/

[10] Stufi, M. and Bačić, B. (2021). Designing a real-time IoT data streaming testbed for horizontally scalable analytical platforms: Czech post case study. In: *Proceedings of the 11th International Conference on Sensor Networks*, pp. 105–112.

[11] High-Level Real-Time IoT Data Analytics Architecture Diagram. https://www.baeldung.com/iot-data-pipeline-mqtt-nifi

[12] Mosquitto. https://mosquitto.org/

[13] StreamSets. https://streamsets.com/

[14] Google Cloud Accomplishes Real-Time IoT Data Processing in Google Cloud. https://www.xenonstack.com/blog/iot-analytics-platform

[15] Lightweight Machine Learning (ML) Architecture for IoT Streams: Håkon Hapnes Strand. https://towardsdatascience.com/a-lightweight-machine-learning-architecture-for-iot-streams-bd1bf81afa2

Index